Shenandoah National Park
AUG 03 200?
Luray, VA

Cuyahoga Valley National Park
AUG 08 2004
Hunt Farm

scayne National Park
JUL 29 2004
Homestead, FL

Acadia National Park
AUG 13 2004
Bar Harbor, ME

Great Smoky Mountains National Park
AUG 0 2 2004
Sugarland VC
Tennessee

ROADSHOW

by Neil Peart

LANDSCAPE *with* DRUMS

A Concert Tour By Motorcycle

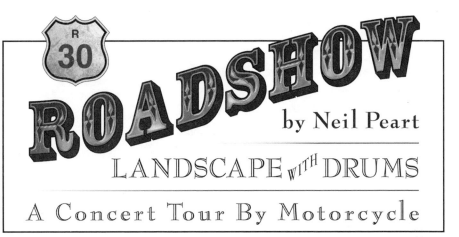

ROADSHOW

by Neil Peart

LANDSCAPE WITH DRUMS

A Concert Tour By Motorcycle

ROUNDER

2006

Copyright © 2006 by Neil Peart

Published worldwide by Rounder Books

an imprint of:
Rounder Records
One Camp Street
Cambridge, MA 02140

ISBN: 1-57940-142-2
Library of Congress Control Number: 2006926680

Editorial advisors: Paul McCarthy and Danny Peart
Copyeditor: Kevin Connolly
Cover and text design: Hugh Syme
Typesetting: Swordsmith Productions
Project director: Brad San Martin

Peart, Neil
Roadshow: Landscape with Drums—A Concert Tour by Motorcycle
1. Peart, Neil—Journeys—North America and Europe 2. Motorcycling—North America and Europe 3. Rush—Rock Band I. Title

First Edition
ISBN 1-57940-142-2

9 8 7 6 5 4 3 2

To my bandmates and brothers,

Alex and Geddy,

for thirty years of collaboration and laughter,

and to my loyal, entertaining,

and crashworthy riding partners,

Michael and Brutus

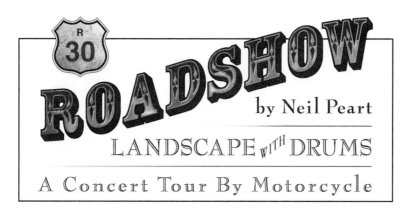

ROADSHOW
by Neil Peart
LANDSCAPE WITH DRUMS
A Concert Tour By Motorcycle

"The music business is a cruel and shallow money trench,

a long plastic hallway where thieves and pimps run free,

and good men die like dogs.

There's also a negative side."

Attributed to Hunter S. Thompson (1937-2005)

"Mommy, when I grow up I want to be a musician!"

"Now honey, you know you can't do both."

Anonymous

ROADSHOW
by Neil Peart

LANDSCAPE WITH DRUMS

A Concert Tour By Motorcycle

the story so far

By 1976, I was twenty-four, and had been playing drums for eleven years. During the previous two years, I had actually been making a living at it (most of the time), touring and recording with my bandmates in Rush, Alex and Geddy. During that brief, frenetic time, we had played hundreds of concerts across the United States and Canada, and recorded three albums together. More or less by default, I had ended up writing nearly all of the lyrics, an unexpected sideline growing out of a youthful obsession with reading.

The band's first, self-titled album had been recorded just before I joined, and when it sold 125,000 copies in the United States, the record company pronounced it "a promising debut." When the next one, *Fly By Night*, sold 125,000 copies, it was "a solid follow-up." But when the third album, *Caress of Steel*, sold 125,000 copies, they called it "a dog."

We were urged to be "more commercial," write some "singles." So, in our contrarian fashion, we recorded an ambitious and impassioned side-long piece about a futuristic dystopia, along with a few other weird songs, and released our fourth album, *2112*, early in 1976. It was considered by the bean-counters to be our last chance, and without any promotion from them, it was something of a snowball's chance.

However, constant touring and word-of-mouth began to build our reputation. When *2112* surprised everyone (including us) and sold 500,000 copies in the United States, a Gold Record, and attained the same relative status in Canada (50,000 copies), we were free to choose our own directions. From then on, almost no one thought they had the right to tell us what to do, and we went our own way. Miraculously, our audience went that way, too.

With a little success, life began to grow bigger, even as it became so much busier. Emerging from the tunnel of my music-obsessed adolescence and teenage years, I was starting to think about "life beyond the cymbals," to use Bill Bruford's perfect phrase.

But at first it was hard to get much beyond the cymbals. Traveling most of the time, from arena to club to college gymnasium, crammed into a small camper-van (misnamed by its makers the "Funcraft") while each of us drove three-hour shifts through the night, it was hard enough just to stay *entertained*. In the old analog days, we had no video games, satellite TV or movies, no CDs, DVDs, or iPods. Usually there was only the radio on the dashboard, crackling out '70s pop hits and Bible-Belt evangelists. Even reading was difficult in the dark, bouncing van, a crowded dressing room, or a shared room at the Holiday Inn.

Our popularity increased slowly, more or less gradually, but still eventually brought strange changes in the way people around us behaved. One afternoon, before a show at a small arena in the Midwest around the spring of 1976, three or four of us from the band and crew were on a lawn outside the venue, throwing a frisbee around. Young long-haired males began gathering, just *staring* at us, apparently fascinated by our frisbee-playing. We exchanged looks, but kept throwing and catching. Then some of the watchers started yelling out our names, and calling others over, until there were dozens of people around us. That kind of appreciation was what we were out on the road working for, of course, but not so much for our frisbee-playing, and as the crowd grew bigger, the fun seemed to go out of the game.

Similarly, in those early days, I sometimes liked to walk from the hotel to the venue, exploring the streets of San Antonio or San Francisco, but suddenly (it seemed) the "reception committees" outside the stage door became too large, too clamorous. Again, naturally you want people to admire your work, but not so much your walking around. I was simply not easy with that sort of attention; I felt embarrassed and uncomfortable.

Typically, that is the point in one's career when it is customary to lose your way, feel alienated, and start drinking too much, or taking a lot of drugs. Mostly that kind of behavior just made me throw up, so I hid out and read books. Devouring everything from the great novels to overviews of history and philosophy, I read in a fever of distraction and the drive of a high school dropout's pride—to make up for lost time and learn something, preferably *everything*. Many of the old paperbacks in my library still have stick-on stage passes in their inside covers, from bands we opened for like Aerosmith, Kiss, Ted Nugent, Blue Oyster Cult—and most of my library still consists of paperbacks, carried around on various journeys.

As our modest success continued, we stepped up to larger modes of touring transportation, from a small RV (the infamous "Barth") to a series of Silver Eagle tour buses. Eventually, we even had our own rooms at the Holiday Inn. Along the way I tried various other pastimes that were portable, like a model-car-building workshop in a small road case, with a surgical array of miniature tools and an aerosol-driven airbrush. I would set it all up in my room on a day off in Jumer's Castle Lodge in Davenport, Iowa (or similar), and build intricately detailed model kits. I spent weeks on one replicating Alex's 1977 Jaguar XJS, white with red interior, with full engine plumbing, working suspension and steering, and even articulated seats that folded forward and slid on little rails.

Brief fads sparked and faded among band and crew, like roller-skating around backstage corridors, racing radio-control cars on courses marked with gaffer tape, and even playing ice hockey in rented arenas after concerts. In the early '80s, I started carrying a bicycle with me on the tour bus, and that not only gave me a welcome outlet of freedom and independence, it made my world much bigger. I spent my days off roaming the country roads of South Carolina or Utah, and show days visiting art museums in Worcester, Massachusetts, Kansas City, or Seattle.

Over the years, my "mental map" of American cities was a changing network of not just hotels and arenas, but local hobby shops, bookstores, bicycle shops, art museums, and more recently, BMW motorcycle dealers.

During our *Roll the Bones* tour in 1992, I formed a backstage lounge act, the Murphtones, with one of our crew members, Skip. We would meet in a tuning room before the show and play jazz standards, Skip on guitar, and me with wire brushes on my little warm-up drums. On a later tour, *Counterparts*, in 1994, Skip and I published a semi-regular tour newsletter, *The Vortex*, lampooning touring life with humorous contributions from crew members and drivers.

The title came from a conversation in my hotel room in Pensacola, Florida, during rehearsals before that tour. Sitting around after work with Alex and a couple of the crew guys, I mentioned that I was already starting to feel that on-the-road mentality, of the world closing in on the narrow reality of performing, traveling, and just *surviving*.

Alex said, "I know what you mean. It's like a . . . vortex."

I nodded, "Yeah, it sucks you in."

Tour manager Liam said, "No—it just sucks."

When Skip and I put together the newsletter, that became our masthead and our motto: *The Vortex*, "It Sucks."

Under that, it said, "Price: Being There."

For a couple of tours in the early '80s, Geddy and Alex and I studied French before every show, our office arranging with the local Berlitz school to have teachers sent to the arena.

During a couple of long tours with Primus in the early '90s, both bands would gather in the tuning room before the show and stage tumultuous jam sessions. Everybody played unfamiliar instruments, banged out incidental percussion on lockers and bicycle frames, and guitar players Alex and Ler brought in pawnshop accordions, violins, and flutes. It was not always terribly *musical*, but it was a lot of fun.

Back in 1976, though, I decided my on-the-road hobby was going to be writing prose. In the same way that loving music had made me want to play it, it seemed that because I loved to read, I wanted to write. In a pawnshop in Little Rock, I bought a clunky old portable typewriter, and on rare days off, huddled in a hotel room in Duluth or Dallas and tapped away at my first experiment: adapting the story from our most recent album, *2112*, into narrative form. That ambition died peacefully in its sleep by about page fifty.

Typically, in the narrative arc of a would-be writer, an abandoned first novel is accompanied by attempts at short stories. That pawnshop typewriter made me think of its previous owners and what they might have written on it, and that suggested other pawnshop tales. I envisioned a chain of stories I was going to call "Pawnshop Guitar." But that didn't fire my imagination either.

So, I followed another well-worn trail and dug some skeletons out of the family closet. "Green Pastures" was a Thomas Hardy-like bucolic melodrama of rural atmospheres, repressed passions, and births out of wedlock. However, I was uncomfortable with the idea of trying to publish that kind of story, because even though the main characters had passed on, there were others who were alive and would recognize themselves, and be embarrassed or wounded. And what would my mother say?

So, the next thing you try is fictionalizing the adventures of your *own* youth, and for the next few years I worked on a series of stories about a character named Wesley Emerson (after my paternal grandfather, who died when I was a baby—I always liked his name). In a typical exercise of "write what you know," my Wes was a musician in a rock band touring the United States (though a singer, tellingly), and not surprisingly, his adventures were based on experiences I had known or heard about.

Wes flew with his bandmates in a chartered jet to watch the first launch of the space shuttle *Columbia*, and Wes and his friend from the band's road crew carried a passed-out stripper from his room back to hers (a story I only *heard* about, I hasten to clarify). In any case, that conceit also died of natural causes: lack of will, or "heart failure," you might say.

Recently I read an interview with a veteran photojournalist, witness to many battles and horrible atrocities, who said that as a young man, he had been certain that if he could just "get the right picture," it would change things. He would make people see how wrong war and genocide were, and they would stop.

I recognized the same secret ideal that had driven me as a lyricist: early on, I had truly believed that if I could just *express* things well enough— injustice, narrow-mindedness, destructive and thoughtless behavior—people would recognize their own folly, and change. Perhaps that naïveté is necessary to a youthful sense of mission; perhaps you *have* to believe that a song, a story, a painting, or a photograph can change the world.

But eventually you learn to moderate your goals. In 1987, I wrote the lyrics for a song called "Second Nature" which included the realization that even if I could not accept compromise, I would have to accept limitations. "I know perfect's not for real/ I thought we might get closer/ But I'm ready to make a deal."

My prose-writing goals were finding their limitations as well, and around that same time, I tried writing about my first experience of "adventure travel," a bicycle trip through China. Although the result was unskilled and unfocused, right away I knew I had found my niche: travel writing. I wanted to try to describe the people and places of the world as I found them, rather than inventing imaginary ones.

It seemed that as I experienced landscapes, cultures, wildlife, and weather, and my own thoughts and feelings, I was always thinking, "How would I describe this in words?" Experimenting with both traveling and writing, I tried to find an authentic way of expressing myself, that elusive "voice," and worked through several experiments along those lines. Between tours and albums, I was traveling the world, often by bicycle, and trying to translate those journeys into narratives.

Many attempts later, from magazine-size stories to self-published books, and fully twenty years after buying that pawnshop typewriter, I began to publish a few books: *The Masked Rider: Cycling in West Africa*, in 1996, then *Ghost Rider: Travels on the Healing Road*, in 2002, and *Traveling Music: The Soundtrack to My Life and Times*, in 2004.

Still, there was one travel story that continued to elude me, the one that represented the biggest journey of all in my restless existence: the life of a touring musician. I had tried to capture that paradigm from the beginning with the Wes Emerson stories, and time after time since then, even in songs like "Limelight," but I had never been satisfied. I kept thinking that if I could just make people see what it was really like, they would understand everything. And, like everybody, I wanted so badly to be understood.

During our *Test for Echo* tour in 1996 and 1997, I traveled between shows by motorcycle for the first time, with my own bus and a trailer for the bikes. I would sleep on the bus after the shows, in a truck stop or rest area, then unload the bike in the morning and ride. My riding companion and navigator was my best friend, Brutus, whose nickname, incidentally, came from him telling me one day that he was going to call his powerful, heavy BMW K1100RS "Brutus." Not being one for naming machines, I said, "Oh yeah? Well . . . I think I'll call mine . . . 'Timmy!' "

He frowned and shook his head, "You can't call it *that*."

So I said, "Well, how about 'Skipper?' "

That didn't stick either, but Brutus did.

Pausing at roadside diners, on the bus, backstage, and in motel rooms, I kept a daily journal of the seventy-six shows and the 40,000 miles of motorcycling between them, and at the end of that tour, in the summer of 1997, I began working on a book I was calling *American Echoes: Landscape with Drums*. Unfortunately, a series of terrible tragedies in my life interrupted that project, and I set it aside.

In fact, I set *life* aside for a few years there, lost in grief and wandering, and when I returned to touring with the band in 2002, after our *Vapor Trails* album, I was content just to *do* it—endure it, survive it, experience it, surrender to the Vortex—and didn't even try to document that tour.

However, early in 2004, when Rush was preparing to launch our Thirtieth Anniversary Tour, I decided once again to try to tell the story of a traveling roadshow, a concert tour by motorcycle.

the mother road

The open road is a beckoning, a strangeness,
a place where a man can lose himself.

William Least Heat Moon

Sunset Boulevard. The name alone resonates like few street names in the world, and few streets in the world were ever as beautiful as Sunset Boulevard at 5:30 in the morning, May 14, 2004, seen from the saddle of my motorcycle. Winding through the predawn twilight, framed by luxuriant foliage, cool, fragrant air, and the solitude of the road, I felt the quiet thrill of beginning a long journey.

From the western end of Sunset, above the Pacific Ocean, my red BMW R1150GS carried me past dark stores and shops, overarching trees and tall hedges of cypress, California fan palms and royal palms, all streaming by under a pearly gray sky. For once, the sinuous dark pavement was almost empty of other traffic, and my motorcycle hummed along, its characteristic "boxer" sound like the purring of a big cat. The wind whooshed past my helmet, filling it with occasional waves of jasmine, and that subtle perfume seemed almost intoxicating, like the lilacs of my childhood in Southern Ontario. The gentle wafts of scent alternated with an aromatherapy yin-yang, the spicier note from the tall columns of eucalyptus.

I leaned the bike into the curves, down through the wooded valley of

Will Rogers State Park, glancing briefly over at the house Dennis Wilson had rented in the '60s, where the Manson "family" had moved in on him. I always wondered what ghosts that perpetually shaded house might harbor, and this time I noticed the walls and roof had been removed—it was being gutted, renovated, maybe exorcised.

Sunset Boulevard snaked its way through Brentwood, trees and hedges obscuring large '50s-style bungalows and ranch houses (the kind realtors were now calling "midcentury classic") with carpets of lawn framed in perfect gardens and asphalt driveways. The pale sky opened wide as the bridge crossed the San Diego Freeway, where headlights and taillights swam rapidly in both directions, early enough to avoid the two-way parking lot that ten-lane highway would soon become.

Back into the tunnel of greenery, around the UCLA campus at Westwood, the gated mansions of Bel Air and Beverly Hills, then into the tall office buildings of West Hollywood, and the shuttered stores and restaurants of the Sunset Strip.

Since my first visit to Los Angeles ("Shakeytown," in the CB parlance of the day, for its occasional seismic events), on tour with Rush in 1974, Sunset Boulevard had seemed like the avenue of dreams. In those early days, touring around the United States and trying to make a name for ourselves, we would play week-long stands at West Hollywood clubs like the Whiskey-a-Go-Go and the Starwood. To save money, band and crew members shared rooms at the Sunset Marquis apartment-hotel, often buying groceries at Ralphs and cooking for ourselves (everyone wanting to room with Alex, the best cook among us), and watching the fabulous wasteland of Los Angeles television. We were thrilled to see old black-and-white shows like "The Twilight Zone" and "The Untouchables" at two o'clock in the morning, in the years when Canadian television at that hour would have been showing test patterns.

One afternoon, that first time in the City of Angels, a few of us drove our rental car out along Sunset, that fabled boulevard, from West Hollywood to the beach. I pulled off my shoes and socks and ran to put my bare feet in the Pacific, then ran right out again. It was so *cold*. Not surprising, seeing it was November, but I guess I thought Southern California would be like a Beach Boys song, "Endless Summer."

That was just the beginning of all I would come to learn about Los Angeles, and about California, as I returned again and again with the band for the next thirty years, always staying at the same old Sunset Marquis. In a rare opportunity for the luxury of independence, we began renting our own convertibles to drive ourselves to shows in the area, at San Bernardino and San Diego. Each time I would drive out on Sunset to the ocean, sometimes in the daytime, sometimes at night, but always with the top down. It was a ritual that never lost its enchantment.

And it still hasn't—though of course I never imagined that one day I would be living near the far end of Sunset Boulevard, in a house over-looking the Pacific Ocean, the beaches of Santa Monica and Venice, and at night, the glittering lights from Century City to Palos Verdes, "the Queen's Necklace," framing the multicolored ferris wheel on Santa Monica Pier. I would never tire of that view.

But now I was leaving that view, and that home, as I had left so many other homes before, to begin a concert tour that would keep me away from it for the next five months. I would be home for a week here and there, but for the most part, I was saying goodbye to my home, my wife, Carrie, our five-month-old golden retriever, Winston, and to the pleas-ant rhythm of everyday life, as seen from one set of rooms, one set of windows.

The traffic lights seemed to be in synchrony with me that morning, and the motorcycle hummed steadily along the empty Strip. I cruised between the rows of expensive shops and restaurants, Tower Records, Book Soup, the little street of Alta Loma that led to the Sunset Marquis, then the rusty metal walls of the House of Blues, and the medieval tow-ers of the Chateau Marmont. Turning up Laurel Canyon, then east along Hollywood Boulevard, I pulled up outside the apartment building where Michael lived, and parked beside his gunmetal gray BMW GS. Michael had agreed to be my riding partner once again for this tour, as he had for the *Vapor Trails* tour in 2002, and although I had stressed to him that this beginning cross-country blitz was optional—just something I wanted to do to reacquaint myself with the country I would be traveling in for the next five months—Michael had insisted on riding it with me.

"I'm down," he said, in the terse hipster lingo of his generation.

In his early thirties, tall and thickly built, Michael was a private inves-tigator by profession, though he laughed and said he only *wished* his life was as exciting as it sounded when he said he was a "Hollywood private eye." Far from any Raymond Chandler or "77 Sunset Strip" fantasy, he spent most of his time behind a desk piled high with computer gear. Michael specialized in computer forensics, for individuals and law enforcement agencies, and personal security for celebrities and their homes. That was how he and I had met, in early 2000, when I first moved to Los Angeles. Michael had helped me to set up an "anonymous" existence there, as I began my new life with Carrie. Later that year, he handled security at our wedding, in a villa near Santa Barbara, and by then he and I had become friends.

A couple of years later, when the *Vapor Trails* tour was being planned, I was looking for a riding partner to replace Brutus (no longer welcome in the United States after certain legal difficulties, as described in *Ghost Rider* and *Traveling Music)*, and with a minimum of arm-twisting, I convinced Michael to buy a motorcycle and join me for that adventure. We had got along well, traveling together like that, and Michael had enjoyed himself. Now, once again he was passing his caseload to trusted colleagues and taking a sabbatical to be my riding partner and the band's security director, for our Thirtieth Anniversary Tour (already abbreviated to the logo icon of "R30").

As I stood by the bikes, Michael emerged from the building with his silver helmet in hand and tankbag under his arm, dressed for the road in his new Alpinestars armored suit, bulky in gray, black, and white. In our usual sophomoric "girl talk," I teased him: "I like your new outfit—it looks *cute* on you."

He did a slow pirouette, "You don't think it makes my butt look big?"

I shook my head, "Ain't nothin' gonna help that, honey!"

He pouted and whimpered, "Why do you always have to *hurt* me?"

"Because it makes me feel good," I said, then offered him my package of Red Apples. Our nickname for cigarettes came from the fictional brand in some of Quentin Tarantino's movies—the kind of trivial detail only Michael would pick up on. He could recite whole scenes from his favorite obscure movies with frightening accuracy, making you want to back away from him carefully, wondering, "Jeez—how many times has he *watched* that?"

Though it must be admitted that my bandmates and I could also repeat plenty of dialogue from movies we had watched so many times on the tour bus over the years—Mel Brooks's *Blazing Saddles*, *High Anxiety*, and *Young Frankenstein;* Steve Martin's *The Jerk;* David Lynch's

Eraserhead and *Blue Velvet; Moon Over Parador,* and any episode of the Canadian comedy series, "SCTV." Lines from those became a kind of shorthand among us, sometimes to convey our feelings about a situation; sometimes just to get a laugh.

In what passed for his "normal life," Michael tried not to smoke, and I pretended not to, but when we were traveling together, we both liked to play bad boys. And in truth, there *was* something about being on the road that encouraged, or at least allowed, arrested development. The shaky reality of being rootless and unsupervised, maybe. One time, Michael's girlfriend, Jae, was visiting him at a show, and as they walked through the backstage area he pointed at our motorcycles in the trailer: "That's the one we call 'Bitch,' that one's 'Ho,' and mine is 'Pimp Daddy.' "

She looked up at him, her canted face twisted with mild disdain, "What *are* you guys—in *high school?*"

I must admit, sometimes it felt that way.

Michael had grown up in the Midwest (on a day off during the *Vapor Trails* tour, I was treated to a motorcycle pilgrimage to his boyhood home in Verona, Kentucky) and in Hawaii, where he went to college. Early jobs had included crewing on charter boats, playing drums in lounge bands, and—surprising to anyone who knows him now—a stint of modeling, which took him to Europe and Asia. (I tell him, "Oh yeah, your big butch act, with your guns, your motorcycle, your Corvette—you're fooling *no one.*")

After finding his vocation as a private investigator, Michael continued his education in philosophy at Loyola, and music studies with summer courses at the Berklee School of Music. Our conversations, in restaurants and while riding on the bus, sometimes elevated to pseudo-intellectual flights of philosophy and literature. But in the on-the-road state of mind, much of the time we were just a couple of boys "lighting out for the territory," like Huckleberry Finn.

Michael's apartment, his "Hollywood bachelor pad," was in a shabby, neglected building, in a '70s collectivist style (and indeed, most of the present-day tenants were Russian). Its falsely elegant name, The Martinique, was spelled out across a cheaply built plaster-and-plywood façade. Behind the wrought-iron security doors, in the barren concrete courtyard, a stern wooden sign stated the obvious: NO CHILDREN PLAYING. Behind a rattling aluminum screen door, Michael's small front room was furnished only with his desk and computers, a full set of left-handed drums (covered with pads to muffle them), and a wall unit with TV and stereo.

Maybe not high school, but definitely college.

Another interesting thing about our friendship was that the only reason we had ever met was because Michael's gay friend knew my gay friend. That said something about each of us, I'm not sure what. We thought of ourselves as "manly" guys, more interested in motorcycles, cars, computers, drums, and side arms than in hair products and exfoliation, but our banter was, to paraphrase the old song, "gayer than springtime." I didn't talk like that with any of my other friends, even the gay ones, but somehow it just worked for Michael and me. And we could be alarmingly good at it.

If I was cranky and scolding Michael for some navigational error, he would look at me with doe eyes and say, "There's no *love* in your voice anymore."

I could only laugh and shake my head, disarmed.

If Michael had forgotten something I had asked him to take care of, I could vent with a harmless hissy fit, hands on hips and a heavy sigh, "I don't know why I even bother *trying* to communicate with you. You never listen to a word I say. You're so distant and cold, I might as well be alone. You never give a single thought to *my* feelings."

He would look at me and shudder, "Okay—now I'm frightened." Then, a beat later, he would open his arms and whimper, "Just hold me."

As Michael and I stood by the bikes smoking and making last-minute adjustments to bungee cords and cargo nets, he proudly showed me the new electronic device mounted on his handlebar.

"Check it out—GPS."

The Global Positioning System unit was a dark gray metal case, the size of a pound of butter, with a lighted, full-color screen. It combined map information in its onboard memory with links to geosynchronous satellites, and Michael was all excited as he toggled through its functions. He showed me how the screen could show us where we were, and even give us directions—guide our routes, find us hotels, restaurants, and gas stations. He had already programmed it with the locations of every venue on the North American part of the tour, and it was going to "know" where they all were. Michael assured me there would be no more flailing around strange cities while we looked for the job every day, or stopping to call the production office and waiting at the roadside while they found someone who could give us clear directions.

I was a little skeptical, not just because of my native distrust of technology, but because years ago I had owned a primitive hand-held GPS unit and tried to use it for orienteering in the Quebec woods. Given the U.S. military-prescribed "margin of error," I eventually decided that, like an Ouija board, it should have been labeled, "For Entertainment Purposes Only."

Apparently the technology had progressed since then, and in any case, Michael was a technophile by temperament and profession, and possessed a kind of *faith* in technology. If a technological device claimed to be able to do something, he just *believed* it was going to work. And because he believed the GPS unit was going to work so well, he didn't even bother to bring a map, which seemed shockingly hubristic to me. Not that I was a full-blown technophobe: for many years I had used electronic drums as part of my setup, and on the back of my motorcycle that very morning I carried my Powerbook, so I could have it with me in rehearsals and on tour for writing work and e-mails. However, based on years of bad experiences, I remained cautious about really *trusting* these machines. Acoustic drums always worked when you hit them, pen and paper always displayed their memory, and I had reliably navigated through many parts of the world with regular paper maps. I would have to be convinced by this GPS unit; it would be a while before I would learn to trust my place in the world to an electronic device.

In any case, this first ride didn't require much navigating. Under the clear plastic cover of the tankbag on my bike, instead of the state maps or even regional maps I would usually navigate by, I had placed a map of the entire United States. I remarked to Michael that all his GPS unit was going to tell him for the next 2100 miles was "Follow Interstate 40 East." (Like an L.A. bumper sticker I had seen, "IF YOU ♥ NY, TAKE I-40 EAST." Which somehow reminds me of the Waylon Jennings song, "Too Dumb for New York City, Too Ugly for L.A.")

Michael and I were setting out from Hollywood on a 2100-mile journey to that other entertainment capital, Nashville, where the final pre-tour rehearsals would be held with the band and crew, and our full production of lights and staging. I wasn't sure how long this first ride—

another kind of pre-tour rehearsal—might take, given variables like weather and traffic, not to mention unexpected obstacles like flat tires or mechanical problems. I figured if we could average at least 500 miles a day, we could still do it in four days, arriving on Monday in time for rehearsals. Of course, I wanted to do better than that.

By six a.m., Michael and I were merging onto Highway 101, the Friday morning traffic already heavy, and riding toward the towers of downtown Los Angeles. Following the overhead signs onto Interstate 10, we headed east into the hazy gray morning, the orange sun beginning to burn through as it crept upward before us. As I described that stretch of highway in *Traveling Music*, "through the endless suburbs of East L.A., everything blended into a flow of malls, car dealers, warehouse stores, insta-home subdivisions, and fast-food outlets."

Picking up I-15 at San Bernardino, we turned north and climbed through the first Joshua trees and rounded rock formations to the Cajon Pass, then down through Victorville. We passed the former Roy Rogers and Dale Evans museum, a low, dark building beside the freeway designed like an Old West fort, and famous for displaying Roy's horse, Trigger, "mounted." Apparently the museum had been moved to the country-western theme park of Branson, Missouri, making more room for the ever-spreading tract developments even that far away from Los Angeles.

Across the high desert to Barstow, we picked up I-40 and continued eastward on the highway that would be our home for the next few days. In most of my travels around the United States, or anywhere, I tended to avoid the major highways in favor of the more interesting and entertaining secondary roads, but for this journey, we would use the interstate for its proper function, as a "mileage disposal unit."

After every fuel stop we alternated the lead, one of us riding ahead in the front-left lane position, the other back and to the right. The leader set the pace, balancing the road, traffic, and weather conditions, posted limits, and what we thought we could get away with (radar detectors would soon be employed in that equation). As we crossed the creosote-dotted brown of the Mojave Desert, the sun was bright in a clear blue sky, traffic was light, state troopers were few, and we were riding a steady 90 miles-per-hour. The leader also generally kept an eye on the time and distance, planning and choosing gas station stops, rest areas, and Red Apple breaks. Usually the leader would also pay attention to the upcoming route, but that was not an issue that day; it was one road all the way now.

Around ten we rode over the Colorado River into Arizona, the landscape changing to ocotillo, saguaro, and prickly pear cactus, with jagged brown hills in the distance. As we passed that first state line, Michael waved his arm at the "Welcome to Arizona" sign, and from then on, we would often wave at them, hamming it up like excited kids.

Through junipers and ponderosa pines, we climbed to Flagstaff, cool and fresh at 5000 feet, and by two o'clock we were riding through the red rocks of New Mexico, across the Continental Divide (behind us every drop of water flowed to the Pacific; ahead of us, into the Atlantic), and into the Mountain Time Zone, losing a precious hour.

I had traveled long stretches of I-40 before, but always in the other direction, somehow, from east to west. Brutus and I had crossed the country that way twice on the *Test for Echo* tour, in '96 and '97. During the early part of that tour, in November of 1996, after the first three-week leg had ended with a show in Hartford, Connecticut, Dave (my estimable bus driver for three tours now) had driven south through the night. At daylight, after a few hours' sleep on the world's roughest bed— I-95 (Dave had joked, "better put on your Velcro pajamas")—Brutus and I got off at a rest stop in Roanoke, Virginia, unloaded our bikes from the trailer, and headed west. We were riding to meet our families in San Francisco and spend a few days with them in that great city, before the next leg of the tour began ten days later, in San Jose.

My journal note described the landscape across Tennessee that morning. "A dusting of snow, a sprinkling of snow, then a *coating* of snow on surrounding hills and houses. Interstate mostly dry though—and *cold!*" Brutus and I worked our way west on I-40, driving our tired bodies on through bitter cold and rain, wearing all our foul-weather gear and even tucking our feet under the exhaust pipes to try to pick up a little warmth.

Around Oklahoma, we began to encounter references to Route 66 on billboards and road signs. That road no longer existed, officially, replaced from Oklahoma to California by Interstate 40, but all the tourist attractions, restaurants, and gas stations seemed to be filled with Route 66 T-shirts, ashtrays, shot glasses, signs, books, salt and pepper shakers, lighters, postcards, and every kind of merchandising and memorabilia on which they could stick a black-and-white "Route 66" crest. At first I was dismissive about this nostalgia. All I knew about Route 66 was an old song and a '60s television series—what was the big deal?

Just west of Albuquerque, where Brutus and I had paused at a BMW dealer for a quick oil change and a new headlight bulb for my 1100GS, we followed I-40 up the Seven-Mile Grade of the West Mesa into the dwindling twilight. We stopped for gas at a lonely exit called Rio Puerco, where one old gas station made a pool of light in the gathering dark. If we followed our usual habit of getting off the road before dark, it was time to be stopping for the night, but because we had lost a couple of hours in Albuquerque, we wanted to press on a little further.

As I stood by the gas pumps filling my tank, road-weary after two long days of relentless riding, I looked west toward an abandoned girder bridge and old-time Aermotor windpump, with its metal vanes silhouetted against the vivid sunset colors. There had been few opportunities to take photographs on that tour, but on principle, I tried to take at least one every day to add to the documentation of my written journals. As I closed the flap on the gas tank, I pulled my camera out of the tankbag to take a photograph of that poetic scene.

It was then I realized that this dead-end service road was the old pavement of Route 66, and another picture came together in my mind's eye. The ancient gas station, the abandoned girder bridge, and the metal blades of the Aermotor were a kind of memorial, a shrine to the romance and history of the American road. In *The Grapes of Wrath*, John Steinbeck had called Route 66 the "Mother Road," carrying the dust-bowl refugees westward to the promised land of California. Then came the postwar America of finned station wagons and tepee motels, cheeseburgers and carhops, and truckers rolling through the night in big rounded tractor-trailers like my childhood Dinky Toys. As the modern-day T-shirts had it, Route 66 really had been "America's Main Street."

At that moment, and from then on, I *got* it, and began seeing the vestiges of Route 66 through different eyes. I bought many books on its history, full of evocative stories and photographs, the maps, the stickers, and even sought out and traveled long-abandoned alignments of the old highway in Arizona, California, and New Mexico. Thus I joined the thousands of people around the world who were fans of Route 66.

"If you ever plan to motor west/ Travel my way, take the highway that's the best/ Get your kicks, on Route 66." All my life, I had heard everybody from Nat King Cole to the Rolling Stones to Brian Setzer do that song. It was written by Bobby Troup, fresh out of the marines in 1946, and traveling west on that Mother Road to California. Not only was his song a success, but he also became an actor in television and movies.

In 2004, as Michael and I rode east through the empty splendor of western New Mexico in late afternoon, with the sunset behind us this time, I looked for that little set piece of gas station, bridge, and wind-pump at Rio Puerco, only to see that it was gone—swallowed up by a huge, overlit parking lot surrounding a huge, overlit Indian casino spanning both sides of the interstate. It was one of many casinos that had sprung up along Interstate 40 in the previous eight years, nominally on Native lands, and sometimes combined with massive truck stops that seemed to form a kind of garish, outlandish city in the desert, like an outpost on the moon.

Interstate 40 still had a few surviving relics from Old 66, like Jackrabbit's Trading Post, Clines Corners, and such, but they were dwindling even as their legend was growing. Ironically, even as more "Historic Route 66" signs went up along the interstate, the *real* signs of the past were disappearing, or relegated to bypassed stretches of lonely two-lane.

Approaching Albuquerque ("Duke City" in Edward Abbey's novels, because it had been named by Spanish settlers after the Duke of Albuquerque), Michael and I had a decision to make. We had disposed of 850 miles on that first day, which was already the farthest I had ever ridden in a single day, and well ahead of the 500-mile average of my worst-case scenario for that ride. But, I was starting to consider another goal: a motorcyclist's milestone called a "Thousand-in-One," meaning to ride a thousand miles in one twenty-four-hour period. We were so close, just a couple of hours from making that distance, and although I was tired and certainly ready to enjoy a cocktail and dinner, I was powerfully tempted to press on for another 150 miles, and bag that Thousand-in-One.

However, when I went to suggest it to Michael at a gas stop, one look at his saggy face told me he wouldn't be up for it. He'd had a late night celebrating his "farewell" with his circle of West Hollywood friends (mostly Asian lesbians—don't ask why), and he was beat. Against my own wishes, and abandoning a goal that was so temptingly close, I took pity on him and suggested we stop in Albuquerque.

Descending the West Mesa, with the russet Sandia Mountains ahead of us catching the lowering sun, we crossed the Rio Grande (a threaded stream under the I-40 bridge), and saw a sign for a Best Western motel. Our frequent choice, they were predictably of a tolerable quality, and always had a restaurant attached (once we had arrived, we wanted to have a large whisky and *walk* to dinner). So we took the exit and pulled under the portico.

While I waited for Michael to check us in, I looked up at the 10,378-foot Sandia Peak, and the terminus for "the world's longest aerial tram." Michael and I had ridden our motorcycles up there during the previous tour, *Vapor Trails*, on our way from a night off in Taos to the next show in Albuquerque. From the far side of the mountain, we had followed the winding road to the summit and its spectacular view. I was disappointed we wouldn't be playing in Albuquerque this tour, but our manager, Ray, had told me there were two cities we would usually play that he hadn't been able to squeeze into this itinerary, Cincinnati and Albuquerque. A shame, as I liked both cities, their venues, and the "commute" to get to them. But there was always somewhere we didn't get to.

An older American sedan pulled up in front of me, and a man stepped out of the passenger side and approached me. He was slender and stooped, fortyish, and his hair and clothing looked ragged, ill-groomed, somehow impoverished. His severely sunburned face was twisted into a pleading smile as he told me a rapid, heated story about how his car was stranded with a broken water pump on I-25, and waved toward the interstate that ran north-south from Santa Fe to El Paso. He said his wife and two children were waiting in the car while he went for help, but now he didn't have enough money for the parts he needed. I asked him why if he was "stranded," he had just gotten out of a car, and he told me the driver was just a stranger trying to help him.

I wasn't sure what to make of that, and hated to be played for a sucker, but I decided to err on the side of generosity, and gave him twenty dollars. He thanked me effusively, then darted into the lobby of the hotel, then across the street to a gas station, presumably continuing to take up his collection. Whatever his real story was, I felt sorry for him. Maybe he was just down on his luck, as they used to say.

When Michael came out with our room keys, we parked the bikes and hauled our gear inside. Then we followed our long-established ritual from the *Vapor Trails* tour: Michael dropped off his bags and searched out an ice machine, then came to my room with a bucket of ice, and I poured us a generous measure of The Macallan. We toasted the first day of a new journey, smoked a Red Apple, then showered and changed and headed for dinner.

At the end of a long day on the road, I felt the mixed buzz of all-day vibration, overstimulation, and weariness—the underlying awareness of having gone the distance, enjoyed it, and survived it. I had once come up with a refrain that often played in my head: "When I'm riding my motorcycle, I'm glad to be alive. When I stop riding my motorcycle, I'm glad to be alive."

The attached bar and restaurant, the Albuquerque Grill, was a nondescript, square, windowless space decorated in Early American Rec Room. George Thorogood-style rocking blues blasted out of a portable stereo sitting on a barstool in the corner, and the flashing images of a boxing match blared on a television overhead. Thoroughly road-blasted, tired all over from the wind, the vibration, and the hours of concentration, we slouched in our chairs and ordered what our exhaustive surveys had revealed to be the most likely meal to be palatable in a humble American restaurant—steaks—and devoured them sleepily.

Determined to get in another long day, I knocked on Michael's door at 5:30 a.m. with a single bang on the door (a useful code long known among Rush people as the "crew knock"), and we were back on the road by six. In the cool morning, with little traffic, we settled into our steady rhythm from the previous day, cruising by the rolling grasslands at what my Canadian speedometer showed as 150 kilometers-per-hour: translating in these metric-resistant United States to 93 miles-per-hour. The sun rose in a cloudless sky, and arced up and over us through the long day as the miles went by.

Back in the Route 66 days, especially the halcyon boom-times of the 1950s, when so many Americans took to the roads to "See America First," the town of Tucumcari, New Mexico, had campaigned a billboard war to hypnotize travelers into staying there. Billboards were placed for hundreds of miles east and west along the highway, as they still are on I-40, urging the driver and passengers to press on and stop in "Tucumcari

Tonite," listing the number of motel rooms and restaurants the town could offer.

While riding the previous day, considering the possibility of going for that Thousand-in-One, the idea of "Tucumcari Tonite" had made me smile, as it was just about the right distance to make it a thousand miles from Los Angeles. Although our fate had turned out to be "Albuquerque Tonite," I decided Tucumcari would still make a good breakfast stop, and I led Michael off the interstate onto the business loop—old 66—in search of breakfast. It was only a little after eight, and we already had 180 miles behind us.

As we cruised the main drag looking for something suitable—an old-time diner, or a mom-and-pop family restaurant—Michael was eager to show off the capabilities of his GPS unit, and at a red light he pointed to it and said, "there's a diner a couple of blocks away."

Suspending my disbelief, I followed him around a couple of corners to the place, but it turned out to be shuttered and abandoned. I led us back to 66, and we parked in front of an old-time family restaurant. As we settled inside, "Johnny Angel," "Monterey," and other oldies serenaded us while we filled up on pancakes and eggs, then filled up our bikes with gasoline and headed back on the highway.

Soon we crossed another state line, into Texas, losing another hour as we passed into the Central Time Zone. The northern square of Texas is called the Panhandle, but it is really more of a top hat, or perhaps a Stetson. Pale brown scrubland had given way to a semi-desert of red soil and rocks, and now a sweep of green rangeland stretched away to distant horizons. The locals say it's so flat you can see for two days. They also say that if the wind ever drops, all the chickens fall over.

I thought I was seeing occasional traces of snow in the low-lying areas and rimming the small ponds, but the pink water was a clue that these were soda lakes. Minerals leached from the soil and tinted the water, which then evaporated to leave the snowy-white residue.

As we approached Amarillo, we passed the reeking feedlots where cattle were fattened on chemicals and hormones for the last few weeks of their doomed lives (we had probably eaten one of those the previous night). Other familiar billboards for an Amarillo restaurant offered an old Route 66 tradition, a "free 72-ounce steak" to anyone who could eat it in one hour.

Another billboard for a Mexican restaurant editorialized in huge black letters, "THERE'S NO MEXICAN FOOD IN FRANCE/ SO WHY GO THERE?"

Some travelers disparage billboards as a blight on the landscape, but in the wide-open stretches of highway in the American West, I was always glad to see them. Approaching every ten or twenty miles, they were entertaining and informative, and many times on previous journeys I had chosen where I was going to stop and stay from a billboard along the highway. And, thanks to the anti-billboard movement championed by Lady Bird Johnson in the '60s, there were seldom enough of them to blight the landscape. All things in moderation.

Bumper stickers could be entertaining, too, and I smiled at one reading, "PRACTICE RANDOM ACTS OF COOLNESS." Or an oldie-but-goodie, "I BRAKE FOR HALLUCINATIONS." And one of those proud alumnus stickers across a car's rear window, in Gothic lettering: "YOUR COLLEGE SUCKS."

Long days on the "superslab" were not much of an adventure, perhaps, save for the not-to-be-underrated pleasure of just moving across the American landscape. But they did have a certain "zone" about them, an almost hypnotic rhythm of constant speed and passing scenery punctuated by trucks, billboards, and the longer intervals of fuel stops. Sometimes, the miles seem to pass painfully slowly, especially late in the day, as I counted down the distance signs to the next town: 97 miles, then 53 miles, 27, 14, and then it's replaced by another town, and you count it down again, the odometer numbers clicking around in their own steady rhythm. The world centers on the motorcycle and what you can see from it, and later that day, I made a journal note:

> A world so *circumscribed*. Framed, limited, contained, complete unto itself. "The Things They Carried." Only the bike, the riding clothes, the luggage. Nothing else matters except the phone call home.

For me, that long ride was a kind of blessed retreat, a welcome step away from an intense period of rehearsing and recording in Toronto, the preparation of our *Feedback* album, and my own writing and editing work on the final draft of *Traveling Music*. For those few days on the highway, I would take a break from all the work that had come before, and all the work that was ahead of me—the tour that had been so long in the making.

Plans had begun almost a year earlier, with manager Ray juggling dates and cities and fees, tour manager Liam coordinating budgets and crew members and subcontractors for lighting, sound, rigging, trucks, buses, airplanes, lasers, rear-screen projections, pyrotechnics, staging, "soft goods" (curtains and scrims), and the many other individuals and companies working on their separate strands of the flying carpet that made up a twenty-first century rock tour.

Before heading to Nashville for the final ten days of full production rehearsals—and the all-important first show—the three of us and our personal crew of technicians had already rehearsed for several weeks in a warehouse in Toronto. The musical side of the concert was fairly well prepared, but our live show, as always, would be an elaborate production, filling seven tractor-trailers and requiring about fifty people on our traveling crew. Behind the spotlights on the three of us, a lot of other people were performing too—from those very spotlight operators (hired locally), to truck drivers, bus drivers, pilots, riggers, lighting crew, sound crew, laser operators, pyrotechnicians, and merchandisers. We would also have a massive lighted projection screen behind us showing conceptual, atmospheric, or humorous film footage for many of the songs, combined with live camera close-ups of us at work. Many of the visual effects, and even sound mixing, would eventually be computerized, but it all had to be programmed manually and synchronized to the music, and that couldn't start until it was all set up in Nashville.

The development of my drum setup alone was a good example of the attention to detail that had gone into preparing for this tour. The previous September, I had ridden my motorcycle from my other home in Quebec to the Sabian cymbal factory in Meductic, New Brunswick. The purpose of that rainy, 600-mile journey was to spend some time at the factory and meet with the technicians, especially alchemist Mark Love, to develop some ideas for my own line of cymbals.

Our experiments eventually produced an array of original and satisfying cymbals, from ride and crashes to high-hats and effects models, which I named Paragon. The sales people at Sabian wanted to unveil the new line at the big musical instrument makers' trade show, NAMM, in

Anaheim, California, in January. They understood that I would be too shy to attend such an event personally, but asked if they might display my drumset as a showcase for the Paragon cymbals. That sounded fine, but I realized right away I didn't want them to use my old drums, the battle-scarred red-sparkle set that had survived two long tours already—*Test for Echo* and *Vapor Trails*—set up and torn down, in and out of cases, and trucked around for about 140 shows. They still *sounded* good, and I hadn't been thinking about replacing them, but cosmetically, the shells and hardware were a little road-weary. I started thinking about a new set, something worthy of being featured at a trade show like that, and to use on the upcoming Thirtieth Anniversary tour.

Thus inspired, when I traveled back to California, I called my friend at Drum Workshop, John Good, the "maestro of wood," and told him I was thinking about trying to create something really spectacular. I described a theme like the "dream cars" auto companies used to make in the '50s for the annual new-car introductions, to show off their visionary ideas and craftsmanship. At exhibitions like GM's Motorama, those gleaming, futuristic one-offs would be displayed on rotating stages with lights and pretty girls and music and dry ice (so very *rock!*), and the concept of "dream drums" was born.

John was excited and inspired, and immediately started talking about the shells—the wood—and how he might combine subtleties like the direction of the grain in the laminates to achieve maximum tonality and accentuate high or low overtones. When I visited John in his office, among the clutter of wood samples and scattered drum shells, he showed me a drum with twenty-four carat gold plating on the hardware. We agreed that would be nicer, more *special,* than the brass plating I had been using for many years, just to be different from the usual chrome.

It was October by then, and the NAMM show was in late January, so there was time, but not too much. Fortunately, the Drum Workshop factory was only a 45-minute drive from my house (and a *nice* drive, too, up the Pacific Coast Highway), so I started making regular visits as we experimented with different special finishes, with input from master painter Louie and transfer-maker, Javier.

Louie, a big man with a small boy's face, turned out a series of prototype finishes on single shells, starting with a flip-flop purple "Chameleon" and moving through various pearl whites. Quiet, precise

Javier worked on a series of laser-cut logos from several different Rush albums, which could be inset like mother-of-pearl: the man and star from *2112*, the skull from *Roll the Bones*, the bolt and nut from *Counterparts*, the Inuit inukshuk from *Test for Echo*, the "p-over-g" from *Grace Under Pressure*, and the bunny and top hat from *Presto*.

Ideas were coming together, but I still wasn't satisfied. Driving home from the DW factory one day, I glanced at the dashboard of my "dream car," the Z8's black lacquer and red leather, and thought, "Well yeah!" My favorite color combination, after all, and of the eleven or so drumsets I had owned over the years, I had never had one in black. After a few more experiments from Louie and refinements from Javier, we arrived at the final combination of black lacquer with red pinstripes (the same shade of red from my previous set, which had echoed the red-sparkle finish of my first-ever set of drums), framing oblong panels (a deliberate nod to Keith Moon's "Pictures of Lily" set from the mid-'60s, my teenage "dream drums") between the gold tension casings.

The panels featured a sparkly, prismatic "Mira" finish behind the pearlescent logos, and with all those steps to be performed, and twenty or so drums to make, paint, and assemble, the boys were hard pressed to get them done in time for the NAMM show. One January afternoon I stood in the factory showroom as they worked on the final assembly. It was virtually on the eve of the show, but at least we could now see how they looked: like a dream.

A drumset is such a pleasing arrangement of shapes to look at—the circle of the bass drum head facing you, nicely proportioned cylinders of different volumes, and shiny metallic discs suspended on glittering metal stands. Perhaps only a grand piano has the same sort of stage presence as a drumset, but of course, drum setups are much more personal, varying widely from one drummer to another.

Around that same time, early in 2004, bandmates Alex, Geddy, and I started exchanging e-mails on what songs we might like to play for this tour. It was intended to be a thirtieth-anniversary celebration, so we considered the musical content a little differently than usual. On previous tours we were always presenting a new album, a new body of work, and wanted to concentrate on that, but this time we wanted the setlist to reflect some kind of retrospective overview. Even with a three-hour show, any such overview could hardly be comprehensive—drawing on seventeen albums of material, we had scores of potential choices—but we wanted to be open to any possibilities. Medleys had always been a good tool for squeezing more songs into the time available, and I suggested we might arrange a kind of "overture," in which instrumental themes from many songs could be woven together into a powerful opening piece.

Early in 2004, the three of us were also exchanging ideas for old songs by other people, ones we might want to record for the *Feedback* project. We were looking back, or listening back, to the songs we had loved as teenagers, the first ones we had learned guitar parts, drum parts, and lyrics for. We bought reissued CDs by The Who, Blue Cheer, Cream, Jimi Hendrix, Love, Buffalo Springfield, and many more, searching for gems that might work for us in that context.

In late March, I flew to Toronto and moved into a downtown apartment-hotel, ready to start work (or *more* work—since January I had also been working daily with my editor, Paul McCarthy, on the ever-increasing revisions for *Traveling Music*). My usual approach to preparing for a tour was to spend two weeks rehearsing on my own, playing along with the CDs and building up my smoothness, accuracy, and stamina, so I would have a good foundation when I started working with Alex and Geddy. (Geddy once joked, "You're the only guy I know who rehearses to rehearse!")

In the first days in Toronto, I worked out a schedule that would allow me to give time and attention to everything. Over the years, I had learned it was possible to get a lot of work done in a day, but *not all at the same time*. That was the critical distinction. For me, the day had to be divided into discrete blocks, in which one activity would be paramount. That avoided the ruinous effects of stress, along with any guilt about not working on something I wanted to get done, and allowed me to approach the writing and the drumming with full concentration and commitment.

Up at six a.m. to start revising the book, I would open the latest e-mail updates from Paul, who worked through the night (and often around the clock). At eight I would pause for breakfast and watch an episode of "Family Guy" on DVD (a present from my friend Matt Scannell, whose band, Vertical Horizon, had a ritual of gathering to watch an episode together before each of their shows). Watching one of those clever, goofy, subversive cartoons was an important leavening interlude in my day. After that, it was write and revise some more until noon, when I would print out what I had done, send the revised chapter to Paul, and leave for the rehearsal hall. During that thirty- or forty-minute drive, I would listen to various Rush songs as I worked on them, refreshing my memory on fills and transitions.

My drum technician, Lorne (called "Gump," after a hockey goalie from the early '60s, Lorne "Gump" Worsley) would already be there, coffee on. He had spent a few days getting the new drumset sorted out, especially the electronics, which were giving us some grief. Since the early '80s, the band's musical technology had been guided by a Class-A technophile, Jim Burgess, who called his company Saved By Technology (though we and our crew had other names for it). Jim had also introduced me to personal computers in 1983, with the little Radio Shack unit that had almost enough memory (with the maximum "optional" RAM chips totaling about 32K) to hold my address book. As a computer, it was relatively useless, but it did allow me to become comfortable with the way the things worked, and a few years later, Jim would talk me into the Mac Plus. That became a more useful tool for writing lyrics and letters, and eventually replaced that pawnshop typewriter for my prose-writing efforts.

In the same way, electronic drums had progressed from the primitive Simmons noises to sophisticated digital sampling and midi, and I had learned to program and control each new unit as they came along. But of course, like computers, they didn't stop changing. Even back in 2002, during rehearsals for the *Vapor Trails* tour, Jim had shaken his head with disapproval over my antiquated setup of Akai digital samplers running off floppy disks Gump had to keep inserting throughout the show. However, I had been reluctant to change—those old units were reliable and straightforward, and even if we didn't have the latest in high sampling rates and hard-drive memory storage, at least Gump and I could program and control them ourselves. But this time, in 2004, Jim had finally convinced me to update to the "latest and greatest." With that irrepressible technophile faith, he had assured me the transition would be simple and painless, and it would all be *better*. Jim's faith was unshaken by my skeptical smile.

Not that I wanted to be right, but unfortunately, while I played through the old songs all day and struggled with the drum parts, building up my finger calluses and my stamina, Gump was struggling with the new electronics, building up brain calluses and bad words.

After four or five hours of bashing through the songs, I would leave Gump to battle on, and drive back to the apartment through the dense afternoon traffic of downtown Toronto. After parking in the basement garage, I would ride the elevator up to the seventh floor, have a shower, and relax with a Macallan on ice, reading over my work from the morning, red pen in hand for any further thoughts or corrections. That was always a peaceful and satisfying part of the day, one of my favorite states of mind—a combined sense of accomplishment and meditative absorption. (Unfortunately, it was necessary to do all that work in a day to create the conditions for that wonderful interlude; you couldn't just wake up and feel that way—more's the pity—it had to be earned.)

Occasionally I might have dinner and catch up with an old Toronto friend, but mostly I tried to keep the work going. I really wanted to finish that book before the tour started, and the days were ticking away.

For that commute to the rehearsal hall and back, I was driving the old 1996 Audi S-6 I kept at my Quebec house, which my property manager there, Keith, had delivered to Toronto. Although the car was eight years old, given my migratory life, it had few miles for its age, and it had a good Bose stereo. One sunny April day, though, I was stopped at a light, and a shiny yellow BMW R1200GS motorcycle crossed in front of me. It was a brand new model, the first one I had seen, but the motorcycle magazines had been full of reports about it (improved in every way, sixty pounds lighter, fifteen more horsepower).

More than anything, that sight made me want to be on a motorcycle, but it also made me want to be on *that* motorcycle. I hadn't been thinking about getting a new bike, as I had bought an 1150GS for the *Vapor Trails* tour in 2002, and it only had about 25,000 miles on it. My plan once again was to bring out the old 1100GS, the *Ghost Rider* bike, from its semiretirement (well-deserved, at over 100,000 miles) as a back-up for when my or Michael's bike needed service or new tires.

However, the band was planning a run of European dates at the end of the R30 tour, and I had asked our tour manager, Liam, to check into the possibility of renting a bus and trailer over there. I didn't know yet if the idea was even *possible*, but it had already occurred to me that maybe Brutus could be my riding partner once again. He may have been unwelcome in the United States, but European countries were not so fastidious. After all Brutus had been through in recent years—two years in prison and two years of hard manual work pursuing the "straight life"—I thought he would really appreciate the opportunity. Brutus didn't have a motorcycle at present, though, so I would have to provide two bikes. I didn't like the idea of us having to rely on the two older ones, with no backup.

So (I rationalized feverishly), obviously I *needed* a new motorcycle. The following Monday, I called John McBride at McBride Cycle, and told him I had seen a new 1200GS on the street.

"Let me guess," he said. "You want a *red* one."

I laughed. "You know me too well." (I had previously owned four red BMWs, and a red Ducati, so the color was perhaps an easy guess.)

Once I got the new bike, the daily commute to the rehearsal hall and back by motorcycle was much more enjoyable, not only for the pleasure of motorcycling, which was important enough, but because on the narrow streets of Toronto, I was able to weave around stopped cars and squeeze between lanes of turning traffic.

After a week of rehearsal on my own, Gump and I had to pause and move the drums and ourselves to a recording studio on the other side of Toronto. In juggling the schedules of studio time and the availability of coproducer David Leonard, I was breaking up my rehearsal time to start recording the cover songs for our *Feedback* project. As I drove out to Scarborough, I felt the apprehension of a big challenge ahead—recording a whole bunch of songs I didn't know very well, and wanting to do a good job—mixed with the anticipation of seeing "the guys at work."

We laughed when we talked about each other that way, remembering how our fathers or our friends with more "normal" jobs would quote news, gossip, wisdom, or humor that came from "the guys at work." When we were growing up and hearing what "they say," very often we were hearing it from the guys at work.

We could all do the stereotypical Canadian accent, familiar caricatures like Ronnie, Dougie, Kenny, or Gordie, saying, "Oh jeez—I was talkin' to the guys at work, eh, and they were sayin' . . . "

At that time, Brutus had a job in Toronto building photographic sets for catalogs (snow boots, chainsaws, curtains), and he would do imitations for me of the craftsmen, set decorators, and photographers on the crew. I especially liked his impression of the know-it-all who would come up behind him, watch what he was doing, and say, "Oh, you're doing it *that* way, are you? Hmm. Well, I wouldn't do it like that . . . But hey—you're the expert!"

I told Brutus he should put together a one-man play called *The Guys at Work*. It would have been huge. Everybody knows those guys.

After thirty years together, the three of us guys at work had evolved a working relationship that was complicated and multileveled. It included being the best of friends, but was complicated by also being both creative collaborators and business partners. Of course, we didn't always agree on what we wanted to do, or how we wanted to do it, but as individuals devoted to the higher entity of "the band," we had learned to pursue our own goals respectfully—to listen to everybody's opinions, consider them, and try to find a consensus that might satisfy everybody. We had also learned to have fun together whenever we could, and to try to keep things light, so even the dumbest jokes were always welcome.

Inevitably, we had our differences and disagreements—even conflicts and rivalries in the early years. But we had learned to choose our battles, to take a breath and ask ourselves, "Is that worth arguing about?" before we pressed a point that might lead to something more serious— the clichés of "creative differences" that so many bands blamed for their breakups.

Also, we had learned that *too much* familial closeness could create problems, and domestic dramas could affect the working relationship. So we had learned to balance our closeness with a certain necessary distance, and tended to keep a separation of home and work—of church and state, as it were.

After thirty years of being as close as Alex and Geddy and I have necessarily been, it is still daunting to try to describe the two of them. Not that I don't know them well enough, but perhaps too well, like a long-married spouse asked to describe his life partner. Over the passing decades, our association had grown to be somewhere between a partnership and a marriage, a family and a fraternity, and our bonds had been forged in the crucibles of both joy and grief. I can't claim to have been such a great friend to either of them—I am too solitary, independent, and self-involved—but I certainly know what wonderful friends they have been to me. (In good times and bad, I have been blessed with so many really good friends. I don't know why, but I do appreciate it.)

In tenth-grade English, I learned how to judge characters in books by what they did, what they said, and what others said about them. In the documentary part of the *Rush in Rio* DVD, Geddy talked about Alex, and tried to express some of the texture of their thirty-five year friendship.

> Lerxst is my oldest and dearest friend. He's the funniest man I've ever met in my life, and I don't expect to meet a funnier person, ever.
>
> He's an incredibly emotional guy, so he can be rational one second, and the next minute he can be *completely* irrational. He's very sharp, in a very scientific way. As a player, he's not a kind of methodical player, he's a very instinctive player. He can write things without thinking about them.

In turn, when I was asked to talk about Geddy, I gave it my best shot.

> Well, Geddy, like all of us, is a loveable mass of contradictions. We can all be as goofy as can be, and we can be serious and get down to it. Geddy, particularly, when he's constructing arrangements or working on vocal parts, he enters that narrow zone of concentration, but at the same time he's crazy for sports, for baseball, but we share so many interests in art, and literature. Even birdwatching, the two of us can talk about from time to time. All of us have these broad-ranging interests and facets to our personalities, that in the case of the three of us, at least, just happened to mesh so well. We entertain each other, we stimulate each other, and more than that, the *work* actually gets done, by the combination of methods that we all have.

Geddy and I always shared the traditional bonds of bass player and drummer—the "rhythm section"—and so worked tightly in that interlocking part of the music. But we also shared the intimate relation of lyricist and vocalist, with Geddy having to be comfortable singing words that I wrote. So there was a lot of give and take in our relationship, on a lot of levels, and whatever differences might have temporarily divided us, there was so much that tied us together.

Alex and Geddy's "brotherhood" could be more volatile sometimes. In the early years, I would be alarmed when they flared up at each other in brief rages that made *me* back away, but they could forget about them just as quickly. We were all counterpoints to each other in different ways (one intended meaning of our 1994 album title, *Counterparts*). Alex was the perfect balance to Geddy and me, musically and personally. So spontaneous, so ingenious, and so hilarious.

In that same *Rush in Rio* documentary, *The Boys in Brazil,* Geddy offered some thoughts on our collective character:

> The nature of Rush has always been musicianship first. It just has. We always tried to be the best musicians we could, and tried to challenge each other, and I don't think that's really changed. I mean, a lot has changed—obviously we've become much better songwriters and song arrangers and producers, and all those things have taken a more and more important role through the years. So that shows your growth, and your expanding. But at the core of it, we love to play, and we love to play well.
>
> I expect myself to play well, and I expect myself to play *better,* and to do something better than I did last time. And that is a natural part of Rush. It's a natural thing that Alex, Neil, and I share. We want to do things better—that's what drives us. That's what's always driven us.

That was a good characterization of us and our group progression, and for the way each of us felt about our profession, of being dedicated without being too solipsistic. Geddy summed that up pretty well, too.

> Listen, we're musicians. It's not really that noble of a pursuit. So if you can do something that touches someone like that, it's pretty mind-boggling to me.

The guys at work gathered in the studio once again, joking and laughing and fooling around, but as always, the work went ahead, too. The basic tracks and drum parts for the *Feedback* songs were finished in a few days, and while the guys and coproducer David Leonard continued working on overdubs, Gump and I moved back across town to the rehearsal hall and continued my prerehearsal rehearsals.

I stayed away on the Monday Alex and Geddy moved in, knowing they would need time to get their gear sorted out. Tuesday, we got down to business, but we eased into it, sitting on the carpet in front of Alex's pedal board with coffee and donuts, pens and paper and song lists, and tried to narrow down the songs we would work on.

The previous tour's setlist was a starting point, though we immediately turned it upside down. If we had opened a set with a song last time, it went to the end; if we had closed with a song, it went to the beginning. We wanted to play as many songs as we could that were not in the previous tour's setlist, and to bring back some unusual tracks from our past. We also wanted to play some of the songs from the new *Feedback* CD, as we had enjoyed revisiting the songs we had played in our first bands, from "Summertime Blues," combining arrangement ideas from The Who and Blue Cheer, to lighter ones like "For What It's Worth" and "Heart Full of Soul." (With only eight fairly short cover songs, it wasn't quite an "album" to us. We thought of it more like what used to be called an EP, an "extended play" single.)

We worked the same sort of hours that I had on my own, so my mornings were still free for book work. We came in at noon and rehearsed for a couple of hours, then stopped for lunch. That always-welcome interlude was especially delicious this time, as Liam had brought in Frenchie, our chef from the *Vapor Trails* tour, to work in a makeshift kitchen in the warehouse. When Liam had been working out the rehearsal budget (wearing his Scottish "Thrifty McBirt" tam, as always), he had figured that having Frenchie there would be just as "economical" (said with Scottish accent) as sending someone out for a pile of take-out food every day, and a *lot* better. Credited in our tourbooks as our "nutritionist," Frenchie had worked with touring artists from Frank Sinatra to Pearl Jam, and his "nutrition" was always delicious and imaginative. His show-day afternoon soups were especially renowned among the three of us, the source of our jokes in the *Rush in Rio* DVD about the most important element of the tour being the soup. (My brother Danny sent me some good soup quotes for Frenchie: "Only the pure in heart can make a good soup," from Ludwig van Beethoven, and "Soup is such a comfort," from Georgia O'Keeffe.)

After five weeks of hard work, good lunches, and lots of soup, the two long sets had come together, and we could more-or-less play them all the way through, most days. It was a marathon performance for all of us, well over three hours of music, and as the drummer, it was particularly demanding, even *athletic,* for me. The show was longer than we had intended, and certainly longer than I wanted, but despite some creative medleying, we hadn't been able to bear cutting it. We would not give up the standards from our usual live shows, like "Tom Sawyer" and "The Spirit of Radio," or the older treasures we had resurrected, like "Mystic Rhythms" and "Between the Wheels," or the cover tunes like "The Seeker," "Summertime Blues," and a nice acoustic version of "Heart Full of Soul." That song was strategically timed so that after my drum solo, I could take a breather while Alex and Geddy performed "Resist" acoustically, as they had on the *Vapor Trails* tour, then started into "Heart Full of Soul." I would join in on the second verse.

I had also spent a bit of time working after hours to put my drum solo together. I always preferred to arrange my drum solo, to compose a structure that would be consistent for each night's performance, but still allow room for improvisation and inspiration. Often I would listen to the previous tour's solo and think, "I'm not really finished with that structure—I could keep working on that." But as a matter of principle, I forced myself to change it all around, or at least put the parts I liked in a different order.

My drumset was divided into two: the main setup of acoustic drums and cymbals at the front, and a "satellite" kit, the electronic setup, at the rear. To switch between them, I stood up and turned around, while the riser rotated 180 degrees to face the audience. On previous tours I had always started my solo on the front kit, then played a middle section on the back, before returning to the front setup for the ending. This time it happened that the solo came after the song "Red Sector A," which I played on the back kit, so I decided to start from there—that would be different. With much sweat and brainwork, I worked out a musical framework to build the solo on, and figured out the technology with Gump, who would have to switch the electronic programs and do "the spin" of the riser following agreed-upon cues.

In the same way, the song order was subject to so many considerations, from Alex not liking to have two songs in a row in the same key—or with the same *guitar*, it seemed, as he was always changing guitars for different sounds or tunings—to me not liking two songs in a row with the same tempo, to Geddy not wanting to be stuck at the keyboards too much. We also needed to consider the rear-screen visual effects for particular songs, wanting the more vivid films to come later in the show, when it would be dark in the outdoor amphitheaters.

By the time we finished in Toronto, and the crew packed the gear into the cases and loaded the trucks bound for Nashville, the three of us felt pretty confident about our part of the performance. And in any case, we would be playing the whole show at least another ten times in Nashville, smoothing out our own parts while the sound, lighting, and video crews worked on their programming.

Now, on May 15th, Michael and I rode eastward on the Mother Road—or its bland and obese daughter, Interstate 40—carrying us through Amarillo, Groom, McLean, and Shamrock, Texas. Long-distance riding days were tiring, and late in the day I would feel stiff and weary, but again, even on the interstate, a motorcycle ride was never tedious. The billboards, the licence plates, the bumper stickers, the ever-changing scenery, the white-noise jukebox playing in my head ("By the time I make Oklahoma" a constantly repeating line that day), the scurrying creatures and bloody roadkill, the ever-changing sky, the smells in the air (from the perfume of newly-mown hay to the stench of the feedlots), the passing towns, hills, farms, trees and shrubs and birds and clouds.

The thoughts, the ideas, the notions, the questions, the memories, all the whirling music that filled the moving brain. So much I would try to remember, then forget when I got off the bike at the end of the day. I began to wish for some kind of voice-activated tape recorder so I could capture all that I was seeing and thinking. But then I thought about transcribing hours of tapes full of thoughts and observations that no one, not even me, would ever care about again.

And anyway, the more significant points seemed to get written down eventually, and if they occurred to me again a day or two later, they were probably the ones worth noting. Still, one of the most frequent journal notes I would make during that tour was, "I miss so much!" referring to all that passed before my eyes and through my mind that didn't get written down.

Traveling through that narrow crown of the Texas Panhandle set off a far-reaching train of thought. I traced through the kind of aimless memories dredged up by the droning miles and the white noise of cutting through the wind at 90 mph. Reading the signs to other cities and towns, I was thinking of all the smaller cities Rush used to play in Texas—not just Houston and Dallas and San Antonio, but Amarillo, Lubbock, Odessa (where I remember going off with some of the crew guys in search of a laundromat on a rare day off in the late '70s), Midland, Abilene, Beaumont, Austin (playing at a '70s rock club called Armadillo World Headquarters), Galveston, and El Paso. Corpus Christi's Gulf Coast warmth and palm trees had seemed so *exotic* to us Canadians on our first winter visit. We had played several times in that old theater with the Pearl beer signs, opening for Rory Gallagher once, and later, headlining a couple of times.

When Brutus and I were riding through Texas on the *Test for Echo* tour, we had noted some graffiti in a truck-stop rest room, "BILLY RAY CAN'T ROPE WORTH SHIT." A phrase like that had a delightful sense of place, and later that summer, in Quebec, Brutus would scrawl with his finger on the oxidized hull of my rowboat, "NEIL CAN'T ROW WORTH SHIT."

I thought of a band from Texas I liked when I was a teenager, Fever Tree. Their first album had been my favorite for a while, and I still remembered many of the songs. Their minor hit from the summer of 1967, "San Francisco Girls (Return of the Native)," played in my mental jukebox, and I heard snatches of other songs from their self-titled album, like "Filigree and Shadow," and "The Sun Also Rises." It occurred to me what an influence that album had been on my youthful ideals of rock music—literary titles, from Thomas Hardy and Ernest Hemingway, classically influenced arrangements and orchestrations, songs ranging from the R&B standard "Ninety-Nine and One Half" to Neil Young's poignant "Nowadays Clancy Can't Even Sing."

In the mid-'70s, we were touring with the band Mott (formerly "Mott the Hoople"), and I learned the keyboard player shared my enthusiasm for that Fever Tree album. During a break I made him a cassette tape from my old LP. What ever happened to them? (Mott *and* Fever Tree. And LPs and cassettes!)

I made a mental note to look up Fever Tree on the Internet when I got a chance, and it turned out to be a familiar story: rise from oblivion to modest success, then personality problems, drug and alcohol problems, creative problems, and eventually, career problems. A couple of Fever Tree's members had died by 2004, and the rest had long since dispersed, but judging by all I was able to find out about them so easily, I wasn't the only one who remembered the band. Too bad about all those problems.

A journalist once told me it seemed to him that not only had Rush stayed together so long, but we had also avoided the usual problems with personalities, alcohol, and drugs that brought down so many of our peers.

I told him, "Well, it's not like over the years we haven't *been* everywhere like that—we just didn't *stay* there!" Like the Winston Churchill quote, "When you're going through hell, keep going." Or the T-shirt a friend brought me from a bar in the Bahamas, "Rehab is for Quitters."

Michael and I crossed into Oklahoma, pointing at the sign, waving our hands and shaking our helmets like demented kids, in a moment of telepathically shared humor. The first deciduous trees appeared at the roadside, yellow flowers dotted the median, and the landscape began to undulate into rolling, wooded hills. I realized how different it was to be making that journey from west to east—traveling from the open, dry country of the Southwest *into* the land of rain and trees, from arid brown and red to dense greenery, tall, leafy, and shady. This resembled the familiar landscape of my childhood in Southern Ontario, and I realized that living in Southern California for the past four years had made the desert Southwest, and especially the arid chaparral, look natural to me. Now the lush vegetation of the East seemed overwhelmingly green and profuse, almost prodigal.

As we rode through Oklahoma City, weaving through four or five lanes of busy Saturday afternoon traffic, my scan of the road ahead fixed on something moving, a gray and solid-looking object flying high into the air in front of me. Time slowed down as I identified the flying object as a wheelbarrow, fallen off a landscaping truck a couple of lanes over. I tensed-up immediately, ready to dodge in any direction if it came near me, or to avoid other cars that might have to swerve around it. The wheelbarrow hit the road heavily, then bounced high into the air a couple of times, before finally crashing down, upright, in the middle of the lane beside us.

The danger was already past when the adrenaline began to rise, and I shook my helmet angrily over what so easily might have happened there—the difference of a few feet or a few seconds either way might have been fatal for us. Even if another vehicle had veered into our lane to avoid it, we might easily have been killed. I thought about that for miles afterward, angry and outraged, imagining excruciating punish-

50

ments for the kind of careless person who could let such a thing happen, and so threaten others' lives through simple laziness.

Another motorcycling musician, Mark Knopfler from Dire Straits, had been forced to cancel a tour in 2003 after he was cut off by a car in London and crashed his bike, breaking some ribs and his collarbone. At a rehearsal hall in Toronto, I once met Richie Hayward, the great drummer from Little Feat. He was looking over my BMW GS, and told me a story about how one time, he had been traveling by motorcycle on a tour in Texas, and had been run off the road by a pickup. Two guys jumped out of the truck, loaded up his Harley, and left him there in the ditch with two broken legs.

So things could happen—in London, Texas, or Oklahoma—and I was always aware of that. Again, "When I'm riding my motorcycle, I'm glad to be alive. When I stop riding my motorcycle, I'm glad to be alive."

Passing a sign for a turnoff to Muskogee, Oklahoma, I thought of Merle Haggard's '60s redneck anthem, "Okie from Muskogee," and made an involuntary scowl, as if at a bad memory. Haggard had sung about how proud he was to be an Okie from Muskogee, where people liked "livin' right, and bein' free." "We don't smoke marijuana in Muskogee/ We don't take no trips on LSD," and, "We don't let our hair grow long and shaggy/ Like those hippies out in San Francisco do."

In later years, Haggard's reputation seemed to make him almost "cool" (he was even pardoned by then-governor of California, Ronald Reagan, in 1972 for a late '50s stretch in San Quentin for armed robbery), but to me, having been the kind of longhair he was disparaging in that song, and in those times, it was a bad memory. It's hard to imagine now, but in those days, "hippies" and "freaks" were persecuted and ridiculed on the street, even *violently*.

In small-town Ontario in the late '60s, I was bullied and jeered at, threatened in the schoolyard, and refused service in restaurants for having long hair (barely covering my ears). A friend of mine was held down in shop class while two greasy-haired jocks hacked at his hair with tin snips. So in later years, I could never look kindly on characters like the Fonz from "Happy Days" (however decent they portrayed him), or the goons from *Grease*, because they were exactly the type of greasy-haired thugs who made my teenage years miserable. Likewise, Merle Haggard's "Okie From Muskogee" had been the voice of the enemy.

One time, in the mid-'70s, the three of us and our first road manager, Howard, were checking into a hotel in Wichita, and a bunch of good old boys in suits and ties passed us in the parking lot. Snickering at our long hair and colorful clothes, one of them was moved to comment, "There's somethin' you don't see every day—horseshit on legs!"

Like every outrageous statement we heard in those days, it became a laughable catchphrase with us, but still, that's no way to talk to other human beings, just because you don't like their getups. And I'm sure Merle Haggard was soon to discover that people *did* smoke marijuana in Muskogee, and would even let their hair grow long and shaggy.

The Saturday traffic had been heavy through Amarillo, and worse around Oklahoma City. From the "Route 66" song: "Now you go through St. Louis, and Joplin, Missouri, Oklahoma City is might pretty." Well, we hadn't been so impressed with Oklahoma City this time—with that flying wheelbarrow and all—and we were saying goodbye to the Mother Road for now. Old 66 angled northeast toward Tulsa, and eventually, up to Chicago, "more than two thousand miles, all the way."

Strange to think that all the place names in that song seemed so exotic when I was a kid, yet are all so familiar now: "You'll see Amarillo, Gallup, New Mexico/ Flagstaff Arizona, don't forget Winona, Kingman, Barstow, San Bernardino."

The last verse was pretty snappy too, especially for 1946: "Won't you get hip to this timely tip/ When you make that California trip/ Get your kicks on Route 66."

We were still getting our kicks on Interstate 40, but even on the open highway through Oklahoma and into Arkansas, there were some long, one-lane construction zones that slowed us way down. For a while we seemed to thread our way through a corridor of solid semi trucks, including a lot of those Covenant trailers from Chattanooga, each with a large sign on the back, "IT IS NOT A CHOICE, IT IS A CHILD." Other trailers offered quotes from scripture, and once I passed a truck with a big sticker on the back showing a waving U.S. flag with a golden Christian cross superimposed over it. In big letters, the caption read, "WE WANT IT BACK." A little shocked at this blatant mixture of symbols—American equals Christian—I made a wry face and shook my helmet sadly, "You already have it."

For several miles I entertained myself with dark fantasies about other religions being so bold and presumptuous. I pictured semi-trailers on American interstates bearing slogans like "THERE IS NO GOD BUT ALLAH AND MOHAMMED IS HIS PROPHET," or a big blue Star of David with, "THAT JEWISH CARPENTER WASN'T OUR MESSIAH."

Traveling the United States by motorcycle, I always noticed the difference between riding on a weekday, when drivers had places to go and knew how to get there, and weekends—when the "amateurs" were out. Minivans and SUVs choked the outside lanes, then dove across lanes of traffic for last-minute exits, talked on their cell phones, shouted at their children, and obliviously carried the banner of the Anti-Destination League. Statistically, Saturday actually *was* the most dangerous day of the week on American roads, and the afternoon was the worst time of day (July 4 was the deadliest day, August the deadliest month).

So, Michael and I weren't making the same fast, easy progress we had on the first day. Once we crossed into Arkansas (waving madly), finally the highway opened up, leading us through a leafy corridor and across a bridge arching over the wide Arkansas River. Michael was feeling stronger that day, and during a roadside Red Apple break he said he was willing to go for the Thousand-in-One if I wanted. But I was feeling pretty fatigued by then, after riding almost 1600 miles in two days, and suggested we stop at Fort Smith, another hour or two on. That would make about 750 miles for the day. (Later I made a journal note: "Yesterday an easy 850; today a *hard* 750. Tough traveling, really, but I'm loving it.")

Along the interstate I saw a billboard for the Holiday Inn Civic Center ("The Pride of Fort Smith"), but I allowed Michael to lead us to a Best Western, guided by the GPS unit. Like the diner in Tucumcari, however, that Best Western was closed, boarded up, and abandoned, so we headed for the Holiday Inn. It seemed that clever machine had a few things to learn.

"The Pride of Fort Smith" was buzzing with activity on that Saturday evening. Cars and pedestrians swarmed in for a "Freshman Formal" and the Miss Preteen Arkansas Pageant, and no doubt everything else that was happening that night in Fort Smith. While I sat astride my motorcycle and waited to see if Michael would be able to get us rooms, the scene around me was like a *Life* magazine photo-essay. Parents were dropping off their teenagers for the formal, the boys pimply and self-conscious in rented, ill-fitting tuxedos, but the girls positively *radiant* in their ill-fit-ting, homemade-looking gowns, elaborate hairdos and makeup, running up to each other and gushing as they embraced.

At the Civic Center Arena next door, I noticed the lighted sign out front announced, "Willie Nelson Concert Postponed." I wondered about a performer of Willie's stature (and *age*) still playing a small town like Fort Smith, Arkansas. Was he still so hard up after the IRS took every-thing away from him that he had to play anywhere that would have him? I hoped not—I hoped he still "just couldn't wait to get on the road again." (Another kind of Mother Road.)

That sign also flashed advertisements for an upcoming *Beatlemania* performance, with ticket prices of $22.50 plus $3.75 service charge. That seemed pretty expensive for an *imitation* show, but for Beatlemaniacs, it was as close as they were going to get, and no doubt they would be entertained. It was ironic to think that the imitation would probably look and sound better than the *real* Beatles ever had, given the limitations of technology in their day, not to mention the con-stant screaming—one big reason they stopped touring. (That, and being pelted with jelly beans every night, after making the innocent mistake of saying they liked them.)

When Michael came out with our room keys, I went to move my bike down along the front of the hotel to park it, and I was struck, literally, by how fatigued I really was. I had to ride up a sidewalk ramp, and as I steered my front wheel along the curb and onto the ramp, I half-realized that the back wheel was going to catch on that curb. But even as my brain began to process the likely outcome, it seemed I was too tired to think it through, or do anything about it. Sure enough, over I went, the bike and me falling sideways onto the pavement. Michael and one of the bellmen helped me raise the 500-pound bike—no damage done (I was too tired even to be embarrassed), and hopefully a lesson learned. Fatigue makes you stupid.

Over dinner in the Holiday Inn restaurant, I talked to Michael about the European leg of the tour that would come in September. I needed to tell him I was thinking of traveling by motorcycle over there as well, but that I wanted to bring Brutus along to be my riding partner. Liam had located an Austrian company that could provide a bus and trailer, but he suggested we should still bring Michael to Europe to look after security there. At least I wouldn't have to tell Michael he wasn't going—just that he wouldn't be riding. I wanted to tell him about this plan as soon as possible, so he wouldn't hear it from someone else. I was hoping he would understand that it wasn't personal—it was something I wanted to do *for* Brutus, not *against* Michael. It was a rare opportunity for Brutus and me to travel together. To Michael's credit, he accepted the situation gracefully. He was disappointed, of course, but graciously sympathized with how great the experience would be for Brutus, and also saw how it would be better for himself, professionally, allowing him to cover the security end of things more efficiently.

Those two long, tiring days on the road, plus the two time changes we had already crossed, had me asleep by ten, and wide awake at five, eager to get going on the last press to Nashville. Unlike me, Michael was not a breakfast person, save for a caffeine jolt from Red Bull or Mountain Dew, so I let him sleep while I went down to the atrium restaurant, empty so early on a Sunday morning, except for another couple of older guys on their own.

Michael and I had just over 500 miles to go now, so we were already a full day ahead of my worst-case plan. Setting off from Fort Smith, in and out of light rain, we made pretty good time across Arkansas. As we crossed the Mississippi to Memphis, the sky was clearing and the midday sun was hot. While we peeled off our rain gear at a roadside pull-out, I made a phone call to our bus driver, Dave, in Nashville. He had offered to ride out and meet us on his Harley Heritage, and guide us to the hotel. (Or as he would say it, "*ho*-tel.")

Just outside Memphis, I passed a sign on a bridge naming the Wolf River, and recognized it as the river where Jeff Buckley had so tragically drowned, in May, 1997. Inevitably, his songs started playing in my head; "Lover, You Should've Come Over," "Last Goodbye," and especially his haunting version of Leonard Cohen's "Hallelujah." I worked on remembering all the verses, and singing them into my helmet with heartfelt tunelessness, the joyful mediocrity of the talentless singer. "Well I heard there was a secret chord, that David played and it pleased the Lord, but you don't really care for music, do ya?"

Farther along, weaving our way through the dense Sunday afternoon traffic across Tennessee, I saw an exit with a sign advertising the "Patsy Cline Crash Site." This ghoulish attraction for the morbidly curious was the site of her fatal plane crash in March, 1963. Now Patsy's songs started playing in my head, and singing in my helmet—both Cline and Buckley were artists I had written about in the book I was trying to finish, *Traveling Music.*

Apart from the tour rehearsals, which were certainly my professional and personal priority at the time, I had a few other jobs awaiting me in Nashville. During the ten days of rehearsal there, I needed to finalize the last chapter of *Traveling Music* and go through the galleys of the rest of the book, hoping to catch any errors, make corrections, and send it off to the printers before the first show. The long tour was sure to demand all of my time and energy, so I knew if I didn't have the book completed and submitted before the first show, I wouldn't be able to get back to it until sometime much later, like October. That would mean at least another six months before the book could be published, and I was way too impatient for that.

Also, I hated to miss the opportunity to find more *readers* among all those concertgoers, as a modest number of books were sold at every show. But at least, I thought, we would have *The Masked Rider* and *Ghost Rider* on sale for the tour. If I was able to finish my part of the work on *Traveling Music,* it could come out sometime during the tour, and that would be fine.

My publisher was planning a new edition of my first book, *The Masked Rider,* but I had known I wouldn't have time to be involved in that. Earlier in the year, I had bought back the rights from the original publisher, Pottersfield Press, a small company owned by my friend, the author Lesley Choyce. I wanted to have all three of my books in more-or-less uniform editions, published and distributed by the same company, with distribution to American bookstores. Back in February, I had dug through my files in Quebec to find the original photographs, and brought them to Toronto along with the bronze cyclist for the cover, then told the publisher I would have to trust him to put the rest of it together. That turned out to be a very bad decision, but at the time, I felt I had no choice.

Michael and I turned off at the exit where Dave had said he would meet us, and there he was, standing by his blue and white Harley, its masses of chrome glittering in the sun. Medium height, mid-forties, wire-rimmed glasses, neatly trimmed hair and goatee, Dave wore jeans and a sleeveless T-shirt, and a "beany" helmet covered with rude stickers like, "IF I'D SHOT YOU WHEN I WANTED TO, I'D BE OUT BY NOW."

Dave had been my driver since *Test for Echo*, the first time I traveled with my own bus and motorcycles. Early on that tour, in October 1996, Brutus and I invited Dave to meet us at a Holiday Inn in Alpena, Michigan, at the end of a day off, and join us for dinner. To justify charging our meals to the tour expense account, I declared the occasion the first official meeting of the Scooter Trash party.

Raising his Captain Morgan and Coke, Dave said in his deep southern drawl, "Ah guess we better discuss some business, then."

"Okay, we're playing in Auburn Hills tomorrow, right?"

"Yep."

"Motion to adjourn for refreshments."

"Seconded."

"Carried."

Brutus asked Dave where he was from originally, and when he replied, "Cincinnati," I said that his accent seemed unusually deep for that part of the country. Dave chuckled, "Ah worked real hard for that accent." He said that in his twenties, he had played bass in a gospel group out of Nashville, and had found that "the little girls really liked that accent." So he had practiced it day and night with a dedication born of pure lust, and twenty years later, it had become his own.

Not that there was anything artificial about ol' Dave. He was as *real* as they come, a bus-driving, Harley-riding, straight-talking Southern boy, occasionally game for a bit of gambling and drinking, a scrap if necessary. I definitely considered Dave to be one of my circle of brothers, on the road or off, just as I did Michael, Brutus, Geddy, Alex, Ray, Liam, and Gump. Dave was fiercely loyal—*fearlessly* loyal—to me and to everyone on the tour, and though he was not a big man, he didn't back down from anyone.

Later in that *Test for Echo* tour, in the early summer of '97, we were playing at an outdoor amphitheater called the Gorge in Washington state, and during the show, Dave stepped off our bus and saw little Richie ("Itchy"), the lighting crew chief, being threatened by a beefy security guard. Without even knowing what the disagreement was about, Dave put himself between them and said to the security guard, "You better just back away right now, or you're gonna get a whole lotta somethin' you're not gonna like."

The security guard was sent home, hopefully to savor that phrase, as I always have—"A whole lotta somethin' you're not gonna like."

On another tour with a country act in Galveston, Dave had been pulling the bus out of the venue after the show, when some yahoo up in a parking garage started dumping bins full of empty beer bottles down on the buses. Without saying anything to the people he was driving, Dave got out and ran up the stairs to take the guy on—only to learn there were *three* of them. One of them came up behind Dave and broke a bottle over his head, and he went down, knocked cold. He came to with a bloody cut on his head and a concussion, and as he described it, "Ah had a bad headache—and ah decided right then that next time, ah'd have a *gun*."

One day, Dave was stopped at a light while driving the bus through a city, and he watched a wild-eyed panhandler walk purposefully in front of the bus, then yank open the door and step right on board. (Oh, you don't do that!) The guy found himself looking into the business end of Dave's handgun, and hearing Dave say, "You just got on the *wrong* fuckin' bus."

The man threw his hands up, *"No shit!"* and backed right out of there.

All through that *Test for Echo* tour in '96 and '97, Brutus and I had heard Dave talk about how he was going to buy a Harley, and Michael and I had heard about it all through the *Vapor Trails* tour in 2002. But finally, at the end of that tour, he had bought one. For the next two years, he had e-mailed me photographs of the bike as he made improvements (more chrome). Then, just a couple of weeks previously, he had called me in Toronto to ask if I thought maybe we could squeeze *four* bikes into the trailer—Michael's and my 1150 GSes, the new 1200 GS, and, of course, Dave's Heritage. That way, when the bus was parked, he could get out and ride around, too. I told him if he could make them all fit in that little trailer, it was all right with me.

Dave fired up the unmuffled Harley, then rumbled back onto the interstate, leading Michael and me to an Embassy Suites in the suburbs of Nashville. Geddy and Alex were staying at a more luxurious hotel downtown, but over the years I had learned that I could best enjoy my privacy by staying away from "the band"—overzealous fans could often find a larger group of people, even under false names, but one or two guys traveling anonymously could usually maintain a lower profile. Dave had also recommended the suburban location of the Embassy Suites as a good gateway to nice motorcycling roads in the area.

For many years, we had all been obliged to stay in hotels under aliases, to prevent interruptions from usually well-meaning, but misguided fans. We'd had a lot of fun with those names, especially the irrepressible joker, Alex, who had adopted such aliases as Dr. Karl Zborg, Hugh Jas, Hy Hytlor ("No, no, no—that's '*Hite*-lor' "), and, for the R30 tour, Red Meat.

For myself, I always tried to pick a name that was easy for hotel staff to spell and pronounce, but with a tongue-in-cheek reference (nothing *too* silly; I had once tried being Joe Rockhead, from "The Flintstones," but after having to say that name to room service people first thing in the morning a couple of times, I changed it). I preferred obscure characters from old TV shows, like Hank Kimball from "Green Acres," Larry Tate from "Bewitched," or (one of my favorites) Johnny Gilbert, the unseen announcer on "Jeopardy." On recent tours I had been Waylon Smithers, the sycophantic assistant to the nuclear power plant owner, Montgomery Burns, on "The Simpsons."

The *nom d'hotel* I had chosen for the R30 tour was Paul Drake, Perry Mason's hapless investigator, so dashing in his ascots and tweeds, and always trying to hit on Della Street, who was so transparently in love with Perry. (It had been a close contest against the evil infant, Stewie Griffin, from "Family Guy," a recent hero, but Paul had won out. When I first showed an episode of "Family Guy" to Michael, and told him Stewie was my hero, Michael made a face of alarmed disbelief, "You *are* Stewie!")

It was also necessary for better-known employees (those often mentioned in album or tourbook credits, like Liam) to use aliases for the same reasons—they would be awakened in the middle of the night by fans looking for us. Michael had chosen Joshua Falcon, a super-geek character he felt akin to from the 1983 "hacker" movie, *War Games*.

One change in our touring personnel this time was Donovan, who was stepping into the position of "road manager." Liam had lobbied for this new combination of an assistant for him, as tour manager, who could help with logistics like ground transportation for Geddy and Alex every day, as well as being the band's personal assistant, taking care of laundry and other glamorous duties. Donovan was in his mid-twenties, from Minnesota, but now lived in Nashville. He had some tour managing experience on smaller tours, and while working with us up in Toronto for several weeks, he had seemed agreeable, willing, and capable. But he won *big* points with me when I checked into my room at the Embassy Suites and opened a big cardboard box from him containing a carton of Canadian cigarettes ("Red Apples"), a bottle of The Macallan, some bound copies of the *Traveling Music* typescript I had asked him to have made (though the final chapter remained open to revision), a map of the Nashville area, directions on how to get to the rehearsal hall, and all kinds of local information. I was impressed.

I was also impressed, in a different, less welcome way, when I turned on my laptop and logged onto the hotel's broadband link. To my dismay, after three days of being off the grid, I had no fewer than twenty-eight e-mails waiting for me, so I had some work to do. Many of them were questions about the details of book publishing, and there were a bunch about the artwork of *Feedback*. As usual, I had been coordinating the artwork, credits, and liner notes for the cover, working with my longtime collaborator on album covers, Hugh Syme, even as Geddy and Alex had been working on their overdubs and supervising the mixing with our coproducer, Dave Leonard.

Over the years we had established a fine division of labor, in which each of us guys at work looked after different areas of band business, especially those suited to our abilities and tastes. Before a tour, Geddy would work for months with the film companies on developing animation and mood-pieces for the big screen behind our stage, to complement a number of songs in the show. The previous year, Alex had spent weeks of long days in a Toronto recording studio with engineer Jimbo, working on the audio mixes for our *Rush in Rio* DVD. Likewise, apart from drumming and lyric-writing, I would oversee the graphic arts side of things: album covers, tourbooks, and written pieces to accompany album releases and such.

Strange that the drummer ended up being perceived as the literary one in the band, given the usual reputation, especially among other musicians, of those of us who "hit things with sticks." Drummers may be the subject of more jokes than any ethnic group, or even traveling salesmen, priests, rabbis, and blondes. And like the ever-popular blonde jokes, most drummer jokes imply very unkind things about our intelligence.

But they are funny:

Q: What did the drummer get on his IQ test?
A: Drool.

Q: How can you tell if the stage is level?
A: The drool comes out of both sides of the drummer's mouth.

a stage is all the world

To awaken quite alone in a strange town
is one of the pleasantest sensations in the world.

Freya Stark

On a hot Tennessee afternoon, the sky a hazy bluish-white and the temperature nudging 90 degrees, Michael and I rode twenty minutes up the interstate to downtown Nashville, then a few blocks through the city to the rehearsal hall. Other than playing in Nashville every tour, and bicycling or motorcycling around a bit, I had never spent much time there, so I was looking forward to these ten days. The beginning of a tour was a rare opportunity to spend longer than the usual few hours in a city, and on previous tours we had enjoyed staying a week to ten days in Pensacola, Florida, Greenville, South Carolina, St. John's, Newfoundland, New Haven, Connecticut, and Hamilton, Ontario (a slightly more familiar setting, between my home town of St. Catharines and Toronto, and, in fact, the city where I was born, the nearest hospital to our family farm in Hagersville).

For the two previous tours, *Vapor Trails* and *Test for Echo*, we had held the full production rehearsals in a small arena in Glens Falls, New York, on the edge of the Adirondacks. The crew stayed at a nearby hotel so they could go back and forth to the arena easily, and the band stayed about twenty miles north, at the Sagamore resort on the shore of Lake

George. I had especially loved the motorcycle ride back from the arena at night, cool in the spring or fall, woodsmoke in the air, as the dark two-lane road curved along the shoreline of Lake George. I seldom ride at night, for reasons of safety and lack of scenery, but those late-night returns were so enjoyable, cruising along through the chilly darkness and feeling warm under my leathers from the exertion of having just played through the three-hour show.

This time we were trying Nashville, or as it was sometimes called, Nash Angeles, Nash Vegas, and—by the guys at work—"Naishville," in the manner of a longtime bus driver, Whitey, from Michigan. It happened that tour manager Liam had been making a lot of visits to Nashville in the past couple of years, though his dimwitted friends and employers hadn't yet put together the reason (*cherchez la femme*). I didn't even make the connection when Ray told me "we" were thinking of trying a new rehearsal place in Nashville that Liam was suggesting. Apparently it was a purpose-built facility adjacent to the downtown arena, and the management there was eager to develop new business, particularly from the non-Nashville, non-Country world, so they were offering a very favorable deal. I had thought at the time it was a classic "Thrifty McBirt" rationale, but it was the opposite of rationale; it was *love*.

Liam had been going through an unpleasant divorce (is there any other kind?), but he was a very private and discreet man, and it would be *months* before the guys at work would start whispering about a possible secret relationship between Liam and the crew bus driver, Lashawn. Now on her second tour with us, Lashawn was a blonde, Nordic girl from Minnesota who lived in Nashville, and her younger brother was . . . Donovan. (And we *still* didn't figure it out!)

On that first rehearsal day, Michael and I followed Donovan's written directions into downtown Nashville (though Michael pretended we were following his GPS), then turned onto a side street. Dave was waiting there, astride his Harley, cigarette dangling from his mouth, and he led us down the ramp and into the cavernous load-in area where we parked the bikes. George, the tour carpenter and a longtime friend who came from the same small town I did (Port Dalhousie), was working with Dave on installing new tiedowns in our trailer, helping to make it possible to carry Dave's Harley as well as our three BMWs.

I walked past Frenchie's improvised kitchen, the usual Tibetan prayer flags looping across it, and he gave me a big smile as I paused to greet him. Frenchie had a surfer's style of straight, fair hair slanting across his forehead, a big warm grin, and an ever-cheerful, earnest demeanor. He lived in Telluride, Colorado, at one time living year-round in a wigwam—though using his girlfriend's nearby house for some amenities, he admitted, as a true modern-day Thoreau (during Thoreau's stay at Walden Pond, his self-proclaimed "simple life," he was said to have often visited his neighbor, Ralph Waldo Emerson, for meals, laundry, and even dalliances with Mrs. Emerson).

From our early conversations on the previous tour, and from reading my books, Frenchie knew of my love for the American West, and one time he gave me a wand of sage as a gift. He said that when he was in a hotel room or unfamiliar place, he would light the sage and wave the smoke around the room.

Geddy once said of Frenchie, "He has great energy." I thought that was the kind of observation only Californians made, but it was apt.

I walked on into a huge concrete soundstage, on the stage-left side of a raised stage that dominated one end of the vast cubical room. Our drums and amps and keyboards were dwarfed by lighting trusses and banks of speaker cabinets hung from the overhead gridwork. The video crew ran through tests of bright grids and skateboarding videos flashing on the rear screen, and on the narrow screens of diminishing length, called "icicles," that framed it. Sequences of colored lights blinked sporadically from the elaborate array above the stage, and occasional experimental noises whooshed, banged, squealed, and thundered through the P.A. system.

In front of the stage, the floor was littered with rows of empty road cases, leading back to the front-of-house mixing area assembled in the middle. Technicians huddled around the sound boards and lighting consoles, supervised by our front-of-house sound engineer, Brad, and long-time lighting director, Howard, who had joined the band as our first road manager, exactly when I did. So this was his thirtieth anniversary, too.

I said hello to a few of the guys at stage left, the friendly monitor engineer Brent, the quiet young sound technician Beau (both with their short, spiky hairdos), and Geddy's bass guitar tech, Russ, older, heavier, with a kind face and a neat haircut he called his "love sculpture." Jack

Secret came wandering by, long hair and droopy, basset-hound face. Jack was Geddy's keyboard tech, one of our old-time crew members going back almost thirty years.

A corridor at the far end of the soundstage led to the production offices, a kingdom presided over by production manager, C.B., and his production assistant and spouse, Karen. The band had a long history with C.B., going back to our first tour in 1974. We were opening quite a few shows for Kiss back then, and C.B. worked for their sound company, Fanfare Sound, out of Michigan. He still had the same warm, beaming smile, though framed by a few wrinkles these days, and his long ponytail showed streaks of gray as it fell neatly down his back. After stints with such Midwest artists as Bob Seger and Chicago, C.B. had come back into our lives on the *Test for Echo* tour, and again for *Vapor Trails* in 2002. As production assistant, his wife Karen looked after the assignment of dressing rooms; the daily guest-list requests from the local record company people, our Toronto office, press, band, and crew; the phones, fax, and e-mail; and the local "runners," who spent the show-days driving around the city on various errands. Karen also supervised the crew catering and deliveries of drinks and snacks to the buses, and dealt with many a trifling request from crew or band members. Karen and C.B. arrived with the first trucks on the morning of a show, and didn't leave until the last truck was loaded, so their days were long.

C.B. also acted as stage manager, dealing with the local crews of loaders, stagehands, and riggers; and with local building management; problems or complaints from our crew and drivers; as well as getting the show started on time and the band on and off stage. Thus, to many of the people who worked around us, C.B. was the face of the band, and his cheerful and unflappable demeanor was a perfect lightning rod to defuse tensions and maintain a calm working day for everyone. C.B. had "good energy" too. Every afternoon when I arrived at the show and checked in at the production office, Karen welcomed me with a smile. Music played quietly from C.B.'s computer, and incense wafted through the air. It was a friendly place.

The always-harassed Liam had a connecting office, and when I gave him a wave and hello, he looked up through his thick glasses from his incessant work on computer, telephone, and piles of paper. Liam's history with the band was even longer than mine, for he had been part of the two-man crew when I joined (his nose still had a kink in it from a long-ago accident in an equipment truck). Through the '70s and early '80s, as the crew grew larger and more specialized, Liam had looked after Alex's guitars, amplifiers, and effects (which explained his premature gray hair, more salt than pepper these days). Then he moved up to stage manager, and finally to the top spot, tour manager. Along with Geddy, Alex, and Ray, Liam was part of the tight inner circle of the organization, and one of my "brothers."

Ray, for his part, usually worked from his Toronto office and left the traveling to us. He would come out for the first show, and other "selected" appearances during the tour, but if Liam's theater of operations was logistics, then Ray's was strategy. Most of his time was spent dealing with other "generals," mostly by telephone, with occasional meetings in New York with our American record company and booking agency. Ray had been Rush's manager since before I joined, back when we were all ambitious young men. Even as a teenager amid the excitement of the Toronto music scene in the 1960s, Ray had gravitated straight to the more practical—not to say more lucrative—side. In our early twenties, while the rest of us were still struggling musicians, Ray ran a successful booking agency, managed several bands, promoted concerts, and had started his own record label to release Rush's first album—when no one else in Canada would.

In the later '70s, once Ray had sloughed off a couple of unwanted partners, he set up Anthem Records to be our Canadian label, giving us complete freedom and isolation from the big corporations. Even our American recording contracts were so-called production deals, where we agreed to deliver a finished piece of work, music and artwork, and the record company would distribute and promote it. This arrangement kept the wolves from our doors, in both senses, and in terms of the music business, maintained the healthy separation I always liked to see between the words *music* and *business*.

Ray and I had sometimes clashed in the early years, each of us seeing our side of things too narrowly, but we eventually developed a friendly respect for each other. Both of us learned to be more generous, in a way that might be useful for other people to consider: "Even if you don't respect the opinion, respect the person who holds it." For my part, I learned to value Ray's abilities in business—his imagination, his thoroughness, his loyalty, his acumen.

I used to joke that while Ray might not be able to spell Tucson or Albuquerque, you could bet that when we played in those cities, our deals would be maximized to every decimal point. There's a joke about why most popular songs are in 4/4—because that's as high as the drummers can count—and it's true that a page of numbers makes my eyes glaze over. I once told Ray, "I don't have to count, because I can spell. You don't have to spell, because you can count."

Q: What is the difference between a drummer and a savings bond?
A: One will mature and make money.

My friendship with Ray went deeper, too. When I was reeling from the losses of my daughter and my wife, no one was more supportive and helpful than Ray. In recent years, when I lived in California and Ray in Toronto, he and I spoke on the phone from time to time, friends catching up on each other's lives, with business being just *part* of it.

Likewise, the separation of music and business remained strong. Ray rarely visited us in the recording studio, for example (music territory), and it had been many years since I had visited Ray's office (business territory). I liked the people who worked there, though, and Ray's small staff included two other people who had been with us for more than thirty years. Pegi, jovial and gregarious, was a kind of vice president of the whole enterprise, running Anthem Records, supervising new releases and packaging, dealing with other record companies outside Canada, music publishing, and an amazing variety of day-to-day issues from TV and film rights to instrument endorsements. The other rock of the organization was Sheila, working quietly in the background as the nominal "bookkeeper," but her power and influence far transcended that. Sheila had held together the practical side of my life for many years, and everyone, including Ray, was careful to stay on Sheila's good side. There was nobody better to have on your side.

But there was something about offices, like banks and hospitals, that made me uncomfortable. So I avoided them—offices, banks, and hospitals. I was much more at ease in my "office" behind the drums, or on a motorcycle, or even just hanging around in a rehearsal hall in Nashville with my fellow gypsies of the traveling roadshow, the guys at work.

Geddy and Alex arrived in the loading area in a rental van driven by

Donovan. Once they had greeted all the crew members, old and new, we began the slow process of checking out our equipment and playing through a few songs. There was the inevitable wait while Alex fussed with amps and effects, his technician Rick standing by to carry out his wishes to change this, that, and the other, then change it all back again. We heard again the familiar loud *gronk-gronk* of Alex playing chopped chords to test the echoes, choruses, and reverbs. If it went on too long, Geddy and I would look at each other and quote the Monty Python movie: "Run away!"

Another important consideration for Geddy was his "amp line." Alex always had a huge stack of amplifiers and speaker cabinets on his side of the stage, but Geddy's bass guitar setup went through direct feeds and electronic effects, as did the keyboards, so he didn't need any stacks of amplification. He was always looking for amusing ways to balance the stage setup, and on the *Test for Echo* tour, he had put up an old refrigerator (perfect for the fridge magnets Brutus and I collected on our travels) and a selection of vintage kitchen appliances.

On *Vapor Trails,* Geddy had been inspired to have a row of three old Maytag dryers up there, spinning throughout the show with T-shirts he and Alex handed out later to the crowd before the encore—"I GOT THIS T-SHIRT FROM DRYER NUMBER 3." Those dryers had caused considerable wonder from stagehands and fans, and the crew had fun inventing reasons for their use, "This one's for a 'warm' sound, this one's for a 'dry' sound," and the sound crew even set up dummy microphones in front of them.

For this tour, Geddy didn't want to give up those dryers, but at the same time, he wanted something new. Eventually he settled on having only two Maytags, but added an old-fashioned Automat dispenser (another part of Liam's job was locating these relics) with rotating shelves that eventually collected all kinds of interesting items, from presidential bobble-heads to superhero dolls. Some days, soundcheck was held up while he found places to display his latest treasures.

Whenever we began that last stretch of pre-tour rehearsals, we always tried to adapt right away to "show hours." We would arrive in the late afternoon and rehearse a few songs as a pro-forma soundcheck, then eat a light meal from Frenchie's kitchen together in the dressing room, and take a suitable interval for digestion—we often quoted a room-service waiter who once advised us, in a Southern ebonic accent, "Don't let the food digest your stomach."

In a college gymnasium dressing room, I once found the following advice taped up on a locker:

How To Stay Young

1/ Avoid fried meats which angry up the blood.
2/ If your stomach disputes you, lie down and pacify it with cool thoughts.
3/ Keep the juices flowing by jangling around gently as you move.
4/ Go very light on the vices, such as carrying on in society. The social ramble ain't restful.
5/ Avoid running at all times.
6/ Don't look back. Something might be gaining on you.

Leroy Satchel Paige

Some useful wisdom there, from a legendary baseball player (veteran of the Negro Leagues), especially "the social ramble ain't restful" and "avoid running at all times." However, I have never figured out how to jangle around gently as I move. Must be a baseball thing.

When the three of us finally decided to face the inevitable and go to work, we gathered onstage and launched into the first set. We always tried to play it straight through, then take a break for the "intermission," before beginning the second set, which was even longer and harder (especially for me, as it included the workout of my drum solo), and finishing with the extended medley of the encore.

Throughout our career as headliners, beginning in the mid-'70s, we had always played a single, long encore. That policy was partly based on advice given to us back then by the incomparable Mendelson Joe, musician, painter, activist, and all-around artist and gadfly. In Joe's usual stern manner, he had said, "Play one encore, and only play another one if the *police* ask you to."

In modern-day concerts, the encore is simply an obligatory part of the show, expected and delivered. In our early days as an opening act, we had often seen headliners work the audience for as many encores as they could, playing one song and leaving the stage each time, with the house-lights still down. They judged their shows by how many encores they had milked from the crowd. We preferred to construct a tour-de-force encore of fifteen or twenty minutes, then leave the stage and put up the house-lights. After more than three hours of us, most people ought to have had about enough.

As we worked through the show in those later rehearsals, we would only stop playing if we had a train wreck and needed to pause to sort out an arrangement problem, or if we encountered a technical calamity that was too . . . discouraging.

For our band, technology had mostly been a blessing, though it was sometimes disguised as a curse. By the time of our third record together, back in 1976, we were already feeling a bit cramped by the limitations of guitar, bass, and drums. We talked about adding a keyboard player to give us more dynamics and more textures, but we also realized that the chemistry among the three of us was a rare and precious alloy, so we were apprehensive about adding another element. Instead, we decided to do it ourselves.

Geddy acquired a primeval synthesizer, the Minimoog, and organ-like Taurus pedals, and soon he and Alex combined those with double-neck and acoustic guitars while I was bringing in orchestra bells, glock-enspiel, bell tree, cowbells, wind chimes, gong, tympani, timbales, tem-ple blocks, triangle . . . the lot.

We experimented and explored, and sometimes, like any ambitious young band, we used things just because we *could*, whether a new musi-cal accomplishment or a new toy. Like us, the machines continued to develop and mutate, and soon there were digital synthesizers, sequencers, midi (Musical Instrument Digital Interface) pedals, elec-tronic drums, and masses of keyboards. This became a conflict, especial-ly for Geddy, who found himself shouldering a heavy double-neck guitar while he played keyboards with his hands, pedals with his right foot—leaving all his weight on his left—while singing the lead vocals. It was an ergonomic nightmare, a mental tapdance, and it didn't leave him much room for jumping around and having fun.

In the '80s, we again discussed bringing in a fourth member, a key-board player, at least for live shows. But we were still apprehensive about the chemistry thing and, certainly, proud of what we could do with just the three of us. So we decided to carry on ourselves. And once again, technology came to our rescue. Since Geddy's keyboards could now be triggered by Alex's foot pedals (through the magic of midi), or even by one of my drum pads, Alex took on more of the keyboard triggering when he could, and though my hands and feet were usually busy with my own part, sometimes I could spare a beat to trigger a sound or an "event."

Sampling had been a major influence in music during the '80s and '90s, and we had certainly made use of it in our music, especially in live performance. But rather than sampling old James Brown records or orchestral flourishes, we tended to sample ourselves. This was a fine line to walk, and on one extreme, some bands started performing to prerecorded tapes, while others made a big deal about not using synthesizers or samplers at all. Over the years, we had seen bands with guitarists, keyboard players, and background singers hidden under the stage or behind the curtain, like the Wizard of Oz ("Do not look behind the curtain! Do not look behind the curtain!"), and others who sounded bare and thin without all the studio trimmings. Being keen young Aristotelians, we chose the middle route, the Golden Mean.

Even as a drummer, I couldn't resist the benefits of triggers and pads, of having literally any sound I wanted under my sticks or my feet— marimba, church bells, West African djembes, a self-made recording of a plastic water bottle struck by a toothbrush (used in "Tai Shan"), an ominous rumble of thunder to open my solo, a perky ensemble of congas and tribal drums to spice it up, and wailing big-band horns for the climax.

As a band, we used whatever we needed—keyboard samples, background vocal effects, string parts, whatever. The line we drew was that they were all samples of *us,* and every note, or every "event," had to be triggered manually (or pedally, as the case might be) by one of us. It became a matter of choreography, ultimately, and early rehearsals often ground to a halt while Geddy and Alex worked out who was going to hit which pedal, while the programmer assigned the appropriate sample to each different trigger.

One steamy morning in Nashville, I joined Dave for a motorcycle ride in the Tennessee countryside with one of our longtime truck drivers, Mac, who had rented a Harley-Davidson V-Rod for a few days. He had been parking it in the loading bay at work, and I had been admiring that sleek, modern power cruiser, especially pretty in its dark red paint. That

72

afternoon I was riding my new 1200GS, working through the 600 miles of the factory-recommended break-in, and reluctantly keeping the engine RPMs low. I followed Dave and Mac as they rumbled along the country lanes, through a green world of farms and fields, woods and small settlements. Dave and Mac had excellent group-riding manners, the leader in the left wheel-track of the lane, and the others in staggered formation with at least a second between us. I enjoyed the relaxed pace of having no destination and lots of time to get there.

As we wound south along the Natchez Trace, giving due regard to its sternly enforced 45 mph speed limit, we had plenty of leisure to appreciate its pristine beauty. A true "parkway," with nothing around it but dark green woodlands, trimmed grass verges, and occasional time-honored pastures and hay barns, it more-or-less followed the route of the path (*trace*, in French) blazed by the farmers returning from the Mississippi. Floating downriver with their produce, they would sell their goods and their flatboats, then walk back to their homes in the Tennessee and Ohio River valleys. That perfect road winding through such groomed, painterly scenery had me wishing I could cruise like that all day, or at least down to Tupelo and back.

Brutus and I had ridden that next stretch of the Natchez Trace back in '97, on a ramble through the Deep South on a route we had whimsically dedicated to the song "Ode to Billie Joe." Bobbie Gentry's Southern Gothic ballad from 1967, with its cryptic lyrics, hypnotically repetitive guitar, and eerie string arrangement, opened with "It was the third of June, another sweet and dusty Delta day." For Brutus and me, it was the *sixth* of June, and it was raining.

After a show in Nashville, we had slept on the bus in Muscle Shoals, Alabama (famous for its recording studio and rhythm section, who played on Aretha Franklin's "Respect," Wilson Pickett's "Mustang Sally," and Bob Seger's "Old Time Rock and Roll," among many others), and woke up in the rain. We put on our rainsuits, unloaded the bikes, and splashed down the Natchez Trace through Tupelo, where the "Ode to Billie Joe" narrator's brother and his new wife Becky Thompson ended up buying a store. Then across central Mississippi to Carrollton, the seat of Carroll County, where "my brother recollected when he and Tom and Billie Joe/ Put a frog down my back at the Carroll County picture show."

No one was chopping cotton or baling hay on that rainy morning, but the sky began to lighten as we crossed the Tallahatchie River (must have been the wrong bridge—if Billie Joe had jumped off that one, he would only have stubbed his toe). We traversed the flat farmlands of the Mississippi Delta, then crossed the wide river itself, the Father of Waters, which always felt like a great American Divide.

After a fine and funky barbecue lunch in Forrest City, Arkansas, the rain cleared away, and we had a fast, fabulous ride up through the Ozarks to a motel in Jefferson, in easy reach of the next day's show in St. Louis.

After that long day, during which we had covered over 600 miles of mostly back roads, and spent fourteen hours on the bikes, traveling through so much southern Americana, I made a journal note.

And about those who bewail the loss of "regionalism" in America. Whether or not it's worth regretting, it's definitely still *there*—if those armchair anthropologists would get off the interstate! Away from the cities and beltways, away from the suits and logos and trailer-trash TV talk shows, there are still a million pockets of "Americana" out there, small town gas stations and diners where you will meet hillbillies, aristocratic southerners, weathered ranchers, overalled farmers, solitary fishermen, burly loggers, apple-cheeked grandmothers, and friendly, decent folks. And a million landscapes, from snowy mountains and starkly majestic deserts, to white picket fences and maple trees on Main Street.

Consider Roy's Motel on Route 66 in Amboy, California, the Queen's Kitchen in Fairview, Oklahoma, the Wheatleigh Inn in Lenox, Massachusetts, the Hammond Family Restaurant in Madison, Indiana, the Cowboy Café in Tilden, Texas, and "La Maison de Saucisse de Lac Artur," in Louisiana's Cajun country. All part of the Great American Theme Park.

But Dave and Mac and I had no time to visit Elvis's hometown, Tupelo, that day. It was a work day, and I had to get to the rehearsal hall later that afternoon. After about 100 miles of relaxed cruising along the Natchez Trace, we stopped at a roadside picnic ground and agreed to loop back from there.

An unmarked ranger car pulled in behind us, and I was worried for a second, but it turned out the ranger was a motorcycle enthusiast, and perhaps lonely. In a deep southern accent (for example, he said the busiest month of the year around there, and the hottest, was *"Jew*-lye"), the ranger talked about motorcycles for a while, and he knew all about my new 1200GS. He told us how he kept hinting to his superiors that he would like to be transferred to motorcycle patrol, but so far, no luck.

Heading back toward Nashville, Mac and I traded bikes for a while. Again I fell in behind the two of them, and sometimes lagged well back, just so I could twist the throttle and feel the gathering surge of the V-Rod's power as I roared up behind them again.

During one roadside conversation, Mac mentioned he had first started driving for the band in 1977, in the course of recounting a story from that tour, *A Farewell to Kings.* In those early years, we hadn't yet learned to demand such touring amenities as an occasional day off, so we would play six, seven, even ten one-nighters in a row, traveling overnight between each one. By that time, we had our small RV, the Barth, and a driver (Jwerg, a nice young man, though he did scratch himself a lot), but following that kind of itinerary for months on end became a soul-destroying ordeal of constant driving and working. The crew had T-shirts made calling it the "Drive 'til You Die Tour."

Mac described himself as "a green young rookie" back then, and he had decided to drive his tractor-trailer up the Pacific Coast Highway near Big Sur, which I knew to be a particularly tortuous coil of road clinging to the contours of that rugged coast, its bends too tight and narrow for a long truck and trailer. Mac's wife, Candy, who still sometimes came out to ride with him, had been with him then, and Mac told Dave and me, "Candy was hanging out the window just freaking out—and I mean *freaking out!*"

I had ridden with Mac in his truck myself a few times in the early days, and other truck drivers too, just for the adventure of it. One time I rode all night across Newfoundland with Mac, heading for the ferry to Nova Scotia at Port-aux-Basques. The band had started our *Hold Your Fire* tour in St. John's that October of 1987 (I know, because I recently came across my certificate from The Royal Order of Screechers, testifying that I had been "enrolled" by fulfilling the rituals of kissing the cod and swallowing the shot of harsh rum called "Newfie Screech"), with a week of production rehearsals and the first show at the Memorial Arena.

In the afternoons, before going to work, I rode my bicycle all around

St. John's, and down to Cape Spear, the easternmost point of North America. There I saw two snowy owls—the kind on our *Fly By Night* cover, which I had never seen in the wild before—sitting on the open meadow beside the lighthouse. That had been our first visit to Newfoundland, and all of us were especially charmed by the people, so friendly and open-hearted.

After the first show in St. John's, we had a day off to travel to the second show in Sydney, Nova Scotia (birthplace of Brutus, though they haven't put up the historical marker yet). My bandmates would be flying from St. John's to Sydney, but I wanted to avoid that dreaded short flight, and see more of Newfoundland, so I hitched a ride with Mac. I don't know why I thought I would see more of Newfoundland driving all night in a truck, but I will always associate that long drive with the music of Percy Sledge, playing on Mac's tape deck while I tried to sleep in the bouncing sleeper.

In the inevitable exchange of road stories among longtime professionals like the three of us, Mac also told Dave and me about a recent tour he had driven with ZZ Top. The band had had a day off in Minneapolis, and early in the morning, guitarist Billy Gibbons came down to the hotel lobby, gathered up some of the drivers who were around, and invited them to go for a ride with him in his limousine. Billy gave the driver directions, and they drove for an hour into the wilds of Minnesota, getting deeper into the woods on gravel roads—left here, right here—until they pulled up at a lakeshore, at the foot of a dock.

Tied at the far end of the dock was a vintage 57-foot Chris-Craft cabin cruiser, a gleaming vision in teak, mahogany, and brass, which Billy had bought from its owner *twelve years earlier,* and had never been back since. He had been sending the former owner regular checks to look after the boat for him, and when Billy and the drivers walked out on the dock, the guy was there working on the boat. When he saw Billy, he was shocked, and said, "I thought I'd never see you again!"

Hearing that story, I remembered Mac had also experienced *my* nautical folly, the 75-foot schooner *Orianda,* which I had owned for a few years in the mid-'80s. Mac and Candy lived in Rhode Island, and at the time I was trying (desperately) to sell that great wooden money-magnet, having it moved from its home port in the British Virgin Islands to Fort Lauderdale, and then to Newport for the summer, seeking a buyer. One week in August of '86, I went down to Newport with a group of friends from Toronto (the parking tag from Newport Yacht Club still hangs in my garage, and my favorite song at the time was "No Promises," by an Australian band called Icehouse—I remember playing it again and again as I drove my Porsche 911 convertible through the White Mountains of New Hampshire). We enjoyed a few days of sailing around Nantucket Island and Martha's Vineyard, and one day I invited Mac and Candy for a day-sail.

My history with that boat was checkered, but its own history was impeccable: built in Europe in 1937 as a racing yacht for a member of the Norwegian royal family, it had been launched as *Ragna IV* (as attested by the compass rose). After several decades in the Mediterranean, and a few name changes, *Orianda* remained sleek, shapely, and beautifully appointed, but its all-wood hull, decks, rails, deckhouses, masts, spars, and staterooms were *ruinously* expensive to maintain. And in any case, I had certainly never had any desire to buy a sailing yacht. The scheme had been cooked up by some friends of mine, brothers-in-law Steve and Keith, and Captain Mike, and the plan was to pool our resources and buy a sailboat, then charter it in the British Virgin Islands with Mike as the captain.

Well, that sounded fun. I had been down to the Caribbean once before and sailed with Captain Mike around those beautiful islands, and I loved the tropical boating life. The plan sounded workable (for all I knew), and I agreed to be a fourth partner. The four of us flew to several Caribbean islands looking at sailboats, playing Cuban dice and drinking daiquiris along the way, and ended up buying *Orianda* from an old Frenchman in Antigua.

However, when the bill-of-sale came due, my partners were suddenly unable to put up their part of the money, and, just like that, I became the owner of a big wooden sailboat. Alas, the charter business didn't *begin* to pay for the upkeep of that graceful wooden albatross, let alone hiring and feeding a crew of four, the semiannual haul-outs at the marina and inevitable repairs, and Captain Mike's regular presentations to me of three-ring binder "wish lists" full of brochures for new dinghies, new generators, new sails, and other never-ending bills and expenses. By the time that enterprise had drained me of five times the original investment, my keen financial mind decided it was time to sell that boat.

Still, I did have some wonderful times on *Orianda*, magical interludes with family and friends sailing among those unspoiled tropical isles, with their warm, clear water and spectacular coral reefs for snorkeling. On one European tour in the early '80s, just after buying the boat, I carried around a copy of the sailor's bible, *Chapman Piloting*, and tried to learn something about nautical terms, seamanship, and dead reckoning. "Some knowledge of nautical lingo identifies a person with an ancient art, one that has had great influence on human history, but it would be mere vanity to learn the language of the sea for such a reason."

During a break in one of our tours in the early '80s, I hosted the guys at work—Geddy, Alex, Liam, frequent coproducer Terry Brown, and occasional pilot Brian Laski—for a riotous week of sailing around the Virgin Islands. Sailing, snorkeling, drinking, and laughing at Alex's nautical terminology (the generator exhaust was the "raging aft-hole," the boom, a "head-smasher log"), we shared yet another unforgettable time together.

One afternoon, Alex and Geddy were lazing on the deck, curled around the foot of the mainmast and drinking whisky as we sailed along. After a while, they called me over and drunkenly told me they had figured out each of our "essential natures," and could define those fundamental characters in one word each. Those one-word definitions boiled each of us down to a very unflattering essence, and there was some rue in our laughter. Like the secret names of God, those words were never to be uttered, but that mutual recognition, however harsh, forged a deep understanding among the three of us forever. We were like those long-married couples you see in restaurants; they know each other's worst sides, and still prefer to stay together.

The late '70s and '80s were our "exotic" period in recording projects, as we often went away to record our albums in rural England, Wales, or Quebec, many times in London, and even in Paris and the Caribbean. In May of 1985, we were working on our *Power Windows* album, and had finished the basic tracks (everything but the vocals and guitar overdubs) at the Manor studio in rural England. After that, we took a couple of weeks off, then moved to Air Studios on the island of Montserrat (before that paradise was devastated by its volcano).

I flew from London to meet my family in the Virgin Islands, and we and the crew spent a few days sailing *Orianda* down through the Leeward Islands, from St. Martin and St. Barthélemy to St. Kitts and

Nevis, a long tack toward Antigua, then a long windward beat to Montserrat. That was a glorious way to arrive at work, of course, but all things considered, I could have bought a lot of adventures for the ultimate price of those few interludes, and I was relieved when the boat finally sold—for less than half what I had put into it.

The worst loss, however, came a few years later, when Captain Mike passed away. He was only in his early forties, and left a wife, Pat, and two children, Elizabeth and Alex. Mike's health had been declining for a few years, weakened by the congenital heart defect that had claimed his father, two of his brothers, and his sister, one after another. All of them were exceptionally tall (a friend compared being around them to standing in a redwood forest), Captain Mike stood about six-foot-ten, and all of them had the long, spidery fingers characteristic of Marfan's syndrome, their fatal flaw.

Mike had grown up in my hometown, St. Catharines, and I remembered seeing him around when we were teenagers—extremely tall even then, with long dark hair and mustache, striding loose-limbed and barefoot on summer afternoons on St. Paul Street downtown, with his big Irish setter. Sailboats had been for Mike and his brothers what motorcycles or sports cars were for other young men—something to cobble together and get around on during our brief Canadian summers.

Mike's father was the owner of a factory in St. Catharines, Canada Hair Cloth, which made upholstery stuffing and such, and supported a fairly aristocratic family lifestyle in our toniest neighborhood of the times, Old Glenridge. Mike told us that as children, they were never allowed to put cereal boxes or ketchup bottles on the dining table—nothing so crude as a *label*. However, his advantages did teach him to appreciate the good things in life; in later years, he and Pat would sometimes go without a few necessities to buy a good bottle of champagne. (Like a quote from Frank Lloyd Wright, "I like to do without the necessities of life so I can have the luxuries.")

Mike was educated in private schools, then boarding school (which he claimed to have enjoyed, unlike most accounts of that experience), and that combination of upbringing and education, with his natural looseness of demeanor and teasing sense of humor, made Mike a perfect charter-boat captain. In addition to his sailing knowledge and experience, he was able to put guests at their ease, take an interest in whatever interested them, while seeing that they were treated with courtesy, consideration, and that ineffable quality of "class."

However, that combination of easygoing refinement and casual sophistication in Captain Mike meant that he wanted the best of everything for *Orianda,* and his own natural generosity meant that he had trouble with the concept of economy. Though it wasn't Captain Mike's fault that *Orianda,* like all wooden boats, was "a hole in the water into which you throw all your money." (Another definition of sailing: "Standing in a cold shower with your foul-weather gear on, tearing up hundred-dollar bills.")

In any case, the *Orianda* episode was a good example of several unfortunate experiences I had investing in friends' businesses, and even my whole financial history. I usually managed to lose money even in the typically reliable enterprise of buying and selling homes, and even my professionally-administered investment portfolios had a distressing habit of shrinking instead of growing. Economic instability, bear markets, rising interest rates, I don't know, I was never very interested in such matters, but as my riding partner Michael likes to insist, "a girl's gotta eat."

At least I still had a job, and could make a decent living, if I was willing to work hard enough. And in May of 2004, I definitely felt like I was working hard enough.

A journal note.

Monday, May 24, 2004
Different kind of pain today, after almost two months of hard playing—not pain of *abuse,* but just *exertion.*
Still, it's *pain!*
And even after a day off. Though I played *hard* Friday night, knowing there were only two rehearsals left. And still some nagging technical problems—triggers, internal balances, monitors. Playing well, though, that's the main thing.
Book sent off yesterday, after page proofs filled with pink Post-its. Tired eyes.

After a week of playing the three-and-a-half-hour show every night, we had been obliged to take a day off, because the arena adjacent to our rehearsal hall was hosting a concert with the pop-country entertainer,

Alan Jackson. That was an amusing coincidence to my editor, Paul, because, at his urging, a little rant on Jackson had recently been cut from *Traveling Music*. In a forum like that book, where I was writing about music I loved, it was hard to resist talking about music I didn't love, but Paul had inspired me to rise above that, to celebrate excellence, rather than lamenting its lack. I was more drawn to what English writer Kingsley Amis said, "If you can't annoy somebody, there's little point in writing," but I could see Paul's point, and acquiesced reluctantly.

For their part, the arena management was concerned that Jackson's audience might be disturbed by our racket next door, but perhaps we could have drowned out his cheesy cover of "Summertime Blues" with *our* cheesy cover of it. (Editorial objection overruled.)

Carrie flew into Nashville for the last few days of rehearsal and the first show, and out of deference to Her Ladyship, Michael and I moved to a slightly nicer—or at least more central—hotel. Before Carrie and I met, in 1999, all she knew about the band was a teenage memory of hearing "Tom Sawyer" or "The Spirit of Radio" on car radios, but she liked to watch our shows. At the Nashville rehearsal hall, she put in her earplugs and joined the small audience sitting in a handful of chairs in the middle of the dark, booming soundstage, and watched us go through the show. I liked being able to look out and see her there, my pre-Raphaelite beauty giving me a smile and a wave.

The young man beside her, with the unmistakable shaved head, was my dear friend and hiking partner in Los Angeles, Matt Scannell, who had recently dissolved his band, Vertical Horizon. Matt was planning to make his own album eventually, but first he was eager for new experiences, accepting session work as a guitar player, and even as a singer, collaborating with other songwriters, maybe producing a young artist. He continued his training with a vocal coach he saw every week, and worked on his own songs.

I admired the way Matt had handled his meteoric success with the Vertical Horizon *Everything You Want* album; he had been so *sensible*. As the band's principal songwriter, Matt's combination of income from record sales and publishing had been sizable from just that one hit album, but instead of throwing the money around and buying things like Ferraris and mansions (and big wooden sailboats), Matt had invested his money (what we in Rush always called a "wedge"). He was determined to live modestly on his income, while devoting himself to music without any economic pressure.

In Nashville, Matt was combining a social visit with some meetings, interested in trying to collaborate with other writers, just to broaden his horizons. But, so far, Matt wasn't too impressed with the horizon in Nashville—he described sitting in an office with a slick-haired record-company executive who wore cowboy boots and chrome-framed, Elvis-style sunglasses. Matt had been sorely tempted to reach over the guy's desk and grab those sunglasses: "Just take those *off!*"

Beside Matt, the diminutive, squarely-built Englishman with the neatly-trimmed beard was our longtime friend Peter Collins ("Mr. Big"), coproducer of several of our albums in the late '80s and early '90s, and one of our favorite people. Though Peter was a born Londoner, cosmopolitan and sybaritic, a complicated life trail had resulted in him living in Nashville (again, *cherchez la femme*). Peter worked with artists in Los Angeles once or twice a year, and he and I always tried to get together for breakfast or dinner in Venice or Santa Monica.

Another audience member (the last time I would be able to introduce them all individually!) was John Virant, from Boston, the tall, narrow, boyish president of an independent record company, Rounder. John was a friend of ours, and his company had been involved in the release of our *Rush in Rio* DVD, and was also publishing Carrie's book of photographs, *Rhythm and Light*.

One of my longtime criteria in appraising people I meet is whether you can look at them and imagine the child they used to be. Looking at the grownup, can you picture them as a ten-year-old? It seemed to say something about a person's character if I was able to detect that, but in John's case, it was too easy to tell what he had looked like when he was ten years old, because his face still *looked* about ten.

The production around us had been growing in magnitude and complexity every day, as the lighting crew worked through the nights programming ever-more-elaborate displays to accompany the music (though, in the minds of lighting people, the music accompanies the *lights*), with sweeps of colored beams moving in automated unison, needles of green laser light mirrored around the room, and towers of fire at the end of the first set, before I started the drum intro to "One Little Victory."

I have always loved fireworks and pyrotechnical effects, but Gump was not so enthusiastic. In fact, what he said was, "I *hate* pyro!" During the show, Gump sat behind Geddy's dryers, changing the programming for the electronic drums, keeping an eye on the mechanical bits, and passing me a towel between songs. So he was even closer to the propane-fueled flames than I was (they gave off a serious blast of heat), and when they went off, he either scurried off to stage left, or draped towels over his head and hunched glumly through it.

Various pieces of film had been arriving throughout our time in Nashville, delivered by Geddy's brother, Allan, who was involved in their production. In the afternoon or evening, before we started rehearsing, we would gather with the crew out by the front-of-house mixing platform to watch the latest piece. The footage that opened the show was an animated dream sequence of our album covers, leading into a "dream dissolve" of comedic actor Jerry Stiller waking up, confused ("What did they put in my *tea*?"), worrying that he had missed the show, then calling us to the stage.

Another little movie, *That Darn Dragon*, would open the second set, with puppet animation of three bobble-head dolls of us (in '70s regalia of long hair and kimonos) doing battle against a puppet version of the dragon from *Vapor Trails*. It was a little like an old Japanese monster movie, but with puppets—*Godzilla* meets "Fireball XL-5" (which Geddy and Alex and I used to watch every morning in the rented house we shared in Chelsea during an '80s recording project).

One of our in-joke slogans for the R30 tour was "more comedy, less music," and though that wasn't quite true—there was more comedy *and* more music—I could see we were going to have a very entertaining show, and congratulated Geddy and Allan on their work. As Alex remarked in *The Boys in Brazil* documentary, referring to one of the other comical videos in our set, "You'll be playing the song and you can see people laughing in the audience, and that's so great to see. You wouldn't think you'd want people laughing in your audience, but definitely—you know, I want it to be *fun,* going to a Rush show."

Now that we were getting close to opening night, Alex, Geddy, and I played through that show with earnest dedication to getting everything right. I was giving it everything I had, straining and sweating, and in fact, I was already playing for an audience, though they were imaginary. It is a defining trait in my character and attitude toward performing that no audience is more unforgivingly critical than an imaginary one. They knew exactly how well I was supposed to play, and whether I had or not.

People sometimes misunderstand the difference between doing something for fun and doing it at the highest possible level. With memories of Little League, or just a necessary fantasy to hold onto, people like to imagine that it must be fun to be a professional athlete or performer, not realizing the difference between a pastime and a profession. It is probably safe to say that any job done professionally is never going to be fun, exactly—because it's a job.

Don't get me wrong, I love my work as much as anyone ever could, but it is still *work*. As the great American journalist Ernie Pyle used to say, after describing someone's difficult job, "Try it sometime." Late in his life, Buddy Rich was asked if he considered himself the world's greatest drummer, and he gave an inspiring reply: "Let's put it this way: I have that ambition. You don't really attain greatness. You attain a certain amount of *goodness,* and if you're really serious about your goodness, you'll keep trying to be great. I have never reached a point in my career where I was totally satisfied with anything I've ever done, but I keep trying."

Amen. And it's the trying that's so hard, especially in live performance. Every night you push yourself to your absolute limits, mentally and physically, and as the standards rise, you're like a high-jumper continually raising the bar. On a good day, you might clear it, but the rest of the time you just fall on your ass.

And *trying*, the philosophy of Tryism, is the key to much about me, my attitude toward fans, other artists, and my own self-image. If I am uncomfortable with strangers making a fuss about me, and feel embarrassed by any show of admiration, people sometimes accuse me of thinking I am "too good." In fact the opposite is true—I don't believe I deserve that kind of attention. I have never thought I was very good at *anything;* I just tried hard. And nothing came easily. Having one's childhood personality shaped by being inept at every sport is a cliché, but it had its effect on me. What else do people judge you by at that age?

Later, in my early teens, my first drum teacher encouraged me by saying I had a natural talent, and that meant a lot. But no matter how much I practiced and played and showed off, the more praise I received, the more I felt like a hacker, a sham, and a fraud. One time in 1977, we were playing in Glasgow, Scotland, and that day I heard I had been voted "Most Promising New Drummer" by the readers of *Modern Drummer* magazine. I was pleased, of course, but onstage that night I played so *badly*—or at least, it felt like I did, because I was measuring my performance against an undeserved honor. I felt like a hacker, a sham, and a fraud. Still do, sometimes, but the important thing was that I kept trying. After almost forty years of playing the drums, I had started to feel a modicum of confidence. Though even that still varied from night to night.

That sense of self affects my outlook in so many ways, rooted in the deep-seated belief that I am nothing special, and anyone could do what I do, if they only tried. It may not be true, but it is how I *feel*, and thus I don't overvalue what I do, or what I am. I hit things with sticks—big deal.

Likewise, many successful people feel that others could achieve what they have, if they just worked harder. It doesn't matter whether or not it's true, the way they feel affects how they treat others—perhaps looking down on them for not working hard enough. And in return, they are accused of being "just lucky." That can be a common division between haves and have-nots, one looking down and thinking, "They could be successful too, if they only tried," the other looking up and sneering, "I could be successful too, I just never got the breaks."

There is such a thing as "luck," of course, good and bad, but it is never the *only* thing. When I was in grade school, the lowest mark you could get on your report card (if you were very "unlucky") was an "E." My siblings and I used to make fun of my dad's old report cards, for they were all "E's." In his day, that stood for "Excellent."

In the School of Tryism, "E" can also stand for "Effort."

Tryism also has a big influence on my response to the work of other musicians. As a music-lover with forty years of experience in music-making, I believe I can tell something about a musician's character, motivation, and talent just by listening to a few of his or her songs. Some artists have clearly worked for years to maximize their rare gift, and that is most inspiring, but I also appreciate the less gifted—those with a limited "voice" who have combined hard-earned technique, taste, and sensitivity to make compelling music. In any case, all of those musicians are trying to *communicate* to an audience, hoping to entertain and, perhaps, inspire.

As Bob Dylan said, "The highest purpose of art is to inspire. What else can you do? What else can you do for anyone but inspire them?"

Well, some don't aim that high. There are talented performers who are capable of making good music, but waste their abilities by contemptuously "dumbing down" their work for a mass audience. When I hear that kind of market-driven music, produced and sold as a mere commodity, like any other, by those who could do better, I feel it in my *skin*, like a physical revulsion. To a discerning listener, such music is tainted by a fundamental dishonesty, a shallow aspiration for fame and riches— at any cost.

A girl's gotta eat, as Michael likes to say, but a woman has to feel good about herself. When I look at the world around me, people's lives and the way they look and behave, it seems rare for anyone to feel truly comfortable about admiration they haven't earned—haven't *tried for*. (Then again, however hard I try, I am not too comfortable with admiration either!)

The same philosophy applied to anything I took up, from motorcycling to telemark skiing, writing to drumming. I felt my own lack of mental agility and physical grace could only be overcome by unstinting effort. That attitude made me receptive to watching and listening to others, eager about learning and practising, and open to being *taught*. I had been helped in all of those disciplines by a series of important teachers.

In motorcycling, it was an instructor at Humber College who helped me with low-speed turns. In telemark skiing, a guy named Chris who froze all day on a Quebec ski hill as he tried so hard to teach me, while I tumbled and rolled my way down the hill, again and again. In writing, I had been guided and improved by the advice of my brother Danny, Mark Riebling, and Paul McCarthy, and by reading so many books. In drumming, there had been my first teacher, Don George, and in later years, Freddie Gruber—and of course, the many drummers I had heard on records or in concerts.

Our band's success had largely been built on live performance, and we were proud of that, but it was a hard-won reputation. For us, The Show was an omnipotent deity, and she could be demanding, unforgiving, and cruel. Every show we had ever played, in any venue, for any size crowd, had always been the very best show we could deliver that night. However short a given performance might fall from our own idea of what was "great," at least we had the cold comfort of knowing that it had been our best, and we had given our all. But it still didn't always feel good.

For the three of us, performing was an all-consuming state of mind, in which every note and every beat was a matter of complete focus, analysis, and effort—a total commitment. After one show on the *Vapor Trails* tour in which I hadn't been feeling well physically—nauseous and lightheaded—I said to Alex that I had thought I was having a heart attack or something. But, I said, "My fear wasn't that I was going to *die*. I was worried that I was going to wreck the *show*."

Alex laughed and shook a finger at me. "Yeah—whatever you do, don't wreck the show!"

But, in its essence, that feeling was real. In the consummate self-immolation of every life-or-death performance, I really would rather die than wreck the show. But I guess that would wreck the show, too.

Another trial of being on the road was that when a friend or family member was having trouble, you couldn't always be there. In thirty years, we had all missed a shameful multitude of birthdays, anniversaries, weddings, births, deaths, and family emergencies, and that had caused an equal number of feelings of guilt and frustration.

One day in Nashville, I walked into Liam's office and saw him looking serious and downcast, giving instructions to Karen and Donovan.

"It's my mother," he told me. "She's in the hospital, and not doing well. They don't think she'll make it."

At least by this point in the tour preparations, Liam had things so well organized and delegated that he could go, and he was flying back to Canada to be with his mother and his family. I knew what a wrench it would be for him to tear himself away from The Vortex, but it was good that he was able to—though terrible that he *had* to.

The next day, I checked in with C.B. for any news about Liam. C.B. told me his mother was still holding on, but failing, and the family was with her at the hospital in a kind of vigil.

"What a terrible situation for them," I said. "Wanting it to be over, yet *not* wanting it to be over."

C.B. nodded in agreement.

The guys at work were all thinking about Liam that day, asking each other, "have you heard anything?" The next day, May 24, Liam's mother finally passed away, and the funeral was scheduled for two days later.

C.B. said Liam would be back in time for the second show, in Charlotte.

On Monday, May 25, the crew moved the whole production out to the Starwood Amphitheater—at least, that's what it used to be called. It now wore a corporate name instead, in the twenty-first century fashion of selling companies the right to put their names on entertainment venues. But they will get no free advertising from me. I'll call it the Financial Services Corporation Amphitheater.

This shift in location gave the crew a chance for a rehearsal load-out and load-in, and the opportunity for us all to put on the show in the same sort of venue as most of the shows on this summer tour. We had played that amphitheater several times on other tours, and I remembered bicycling around Nashville one of those times, out to see the full-scale model of the Parthenon (one of those weird and wonderful bits of Americana, like the upended Cadillacs on Route 66 in Texas, and the full-scale Stonehenge of poured concrete built by Sam Hill in Washington state).

The road leading out of Nashville toward the amphitheater let you know right away what part of the country you were in—any place with an address of Murfreesboro Road was likely to be in the Mid-South.

We got through that final rehearsal fairly smoothly, and faced up to the ultimate challenge: the first show. May 26, 2004, Financial Services Corporation Amphitheater, Nashville, Tennessee. Every show is a Sisyphean undertaking, but none is ever as hard or as nerve-racking as the first one.

I was nervous and on edge from the moment I woke up that day, and that agitation and intensity only increased as the day went on. In the afternoon, I got Michael to join me for a relaxed motorcycle ride down the Natchez Trace, then we turned east and north to Murfreesboro Road, and the amphitheater.

The backstage area was dominated by a line of seven white trucks backed up to the loading dock, and a row of four buses painted in swirls of copper and black, three buses for the crew, and one for me and Michael. We parked the bikes beside our new home-away-from-home, and started moving aboard.

The crew buses carried eight or ten people, and were configured with a front lounge, double or triple stacks of bunks in the middle, and a lounge at the rear. Mine, called (embarrassingly) a "star bus," had a similar layout to the ones I'd had on *Test for Echo* and *Vapor Trails:* a front lounge with sofa, chairs, table, small galley, and entertainment center, then back to a row of stacked bunks either side for Michael and Dave, with a couple of "junk bunks" left over for our riding gear and helmets and such. There was a small head for them, then a door to my stateroom, which had a private shower and head, a plasma-screen entertainment center, and a big bed. If you have to bounce down the highways of America all night, and be away from home for five months, this is the way to do it.

"Hmm," said Michael, with queenly envy, "Is that a *queen* size bed? How *appropriate*."

"Shut up," I said, with manly eloquence.

Shelley, from our Toronto office, was in the production office, working on the guest list with Karen, sorting out ticket and pass requests. As she had on *Vapor Trails,* Shelley would travel with Alex and Geddy (and Liam and Donovan) on their chartered jet, handling "artist liaison" with the local record company people, press, photographers, and our office in Toronto. Shelley also organized the daily "meet and greet" sessions, in which Geddy and Alex would take a few minutes before the show to meet some contest winners. Shelley had made a deal with Kodak to supply hundreds of disposable cameras, and Geddy and Alex posed for a photo with each winner, who took the camera home with them. It was a measure of the difference in our characters that Alex and Geddy didn't mind that daily ritual, while it would have been an uncomfortable ordeal for me. So I stayed away.

Interviews were a different story. In former years, we had divided that task among the three of us, Geddy and Alex often handling the radio and TV requests, while I talked to the daily press, usually through phone interviews a week or so before our scheduled appearance in a city. I never minded working a couple of phoners into my days, and the conversations could sometimes be stimulating, but in the wake of my tragedies in 1997 and 1998, it became too sensitive for me. Even the most innocent questions couldn't avoid touching on that time—the band's five-year hiatus, our return to work in 2002 with *Vapor Trails*—and these days I just had to stay away from all that. It was too painful to face over and over again, especially with strangers, and I had found it was better just to keep my head down and do the job.

Back on the bus, I dragged my big suitcase down the corridor and started emptying it, filling drawers and hanging lockers with clothes and books, then finding a place for my helmet, leathers, and riding boots. For the next few months I would basically be living on the bus, transferring what I needed into the bike's luggage cases for days off. Even when I flew home for breaks between legs of the tour, I would only pack a carry-on bag, and leave everything else on the bus.

All that mindless organizing helped keep me occupied during those anxious hours. I warmed up for a while on the little drumset in my tuning room—with a sign on the door reading "Bubba-Gump," after the fictional shrimp company in *Forrest Gump,* and using the logo of the real San Francisco seafood house. This combination had occurred to me when I had first hired Gump, in 2001, because one of my nicknames among band and crew was "Bubba," bestowed upon me for inscrutable reasons by Andrew, our longtime photographer and personal assistant on a couple of tours in the early '90s.

It was common for any of us in the band and crew to have several nicknames, sometimes alternated for variety, sometimes varying with different members of the organization, and visitors could be confused. Over the years, I have been called Bubba, the Professor (after the "Gilligan's Island" character), the Submariner (after my hairline, which allegedly resembled the superhero's vee-shaped cowl), and Pratt, which was a play on the various butcherings of my simple Anglo-Saxon surname, "Peert," which the other guys were amused to hear everybody, from hotel staff to fans, insist on pronouncing "Pert," "Part," "Pairt," and even "Pee-art." (I prefer to think my friends' choice of nickname for me has no relation to the English slang word "prat," meaning "ass.")

The riotous English band, UFO, did a long tour with us in the early '80s, and their loveable cliché of a drunken bass player—Pete Way, right out of *Spinal Tap*—had another nickname for me. Noticing how I dodged attention, kept to myself, and socialized less than the other two, he used to call me "the Third Man, Harry Lime."

But Pratt was the name that endured, morphing into Nels Pratt, then just Nels, which Alex and Liam usually called me, or Mr. P., as Geddy preferred. To the rest of us, Alex was usually "Lerxst," which came from a long-ago, exaggerated pronunciation of his name as "A-lerxt." Geddy was commonly "Dirk," which derived from an invented name for an archetypical rock bass player, or secret agent—Dirk Lee.

Those nicknames had passed into use as slang among us, as names for our companies, and even as characters in the puppet-animated film that started the second set, *That Darn Dragon,* as the names Dirk, Lerxst, and Pratt popped up on the screen above the bobble-head dolls.

After the traditional afternoon bowl of Frenchie's soup in the dressing room, I went to Bubba-Gump and changed into my drumming shoes—actually *dancing* shoes. My drum teacher, Freddie Gruber, had once shook his finger at me and said, "Don't play drums in *sneakers!*" The essence of what Freddie taught me was how to dance on the drums, so I thought I would try the soft-shoe style of dancing shoes. They had worked great for me, giving me glide and sensitivity on the pedals.

My big black wardrobe case stood neck high, its open doors lined with taped-on photographs, cartoons, and a little art gallery of postcards of paintings from different museums I had visited on my bicycle over the years. One side of the case held a row of hanging black pants and T-shirts—my stage clothes—beside a stack of drawers containing several pairs of dancing shoes, a wide variety of African-style hats (made for me by a Toronto milliner named Sheila, they were based on prayer caps I had collected in Africa, and an Israeli version Geddy had bought for me on his travels—they were great for keeping sweat out of my eyes), hard-to-find Elastoplast bandages (the only brand that survived both sweat and drumstick abrasion), yellow reflective bicycle clips to keep the bass-drum-pedal beater from getting caught inside my right pant leg, and other such necessities.

At five o'clock, we did our usual soundcheck, starting with the acoustic numbers, "Resist" and "Heart Full of Soul," then playing through a few songs we felt still needed review—the cover tunes particularly, like "Summertime Blues" and "The Seeker," that we were playing live for the first time. As always, we played a bit of "Red Sector A" to check out keyboards and electronic drums, then finished with the opening number, the "R30 Overture," so our sound mixer, Brad, could have everything set for the beginning of the show.

While we worked, the building staff began to assemble in the empty house, cleaners working through the rows of seats, groups of security people in matching jackets, and small utility trucks delivering merchandise and catering supplies. In all, more than 300 local people were employed for the day and night, when you added in stagehands, building and parking staff, police and medics, and cashiers at refreshment and merchandise stands.

Among the many family associations in our organization was our current chief rigger, Brian Collins, whose father, Billy, had been our original rigger, starting back in the '70s when our show first started getting big enough to require hanging light trusses and speaker cabinets. Also spanning the generations, our merchandising operations were run by a young Canadian named Pat McLoughlin, whose father, Mike, had started traveling with us, selling T-shirts and tourbooks back in the mid-'70s. We had first encountered Mike as the owner of a small dance hall in Port Dover, Ontario, where we played in 1975, and a few years later he became one of the pioneers in the tour-merchandise business, touring with us until his untimely passing in 1998.

I often think of Mike when I swim my laps at the Y, as he had been a keen long-distance swimmer, and had given me some good coaching. In the '80s, when I was first getting interested in endurance sports, Mike had counseled me to try to develop a relaxed breathing pace of three strokes to every breath. The advantage was that I would surface and breathe on opposite sides, rather than the typical "left, right, breathe, repeat" rhythm, where you always turned your head to breathe on the same side. Sure enough, once I mastered the cadence of holding and releasing each breath exactly right, that three-stroke rhythm became a relaxed, comfortable pace I could maintain for miles.

Unfortunately, that day Pat brought me some bad news. During the past month, while I had been busy with the rehearsals and the desperate drive to finish *Traveling Music,* my Toronto book publisher had been evasive and noncommittal with me about the status of the new edition of *The Masked Rider.* I hadn't had time to worry about it, but now Pat told me the book wasn't ready, and wouldn't be for a while. Apparently the publisher had been holding off, waiting for *Traveling Music* to be finished, so he could get a "gang-printing" discount on all the books, and that meant there was even worse news. The publisher hadn't reprinted *Ghost Rider* either, and now Pat had very few copies of the one book that was in print.

I was shocked and disgusted at that information, and felt deceived, betrayed, disappointed, and fiercely angry. I felt my pulse and blood pressure rising toward rage, but then an almost autonomous mechanism kicked in, setting that issue aside: "I can't worry about that today." Today, there is only The Show.

Even then, I was surprised at how easily I was able to shunt that anger, rather than letting it come screaming out or bottling it up inside. Whether from my long experience at handling stress, or simply the mellowing of advanced years, I had evolved some healthier methods of handling anger. Generally, I had always found that anger cost me more than it was worth, upsetting me more than it did the person I was angry at.

If there was something bothering me that I couldn't do anything about, and didn't urgently *need* to do anything about (because it wouldn't do any good anyway), I could set that problem aside and worry about it another day. Such adaptations were easier said than done, but it seemed that kind of detachment could be practiced and learned. It would serve me well.

That afternoon, I simply sent a brief e-mail to Paul McCarthy, who was my literary agent as well as my editor, and informed him of this disaster. There was nothing more I could do—though I did tell Paul, referring to the publisher, "I will never have anything to do with him again."

Later, I composed an angry letter, but never bothered to send it. He wasn't worth it, there was no point in "dialogue," and I remembered the advice, "Speak in anger, and make the best speech you'll ever regret." In my whole life, there had only been a handful of people I had ever broken with like that, but to me, when someone betrayed themselves as no kind of a friend, it was simply over. It wasn't the first time I had felt compelled to write that kind of letter, nor the first time I had elected not to send it.

Around six, the three of us gathered in the dressing room for dinner, delivered by Frenchie and Donovan. On recent tours, when I had traveled separately from the other two, dinner was the only time of the day when the three of us would just hang out together. While we ate, we caught up on what we had been doing on the show days and on days off.

The dressing room was always equipped with a television, and when Geddy was around, it was nearly always tuned to a baseball game. Geddy would also have his computer open and on-line, watching the box scores of other games. Not only an avid fan of the real game, Geddy was also involved in a fantasy league, in which a group of his friends assembled imaginary teams of players they drafted, bought, or traded, then "competed" with each other according to their chosen players' real-life performances. (I think that's how it worked.)

After dinner, with another hour to go until the show, I tried to take a little quiet time on the bus, though my nerves were anything but quiet. As the minutes until show time ticked by, I felt myself winding up tighter and tighter. The roaring in my ears kept building, my pulse was racing, and an electric tension tightened every muscle in my body. It was an awful feeling, one of the worst parts of being a performer, and time dragged in an edgy, uncomfortable void. At seven, I went to the Bubba-Gump room again, and sat down at the drums to warm up for a while, hoping to work out the nervousness a little bit.

Buddy Rich's featured saxophonist for many years, Steve Marcus, told me that one time he had been standing beside Buddy, then in his sixties, as they waited to go onstage. Buddy had been a child star in vaudeville as "Traps the Drum Wonder," and had been performing all his life, on stages from Carnegie Hall to the Royal Albert, on television, and in movies. But next to the stage of that small club, Buddy showed Steve his shaking hands. "You'd think after sixty years of doing this I'd get over it."

But of course, you never do. In fact, it often gets worse. A Broadway actor once told me Sir Laurence Olivier had been afflicted with terrible stage fright in his later years, and I remember reading as a child that Glenn Hall, goalie for the Chicago Black Hawks, used to throw up before every game.

As the years went by, before a show I felt *more* nervous rather than less—always expecting more of myself, and feeling that the audience did, too. All those sensations of anxiety and incipient panic were not pleasant, and it was only the application of will that made me go through with it—a sense of professional obligation and pride.

In the early '90s, I was asked by Canada's music television channel, MuchMusic, to interview one of the candidates in the upcoming federal election on live TV. That was pretty daunting, and at first I said I would talk to the Green Party candidate, to keep it low key. But then I thought, "If I'm going to put myself through this, I want to talk to the *winner!*"

So I agreed to interview the leading candidate, and eventual prime minister, Jean Chrétien. As I stood in a hallway at MuchMusic's studios, waiting to walk out into the lights, camera, and live audience, I had a sudden attack of panic. I thought, "I could just run away, right out of here, and there's nothing they could do. That's what I'll do, yeah, I'll run away!'"

But of course I stayed, and made myself walk out there, and it went pretty well. But it sure wasn't easy.

When you watch a performer of any kind on television, or onstage, it is easy to forget how difficult it is just to get up there, in front of a crowd of strangers, and display not only whatever talent or accomplishments you have, but also every error and all-too-human flaw.

Jacob Slichter's fine book, *So You Wanna Be a Rock and Roll Star,* recounts the rise and fall of his band, Semisonic, in familiar tales of record company incompetence and politics. His story is funny, sad, and true. He also describes his own battles with onstage panic attacks, and to those people whose fantasies ignore the less-glamorous aspects of performing, or the cynics who dismiss the difficulty of it, once again I can only quote Ernie Pyle—"Try it sometime."

As soon as the doors were opened, there was a change in the atmosphere. Wherever we might be playing, arena or amphitheater, all day the building had belonged to the professionals: the riggers, the stagehands, the various crews, the band, and the building staff.

But once those doors were opened, the place belonged to the audience. That night in Nashville, almost 8,000 people streamed through the turnstiles and the seats filled gradually, like a mosaic. Recorded music from my private "radio station" (as described in *Traveling Music,* a collection of modern and classic rock songs programmed by me and compiled by my "engineer," Michael), percolated from the PA system, and you could feel an electric charge of anticipation growing.

Then there was that mighty roar when the houselights went down, a physical wave against keyed-up nerves as I ran onto the stage into the twilight, and settled behind the drums while the opening movie played through ("What did they put in my *tea?*").

Those audience responses created a *sensory* buzz greater than any sense of personal vanity, and that was part of the addiction that crept into your soul over the years. That atmosphere was exciting and contagious, and never got old—despite all the stress, the fatigue, the performance anxiety, and the sheer repetition of doing it night after night. A rock concert remains one of the most exciting events I have ever experienced. Though I must admit, I have always had a secret wish just to *be there,* to watch and listen and not have to work. But I guess that might not be quite so exciting—at least after the five hundredth time.

The hardest show of the tour is always the first one, with all the preparation it takes to bring everything to that point of readiness, and the pressure of actually *doing* it, just once, in front of an audience. The *first* stage, in many ways, was the *final* stage. After that, no matter how difficult it was to perform at that level every night, it could never be as uncertain, or as exciting, as the First Show.

It seemed to last forever, and to be over in a flash. One by one, we played through the songs we had rehearsed so many times, and after each song we got through, I breathed a silent "okay." My focus was mainly inward, but occasionally I glanced out at the cheering, rocking audience, catching brief glimpses of Carrie's radiant smile and Matt's radiant bald head. I noticed some other familiar faces, fans who had attended many shows on previous tours. The average age of the audience was probably about forty, but that average included many both older and younger.

For reasons I have never understood, our audience has always been predominantly male, 90 percent or more. Some speculate that this gender divide is because our music is "aggressive," or because it is technical, and in the '70s, a fatuous record company executive once even referred to our music as "cock rock." It is a mystery to me, although it does seem that the female fans we do have often understand our music in the deepest possible way, appreciating not only its technicality, but its passion, too. They are also often more sensitive to the lyrics—which naturally pleases their author! Perhaps because of their scarcity, I always loved to see females in the audience singing along, or air-drumming, or even dancing. However, given the complexity and constant changes in our music, even their dancing had to be absorbed in the music—no mindless twitching to a metronomic beat. In our song "Force Ten," I had expressed my appreciation for that absorption, "Cool and remote like dancing girls, in the heat of the beat and the lights."

Bandleader Artie Shaw passed away in 2004, and I read an on-line obituary: "A volatile and superbly intelligent man, Shaw hated the loss of privacy that stardom brought, had little use for signing autographs, and once caused an uproar by calling jitterbugging fans 'morons.' He later said he was just referring to the rowdy ones. 'I could never understand why people wanted to dance to my music,' he once said. 'I made it good enough to listen to.' "

I understood what Artie was talking about, but I was always glad to see a few girls dancing out there.

Twilight deepened during the first set, from 7:30 to 8:50, especially under the roofed-over part of the amphitheater, and my view of the audience narrowed to the first twenty rows or so, when the stage lights shone out on them. They were cheering and clapping and rocking along with us, laughing at the funny movies, at Alex's antics, and obviously having a good time. Toward the end of the second set, when we felt we could finally relax a little, we started having a good time, too. The last few songs were deliberately chosen to be looser and easier, technically and technologically, and allow us just to play.

In one part of the long instrumental "La Villa Strangiato," Geddy and I played a quiet jazz riff while Alex stepped to the microphone and told a little story. As on the previous tour, his monologues would be different every night, springing from the endlessly inventive and spontaneous brain of our "musical scientist." That night, he recounted a story about his adventures that afternoon, flying radio-controlled airplanes with Peter Collins. Alex was a licenced pilot, and had built several radio-controlled airplanes himself, especially in the early '80s, during long stints in the studio while we worked on our *Permanent Waves* and *Moving Pictures* albums. However, that afternoon he had apparently crashed not one, but *two*, of Peter's model planes, and though they could be repaired, the next day he would send Peter an expensive and sophisticated new one.

At the beginning of that R30 tour, I was experimenting with various ways of capturing my Important Thoughts, and the day after that first show, at a motel in Sweetwater, Tennessee, where Michael and I had parked for the night, I tried recording an entry on a microcassette recorder.

First show last night went pretty well. One minor train wreck in "Earthshine," not sure whose fault it was, and maybe don't *want* to know! We'll sort that out tomorrow. Otherwise, went very well, everything seemed to work, including me.

Best Western, right by the interstate, and *conveniently* next door to the Cracker Barrel (ha ha). First long "free" ride today, rambling around back roads and not knowing where we were going to end up, and mostly on two-lanes. Very nice, even slowing down through towns and all that is just part of the rhythm.

Carrie hadn't left until that morning, so Michael and I stayed over in Nashville after the first show (almost the last time on the whole tour we would ever stay in a city after a show). In the afternoon we loaded up the bikes, then followed a meandering route I had written down from the map. Small two-lanes carried us east and northeast of Nashville, then curved southeast toward the corner of the state, in the direction of the next day's show in Charlotte, North Carolina.

All that day I felt a wonderful sense of freedom, as expressed in that voice recording. After the ordeal of getting through that first show, a burden had been lifted, a dreaded challenge faced. Now I could enjoy the pleasure and lack of pressure of meandering around unfamiliar roads on a day off.

Another pleasant thought occurred to me when we were parked at the motel, enjoying the Macallan and Red Apple time.

I smiled as I wrote it down—"Nobody even knows where we are."

midwest state of mind

If thine enemy wrong thee, buy each of his children a drum.

(Chinese saying)

Signs on the front of churches, especially in the South, were often thought-provoking to a passing motorcyclist, though not always in the manner intended. In eastern Tennessee, I noticed one that read, "JESUS CHRIST—THE SAME YESTERDAY, TODAY, AND TOMORROW," and remembered that I used to see that same message outside a church on the way to my dad's farm equipment dealership. As a teenager, I worked for Dad summers and weekends, rising at painful hours of the morning and riding in the pickup with him, then spending the day cleaning parts bins, polishing tractors and mowers, sweeping floors, and restocking shelves. In my dozy, teenage ennui, the hours seemed to pass so slowly, and when I saw that sign on the way to work, "THE SAME YESTERDAY, TODAY, AND TOMORROW," I decided that was exactly what I *didn't* want. Be careful what you wish for . . .

The three days after the Nashville show went by in a blur, a kaleidoscope of experiences and impressions, on the bike and on the stage. The Vortex. My only journal notes were dates, cities, and mileages, 468 kilometers (290 miles) to the Cellular Telephone Network Amphitheater in Charlotte, North Carolina; 395 kilometers (246 miles) the next day, to the

Cellular Telephone Network Amphitheater in Virginia Beach, Virginia. Another day off brought Michael and me to Elkins, West Virginia, after 419 kilometers (261 miles).

I did remember a humorous/ painful church sign we passed in North Carolina: "To PREVENT ETERNAL BURNING, USE SON BLOCK."

When Liam returned to the tour, in Charlotte, I went by his office in the afternoon to commiserate a little. As an experienced griever, I had unfortunately learned to be comfortable with such situations.

After two shows in a row, and riding in between them, I really wanted to get caught up on everything, journal-wise, and when Michael and I arrived in Elkins, West Virginia, I delivered a monologue to the microcassette.

The major flaw in this plan to document the tour is that life is so full there's no time to document it. Thinking yesterday about conversations with people in passing—crew members, drivers, and strangers—that would be worth writing down, worth making part of the real-life touring story, but no time to do that. By the time you get there and look after the bike, look after yourself, and look after the drums, and do the job and get on the bus and recover, it's about all you can do.

Great ride today. Threatened rain all day, but didn't happen until . . . right now!—just as we checked into the Days Inn in Elkins, West Virginia. Riding across minor roads through Virginia and West Virginia, we managed to avoid pretty much any hint of Memorial Day throngs. Combination of maps and the newly christened [by me] Doofus, the GPS unit, with its virtues and its . . . flaws.

Beautiful winding up to the Virginia-West Virginia border, a river flowing alongside that I remember, in the other direction, last tour, stopping somewhere along there, just as we did today, for a (ahem) water-making and smoke-taking session.

Twenty-five hundred kays on the new bike at this point, and I can feel the engine starting to loosen up, and the whole thing just working together as a unit. Comfortable and fast and great handling, on a lot of winding roads today—most of the way, in fact. Very few straight stretches, now that I think about it, and so green, too. Once again, that contrast to "western eyes," I guess it must be—not something that I used to notice on bicycle or motorcycle, but riding through those lush green forests, everything at this time of year is so green, before any flowers or blossoms and such have appeared. Just one solid mass of dense, green foliage.

The show last night so nearly perfect, really, already felt that autopilot mentality, the pleasant flow of things coming out of me without having to . . . be *provoked*.

Especially the drum solo, finally got everything I wanted in there, in terms of elements and transitions, each of them very spirited, and free-spirited—truly improvised. What I've been trying to get into the waltz section, of interposing the odd times over it, I managed to get a really nice pattern of seven going over the three, and now it's time for five. And the four over three too—got it perfectly together. The whole solo, the big band section and everything, was what I had wanted it to be for the last seven weeks or so.

And then I get to the very climax of the "One O'clock Jump" bit and hit that sample, and . . . it doesn't go!

And I hit it again, and it *still* doesn't go.

Not knowing what else to do, I just played on to it in my mind, I guess you'd say, and played through the drum part, climaxed with it, and—poof.

Disappointing. Poor Gump, I felt worse for him, he took it harder than I did, I think, but I was certainly disappointed in that major flaw in the show, and of all the samples not to work in the course of a whole show, that's probably one of the worst. [Just as Alex and Geddy were starting "Resist," on quiet acoustic guitars, the sample finally triggered, too late and too *loud*, blaring through the monitors as Gump scrambled to shut it off.]

Strange this ongoing sampling problem that never occurred once last tour—not once. Makes me wonder where the loophole is. It's making Gump crazy, and me, I guess, *uneasy*, not being able to trust, the way we could last tour, that things would simply work.

So difficult to get a real sense of the weather we're in for right now. On-line weather reports look like they're going to be the only answer, now that local cable is disappearing. Satellite feeds only have the national picture, one major city at a time, which doesn't really help. We need to know what we're in for weather-wise in terms of the distance we can do, plus also, crucially, in terms of *wardrobe!*

So that's been puzzling, spending so much time watching unimportant weather news, just trying to glean the few details that will be helpful. By the national forecast, we were supposed to be under a huge blanket of rain in this part of the country, and wore our rainsuits all day. But in reality, we wouldn't have needed them until . . . now! When we're *here!*

Oh yes—the *pain* this morning, after two difficult shows in a row, and some long bike rides too. But it's definitely the drumming that kills. Start off the day with two multivitamins and two vitamin B (for Bufferins), and they really do work, I've noticed in the last two days, having compared Advil the first couple of days, where it seemed to *lessen* the pain, but Bufferins—here comes the commercial!—seem to *obliterate* it. So I didn't think about physical stiffness or aches and pains, for the whole day on the bike yesterday and today.

So . . . there's a testimonial. [Where's my money?]

On the bus ride out of Charlotte, Dave told me about a conversation he had with three hardcore fans who were friends of his. The first one, a woman who had seen dozens of Rush shows over the years, said it was the best Rush show she had ever seen. Another guy said it was great, "except for the cover songs" (obviously a purist of some kind). The third one said, "Hey, I don't care if they play 'Yankee Doodle Dandy,' as long as they keep *playing!*"

That's the spirit.

The first night I spent on the bus, after the Charlotte show, had been strange. No matter how familiar the rhythm of the road had been in my life, it still took some getting used to, and as Dave piloted us through the night and I cooled down in the front lounge with Michael, I found myself restless and unable to relax.

Later, I discussed it with my therapist, the tape recorder.

That ongoing, craving sense of—I don't know, must be some sense of discontent and rootlessness, that "I want, I want," and trying to make it *good* or something. Okay, have a drink, have a smoke, have a sandwich, and now what? Some potato chips. Okay, I used to like them on the bus. Some peanuts, I used to like them on the bus.

[With all the sweat that poured out of me in concerts, I always craved salty snacks.]

Couldn't even play music that first drive, with the ridiculously complicated "entertainment system" that even Dave didn't know how to work. [Not having driven that particular bus before, Dave called the shop to find out how we could do a simple thing like play some music, and when he complained that it was "too technical," one of the guys there said, "Hey, entertainers *like* technical." The plain-spoken Dave replied, in two distinct syllables, "Bull . . . Shit."]

So I automatically felt that . . . desperation for diversion, I guess, or entertainment, or "Now what?" Again, something to get *excited* about.

That road mentality, The Vortex, certainly contributes to people's problems in dealing with the . . . less agreeable diversions.

Last night we finally got the stereo working, the five-channel setting seems to be the only way the unit operates. Actually sounds really good, listening to Patsy Cline and Jeff Buckley up really loud, and Porcupine Tree, too.

Slept on the bus last night just outside Charlottesville [Virginia], to set us up for a little road that would go by Monticello [Thomas Jefferson's residence, which I had always wanted to visit]. On a Sunday morning, though, it was jam-packed, and the place itself wasn't visible from the parking lot or the road, so we kept going.

But some wonderful roads from then on, combined with my mapped route and the ability Doofus has to find roads that aren't numbered on the map sometimes, or twists and turns that aren't adequately signed. That's certainly been one of the strengths of the Doof. [Though the GPS unit did direct us to turn up some farmer's driveway, and to turn left in the middle of a bridge—hence, "Doofus."]

Our mornings on the bus began with the beeping of my Swiss Army alarm clock. After a show, by the time I cooled down, had a shower (always an adventure on a moving bus!), and read a little, I would get to sleep around two. I usually tried to plan our dropoff point to be a two- or three-hour drive, so that by the time I was going to bed, Dave would be parking the bus in a truck stop or rest area. Apart from the pleasure of sleeping in a *stationary* bed, I always liked to hear the death rattle of the main engine shutting down, then the generator starting up, its distant hum blocking any outside sounds. Over the years of bus travel, it always seemed to me that an hour of sleep on a stationary bus was worth *three* hours on a moving one.

Wanting to make the most of the riding day, I would set the alarm for eight, so there was never enough time for sleep, and I would have to force myself out of that soft, warm bed. Going forward to start the coffee, which Dave had set up the night before, I squeezed two oranges into the little electric juicer, and poured out some cereal. Only then would I go back and rattle the curtain over Michael's bunk—"Come on Wendy, it's time for school!" After a few groans and protests, he would stumble out to crack a Red Bull or Mountain Dew.

Then, all amped-up, sometimes Michael would jump into his riding clothes and go out the door and back to the trailer to unload both of our bikes. He had never done that once on the *Vapor Trails* tour, and the second time I walked off the bus to find both bikes ready to go, hard bags installed, I asked him, "Have you changed your meds or something?"

"Ha ha, nice talk. What do you mean?"

"Well, don't think I'm complaining, because I love it, but it never happened *once* last tour."

"Why can't you just *appreciate* something I do," he pouted, "without *criticizing* something else?"

"Sorry, honey."

That day's route through Virginia and West Virginia was absolutely sublime, combining twisty mountain roads that followed ridges and rivers through dense forests, then opened into pastoral valleys with centuries-old farms in picturesque array.

In the ever-changing Rorschach pattern of each tour's itinerary, the routing could vary almost infinitely, due to factors like building availability on a given night, venues that preferred certain days of the week (everybody wanted Friday and Saturday, of course), and (the drivers' explanation) the dartboard on our manager's wall. So the nature of the journey could be very different from tour to tour, and on the *Vapor Trails* tour, it happened that Michael and I rode across Virginia about four times, and I became enraptured with the area, and still consider it some of the best riding in the East. Cruising on one of those winding two-lanes out of the forested mountains into a long valley with tidy barns and fences, I would see a farm for sale, and think, "Hmm . . . I could live here."

However, I have thought that about at least a hundred different places in the world, and in the end, I always follow the line of least resistance, and settle where my wife wants to live. When you are away from home so much of the time, you can't go stranding your wife in a place that has no photo labs, no yoga classes, no organic food, no Peet's coffee, no family, no shopping, and no gay friends.

Along those back roads in Virginia and West Virginia, Michael and I encountered quite a few groups of motorcyclists, off on a Memorial Day Weekend tour together. Even though we had avoided crowded interstates and busy towns, the holiday was apparent in two kinds of signs we passed frequently: those advertising yard sales, and those reading "NO VACANCY."

With late afternoon suggesting cocktail time, we settled for the Days Inn in Elkins, West Virginia. It didn't have the requisite restaurant nearby, but it did have rooms. A neighboring church featured a sign that perplexed and delighted with its refreshing honesty, "WE HAVE NO NEW MESSAGES."

We arrived not only right before a torrential rainstorm, but just ahead of a large crowd of motorcyclists on big touring rigs, some with passengers and towing little trailers. They would have caused us a long wait, and possibly another "NO VACANCY" sign.

When we asked the slack-jawed twenty-something at the front desk about restaurants, she said most of them were closed on Sunday, but directed us to one that was open. I asked her the name of the street it was on, and she said, "I don't know . . . it's the main street of Elkins." That's all you needed to know.

After a long walk, we found the restaurant, but there were dozens of people already waiting for tables. We thought we might be waiting a long time, and even discussed giving up and settling for the Subway we had passed, or trudging back to the hotel and ordering a pizza. But apparently twenty-one of those waiting people were the group of motorcyclists from our hotel, and they were waiting for one table for *all* of them.

We were relieved when we were led to a table after only a few minutes, but perhaps we would have been better off with Subway, or a pizza.

After decades of road food, from American franchises to African street stalls, I am not a fussy eater or drinker, so it was not very often that my journal contained a review like this: "Such an *awful* meal. House wine, 'Lambrusco,' tastes like syrup, pasta like canned spaghetti with chicken and Chinese sweet-and-sour sauce. After that long walk, too."

Two of the motorcyclists, a middle-aged couple, came over to our table, and asked if I was "Neil Pert." When I said I was, they told me they had recognized me because their sixteen-year-old son was a drummer. They asked for an autograph, and I signed it to him with my usual salutation to drummers, "Happy Drumming."

As so often happened, a few minutes later they were back, standing at the end of our table. This time they asked if they could take a photograph with me. Always uncomfortable posing for a stranger's camera, especially attracting that kind of attention in a crowded restaurant, I politely declined.

The next morning was cool and rainy, as we wound our way north toward a little wedge of Maryland. We stopped for breakfast at a small restaurant just over the West Virginia line in Oakland, Maryland, which apparently gave the establishment its name, the Oak-Mar. Looking around at the other diners that Memorial Day Monday morning, I thought again about the nature of regionalism, and the difference between saying, "I am from Maryland" and, "I am from West Virginia."

Superficially, Maryland was the Chesapeake, Annapolis and Quantico, horse farms, and the Cumberland Gap, while West Virginia was a thinly populated, hillbilly Appalachia with wild scenery occasionally blighted by mines and chemical factories.

The people in the Oak-Mar might have been natives of either state, as alike as any neighbors, but whether or not they conformed to any generalization, their licence plates and convention name tags would "label" them. The more I traveled through the states of the union, the fewer generalities seemed to apply; if asked what I thought of a particular state, even Maryland or West Virginia, my answer would fill an essay—or a book.

In the mid-'80s, I remember a hundred-mile bicycle ride up the Kanawha River out of Charleston, West Virginia, on the day of Halloween. The roadside trees were in full autumn splendor, the houses decorated with jack-o'-lanterns, speckled cobs of dried maize, ghosts and witches, and the children ran out of small-town schools in their costumes.

I saw a couple of guys fishing downstream from a huge chemical plant, and noted in my journal, "Whatever they catch, I sure hope they don't eat it." That night, our bus and truck drivers hosted a dinner for the three band members, the Annual Drivers' Dinner, in a private dining room at the hotel, and it was a riotous feast.

Several times I had bicycled from downtown Washington, DC, to shows at the old arena, the Capital Center, in the Maryland suburbs. I remember a rainy afternoon at the Baltimore Art Museum, marveling at the European masterworks collected by the Cone sisters. Motorcycling down the Eastern Shore to Delaware, or across the Chesapeake to Virginia, or through a misty valley of rich green pastures and country homes—there was so much. I always liked to tell people, "There are great roads in every state, you just have to look for them." Same with the people.

After pancakes with two eggs over easy, and some carnal grease-fest for Michael, we filled the bikes with gas and he led us north through occasional rainshowers across the Appalachian corner of Maryland, then into the woods of southern Pennsylvania, not far from the state's highest point, Mount Davis, at 3213 feet. Among the deeply forested valleys, we passed the sign for Fallingwater, a house designed by Frank Lloyd Wright in 1936 that was considered a masterpiece, now open as a state park.

Until then, I hadn't realized I had been on that road before, but Brutus and I had stopped at Fallingwater on *Test for Echo*. On a cold autumn day, we had been on our way up from West Virginia to Pittsburgh, and I had noticed the sign as we rode by. Quickly deciding we had time for a look, I waved Brutus over. We parked our motorcycles and walked around a little in our riding suits, marveling at the way the house was set over a waterfall, the interior so perfectly proportioned and open to its woodland setting.

In 2004, though, it was somewhere around there that Doofus really earned its nickname. Or its operator did. From previous tours, I knew the Local Newspaper Amphitheater was well to the west of Pittsburgh, in a rural area. For some reason, though, it seemed Michael was leading us *east* of the city, and by the time I got him stopped to look at a map, we had traveled twenty-five miles in the wrong direction. We would now need to ride through the middle of downtown Pittsburgh, and traffic on that holiday Monday had grown increasingly dense all day.

The occasional rainshowers tapered off as we crossed the city, and I glanced over at its modern skyline, the triangle of green, Three Rivers Park, at the point of land where the Monongahela and Allegheny Rivers became the Ohio, and Three Rivers Stadium across the Allegheny. Among the sleek buildings that indicated Pittsburgh's successful transition from Iron City to a technological center, I caught a glimpse of the low dome of the Civic Center Arena. That was where Alex and Geddy and I had played our first show together, on August 14, 1974, opening for Manfred Mann's Earth Band and Uriah Heep in front of about 11,000 people. Among the many memories of that life-changing experience, I would never forget standing on the floor beside stage left while Uriah Heep played "Stealin'." The big dark building, colored lights on the heroic figures up on the stage, the roaring audience, the sheer electricity in that place. Halfway through their show, the retractable dome of the Civic Arena had peeled back, open to the summer night.

Some other memorable buildings in Pittsburgh existed only there—in memory. An old hotel called the New Webster Hall had been the first hotel we had ever stayed in together, and several times we had played at an old vaudeville theater, the Stanley Warner, as both opening act and headliner (I remember the rats in the back alley by the stage door).

The rain came down again as Michael and I rode west toward the venue, and by the time we were parked by the bus at the Local Newspaper Amphitheater, it had been a long, cold, wet 220 miles.

Between rain showers, crew members lined up at an impromptu "driving range" in the backstage area, driving golf balls across a small lake. I recalled that on the previous tour, the Local Newspaper Amphitheater had been the scene of a little friction betweeen Dave and Michael. Dave was like a ship's captain, and kept high professional standards for the bus's cleanliness, while Michael tended to bring aboard his bachelor apartment habits. That day, Dave had decided the front lounge had become too crowded with Michael's computer components, cases, and personal items, and he shifted them all into the production office. Michael had been shocked and mystified, and looked to me for help, but I wasn't sure how to resolve this standoff (it's not always good to be the king!). I often take it for granted that two friends of mine are going to be friends as well, but of course it doesn't always work out that way.

In any case, the three of us talked about it and reached a compromise—from then on Michael kept most of his stuff in the luggage bay, peace was restored, and I was glad that by the time of this tour, Dave and Michael had evolved a good working relationship.

I was also glad that I had been able to lay off the Bufferins (though I moaned and groaned a lot on the bus after the show, and in the morning), but I was having trouble with my hands. Through the rehearsals I had built up the usual peanut-sized calluses on thumbs and fingers, but some of them were now cracking open, perhaps from the heat and humidity. During the show, salt would work through the cracks and into the tender flesh beneath, and it *burned*. Both hands were tender all the time, even on the handlebars of the motorcycle, and swollen so that I couldn't even close my hands all the way.

I didn't know what to do about that, but at least the audience didn't have to worry about it. They seemed to be having a good time every night. The past few shows had continued to average about 8,000 people, and that was respectable. That night at the Local Newspaper Amphitheater, Geddy thanked the audience for helping us celebrate our thirtieth anniversary, and when he mentioned our first performance together had been in Pittsburgh, they gave a big cheer.

I had been noticing a lot of *families* in our audiences. Sometimes the parents were obviously the fans bringing their kids along, but other times it was the preteens or young teenagers who were the fans—the parents were there because the kids were not allowed to go to a concert alone.

During the pre-show dinner with Geddy and Alex, we were talking about some of the familiar fans we remembered from many shows and many tours, and joked that we were starting to talk about their *social lives* — "That blonde girl who's always waving the Rush licence plate has a new boyfriend. He looks nice."

Or one fan Geddy called "the happy guy," who showed up wearing a different Rush T-shirt every night, always in the front row or two, and just smiled and laughed and danced his heart out.

However, one night he was wearing a dress shirt, and he had brought a date. She was very obviously *not* a Rush fan, and just stood there, without comprehension or interest, while the Happy Guy's spirits visibly sank. She would even lean over and start yelling into his ear in the middle of a song, his smile fading even while his eyes still followed us. We recognized the familiar "fan's girlfriend" syndrome. Sometimes we would look out from the stage and see them sitting there, arms folded, as they scowled at us all night—not just hating us, but resenting our place in their boyfriends' affections.

We would see the Happy Guy many more times, but never again with that girl.

Around that time, I started to hear some stories about Donovan, who was apparently a tireless pickup artist. In his mid-twenties and unattached, Donovan had once said, "Hey, for a guy who's not that great looking, and could lose a few pounds, I do pretty well."

Alex and Geddy told me that Donovan showed absolutely no fear of rejection, and took it as a challenge never to use the same pickup line twice. They laughed as they told me about watching him approach a table of several attractive and prosperous-looking women in a hotel bar. Donovan walked straight up to one of them, looked her in the eyes and said, "You look like the kind of woman who could use a pool boy."

I don't know if that particular gambit was successful, but from then on, Donovan had a new nickname: "Pool Boy."

The next day was another day off, the first of June, and I had arranged to visit my brother-in-law Steven and his wife, Shelly, at their home in a small town ("Podunk," Steve called it) near Columbus, Ohio. Michael also had relatives in the area, and wanted to visit the BMW dealer the next morning for some service work, so after sleeping on the bus near Zanesville, Ohio, we split up for the day.

I set off down the Muskingum River for a couple of hours, then zigzagged west on little two-lanes through the Wayne National Forest and southeastern Ohio. Hills and curvy roads shaded by hardwood forests, occasional tidy farms and meadows—it was probably the most scenic part of the state. Eventually I veered to the north, making a point of passing through Rushville (named after some old farmer, not some old rock band), then into the farm country east of Columbus.

It was a warm, sunny day, and I paused for a siesta beneath a tree in a cemetery, undisturbed by the slumbering spirits of the Buckeye State. In mid-afternoon, after a pleasant 125 miles of solitary riding, I saw the sign for Steven and Shelly's little town, "BIG CITY CLOSE, SMALL TOWN COZY," and followed the directions Steve had given me to their "small town cozy" house.

Steven and I had known each other since our late teens in St.

Catharines, and at the time of joining Rush, in 1974, I was sharing a house with Steve, his brother Keith, and our friend, the Bear. A couple of years later, I would be sharing a house with Keith and Steve's sister, Jackie, and in 1978, she would give birth to our daughter, Selena.

In more recent years, Steven and I had lived through the deaths of Selena and Jackie, and mourned and commiserated in Toronto, London, Barbados, Belize, Quebec, and Baja California (traveling through the Christmas of 1999 in Shelly's father's Hummer). Even more recently, during the pre-tour rehearsals in Toronto, I had been with Steven for the funeral of his 15-year-old son, Kyle, who had died after a long and terrible battle with bone cancer.

Steven and Shelly, an emergency-room doctor in a nearby hospital, were still reeling from those tragedies, but we did our best to have a good time together. Shelly regaled us with a homemade dinner, a welcome treat for me, as was their comfortable guest room. Shelly made me laugh with doctor stories about men who showed up at the emergency room with some work-related wound, then just before they left, would turn and say, "By the way, Doc, I've got this rash. Maybe you could have a look at it."

As they unbuckled their belts, Shelly would be thinking, *Here we go*, as she asked them, "How long have you had it?"

"Oh, a *year* or so . . . "

The next morning, Michael and I met up at the American Motorcyclist Association's Motorcycle Hall of Fame Museum, just east of Columbus, and walked through their displays of historic machines, dirt bikes, racing bikes, and an exhibition devoted to the long-gone British make, BSA (for Birmingham Small Arms, originally a gun-maker).

From there, I agreed to trust Doofus one more time, and that day, he succeeded in navigating us to the venue. Formerly called the Polaris Amphitheater, it was now the Import Auto Dealer Amphitheater.

After the Columbus show, which was another very good one for us and the audience, we had another day off, establishing a typical rhythm for this tour: two shows, day off, one show, day off, then two shows again. Dave drove us south to a truck stop near the Kentucky border, and the next morning Michael and I rode a long loop down through the Daniel Boone National Forest and around Lexington, with its vast, park-like horse farms on manicured lanes. (Last tour I wanted to move to Virginia; this tour it was Lexington.)

The day also gave me one of my all-time favorite church signs, "IF YOU TAKE SATAN FOR A RIDE, PRETTY SOON HE'LL WANT TO DRIVE." That is *so* good.

The little town of Eminence, Kentucky, had been badly damaged in a tornado just two days earlier, and it was like riding through a disaster area. Trees were shattered, and had crushed a couple of houses under their heavy trunks. Broken branches were everywhere, sometimes chainsawed and stacked already, if they had been blocking the road. Many roofs had been damaged, power lines were down, utility trucks flashed their yellow lights, and workmen and police blocked lanes and directed traffic.

Back at the Ohio River again, maybe 100 miles downriver from where we had started that morning, we stopped for the night at a motel in Madison, Indiana. The Hillside Inn sat high above the steep, forested bluffs along the Ohio, overlooking the ancient girder bridge we had crossed from Kentucky into Indiana, the only crossing in about sixty miles, between Louisville and the Markland Dam, well upriver.

It had not been a very long day, only 260 miles, but by mid-afternoon I felt weary. Those little two-lanes in populated areas demanded constant alertness for hazards, like tractors and driveways appearing out of the trees. Such roads required a lot of *passing*, too, around crawling tractors, laboring trucks, and every car who didn't match our pace (all of them). Such active riding necessarily kept us vigilant and on edge, forever calculating how much clear road we needed to make a safe pass. It was fun, all right, but tiring.

When we checked into the Hillside Inn, with cicadas shrieking in the trees all around, we learned we had crossed into the Central Time Zone, and had gained an hour. Good, I thought, time for a nap before dinner.

The next morning, in a classic little restaurant on Madison's main street (mentioned earlier, by coincidence, in that litany of Americana from a previous tour), I made some journal notes.

June 4, 2004
Just had to look up the date in the itinerary (unaccountably, I *did* know it was Thursday).

Limestone outcrops through Kentucky, I think, like Tennessee, though I remember granite somewhere—maybe in West Virginia and Pennsylvania.

Breakfast at Hammond's Family Restaurant, a truly classic diner, where Brutus and I stopped in '96 or '97—probably on our way up from Lexington to Indy. Kind of place the same people, mostly men, come to every day. Two hefty daughters cooking and serving, one small grill. Jerry Springer on TV.

Antique Mason jars, painted metal ads for "Bambino" cola ("It's a hit!"), yet the Babe also touts Red Rock Cola, "It's the finest cola drink I've ever tasted."

Ted Williams says, "Make mine Moxie!"

The ride up to Indianapolis meandered through 180 miles of rural Indiana, through tiny towns with names like Pumpkin Center, Surprise, and Gnawbone (near Acme and Spraytown, not to mention Rush Creek Valley), to another Nashville—the second of four we would eventually ride through.

The day's church sign: "WHAT'S MISSING FROM CH_ _CH?"

"U-R"

We had played the Deer Creek amphitheater (the name now replaced by a Cellular Telephone Network), just north of Indianapolis, quite a few times before. I had even arrived there by bicycle a couple of times, so I knew exactly where it was. On a bicycle, I never took any chances with navigation and directions, as a wrong turn wasn't just a nuisance; it meant more hard pedaling. However, I let Michael and Doofus pretend they were leading us to the venue.

I had wanted to arrive early that day, as the 1200GS was due for an oil change. We had racked up over 3000 kilometers since the first service in Nashville, so it was time. I kept a mileage record in the back of my journal, as well as on a dry-marker board in the trailer, to record maintenance done on the bikes, when new tires were installed, and any service work or supplies we needed.

As usual, just before reaching the venue, Michael and I pulled over and dug out our laminated passes and strung them around our necks. As we crawled through some heavy traffic in suburban Indianapolis, a guy in a van behind us started crowding close, yelling my name out the window, perhaps spotting my tell-tale Ontario licence plate (by pure chance, its number was "666B9," marking me as the "benign devil"). Michael's security instincts took over, and at a red light, he led me out and around the line of traffic to the front, then we sped off when it turned green.

We waved our passes at the security guards as we rode through the backstage gates, and I pulled my bike under the awning beside the bus. While I changed out of my riding gear, Dave opened the luggage bay and brought out the necessary tools, the plastic drain pan, oil, and a new filter.

Of the many oil changes I had performed in backstage loading areas and parking lots, I always remembered one at the Omni arena in Atlanta, during the *Test for Echo* tour. Lying on the floor under the bike, I was installing a new filter and the drain plug, when a formidable black woman in an Omni uniform loomed up beside and above me.

I looked up and said, "Hello."

She pointed to another security guard across the backstage area, and said, "*He* says you the best drummer in the world."

I laughed, "Well, I don't know about that—maybe the best drummer, um, under this motorcycle right now!"

"Hmm," she said. Then she put her hands on her ample hips and shook her head, "You the only rich man I ever saw change his own oil!"

I laughed again. Changing the bike's oil was just something I enjoyed doing, and one of the few mechanical procedures I *could* do. I was no mechanic, and there wasn't much else I could do on the bike—plug a puncture if I had to, remove a wheel for repair. I never felt like I had to change the oil in my cars myself, dealing with jacks and blocks and crawling underneath (though I used to when I was young and poor). But as a motorcyclist, my relationship with the machine was more intimate, and it seemed necessary to be more *involved* with it.

In any case, it was a fairly simple task. While the oil was still hot, for easy flow and while any contaminants were still in suspension, I would crawl under the bike, remove the crash plate, undo the drain bolt, and try not to get my hand caught in the sudden flood of hot, burned-smelling black liquid as it poured into the drain pan. Remove the old filter, fill the new one with fresh amber oil and screw it in, replace the plug, fill the crankcase, then button it all up again, and start the engine to check for leaks and proper oil level. After the first few seconds of clatter from the oil-less engine—a terrible sound—it would settle into a smooth hum. Shutting it down, I would enjoy the small satisfaction of noting the mileage in my journal, and on the board in the trailer.

While I worked, one of the drivers, or a crew member who had a spare minute, would stop by for a chat. It had been Mac, years ago, who had advised me to smear the gasket of the new oil filter with *old* oil—I didn't know why that would make a difference, but a truck driver should know, so I did it.

Truck drivers were interesting characters, and they came in all kinds. On past tours we'd even had a couple of female truck drivers, and a couple of gay ones (one "out," one not). You would think the nature of the job—driving alone through the night for thousands of miles—would attract a quiet, solitary person, but in fact, they were among the most sociable crew members. During my afternoon errands around the backstage area, I would pass the line of trucks backed up to the loading bay, and often two or three of the drivers would be gathered in one cab for a gab and a smoke. They often sat together in the catering room in the mornings during load-in, in the afternoon for crew meal, and after the show during load-out. They even "camped out" together on days off, parking the trucks and buses at the next venue, chipping in for steaks and beer. (They were paid a hotel allowance every day, and if they didn't use it, they kept it.)

During one oil change on the *Test for Echo* tour, I was talking with a bus driver named Paul, who shared my interest in the history of Route 66. He said he thought that when Steinbeck called it the Mother Road, he hadn't intended the name in a romantic or nostalgic way, but as a symbol of desperation. The dust-bowl refugees were abandoning their homes, their lands, and "running for Mother."

That day in Indianapolis, Mac told me a story from the previous tour, during the time we had interrupted the American run to play a single show in Mexico City. All of our truck drivers had to deliver the equipment to the Mexican border, where the trailers were transferred to Mexican trucks and driven under armed escort to Mexico City. Our American drivers had to wait for a few days until the trailers returned, and Mac, for one, was always eager to make his job as interesting as he could. He had told me before about adventures like camping his way across the country during a break in a Neil Diamond tour—four tractor-trailers pulling up at the national parks and wanting to camp. The rangers had been bemused, but had usually found them a place they could get the trucks into.

From the Mexican border in McAllen, Texas, the drivers drove their tractors to South Padre Island, on the Gulf Coast of Texas (Brutus and I spent a night there on *Test for Echo*, our hotel rooms right above the surf). They parked in a row on the sandy beach, and after a night of barbecueing and drinking, retired to their sleeper cabs—only to be awakened in the night by waves lapping at their doors! Fortunately they had time to get the trucks out of there, though at least one had to be towed, and the drivers vowed not to tell their employer, or Liam.

"Now it can be told," Mac said, and showed me photographs of surf breaking over the line of white trucks.

Oil change completed, I showered and changed on the bus, then carried my Powerbook into the Bubba-Gump room to check my e-mails—mostly book business from Paul McCarthy and Hugh Syme. On that tour, Rick, Alex's guitar tech, had managed to set up wireless broadband in most venues, which was much better than the old way of doing things, with everybody lining up in the production office for the one designated phone line. When I went back out to the bus, Dave and Michael had washed the bikes, so we lined them up in front of the bus for a group portrait.

The shows by then had become almost routine, though not in the sense of being tedious or unimportant. It was just that all the little bugs, musical and technical, had been worked out, and the crew and band simply showed up at work every day and did the job.

Michael and I had also evolved a smooth system for route-planning and navigating. On the bus after the show, following the sequence of rewards (drink, smoke, sandwich), I would look over the map for the next day, choose a route, and highlight it with a yellow marker. Michael would trace it out on his computer maps, then download the route to Doofus. I still didn't quite trust that guy, though (Doofus, not Michael), so if I was going to be leading, I would write down the route numbers to follow.

The next day's ride was an easy amble through rural Illinois on a hot, sunny day. Looking at the sprouting cornfields, I thought of the farmer's adage, "knee high by July," and noticed the corn was already knee high, on June 5. The day's amusing church sign was, "FORBIDDEN FRUITS CAUSE MANY JAMS."

It was a Saturday, and a line of Amish horse-drawn buggies stood outside a grocery store near the little town of Arcola. As we approached Chicago, we began to see a lot of motorcyclists, and I gave them all the usual fraternal wave (Brutus always made a low, sideways peace sign, and I copied him). The bikes were mainly cruisers, shiny Harleys and clones, rumbling along in groups, their riders obviously taking advantage of the state's lack of a helmet law. Seeing a bareheaded motorcyclist was like seeing a naked skier—they were so *vulnerable*—yet nine out of ten of them, and their female passengers, seemed to think it was fine.

Later Dave told me he saw about 150 motorcycles in the parking lot before that Chicago show, eighty-five percent of them Harleys, and it was nice to think Michael and I might have passed some of them that afternoon. I was pleased the band was attracting such a large two-wheel crowd, though that was only one percent of the audience. In the '50s and '60s, "one-percenters" was what the organized motorcycle clubs used to call the outlaw gangs, resenting the way they tarnished their image as bikers. The outlaws, of course, took this up as a badge of honor, and would wear embroidered patches reading "1%."

After 240 miles of country roads, and even a stretch of old Route 66 near Chicago, we were less than a mile from the amphitheater, just about to turn left on a green arrow. Fortunately we paused before making that turn, as a giant semi came roaring through on a red light, straight toward us.

Like the wheelbarrow on the highway in Oklahoma City, it was one of those moments that make you take a deep breath and think, "What if?"

Formerly the World Amphitheater, now the Consumer Electronics Chain Amphitheater, this was another venue we had played several times. In fact, it had been the final stop on our *Roll the Bones* tour, in 1992. I was wearing bandanas on my head on that tour, to keep the sweat out of my eyes, and before the show, I got Andrew to shave my head into a Mohawk, which I kept hidden until the encore. Then I pulled off the bandana and got a big laugh out of Alex and Geddy and the crew.

I kept that Mohawk for a couple of weeks that summer, just for fun, beginning the family vacation in Quebec. Selena, then fourteen, had been mortified, and wouldn't let me go anywhere in public without a hat. I got her to help me shave it off, and enjoyed the sensual pleasure of a naked head (especially in the lake, or in the rain) for the rest of the summer. From then on, I often made it a summer ritual—shaving my head on July 1st, then letting it grow back the rest of the year.

The Chicago show also went well, in front of the largest audience so far, 13,346 people. We had a special guest on the dryers, Alex's friend Mike, who played the character "Bubbles" in the irreverent Canadian TV show, "Trailer Park Boys."

The next day, Michael and I didn't ride *anywhere*.

At least once in the course of a three-week run of shows, I tried to spend a day not moving, preferably in a big city, in a fabulous hotel with a spectacular view. A day of rest and luxury, seeing no one but the room service waiter, catching up on sleep and e-mails, and browsing through the feast of the Sunday *New York Times*—the crossword puzzle, William Safire's column "On Language," Randy Cohen's "The Ethicist," and the Book Review.

Back at Steve and Shelly's house, I had been showing them my abused hands, cracked and swollen, and they had recommended a product Shelly's father used, "Bag Balm." Apparently, Vermont farmers had developed the formula to keep their cows' udders from drying and cracking in the winter, but they found it kept their hands nice, too. Michael went out on some errands in downtown Chicago, and he brought me back a small, square tin of Bag Balm, lisping that I should remember it was only for my *hands*.

The next day, I made a journal report: "Seems to have helped—hands only slightly tender today, and I can *close* them."

On that blissful day off in Chicago, I also took advantage of the opportunity to listen to a CD Brad had recorded of the house mix from the Indianapolis show. From time to time, I always tried to check up on how we were playing—especially me—and how everything sounded. The Indy show had been a good one, and I was glad to hear that, in general, the song tempos were well locked. I noticed certain areas that could be improved—transitions that felt pushed, that kind of thing—but I knew the next night I would remember those parts and adjust them.

The next show was just up the road in Milwaukee, so rather than unload the bikes in the middle of Chicago and fight our way out of one city and into another, Michael and I rode up on the bus with Dave. Backstage at the Lodging and Entertainment Corporation Amphitheater, Pat McLoughlin came by with some paperback copies of *The Masked Rider*, which had finally made it to print after missing seven shows of potential sales. *Ghost Rider* had been selling about thirty copies every night, even after being on sale all the previous tour, and the time in between, in bookstores and on-line.

But never mind, here it was. The cover looked okay, and all the pages seemed to be there, so I told Pat to go ahead and put it on sale that night. But after dinner, when I had a chance to give the book a closer look, I noticed something awful, and my heart sank. Where were the *photographs*? Each chapter was supposed to be introduced by a full-page black-and-white photograph, with a caption, and they were *all* missing.

And where were the new maps I had been promised? Here were the same crude line-drawn maps I had made myself, on my computer, back in 1996. And why was the section title, "White Man, Where You Going?" (a quote from an African in the story), changed to "White Man, Where Are You Going?"

I was terrified to read further and see what other solecisms the book contained, but this was enough. I asked Michael to contact Pat on the crew radios, and tell him to stop selling the book. Then I lugged my computer back into the Bubba-Gump room and sent an e-mail to Paul—a long tirade of outrage and disappointment, ending with, "I am crushed."

It took a while for Paul to twist the publisher's arm to agree to recall all 5000 copies of that first run, and have them pulped. It took until the end of the North American tour for Paul to personally supervise a corrected edition, and get it on sale.

(When the book *was* finally available, I placed an offer on the band's Web site to replace each of the twenty-six copies of *The Masked Rider* Pat had sold in Milwaukee for a signed hardcover copy of the corrected edition. So far, almost two years later, only two takers.)

After the Milwaukee show, where we played well for 8,750 people, the bus headed down around Lake Michigan and eastward, parking in a truck stop in western Michigan, ready for Michael and me to get back to riding the next day. Our boy Doofus really came into his own that day (or his operator did), managing a very complicated route, 240 miles of tiny roads, constantly changing their names and numbers, as we rode through Michigan's farmlands, woods, small lakes, and tiny towns (including Nashville number three).

That day's church sign, "FAITH IS A HIGHER FACULTY THAN REASON," later inspired some discussion between Michael and me. We had trouble with that concept, but I guess that was to be expected—mere reason trying to grapple with faith.

It was 90 degrees that day, and I was feeling a little under the weather, with a sore throat and what my journal described as "a 'bug' trying to get me." I was glad when we arrived at another frequently played venue, Pine Knob—an older amphitheater (now called the Natural Gas Corporation Theater) at a ski resort north of Detroit—early enough for a brief nap on the bus before soundcheck.

We had a lot of history with Detroit, beginning with the old downtown theater called the Michigan Palace, the first sizeable venue we had ever headlined. We still joked about the gay promoter at the Palace hitting on Alex, looking him in the eyes and quoting the Olivia Newton-John song, "Have you ever been mellow?"

Around that time, Alex, Geddy, and I attended a night-off showing of *The Godfather, Part II* at a movie theater in downtown Detroit. The theater was crowded, and when the lights came up at the end, we couldn't help noticing we were the only white people in the place. People stared, of course (and not just because of our skin color—I'm sure our hair and clothes were "outstanding" too), but seemed more welcoming than threatening.

In later years, we played the downtown arena, Cobo Hall, a few times, then the newer Joe Louis arena, an even larger one in the suburbs of Auburn Hills, and several times at the ski-hill amphitheater of Pine Knob.

This time, the audience was large, 10,835 people, and enthusiastic, as Detroit audiences always were. During the second set, I noticed a guy holding up a sign reading, "NEIL—ANY SPARE LUMBER?" That was an original way to ask for a drumstick, and made me smile, so after my solo, when I was resting behind Geddy's dryers while he and Alex played "Resist," I called Michael over. The fan was also wearing a T-shirt from my former cymbal company, and I asked Michael to take him a pair of used sticks and a Sabian T-shirt. Michael couldn't resist telling the guy he had to put on the Sabian shirt *now*, and when I hopped back on the drum riser to join in on "Heart Full of Soul," I saw the guy clutching his sticks, wearing the shirt, and looking happy, if a little confused.

We parked the bus that night in a mall parking lot in Ann Arbor, and the next day, Michael and I had our first guest rider, Tom Marinelli, a man I had never met. My invitation to Tom to join us for a ride had been a direct result of our one previous guest rider, Brian Catterson, from

Cycle World magazine. Two summers before, on the *Vapor Trails* tour, Brian had joined us for an adventurous two days of riding from Gallup, New Mexico, through Arizona and Utah, to a show in Salt Lake City. He had written a story about that adventure, "Riding With the Ghost Rider," for the magazine.

A few months after the story appeared, Brian forwarded a letter to me from a Michigan motorcyclist who had asked his help in getting a signed copy of my book, *Ghost Rider.* The motorcyclist said it was for a friend who had lost his own daughter within a few weeks of Selena's death, at nearly the same age. He too had moved to Europe with his wife to mourn in exile, and he had gone motorcycling on a BMW with his wife, who was now ravaged by the wasting effects of Multiple Sclerosis.

Moved by the story of the man's parallel tragedies, shortly before Christmas 2003, I sent an inscribed copy of the book to Tom, and received a letter in reply—a letter that gave me a feeling I might just *like* this guy. Very close to my age, Tom had worked in the auto industry all his life, rising to the upper management of the oft-reborn Chrysler Corporation. He knew little or nothing about the musical side of my work, but because of the way I had expressed myself about loss in *Ghost Rider,* and the shared tragedies in our lives, he too had a feeling I was a kindred spirit.

Of the hundreds of letters I have received from strangers over the years, and the hundreds I have answered, only three or four times have I felt moved to continue the relationship beyond that one polite reply. (In fact, I was always careful not to answer people more than once—having a good memory for names and towns—partly out of fairness, in wanting to answer as many letters as I could, but mostly because such people so easily got the wrong idea. See Eminem's song, "Stan.")

But the few times I have offered my return address, my instincts have been correct, and I have made good friends for life with a few people who will appear later in this story. So, I took a chance and invited Tom to ride with us. When a dark red BMW touring bike pulled up outside the bus in Ann Arbor that morning, the rider dismounted, tall and slender in his Aerostich riding suit, and took off his helmet to reveal a shaved head and angular, composed features opening in a warm, shy smile. I liked him right away.

As with our previous guest rider Brian, on the last tour, what a *ride* we took Tom on. I had planned on rambling down into Indiana, to the classic car museum in Auburn, then over into Ohio, to spend the night on the tiny Bass Islands, in Lake Erie.

It didn't quite work out that way, and again that night, I tried to capture it all on my tape recorder.

Well, again, so much gets away in the course of the passing days, so much going on there's no time to actually *record* it. That is a shame, as there is much worth recounting and trying to distill down to essences that a reader could understand and maybe relate to.

Anyway, a day of *strange* adventures. Meeting Tom Marinelli in Ann Arbor this morning, riding down to Auburn to the Auburn-Cord-Duesenberg museum on a hot day, and a pretty elaborate route of thin red lines and gray-line-type roads [on the Rand McNally maps]. Those are definitely preferable, especially in the populous East.

When we did accidentally get onto a "thick" red road, I think Highway 12, thanks to Doofus and his "friend" [Michael], it was just wall-to-wall trucks, avoiding the toll-paying Ohio Turnpike. [Actually overloaded trucks avoiding the *scales*, according to Dave.]

So that was unpleasant, and a good lesson learned. As it was when we almost ran out of gas.

We got back on the original plan of gray roads and thin red lines, and had some really nice riding through farmland and small towns. Not that exciting, but always enjoyable, especially when you contrast all the other kinds of riding, in the mountains, along rivers, in the West, it makes a pleasant change.

A few Amish communities again today, buggies going down the road—in western Ohio, I guess that would be, not too far from where we crossed from Indiana.

Then, after 434 kays [286 miles], we arrived here—Port Clinton, Ohio, is where "here" actually is—but a little beyond here, to the ferry dock, just as a giant thunderstorm was looming toward us, and just as the ferry was leaving. The dock workers said even the next ferry might not carry us, if the lake was too rough, and in any case, they could only take two bikes at a time because of their limited chocks and tie-downs.

Seeing the weather coming, I said, "It's going to get *real* bad pretty soon, let's just stay here."

So we turned around and raced back to the Holiday Inn Express, and once again, almost unbelievably story-like, arriving just as the storm broke above us, blowing in horizontally. Sheets of rain, literally, against the windows. Big potted plants below me, heavy clay pots, blown over.

Tom was concerned about which way to park his bike so it wouldn't be blown over. I knew it wouldn't get *that* serious, as a typical East-Coast Great Lakes thunderstorm, but still, it was as serious as *they* get, as brief as it lasted. The power flashed out at the hotel on our way up, just before taking the elevator. Yikes!

Plenty of drama of different sorts today, but altogether a rich, rewarding, and well-spent day. Also another 90 degree one.

Note how loud the background vocals [crowd] were last night for "Heart Full of Soul." Seems to be an audience-participation act that's catching on more and more night by night.

It's a cool one!

[That was the last time I felt moved to use that tape recorder. From then on I stayed with written notes in my journal, proving that I really do prefer writing to talking—even to myself!]

A couple of church signs also made the list that day—"RSVP FOR ETERNITY," and, "TO BELITTLE IS TO BE LITTLE."

After dinner at a nearby restaurant, Tom held out a handful of cigars, and invited us back to his room. I was beat and headed for bed, but Michael joined him for a while. Tom and I agreed to meet for breakfast the next morning.

We walked across the road to a likely looking breakfast place, and had a remarkably deep conversation—considering we had only known each other for one day. But we also shared some hard-won understandings about life and loss, and so could talk about such things easily. Tom had planned to ride home that day, but accepted my invitation to come to the next show with us.

The previous night's thunderstorm had opened the floodgates to a series of heavy rainshowers, and all that day we rode in and out of teeming curtains of rain. The aforementioned bug was still attacking me, starting to feel like it might develop into a full-blown cold, so I was feeling a little thick-headed, but at the same time, needing the concentration and caution of riding a motorcycle on wet roads.

"WHY WORRY WHEN YOU CAN PRAY?" the church sign said.

"Phooey," answered the passing motorcyclist.

Our route was beautiful, even if the weather wasn't, and Tom and Michael and I rode together over hilly country roads, past neat farms and some charming, small Ohio towns. Whenever I found myself riding in that part of the country, there were two little towns I always tried to pass through. One of them was Mount Eaton, which had been the turnaround point on my first-ever 100-mile bicycle ride—a "Century"—on the Fourth of July, 1984.

In those days, when we all traveled together, I often waited on the bus for hours after the show, while my bandmates socialized in the dressing room. It had been like that after the show in Indianapolis on the night of July 3, 1984, so it was an all-night bus ride to the Holiday Inn near Cleveland. After only a few hours of bouncy sleep, I unloaded my bicycle from the luggage bay and set off into the morning. I rode fifty miles south on little Highway 94, past farms and pretty Ohio towns decorated for the Fourth of July, waving to Amish farmers behind their horses in the fields.

In Mount Eaton, I bought a sandwich from a small store and ate it in the local park, with its picnic pavilion and baseball diamond. Then I started north again, still nervous (especially worried I was going to get a flat, because I didn't yet know how to fix one). When I finally arrived back at the Holiday Inn, with my first Century accomplished, I felt triumphant and relieved (and wondered why there were no cheering crowds for *that* performance). I would always remember that ride, that road, and Mount Eaton, Ohio.

On the *Test for Echo* tour, Brutus joined me for the second Mount Eaton pilgrimage, this time by motorcycle, and we stopped in that same park for a few minutes. As often happened, an older man wandered over to look at the bikes, and told us about coming home from World War II and buying a new Indian Chief motorcycle, and how his friend bought a new Harley, for $850. Their bikes had arrived in crates by train, and they had ridden them all over, at a time when all the local roads were unpaved.

The other Ohio town I liked to pass through was Beach City, just to the east, near Canton. The summer before I turned fifteen, my family camped outside Montreal to visit the World's Fair, Expo '67, and at the campground, I met a girl from Ohio. Her father was extremely watchful (warning her that Canadian boys had "Roman hands and Russian fingers"), and we never even kissed, but I fell hopelessly in fourteen-year-old love, and wrote to her all that summer, to Beach City, Ohio.

I remember sitting on the front steps of our house waiting for the mailman, and when her letters trickled off, I was devastated. Maybe her father made her stop writing to me. In any case, I always remembered her ("the fawn-eyed girl with sun-browned legs" in the song "The Analog Kid"), and the name of that town in Ohio. On a day off on tour in 1987, twenty years later, I set out on another Century ride, from Akron this time, and I mapped my route to go through Beach City.

Actually going there after all those years affected me in a strange and powerful way. On a warm summer day, I sat on the steps of the general store in Beach City eating a sandwich and drinking a Coke, and I suddenly felt an overwhelming compression of time, a rare sense of *relation* to myself as a boy, so many years and so many experiences ago. I was transported from the steps of that store right back to the steps of our house on Gertrude Street in Port Dalhousie, waiting for the mailman with fading hope.

At thirty-five, I was a successful, hard-working absent father, leading an "interesting" life, presently riding my bicycle through Ohio on a day off in the middle of an American concert tour. The boy I had been at fourteen had been so ignorant and inexperienced about everything, and his heart had been broken for the first time.

But not, of course, for the last.

As Tom and Michael and I rode through Mount Eaton and Beach City, the rain poured down, growing heavier all the time. At one red light Tom pulled up beside me, and I raised my steamed-up faceshield and looked over at him, smiling and shaking my head. "Just like riding in Europe, isn't it?"

He smiled and nodded.

Michael and Doofus led us along narrow roads overhung with dripping trees, and we rode into Cuyahoga Valley National Park—in the middle of which, uniquely, was the venue, Blossom Music Center, unsullied by a corporate name. A couple of months later, that park was going to figure in my destiny again. Later still, so was that comment about the rain and riding in Europe.

Even after we arrived at the Blossom Music Center, heavy rain continued through the afternoon, puddling in the backstage parking lot and filling the bus's awning, so that Dave had to keep rolling it in to empty the water. Fortunately the rain cleared away by evening, especially for the part of the audience on the uncovered lawn, and we had a good show. As my next-day journal note reported, with rare self-satisfaction: "Played well last night. Not *great*, but well."

Some wittier members of the audience entertained us with clever signs. One reading "SHRIMP COT?" referred to a routine between Alex and Geddy in the *Boys in Brazil* documentary. When Alex complained on camera about having "a shrimp caught in my teeth," Geddy replied, "What's a shrimp cot?" Both of them already collapsing in laughter, Alex held his fingers up, a few inches apart, and explained, "it's a tiny, little bed . . ."

Another sign sticking up in the crowd, "WE BROUGHT SOUP!," referred to the ongoing jokes in the documentary about our reliance on Frenchie's soup to get us through the tour.

The maker of a third sign, "I WANT TO MEET NEIL," was doomed to disappointment, if I had my way—and probably just as much disappointment if she had hers. I would think, anyway.

After my runner off the stage and into the bus, Tom followed us out of the parking lot on his motorcycle, heading for a nearby motel. I felt I had made a valuable new friend, and hoped we would stay in touch (we have). Dave drove Michael and me on a long ride south, the bus not stopping until five a.m., and it was a rough, bouncy sleep until then. There were few nicer times of the day than finally stretching out in that big bed, but that didn't mean I would have an uninterrupted sleep—not as long as the bus was moving. The vibration of the engine could be restful, but not the bouncing and rocking, or waking up in midair as the bus pounded over a rough road.

When the Swiss Army alarm clock beeped me awake at eight, I felt tired, unwell (sore throat, croaky voice), and miserable. So I got up, had breakfast, and went for a motorcycle ride.

Michael and I started out just north of Louisville, on the Indiana side of the Ohio River. We planned to loop south through rural Kentucky, then west through the Land Between the Lakes (courtesy of the Tennessee Valley Authority). From there, we would aim for somewhere near Missouri to spend the night, and on to the next day's show in St. Louis.

We followed a perfect country road along a high bluff, with fields on our right and panoramic views to our left, down over the river and across to wooded Kentucky. I remembered that stretch of road from the spring of '97, riding it the other way with Brutus, and taking a photograph from beside the Overlook Restaurant.

"HE IS NO RESPECTER OF PERSONS," said the church sign.

"Who?" I wondered. "The *Debble*?" The quote was attributed to the book of Acts, and I decided to look it up. It turned out to be God who was no respecter of persons, meaning that when it came to Judgement Day, he didn't care who you were.

At the time of looking that up, I happened to be reading Walter Kaufman's *Critique of Religion and Philosophy*, and noted a passage that put an ironic spin on that reference.

Analytic philosophy does not only develop the intellectual conscience, train the mind, and combine subtlety with scrupulous precision; above all, it teaches people to think critically and makes them instinctively anti-authoritarian. There is something democratic in this way of thinking: a proposition is a proposition, whether written by a student, a professor, or a Plato; the laws of logic are no respecters of persons.

Now—speaking of "analytic philosophy"—I had only intended to quote those church signs in an *observational* way in this book. Although I am certainly "instinctively anti-authoritarian," I truly meant to stay away from any editorializing about organized religion. The church signs were going to be reported as part of the American landscape, without comment.

In thirty years of traveling around the United States, I had seen how entrenched evangelical Christianity was in American life. Just before setting off for Nashville, I had read that eighty-three percent of Americans called themselves Christians, and half of Americans believed that God created humans pretty much in our present form at one time within the past 10,000 years. It seemed pointless to try to fight that tide of faith, even with the weapon of the "laws of logic," and I thought, "I give up." My blustering was not going to change anybody's mind, and there was no sense alienating people and making enemies. You can reason with people's minds, but you can't argue with their faith.

I even resisted commenting that first day off, when Michael and I passed near Dayton, Tennessee—the site of the famous Scopes "monkey trial" in 1925. At the time, Tennessee had passed a law against teaching Evolution, and the American Civil Liberties Union announced that it would defend anyone charged with that "crime." Boosters and Babbitts in Dayton saw an opportunity to put their little town on the map—though they had no idea how *much* attention the issue was going to attract—and convinced a young high school science teacher, John Scopes, to face the charges.

The resulting struggle between champions of Creation and Evolution made national headlines at the time, just as it has in the early 2000s, over school curricula from Kansas to Georgia. (The term "Bible Belt" was coined by a famous journalist, H.L. Mencken, who traveled to Dayton to report on the trial, along with about 200 other newsmen.) The case was argued—sometimes *outdoors*, as it was so hot that summer of 1925, and the courtroom so crowded—by famed lawyers Clarence Darrow and William Jennings Bryan, and later dramatized in the movie *Inherit the Wind*.

A recent issue of *Smithsonian* magazine commemorated the eightieth anniversary of the trial, and the writer, Steve Kemper, visited Dayton and interviewed some of the locals. One of them was a "science" professor at William Jennings Bryan Memorial University, educated at Harvard under the renowned paleontologist and evolutionist, Stephen Jay Gould. This professor believed, and taught his students, that God created the world and everything in it 6,000 years ago. According to him, the Grand Canyon was formed by Noah's flood "in about three weeks." His justification for filling impressionable young minds with his creationist beliefs was that "scripture trumps interpretations of physical data." Like that earlier church sign, "FAITH IS A HIGHER FACULTY THAN REASON."

Humbug. At this point in recounting my American travels, I begin to think that even if the voice of reason *is* increasingly drowned out by the evangelical crowd, that is all the more reason to speak up. Spiritual yearnings are natural to many people, and may give them solace or hope, but extremists of any stripe are not content with faith as armor; they must forge it into a sword.

In one study, more than half of Americans agreed with the statement, "It is very important to convince non-Christians to become Christians." Not only do these people believe in their "higher faculty" of faith, they *know* they are right, and they want the rest of us to be more like them.

The clear translation of "scripture trumps interpretations of physical data" is "faith beats facts," and that seems like a profoundly frightening, and fearful, view of the universe. Yet these same religious extremists dominate American politics, try to control the schools and the media, and their ever-increasing numbers give them ever-increasing power. Greater power gives them greater influence, and now their faith-based crusade spreads like kudzu, an introduced vine from Asia that has overtaken large areas of native foliage in the South, blanketing whole valleys of treetops and power lines in eerie green monotony.

Now the "introduced vine" of radical religion threatens to stifle, even outlaw, the ideals of freedom and variation in American life. In the face of all that, to be silent is to let the forces of unreason triumph by default.

Like another church sign, "WRONG IS ALWAYS WRONG, EVEN IF EVERYBODY DOES IT."

And indeed, I have come to know there *is* a point to speaking out, for in the past I have acted (however unknowingly) as a counterpoint, a voice of reason. One young man told me about being raised a strict Catholic, sure that his faith and received doctrine were the only truth. Then he started listening to some of our songs, like "Free Will" ("You can choose a ready guide, in some celestial voice / If you choose not to decide, you still have made a choice / You can choose from phantom fears, and kindness that can kill / I will choose a path that's clear—I will choose free will"), and began to consider that it was possible to believe differently.

Not long ago, a former Mormon wrote to me recounting a similar experience, of being brought up and simply accepting what he was told, until his independence of thought was kindled by our music. In fact, I had the same experience myself as an adolescent, when a friend showed me a book called *The Passover Plot,* and I realized for the first time that not everyone believed what I had been taught in school and church. It was possible to think differently. I remember how it felt to discover that not everybody was an identical unit in the narrow Protestant world I had perceived as a child—that realization was deeply jarring, yet liberating.

So you've got to speak up, even just to be counted against the flood of unreason and antilife poison that fills the media, the pulpits, the government, and church signs. Fight the power! Others are doing it, and I am always encouraged when I hear them speak out, in the newspapers, on television, on the Internet, in modern music—Todd Rundgren's *Liars* a great example—or on a particularly great bumper sticker: "PLEASE DON'T PRAY IN OUR SCHOOLS, AND I PROMISE NOT TO SPREAD KNOWLEDGE IN YOUR CHURCH."

So, let the record show that this formerly neutral reporter will now have to be considered a "hostile witness."

"HE IS NO RESPECTER OF PERSONS."

A winding, tree-lined lane carried Michael and me down the bluff to the riverbank (spectacular riding, especially for Indiana), then across the river and into the rural two-lanes of Kentucky. Between woodlands, the cornfields were often shoulder high, which hopefully pleased the farmers, as it was still only June 11. It was also a Friday, certainly the second-most dangerous day of the week, and the little roads curving through the obscuring trees demanded infinite attention for the usual driveways, tractors, lawn mowers, parked vehicles, and erratic drivers.

It was also 90 degrees again, steamy and draining, and by afternoon I had a strong craving for a milkshake. I started watching for a Dairy Queen (not the best milkshake in the world—*I* make that, on the old Hamilton Beach mixer my brother gave me—but DQ's were at least consistently acceptable), but none appeared for *hours*. Eventually, desperate, I settled for an unpromising looking "Dairy Bar." My journal felt my pain: "Lame glop of frozen goo in styrofoam cup supposed to be a chocolate milkshake."

"DON'T TRY TO CHANGE THE BIBLE, LET THE BIBLE CHANGE YOU," said the church sign.

"Phooey," said the motorcyclist. (What does that even *mean*?)

Doofus, our minor deity, was mostly successful that day, only once leading us down a diagonal street that didn't connect with the main road. However, the sidewalk did, and we took advantage of being "motorcycle hoodlums," and flouted the law. (Don't try to change Doofus, let Doofus change you.)

There was a spot on the map I had long been curious about: the confluence of the Ohio and Mississippi Rivers. I wondered why a metropolis had never grown there—like St. Louis at the Missouri and Mississippi, Pittsburgh where the Monongahela and Allegheny converged into the Ohio, or even the Tri-Cities of Kennewick, Pasco, and Richland, where the Snake flowed into the Columbia. There was a dot on the map called Cairo, but I knew nothing about it except a mention in one of Bill Bryson's books, saying that the locals pronounced it "Cay-ro."

Unfortunately, when we got to Cairo, as Gertrude Stein once wrote about an Ohio town, "there was no there there," and it was easy to see why. We had ridden to the town across a vast floodplain, and presumably Cairo had been inundated too many times to grow, or even to survive, by the look of it. There was one shabby-looking motel, but no restaurant we could see.

The map showed no nearby towns, and even Doofus thought we would have to travel on a ways to find accommodations, so we hopped on the interstate to dispose of some miles. In an hour or so, we fetched up in what my journal called "Somewhere, MO." It might equally have been called Nowhere, MO. But we didn't care; we had ridden 541 kilometers that day, 338 miles, all of it on demanding back roads, and were glad to settle for what my journal called, "a generic freeway off-ramp cluster of gas, food, lodgings."

We parked in front of the numbered doors and carried our stuff inside, did the ice and Macallan and Red Apple thing, then I had a shower and simply passed out for an hour. All those days of too little sleep and too much activity had been draining me, and I was starting to feel exhausted all the time.

I asked my journal, "Which is harder, the shows or the rides?"

I decided they were the same, in different ways, "Equally *ordeals*." About the motorcycle itself, I noted, "Over 6000 kms now, and perfect."

The motel was some Ramada clone, charmless and bleak, with a Ruby Tuesday's franchise restaurant next door. We did okay there, reviving ourselves with the salad bar, shrimp pad thai, Kendall-Jackson chardonnay, strawberry shortcake, and coffee. The waitress was amazed at my constant requests for more water.

Before passing out again, I made a final journal note: "No voice today—no problem most of the time, except for yelling at Michael [through earplugs and helmets] or talking to Carrie!"

My next words were written in the morning, after I walked over to the smaller restaurant attached to the hotel and joined a few older couples and some extended families for the breakfast buffet. It was grim. "Feel just awful this morning. Awake with bad coughing spells during the night, then headache, bit of fever, diarrhea."

Our ride that day must have been lovely, 350 miles through the northern Ozarks, parts of the Mark Twain National Forest, through places with names like Buckhorn and Cherokee Pass, but I remember none of it.

Only that it was hot, and I felt bad. And it was Saturday. I had a fierce craving for orange soda, for some reason, which tormented me for a couple of hours, until we stopped for gas and I was able to buy some.

And despite everything, I could still laugh out loud at a particularly clever church sign,

GOD IS DEAD
   — NIETZSCHE
NIETZSCHE IS DEAD
   — GOD

St. Louis wouldn't make too much of an impression on me that time, but I had always liked the city, its waterfront, the Gateway Arch, Forest Park—one of the nicest city parks in America—and a fine art museum. I had some good memories, too; a riotous after-show party at the Chase Park Plaza in 1974, a day off in about '78 when the band and crew wandered around the zoo on a spring afternoon, then saw a laser show (probably set to Pink Floyd's *Dark Side of the Moon*) at the planetarium that night. I remember roller-skating around the old Checkerdome arena before a show in the early '80s, falling badly on a concrete floor and hoping I wasn't going to wreck the show (I was fine). Preparing for my first bicycle Century in 1984, I did a seventy-five-mile ride southwest of St. Louis, and in the years since then, several times I had bicycled out to the Riverport Amphitheater—now known as the Financial Services Corporation Amphitheater.

On the *Counterparts* tour in the spring of '94, Selena was traveling with me on the bus for a few days, and we had a day off Easter Sunday at the Ritz-Carlton in St. Louis. Even though she was almost sixteen, I had to hide some chocolate eggs around the hotel room (how she clung to those childhood rituals of Easter and Christmas). Later that day, we walked through Forest Park, its rolling lawns blanketed by a freak snowstorm, and into the Museum of Art for an hour—trying to make it a brief and positive experience for her. I love those memories. And hate them, too.

This time, St. Louis was just something to *get* through. During the intermission, I scrawled a few notes.

> Signer for the hearing impaired, a light on her as she dances and gestures the lyrics.
>
> Biker couple, man with beard and T-shirt from the band Alabama, woman with West Coast Choppers T-shirt. Both of them extra large, and older, maybe contest winners—seem kind of mystified, but having a nice time! Smiling along.
>
> Many different vintage Rush shirts every night, and homemade ones: "Got Rush?" and "Stick Please."
>
> Gump in bad back pain.
>
> Cracked 18-inch cymbal at beginning.
>
> Crowd singing along with "YYZ," à la Brazil.

On the R30 tour we noticed how the American audiences had been influenced by watching our Brazilian audience in the *Rush in Rio* DVD, released the previous year. One of the unique reactions of the Brazilians was how they sang along with *instrumentals,* tens of thousands of them in a wordless chant, and now our American fans had picked up on that, too. It sounded great.

The final show on that first leg was in Kansas City, another city I liked, and of which I had good memories. One time in the mid '80s, I got our bus driver, Whitey, to stop the bus at daybreak, 100 miles out of Kansas City. I unloaded my bicycle and rode the rest of the way into town, following the old Santa Fe Trail through Malta Bend, Napoleon, and Harry Truman's hometown of Independence, Missouri. Kansas City also had a nice art museum, the Nelson-Atkins, which I had bicycled to a couple of times on past show days on my way to the Kemper Arena, down by the old stockyards.

The guys at work and I had always been fans of Gates Barbecue in

Kansas City, and one time, in the '70s, we even went there for *breakfast.* The spicy ribs had made my forehead sweat. As I did every tour, this time I asked Dave to pick us up a case of each of their barbecue sauces—he and I would split a case of Regular and one of Extra Hot, both so delicious on my home-grilled steaks, chicken, or pork chops, and always a reminder of Kansas City.

On *Test for Echo,* in the spring of '97, Brutus and I had started a motorcycle ride in nearby Jefferson City, passing the cool, shady bluffs along the Missouri River, and that morning we saw a huge, prehistoric-looking snapping turtle in the road.

On that same *Test for Echo* tour, I did an advance phone interview with a journalist from the *Kansas City Star,* the newspaper Ernest Hemingway began his career with as a cub reporter. In later years he recounted the style sheet he was given by the editor on his first day: "Use short sentences. Use short first paragraphs. Use vigorous English. Be positive, not negative." He said later those were "the best rules I ever learned for the business of writing."

My young-voiced interviewer from the *Kansas City Star* opened with, "So, you're coming to Kansas City?"

"Yes," I said, deadpanning. "They've got some crazy little women there, and I'm going to get me one."

Silence.

He didn't get it—a so-called music writer who didn't know the classic song named after his city. I had to explain that it was a song, that I was *joking.* That's never good.

> I might take a train, I might take a plane
> But if I have to walk, I'm going just the same
> I'm going to Kansas City, Kansas City here I come
> They got some crazy little women there, and I'm going to get me one

Composed by the legendary Leiber and Stoller, writers of many Elvis Presley hits, "Kansas City" was released by Wilbert Harrison in 1952, became a hit for Little Richard in '54, then for the Beatles in '64, and for decades, it was a staple of many a bar-band repertoire. Interestingly, the song was said to be about prostitutes, and one version of the chorus ends with, "They got a crazy way of lovin' there, and I'm gonna get me some."

After the St. Louis show, Dave parked the bus halfway between St. Louis and Kansas City. Early on a Sunday morning, already hot and humid, Michael and I rode south toward the Lake of the Ozarks region. I was still not feeling well, with a sore throat and general malaise, but I wasn't going to do anything as sensible as resting on the bus—just one more ride, one more show, and we would have a break.

I hated to miss anything, and I could rest next week at home.

The Lake of the Ozarks area was pleasantly scenic, though busy on a summer Sunday, and Michael and I gradually angled back to the northwest, through the farms and woodlands of western Missouri.

"IF GOD HAD A WALLET, YOUR PICTURE WOULD BE IN IT."

That's pretty good, I must say—kind of "lyrical." Could be a line from a song, maybe by the New Main Street Singers in *A Mighty Wind*.

Near the venue, west of Kansas City on the Kansas side, we met Dave out for a cruise on his Harley. He led us around to the hidden backstage entrance on a back road, and as we waited to turn, we were passed by about a dozen Japanese sport bikes, "extreme" street riders, all in a pack. Some of them went roaring by with their front wheels in the air, some rode with both feet on one side, strap-on metal soles sparking on the pavement. Others were performing acrobatics, up out of the saddle with hands and feet extended. I winced to see those young men doing crazy stunts on some of the fastest motorcycles in the world, while wearing jeans, T-shirts, and sneakers.

Though in the 90-degree heat, I admit I was certainly *warm* in my armored leather suit, even with its summer "perforations." I was grateful to arrive at the air-conditioned bus and peel it off, have a shower, and curl up for an afternoon nap.

We had covered just over 300 miles that day, and our total for the first leg was 6035 miles.

Before I went into the Cellular Telephone Network Amphitheater for soup and soundcheck, I made a quick journal note. "Realizing in the last few days, I'm ready for a break—big time."

Once again, I scrawled down some notes during the intermission, and that night, I waxed all lyrical.

Carrying on, but deeply fatigued. Every millisecond of performance *evaluated*, weighing too much. And yet, the whole thing is *elevated* now, among the three of us, to such an intricate, interactive communication, millisecond by millisecond, that it's inevitable the self-criticism is also going to operate at that rarefied level. Only way it can be.

Incredible, really, objectively speaking, what we pull off night after night. Thinking of it tonight, looking at "recidivist" people in audience, show after show, tour after tour.

But I get it.

If you can do it (how do they?), it's probably a "repeatable" experience.

But I just want to go home!

magic shows and golden roads

A Texan, visiting Newfoundland, told a local about the size of his ranch.
"I can drive my pickup for a day and a night, and still not leave my land."
"Oh yeah," said the Newfie. "I used to have a truck like that."

As Brutus would say, "Ah, the old jokes . . . "

But Texas really *is* big, and the state map can be so deceiving. If you look at Texas in the road atlas, say, like you'd look at another state (though it spans four pages), it is easy for a traveler to underestimate its sheer scale.

Michael and I flew into Dallas-Fort Worth airport the night before the show, and I wanted to take a casual ride on the show-day, to get back in the rhythm. In the airport hotel room, I looked over the map and drew a loop around Dallas and Fort Worth, just trying to get out onto the gray and thin red roads for 150 miles or so. When Michael added up the mileage of that little loop, it was almost 400 miles.

"What?"

I tried again, and it was still 300 miles. So I cut it again, to about 200, and in the morning we set off, basically tracing the far suburbs of the vast "metroplex." Scissortail flycatchers perched on the wires, their freakishly long tails dangling. Vultures circled high in the gray Texas sky.

A church sign advised us, "No Jesus, No Peace. Know Jesus, Know Peace."

The break at home had been too short. Our touring schedule was supposed to be three weeks of shows, then ten days off, but Ray—otherwise so aware of every decimal point and percentage—could be a little sloppy with those numbers. It was June 23 now, and there had been nine days off, but two of them were travel days, which assuredly did not count.

On the plane flight to Dallas, Michael told me about our latest security threat, a woman who was stalking *me*. Each of us had attracted these unwelcome strangers before, of course, and this one followed a familiar pattern. She had been calling the office in Toronto claiming a personal relationship with me, demanding to speak to me or Ray, and threatening all kinds of blackmail and violence if she didn't hear from me soon. Michael showed me her latest letter. The woman, in her fifties, wrote with weary resignation that she guessed I wasn't "showing up," and advised me that I should run far away, and take lots of money, as "they" would be coming after me.

Michael had collected the woman's name, address, phone number, social security number, driver's licence, driving record, job history, criminal history, and a map to her home. He was trying to decide if the case merited a "personal visit." With such obvious schizophrenics, Michael could sometimes placate them just by paying attention to them—going to their homes as a representative of the band. That made them feel important, and that their messages had been "received." Michael would try to explain that their behavior was hurtful to their beloved idol, and from then on, he would keep track of ticket sales to these individuals, find out where they were sitting at concerts, and keep an eye on them.

My one regret about taking up lyric-writing was that it attracted the attention of that kind of schizophrenics much more than drumming did. Such people rarely found secret messages in drumbeats, but words were so powerful, for good and ill. Drummers only tended to attract other "drumheads," who were generally harmless, but when I was approached by a stranger, I couldn't know if they were attracted to me as a guy who hit things with sticks, or as a "visionary messenger" who planted secret messages for them alone in my song lyrics.

That lunatic fringe had been around for years, and generally I tried not to worry about them. However, I had noticed that if I was onstage and caught an unfamiliar movement in the corner of my eye, a crew member ducking onstage to fix something, or even a moving shadow from the lights,

I immediately feared an invader—one of the people who find a way to climb past the line of security guards and reach the stage. I was fairly well protected behind a barricade of drums and cymbals, but I always worried about Alex and Geddy—they were so *vulnerable* out there.

A row of security guards was always seated in the pit in front of the stage, and Michael always chose them carefully—no Rush fans, who might be tempted to watch us instead of the audience. From time to time someone did manage to get on the stage, but most of these "stage invaders" were harmless. They just wanted to stand up there and wave to the crowd, and they usually left their performance until late in the show—knowing they were going to be hauled off and ejected. Sometimes, though, they tried to grab onto Alex or Geddy, who would twist and turn around the stage, still playing, until one of our crew dragged the invader away.

A fan once jumped on Lou Reed's stage and expressed his feelings of admiration by biting him on the ass. That was probably alarming for Lou, but no permanent damage was done. Sometimes it could get more serious.

Later that year, on the anniversary of John Lennon's shooting, the former guitarist of Pantera, Darrell Abbott, and three others were fatally shot by a deranged fan at a club in Columbus, Ohio. The mentally disturbed kid had a grudge against the guitarist for "breaking up Pantera," his favorite band, and he also claimed Abbott had stolen some of his songs. Reading about that, Michael and I both saw our professional nightmares made terribly real.

That afternoon, at the the Vodka Distillers Center in Dallas, I got wind of a scandal on one of the crew buses. A longtime crew lothario had a local girlfriend traveling with him, and the other crew guys had learned she was a "working girl"—posting her itinerary (*our* itinerary) on a Web site for potential customers in the area. Boys will be boys, I thought, and a girl's gotta eat, but some of the other people on that bus didn't see it that way. That was the end of that little arrangement.

Pat dropped by my bus with some paperback copies of *Traveling Music*, the first I had seen. Usually that would have been an exciting moment, to finally hold in my hand the product of my labors, whether a CD or a book. It was always a big thrill of satisfaction, mixed with only a *tiny* chill of apprehension—that I might find some little thing wrong with it, a typo in the credits, an error in the text.

This time it was all chill, and no thrill. After the disaster of *The Masked Rider*, I was afraid of what I might find inside. Paul and I had both done our best to oversee this edition, but for the next few nights I would be poring over every page, searching out every little error in the text and noting them, always afraid of finding something *really* bad—a missing page, egregious typo, I knew not what. (I would find a dozen or so small errors, but thankfully, nothing that couldn't wait until the next printing to be fixed. Still, I had been robbed of that gratifying moment.)

At dinner in the dressing room, Alex and Geddy told me they had thrown out the first pitch at a major-league baseball game the previous day. Geddy showed me photographs of the event on his computer, and told me how when he had thrown the ball from the mound to Alex at home plate, Alex had charged the mound, like a furious batter who'd been struck by a pitch, and attacked poor Geddy. Apparently the crowd had loved it.

The first show after a break was always an adjustment back to the Vortex, and I was, as my journal noted, "Nervous about being rusty, forgetful, bad." I went into Bubba-Gump for an extra warmup in the afternoon, Geddy and Alex and I agreed to play a few extra songs at soundcheck, and I made time for a serious warmup before the show.

In fact, I had felt more rusty and unsteady on the *bike* than I did on the drums. Earlier that day, Michael had told me I had gone right through a rural stop sign, causing a truck driver to slam on his brakes and blare his air horn. Fortunately for me, I hadn't even known—long gone down the road—but hearing about that error made me angry to think I had been so careless. I put a warning in my journal: "Watch it, dummy!"

Early in the show, while it was still daylight, whenever I could spare a second to glance out at the crowd, I scanned the faces randomly. Among the 9,222 people in Dallas, I caught some bald heads, some eyeglasses, some smiles, and some intense glares. Down front, I saw one couple enjoying themselves, the girl wearing a T-shirt that said, "I LOVE MY GEEK."

I laughed at another T-shirt, "WHO DIED AND MADE YOU NEIL PEART?" I had seen that one a couple of times last tour, and Michael and I had joked about having them made for the whole crew.

While compiling notes and background for this book, I did an Internet search for drummer jokes, thinking I might be able to use some of them. I came up with the usual stereotypical dumb-drummer jokes quoted already, plus a few other good ones:

Q: What do you call a drummer in a three-piece suit?
A: The defendant.

Q: How do you get a drummer off of your porch?
A: Pay for the pizza.

Now that's just *mean*. I also ran across this one.

Q: How many drummers does it take to screw in a lightbulb?
A: Five: one to screw in the light bulb and four to talk about how much better Neil Peart would have done it!

I repeat that joke not out of immodesty, but to illustrate the kind of *expectations* I felt the audience had for my performance every night, the kind of reputation I carried to the stage and felt I had to live up to, even apart from my own high standards.

One guy in the Dallas audience, wearing a T-shirt from Geddy's solo album, *My Favorite Headache*, held up a neatly printed sign, "AFTER LONG ORDEAL, VT CARPET SAFELY IN CONN."

He must have been referring to the stage carpet from the *Vapor Trails* tour, 40 feet by 12 feet, black, with the "fireball" logo in the middle. At the end of the tour, after three rainy outdoor shows in Brazil, the carpet had become so sodden that it weighed too much for the crew to lift—or to fly it all the way back to Canada with the equipment. The decision was made to leave it there, and later it had turned up on eBay, so presumably this guy was the new owner.

We worked our way through to the song "Bravado," about half an hour into the first set. All three of us were especially fond of that song—it was enjoyable to play, and its blending of music and lyrics was among our best, I thought. We had played "Bravado" on almost every tour since 1991, when we wrote and recorded it for our *Roll the Bones* album, but no matter how many times we played that song, I always *felt* it, emotionally.

"Bravado" also gave us a breathing space, as it began with a mid-tempo instrumental groove, more textural and gentle than what had gone before.

While we played that introduction, I had a good chance to let my gaze wander around the audience, and I couldn't help noticing a scattered few-dozen silhouettes rising and walking away, choosing that song as a good opportunity to get up and wander around—head off to get some more beer, or to "offload" some. That bothered me more than it should have.

As the evening grew darker, usually I could only see the first few rows of people. During one show on the first run, I had a vision of a new kind of concert hall, one in which the audience "rotated." They would be on some type of conveyor belt or treadmill, so that every few songs, a mechanism would move the first twenty rows to the back, and shuffle the others forward.

I haven't quite worked out the details, but it's going to be *great*, for the audience and for the performers.

As usual, we slept on the bus after the Dallas show, and next morning, a day off, I pulled back the curtain and looked out at a tableau of prickly pear cactus, mesquite, barbed-wire fence, grass, yellow flowers, and heavy clouds.

Must be Texas.

Just south of Waco, Michael and I mounted up and headed south for the Hill Country west of Austin. I had traced out a long loop from there into an empty-looking area on the map west of San Antonio, then curving back around to the quaint town of Fredericksburg for the night. That was the plan . . .

We had a couple of hours of pleasant riding through gray-green ranchlands and small towns, lower-lying country showing signs of recent flooding. The road was framed by swollen ditches and streams, mud and debris along the edges, and a few puddles spread right across the pavement in front of us. After splashing through one of those shallow dips—excited to send up all that spray, but fearful of hidden hazards, like potholes—Michael pulled over at the roadside, and I stopped behind him.

"What does it mean when the yellow warning light is on?" he called back.

I shuffled my bike up beside his for a better look.

"That's the alternator light, and it probably means your battery's not charging anymore. Could be serious."

"Maybe something got wet when I rode through that water. I'll try it for a while, see if it goes away."

I had a feeling this was terminal, but followed Michael to the next town, Kerrsville, where we stopped for gas.

"That light still on?" I asked him.

"Yeah."

It was time to consider our situation. We were about to head off into a particularly empty part of Texas, but now we were still near the interstate, where there would be accommodations. It was noon on a Thursday, and we were not too far from Austin or San Antonio, and their BMW motorcycle dealers. We could stop, get Dave to bring the spare bike over, and take Michael's to be fixed.

I said to Michael, "It's liable just to die pretty soon, when the battery goes flat. I think we'd better stop here and get it taken care of. Does Doofus show any motels?"

Doofus said there was a Best Western just an interstate exit away, so we went there, checked in, and parked the bikes in front of our neighboring rooms. Dave had been planning his own motorcycle ride in the Hill Country that day, and I called his cell phone, catching him just as he had stopped his bike to put on rain gear. I explained the situation, but told him there was no hurry. "Finish your ride and bring the 1150 over then." Meanwhile, Michael was on the phone to BMW Roadside Assistance, arranging to have his bike picked up and carried to the nearest dealer, in Austin.

We had only ridden 278 kilometers (175 miles), but once I had accepted the reality of our situation, I didn't mind stopping so early in the day. After a shower, I stood outside and watched the tow truck operator, a friendly bear of a man, winch Michael's bike onto the flatbed. It had been a good decision to stop—by that time, the battery was dead and the bike wouldn't start.

Michael and I walked across the street to the Dairy Queen. Most days we didn't bother stopping for lunch, but since we were stopped anyway, it seemed like a fine idea.

So did a nap. When I woke up and looked out the window, I saw my old 1150GS parked beside the 1200. Michael told me Dave had dropped it off, but with no place to park, he had turned around and headed back to the amphitheater in San Antonio. Once again, the bus and truck drivers were "camping out" at the next venue for the night off, saving on their hotel allowances.

Michael and I went to the adjacent restaurant, KJ's Good Eatin', and for some reason I was touched by the plastic flowers on each table, the attempt at decoration and welcome. Most of the other patrons were older couples of ample proportions, and I whispered to Michael that I had just read somewhere that sixty-five percent of Americans were overweight.

He sighed dramatically, "You're talking about *me*, aren't you?"

"Now, honey, let's not fight. Just this once."

From the ceiling speakers, a generic young male singer droned away, monotonous songs one after another, acoustic guitar, sidestick snare, congas, and soft-voiced vocals. All of the songs seemed so dull to me, rhythmically, musically, lyrically, and sonically. All I heard was a puppy-dog personality so eagerly attuned to what others might like (especially women), that he automatically reduced himself to the lowest common denominator.

That was what this listener heard, anyway.

Michael said, "Well, *I* think he's *cute*."

"You would," I sniffed. "Why don't you just ride with *him* then?"

"Bitch."

"Slut."

Elevating the conversation a little, I wrote down the day's church sign, saying it aloud to Michael, "CONQUER YOURSELF, RATHER THAN THE WORLD."

Michael and I agreed that we would prefer a more Nietzschian interpretation: "Conquer yourself, *then* the world."

When I crawled into the motel's polyester sheets that night, I noticed some little red sores had erupted all over my legs, especially in the tender areas behind my knees and . . . elsewhere. Resembling insect bites, they itched fiercely through the night, and by morning, burned so badly they put my nerves on edge. The inflamed sores looked and felt exactly like the bedbug attack brother-in-law Steven and I had experienced in Belize. Those vicious carnivores were later identified by Steven as *cimex lectularius*, a name burned into my memory by the virulence and duration of those bites.

Well, if these *were* bedbug bites, I could only have picked them up at the DFW Airport Hyatt, or . . . from the bus.

It rained heavily through the night and several times the next day, as Michael and I rode the back roads of Banderas and Medina counties. We saw a sign, "ROAD CLOSED AHEAD," but with few other routes to choose from, we carried on through a flood-ravaged valley. Brown water spilled out of the overflowing ditches and along the shoulders, and often we had to pick our way through debris-ridden puddles and streams. Our progress was slow, and it was a long way around by any other route, so we were relieved to find that the road had just been reopened.

As we merged onto a short stretch of I-35 to carry us south to the Cellular Telephone Network Amphitheater, rain started teeming down, and lightning split the sky ahead of us. Traffic around us was heavy, and the spray coming up from the trucks and cars made the road invisible. My left glove wiped at the drops collecting on my steamed-up faceshield again and again. I had read a story in *Cycle World* magazine recently about a rider who had been struck by lightning and killed. I hadn't even known that was *possible,* and so had never worried about lightning when I was riding, but now I did.

On top of all that, something felt squirrelly with the bike's handling. When we arrived at the venue, I checked the rear tire and found it was almost flat. Picked up a nail, no doubt, somewhere in that 330 kilometer (206 mile) ride, and the tire would have to be replaced.

I told Dave about my attack of *cimex lectularius,* and he said he'd had some bites himself, though Michael had been spared (because of his upper bunk, presumably). Dave also said that during the break he had been working on the trailer in a field behind the bus company shop in Nashville, and maybe he had picked up something there and brought it aboard. He sent the runner out for some canisters of insecticide, and I had to stay away from the bus for a few hours while he fumigated it. Later Dave came by Bubba-Gump with some anti-itching cream he had borrowed from the crew bus driver, Lashawn (Liam's "secret sharer").

In the hallway by the production office, I ran into Pat, and he told me he had sold almost 200 copies of *Traveling Music* in Dallas, and more than thirty copies of *Ghost Rider.* "Great," I said, "Keep it up." It was nice to know all those people were buying my books, but in another way, it was strange to think of all those people *reading* them, knowing so much about me and my life. But I had obviously been willing to share it—on my terms, anyway.

Every time we played in San Antonio, I was reminded of the first time, in 1975. The show, at a country-and-western club called Randy's

Rodeo, was being promoted by a small local radio station, and as we arrived in town, we were amazed to hear them playing nothing but Rush songs (we only had two albums at the time, so there wasn't much variety) all day and night. The radio station and the presentation of the concert seemed to revolve around a bunch of old army buddies, like a Tex-Mex Rat Pack movie, and they were quite a group of characters.

The ringleaders and radio personalities were Joe and Lou, who entertained us generously with food and drink. An older man named Mel was assigned to show us around—to be our "aide-de-camp," as he put it. Mel took us to the Alamo, and on one of the tour boats on the San Antonio River, between the landscaped banks, the Paseo del Rio, lined with parks, restaurants, and hotels. He pointed at the towering needle and huge arena of the Hemisfair complex, and assured us that one day we would be playing there.

(It happened that we did play that arena, fifteen or twenty years later, and Mel showed up and told us that Joe from the radio station had recently died of AIDS. Mel said he understood the disease had originally been caused by African men having sex with monkeys. We could only nod and glance at each other in disbelief. Just before the show, a kid showed up backstage wearing the pass we had given to Mel, claiming Mel had sold it to him for $50.)

A cheerful, ruddy-faced carpenter named Charlie Applegate built some additions onto the stage at Randy's Rodeo (even back then, we had more equipment than the average country band). In subsequent years, Charlie showed up every time we came to town, bringing big plaques of varnished rough-cut wood, and one time full-size benches, made by the high-school woodworking class he taught. These rough-hewn crafts were inset with promotional and album photographs of us, and inscribed with jocular phrases burned and routed into them about us being "rootin' tootin' cowpokes comin' to town."

When we were first "comin' to town," back in 1975, with all that radio hype, the tiny roadhouse was packed (meaning a couple of hundred people), and that performance was the seed of an enduring popularity for the band in San Antonio. But the real drama came after the show. When our road manager at the time, Howard, went to the owner's office to get paid, there was a disagreement about the amount. Joe and Lou from the radio station and their army buddies were on Howard's side, but the owner expressed his disagreement by pulling out a gun and laying it on the desk. Another Charlie, an Air Force veteran, spoke up and resolved the situation with some calming words, and finally Howard was paid the contracted amount. Of course, from that day forward, Charlie earned our undying loyalty. However, also from that day forward, whenever we were in the area, our loyalty earned us Charlie's undying *presence.*

In later years, Charlie moved to Southern California, and for the next twenty years, every time we played anywhere in the Los Angeles or San Diego area, Charlie was there, grinning and talking, in the dressing room and backstage, all afternoon and all evening. Charlie truly was as nice a man as you could meet, friendly and garrulous, but at the same time, he seemed oblivious to the idea that we might like some privacy, some quiet time. A hello and how-are-you was always welcome, but his all-day omnipresence show after show, year after year, became less so.

One time when we were playing at the Los Angeles Forum, I was deathly ill with some kind of stomach flu, and I was lying supine on a sofa in the dressing room, hoping I could make it through the show without vomiting onstage. (I had played with a bucket beside me more than once over the years, trying to hold my stomach down until the lights went out between songs and I could "hurl" in the darkness before counting in the next one.) Charlie came bustling into the dressing room, standing over me and talking and talking, oblivious to my condition, and not even hearing me when I told him how sick I was.

Finally, after twenty years, one day I snapped at Charlie. It was the second of a two-night stand in Costa Mesa, and the last show of the tour, which is always a stressful time (the relief only comes later). I had ridden my bicycle to the venue early, determined to clear out my dressing room case, straighten out my luggage for the flight home (always an ordeal after living on a bus for months), and disassemble and pack the bicycle into its road case. With the urgency of all that to do, saying goodbye to all the crew guys, and the show itself ahead of me, when I heard Charlie coming up behind me, chattering away already—as he had all the previous day and night—I felt my irritation rise.

Even as the words came out, I had time to realize I was going to say something bitter, and tried to soften it along the way. Thus there were

147

mixed tones of humor and anger as I turned and said, "Are you here *again*?"

Without a word, Charlie simply disappeared, and never came back. That was certainly not what I had intended, and now whenever we played in Southern California, I always thought of Charlie, and felt sorry I had so obviously hurt his feelings. He hadn't meant any harm, but like many other people, friends and strangers alike, he couldn't imagine what our lives were like. (Charlie, wherever you are, I'm sorry.)

By 2004, our San Antonio audience had grown from a couple of hundred people at Randy's Rodeo to 11,288 happy fans at the Cellular Telephone Network Amphitheater. For myself, I had a simply *magic* show, and even by the intermission, I was making a journal note:

> Best show yet for me, so far. Strong, solid, smooth, and "effortless" (relatively, of course.)
>> Happy audience, too.
>> Magic word—love to see people who are "delighted."

The next day I completed that review.

> Last night continued *great*, by the way, solo and rest of second set best yet, for me.
>> *Now* can I go home?

It is a harsh fact of a musician's life on the road that out of a tour of fifty or sixty shows, only a handful will be "magic." A sublime performance is as rare and mysterious as an astrologer's planetary confluence, and far less predictable. A set of separate moving elements must coincide at exactly the same time and place, and like the magic which is supposed to result from planetary confluence and sublime performance, it cannot be summoned on demand. Like, say between 7:30 and 11:00 on June 25, 2004, at the Cellular Telephone Network Amphitheater in San Antonio.

All the stars and planets have to be in place, and the moon in its proper house. Internally, the electromagnetic brainwaves have to flow with alacrity, all the little muscle fibers have to twitch together in smooth flex and reflex, and a few little sparks of inspiration have to illuminate the proceedings. Externally, the equipment has to be perfect, the electronics have to be perfect, Gump has to be perfect, and the audience has to be perfectly happy—"delighted." That was a lot to be praying for every night as I ran onto that stage, and those prayers were not often answered.

After thirty years of playing together, every Rush show was a good show. Generally, you don't get to be professional performers without learning to perform professionally, and a certain standard of quality and consistency was simply expected. You learned to deliver at least that, and at the same time aim as much higher as you could on the night. The perfect show, the magic show, is the goal every time you go up there, but stars and planets do not so readily converge.

I often quote Somerset Maugham: "Only a mediocre man is always at his best," and that is some comfort. However, it is our experience that even a mediocre band is not always at its best.

That night in San Antonio, even when I sat down at the practice kit for my seven o'clock warmup, I could feel it—what baseball pitchers call their "stuff." Hands and feet worked smoothly together like they *wanted* to, sticks and beaters struck clean and true, and everything I played flowed out with controlled fire.

I had my stuff, and the stars and planets must have been aligned, too. The show poured out of us like a force of nature, sweeping out in waves from the stage and the lights and the speaker cabinets, ebbing and flowing over a cheering, smiling, delighted crowd. We were all locked together in a long, timeless moment of sublime pleasure, and as song after song played out into the ether, I felt energized and ever more determined to make this *the one.*

After my solo, when Geddy and Alex started the acoustic intro to "Resist," I sat behind the dryers with Gump, and he said, "Nice one." He only said that when it was true, a half-dozen times a tour, and I knew he meant it. "Thanks man," I said, accepting the wet towel he pulled from the tray of ice—a refreshing invention of his, and I wiped my face and arms, then put it on my head.

With three-quarters of the show behind us, and the solo the most critical part for me, it looked like a winner. At the end, as I waved to the audience and jumped off the riser, I put a hand on Gump's shoulder and gave him a smile and a nod, then ran for the bus.

As Dave pulled away, I steadied myself against the bed in my state-room and started working at the double knots on my dancing shoes (Brutus taught me that—I used to put little pieces of duct tape around the knots, which were messy and hard to get off). Blue strobe-flashes from the police escort flickered down the bus as I struggled out of my sweaty clothes and into a dry T-shirt and a towel wrapped around my waist. I leaned my way along the wall and up to the front lounge, to the waiting Macallan and ice.

"Wow, good one!" Michael said.

I was pleased to raise the glass and answer, "It was *magic!*"

During the show, Michael always moved around the building on his security duties, watching the crowd and the security guards, but I knew he always paid attention to my solo. It had occurred to me before that when I conducted my experiments in independence in the part of my solo based on Max Roach's "The Drum Also Waltzes," playing 7/8 with my hands and 3/4 with my feet, and so on, Michael, because of his own passion for the drums (and maybe Gump), were the only people in the building who really understood what I was doing. Not that it mattered too much, as those kind of things weren't so much *musical* exercises as they were a kind of puzzle to help keep me entertained every night. Still, it was nice that *somebody* knew.

As the big Prevost settled into the long swells of the interstate, I sank into the cushions of the sofa by the table, slowly coming down. Now I felt sore muscles, tired brain, ringing ears, but also a lingering glow of elation. That night I had played as well as this mortal could, and that was enough.

As the vibrating, bouncing bus drove on, I relaxed with my humble workman's rewards: a glass of booze and a smoke.

I said to Michael, "You know, if it's true that music keeps traveling out into space forever, then I want some alien dude to pick up *that* show someday. It was the kind of night you'd almost be happy to die after—or at least, if you had to go, you could feel satisfied."

I thought about that for a while, then added, "It's weird. A show like that makes me happy at first, then I get kind of sad—to think that I should have to go and do it again, knowing that the next show can't possibly be as good. It doesn't seem right. If my job was to go out there and play the best show I can, then my job is done. I want to go home now."

150

Michael was accustomed to my manic ups and downs. He just nodded, shook his head, and passed me the map of Texas.

We slept that night on the bus in the parking lot of the BMW dealer in Austin, and in the morning, while I ate my breakfast, I watched the mechanics and salesmen arrive. When they finally opened at 9:30, we unloaded my bike, and they went to work installing a new tire. An hour or so later, Michael and I set off for Houston on the bikes, taking the back roads, while Dave fired up the bus and headed for the interstate. All of us traveled straight into a heavy rainstorm. Even with the 248 kilometers (155 miles) of back roads and suburbs, Michael and I were at the venue long before the bus, hanging around Bubba-Gump and hearing from Dave on his cell phone that he was stuck in traffic on the interstate.

That day's church sign, "JESUS BUILT US A BRIDGE, WITH TWO BOARDS AND THREE NAILS."

That's just *gross.*

After a show like the one in San Antonio, I didn't expect to have another one like that right away, but I still gave what I had. Apparently it wasn't enough, and during the intermission at Houston's Cynthia Woods Mitchell Pavilion (named not after a corporation, for once, but after a Houston philanthropist who actually contributed to its founding), I wrote, "Tedious struggle tonight."

Michael and Dave and I were joined in Houston by Brian Catterson from *Cycle World* magazine, who had accepted my invitation to come out for a couple of days and ride my 1150. Dave cleaned out one of the "junk bunks" for Brian, and he rode with us on the bus to our drop-off point, Fort Stockton, in West Texas.

We had the rare luxury of two days off in a row (a manager usually tries to avoid that wasteful overhead, but maybe once a tour he might slip up). The next show would be in Denver, so Brian and Michael and I were set up for a two-day ride through one of my favorite parts of America, New Mexico and Colorado.

My bedbug bites were still giving me fits of pain and itching, and I counted more than twenty of them. Some of them were starting to become painful sores, so as well as the anti-itch cream, I was treating them with Neosporin to avoid infection.

As life will have it, that morning was the one day on the tour when I could have used a spare bike, and I had given it up to Brian. We unloaded the three BMWs from the trailer, packed our stuff, including my little red plastic gas can, bungeed on the back for rides in lonely country (nice title, "Rides in Lonely Country"), and started the engines. I noticed that the warning light for the ABS brakes was flashing rapidly, meaning the system wasn't resetting. Also, the servo-assist wasn't working, making the lever effort on the front brake—the important one—very high.

Of course, two days and 900 miles later, at a BMW dealer in Colorado Springs, it would turn out to be the simplest thing: the bike's handguard had been jostled by another bike in the trailer, and was just touching the front brake lever, so it couldn't retract completely—by about one-eighth of an inch.

But I didn't know about that design quirk yet, and didn't know what to do. Even Brian, a professional motorcycle journalist, had no idea what the problem could be. After a brief, solitary debate, I decided to set off, hoping it would fix itself, as such problems sometimes did. If not, I would have to ride without ABS, and exert a lot of extra effort when I braked.

The three of us rode north on a long, straight West Texas road in staggered formation, heading for New Mexico under a clear, sunny sky. Few roads crossed the dry grasslands, the kind of sparse country that needed an average of forty acres to support each cow, but we chose the smallest gray lines we could find on the map. We shared those long, straight roads with almost no other vehicles, and like the Texas Panhandle just east of us, it was so flat you could "see for two days."

Unlike the Midwestern roads Michael and I had been riding on the first leg, there were no cornfields, no curves, no buildings, no trees, nothing for danger to hide behind, and we settled into a fast pace between 90 and 100 mph. Brian had been a keen amateur racer, still was from time to time, and liked to ride fast. Michael and I had been riding together for more than 25,000 miles now, nearly every day for the past month, and we liked a fast pace, too.

It was a good opportunity to do a top-speed test on our bikes, and when I looked ahead and saw Michael crouched down behind his windscreen and beginning to pull away, I followed. Later, I noted, "1200 hits 200 kph [125 mph] *easily*, even with bags on."

Sometimes we slowed down a little, to observe the scenery. A few herds of pronghorn antelope went springing away from us like gazelles in the distance, and small families of mule deer stood beside fences, looking confused. Michael had an unfortunate encounter with a vulture, and I knew from experience vultures were *big* objects to run into. Then and now, the vulture got the worst of it.

We decided to be considerate of our guest, and just after we crossed I-40, not far from Tucumcari, we stopped for lunch at a diner, Cherish's, in Logan. As we enjoyed our cheeseburgers, fries, and lemonade, I noticed a sign by the employees' entrance, "AS OF JANUARY FIRST, NO CHILDREN ARE TO BE BROUGHT TO WORK WITH THE PARENT. IF YOU DON'T HAVE A SITTER, CALL AND MAKE ARRANGEMENTS."

Some stories there, I guessed.

Heading into northern New Mexico, the towns were a *long* way apart—fifty-three miles from Logan to Mosquero, then another sixty to Springer—so we kept an eye on our gas. At those high cruising speeds, our fuel economy, and thus our range, were reduced.

We were also gaining elevation all the way, from 3100 feet in Fort Stockton to 3800 feet in Logan, then 5832 feet in Springer. The sky was vast and so was the landscape, sweeping away in broad strokes of short grasses and occasional distant rock formations. The map showed we were riding through a part of the Kiowa National Grasslands, a preserve along the Canadian River that had been rescued from the devastation of the dust bowl and reseeded to natural grama grasses.

A wall of black clouds towered into the sky ahead of us, pierced by jags of lightning. There was nowhere to take shelter or go back to, so we agreed to press on. We stopped to put on our rainsuits, and Michael and I put our radar detectors in our waterproof tankbags.

The wall of rain came at us, clearly visible as it obscured the landscape behind it, and as that curtain grew closer, it marked a black line across the pavement. We passed into the torrent, rode through it for a few minutes, then there was a respite, like the eye of the storm, before it swept over us again.

We passed out of the rain, and right into a radar trap. We saw the highway patrol car coming toward us, then turn around, and race up behind to pull us over. The cop said he had clocked Michael at 78 in a 60, me at 73, and Brian at 70. He gave Michael a ticket for 70, while Brian and I got written warnings. As we pulled away, I saw Michael's ticket blow away and down onto the wet road beside me, and I thought, "Isn't *he* being cheeky?"

It turned out the ticket had simply blown out of his unzipped tankbag, and later he had to meekly call the New Mexico highway patrol to get a copy, so he could pay it.

After filling up with gas in Springer, we followed a scenic little road through an area called the Philmont Scout Ranch, a section of rugged mountain wilderness that had been donated to the Boy Scouts of America in 1941. Near the beautifully-named town of Cimarron ("wild and unruly," apparently referring to the town's character in frontier days), at 6428 feet, we started to see trees again, as we rode into the forests of the Sangre de Christo (Blood of Christ—hadn't seen a church sign all day) Mountains.

And it rained. We followed a winding road through conifer woods, Brian leading now, me and Michael behind. Riding in steady rain, the road shiny in the dim light, I concentrated on keeping a steady *smoothness*—steering, accelerating, and braking (still in high-effort manual). It was not too unpleasant, until we got stuck behind an RV, plodding along and refusing to pull over, for the whole sinuous, rainy, last twenty miles into Taos.

Taos was surrounded by green mountains, a fantastic setting at 7000 feet, below peaks reaching 12- and 13,000 feet. The town's adobe building code gave it a unique character and charm, a sense of place similar to Santa Fe's without being so big and busy. As we splashed into town, I passed Brian to lead us around the attractive main plaza, covered storefronts framing the trees and statues, and park in front of the old hotel, La Fonda.

Brutus and I had stayed there in May, 1997, riding from an overnight on the bus near Lubbock to meet our wives in Durango, Colorado. Back then, La Fonda ("The Boardinghouse") had been fairly funky, in a charming way, but when Michael and I stayed there in the summer of 2002, we found it much improved (making me feel bad about a reference to its funkiness in *Ghost Rider*). This time, a young employee led us to a walled-in area at the back to park our bikes, and we hauled our bags up a couple of long flights of stairs to our rooms, with balconies facing the plaza.

Brian joined Michael and me in my room for the traditional

Macallan, and he raised his glass in a toast, aptly quoting from *Ghost Rider*: "Cheated death again."

Clink, clink, clink.

"Right on."

It had been a long day, 868 kilometers, 540 miles, and my first journal note was, "Once again, too goddamn much *happens* in a day." I went on to list Taos in my "Top Ten Good Places," and speculated, "Could probably live around here . . . someday."

But I always say that.

I was still suffering from those bedbug bites, smearing on anti-itch cream and Neosporin, before joining Brian and Michael for a good dinner in La Fonda's restaurant. We were all pleasantly tired and made it an early night, then Brian and I met for breakfast, letting Michael sleep in.

The day started sunny and cool, the air at those high elevations thin and bracing. We headed west across low sage country to the Rio Grande Gorge Bridge, looking down into a deep, narrow canyon, then turned north toward Colorado. As we entered the southernmost reaches of the Rocky Mountains, high peaks began to rise in the distance, to the east, north, and west, and by Alamosa, Colorado, we had climbed to 7500 feet.

As we rode along a straight stretch of little Highway 17, we paused to check our bearings, and Michael pointed to Doofus and an arrow on the screen that said we were approaching Mineral Hot Springs. Brian and I, who had been watching the roadsigns instead of a screen, knew we had already passed Mineral Hot Springs. Michael preferred to believe Doofus rather than us fallible humans, but we convinced him to turn back and prove us right.

We picked up the promising loop we had wanted to take on Highway 14, which led us on a classic mountain road between forested peaks, winding up to the 10,149-foot North Pass and curving down again, then up to the 11,312-foot Monarch Pass and down again. Brian was leading at a rapid pace, and it was all I could do to keep him in sight.

A little north from there we paused at a crossroads and waved good-bye. Brian and Michael were riding north into Denver, while I was turning east toward Colorado Springs on my way to spend the night with my friend Kevin Anderson and his wife, Rebecca. Seeing a wall of black clouds ahead, I paused to put on my rain gear, then headed east on Highway 24. Up over Trout Creek Pass, at 9346 feet, and Wilkerson Pass, at 9507 feet,

155

the spectacular mountain scenery and cool fresh air continued.

As I got closer to Colorado Springs the traffic became heavier, and the highway split into four lanes at Woodland Park, at 8465 feet. It was then I started to notice the *terrible* left-lane manners of Colorado drivers, so many of them crawling along in the so-called passing lane without regard to anyone who might actually want to pass. Even when there were no cars in the right lane, drivers would putter along in the left, oblivious to me racing up behind. (Later I learned that kind of left-lane squatting had become so widespread in Colorado the state police had started ticketing people for "failing to yield." Two years later, I happened to ride across Colorado, and it seemed much better.)

That manifestation of the Anti-Destination League was especially frustrating late in a long day, when I had already ridden a long distance, still had a long distance to ride, and rainclouds were closing in ahead. Still, I never liked to pass on the right—unsafe and just plain wrong to me—so I tried sitting patiently a few car-lengths behind these oblivious SUVs and cars, waiting for them to do the right thing. But no. A few times I tried putting on my left signal (a European custom Michael favored, and that *sometimes* worked, in other states), but the Colorado drivers paid no attention.

Eventually, I would breathe a curse and swing around them on the right, then signal left and pull in front of them. Then I couldn't help throwing out my left arm in a palm-up signal intended to express "Hello! What are you *doing*?" Sometimes, exasperated, I would pull in front of them and point over my head to the right lane, hoping to give them the idea, but it made no difference—no one ever moved over.

In any case, the dark clouds finally began to release their showers, so I settled into a more relaxed pace as the road descended, just staying with the flow of traffic and taking it easy on the wet road. I began to encounter lines of vehicles backed up at traffic lights, and at one of them, just after Manitou Springs, a small pickup pulled up beside me. A bearded man in a park ranger's uniform leaned over and called through his passenger window, "You dropped one of your boxes back there."

I automatically looked to the rear of the bike, saw that my right-side luggage case was gone, and felt an immediate chill of alarm and fear. The hardshell cases were locked onto the frame of the bike, so one of them coming off was like, say, losing the trunk of your car.

"About a half mile or a mile back," the ranger said.

Thanking him, I made a U-turn at the lights and raced back up the divided highway a mile or so, then turned around and rode back in the drizzling rain, slowly scanning the roadside. At first I hadn't been too upset, thinking I would surely find the case lying beside the road and everything would be okay, but I didn't see it.

Still hopeful, I thought, Maybe I didn't go back far enough.

I turned around again, sped back a couple of miles this time, then turned around and rode slowly over that same stretch of road, desperately scanning for that luggage case. It wasn't there.

I tried again, riding back a little farther this time, but there was no sign of it.

I started to get upset, going over in my head all that was in that case. Some of it was replaceable, of course: a few clothes, the "little black book" of our itinerary, a spare faceshield for my helmet, tire repair kit, some maps, Swiss Army alarm clock, *Cycle World* baseball hat, and the venerable plastic flask half full of The Macallan. (Precious, but replaceable.)

Then I began to add up the irreplaceable items, like my shaving kit and medicines, my phone and address book, a copy of *Traveling Music* with all of my proofreading notes in it, the little Zeiss birdwatching binoculars Jackie had bought for our East African safari in 1987, and—worst of all—the Patek Philippe watch Carrie had bought me for my fiftieth birthday, and the Cartier engagement ring she'd given me in 2000. I didn't wear them when I was riding or drumming, but I liked to have them with me, in what ought to have been a safely locked case.

Where was it?

One corner of my mind knew this wasn't the *worst* that could happen—my imagination always allowed for the possibility of extreme, fatal disasters. But at the same time, having barely survived some tragedies that weren't imaginary had left me permanently fragile, living and functioning inside a thin armor of "adaptation" that was easily pierced. I was feeling bad about this lost case, near tears, and stopped at the side of the road. I lit a cigarette with shaking hands, and tried to think what to do.

Nothing I *could* do, really, except hope. Perhaps some Good Samaritan had picked it up, a fellow motorcyclist tossing it into his van or pickup. As a Canadian, I naturally hoped it hadn't inconvenienced anyone, but maybe the fallen case had landed in the road, blocking traffic, and a cop had picked it up.

From the time the case fell off (caused by the failure of a five-dollar bolt, it turned out) until the ranger told me about it and I raced back there, not more than ten or fifteen minutes could have passed. But I would still hope for the best. It was the way I was made.

At least I still had the directions to Kevin and Rebecca's house in the map-case on my tankbag, and it was getting late in the afternoon, and still raining. I decided to carry on, get to their house, then try to deal with the situation. I followed the directions onto I-25 and north in the chilly drizzle, climbing again from 6000 feet at Colorado Springs to 7000 feet at Monument, before getting lost in a maze of tree-lined roads in the rainy twilight.

Some of the street names made sense, but something seemed to be missing—I couldn't find *their* street. Worse, I didn't have my phone book, so I couldn't even call them. I headed back toward the interstate and stopped at a little strip mall. A dentist's office was just closing, and the nurse gave me the missing piece of information. When I had copied down Kevin's directions from his e-mail, I had missed one line, one street name where I was supposed to turn.

After all that, and 734 kilometers (458 miles) of mountain riding, I was tired, cold, wet, and feeling low. When I pulled up in front of their house, I tried to pull myself together and prepare to be sociable. Kevin walked out into the driveway to meet me—medium height, slender, fair hair receding and neatly trimmed beard—and I began blabbering about what had happened.

The following is the beginning of an introduction I wrote for a collection of Kevin's stories, called *Landscapes*.

In the late '80s, a novel called *Resurrection Inc.* arrived in my mailbox, accompanied by a letter from its author, Kevin J. Anderson. He wrote that the book had been partly inspired by an album called *Grace Under Pressure,* which my Rush bandmates and I had released in 1984.

It took me a year or so to get around to reading *Resurrection Inc.,* but when I did, I was powerfully impressed, and wrote back to Kevin to tell him so. Any inspiration from Rush's work seemed indirect at best, but nonetheless, Kevin and I had much in common, not least a shared love since childhood for science fiction and fantasy stories.

We began to write to each other occasionally, and during Rush's *Roll the Bones* tour in 1992, on a day off between concerts in California, I rode my bicycle from Sacramento to Kevin's home in Livermore, California. That was the beginning of a good friendship, many stimulating conversations (mostly by letter and e-mail, as we lived far apart), and regular packages in the mail, as we shared our latest work with each other—the ultimate stimulating conversation. In subsequent years I would send Kevin a few books of my own, plus numerous CDs and DVDs from my work with Rush, and there seemed to be a fat volume from Kevin arriving about every other month.

Back in 1992, though, Kevin was still working full-time as a technical writer at the Lawrence Livermore National Laboratory. He spent every spare minute working on his fiction, and though he would famously collect over 800 rejection letters, there was no doubt in Kevin's mind about his destiny. Even as a child, Kevin didn't "want to be" a writer when he grew up; he was *going to be* a writer.

And so he was. To date, Kevin has published more than 90 novels, story collections, graphic novels, and comic books, and he still spends every minute *being a writer.* Kevin doesn't write to live, he lives to write.

He has even found ways to weave his recreation, relaxation, and desire for adventure and physical challenge into the writing process, carrying a microcassette recorder on long hikes throughout the West, including the ascent of each of Colorado's fifty-four "fourteeners" (peaks over 14,000 feet).

Kevin and Rebecca had designed their home like a whimsical castle, with turrets and battlements and a full suit of armor in the entranceway. Inside, though, it was entirely modern, with a fantastic view through big windows framed in tall conifers. Looking to the west, the Front Range of the Rockies rose up in a forested wall befitting its local name, the Rampart Range.

A bottle of Scotch stood on the counter, and Kevin invited me to help myself as I called Michael to let him know about the missing luggage case and see what he could do to help.

My one remaining bag contained a few things I needed, a clean shirt, socks and underwear, and a pair of shoes, but I realized I had no pants to wear other than my leather riding outfit, which wouldn't really suit Kevin and Rebecca's plans to go out to a restaurant for dinner. While I showered and settled into the welcoming guest room, Rebecca arranged to borrow a pair of pants from her father, who lived nearby, and who was, it turned out, just my size.

Kevin and Rebecca drove me down to Colorado Springs, talking about life and work all the way, and we enjoyed a fine meal in a favorite restaurant of theirs (Kevin was a longtime connoisseur of microbreweries). I remained jittery and distracted, and faced the unpleasant duty of telling Carrie about the lost case, and the watch and ring. Outside the restaurant, I called her on my cell phone and told her, saying I was still hopeful—there were good people out there, and I would get them back.

Rebecca was a great partner for an obsessive writer like Kevin, supervising the business side of his publishing, acting as his initial editor, and even cowriting several series of young adult books. She also protected his writing time jealously, and Kevin laughed when he told me he had wanted to prepare his famous lasagna in honor of my visit, but Rebecca had insisted it would take too long. He had deadlines to meet.

The house was clearly designed around Kevin, the "writing machine," with his spacious office in a downstairs corner where he could play the loud music he always listened to while writing, and plenty of room to store copies of the dozens of titles he had published. Just inside the main entrance of the house was a cozy library, with hundreds of books lining the shelves that framed a fireplace.

In the morning, while Rebecca went over the day's business with their full-time assistant, Catherine, Kevin drew up a route for me to take that day toward the next venue, near Denver. Not wanting to risk Rebecca's wrath by taking up too much of Kevin's time, I set off in the mid-morning sunshine. I stopped at the Colorado Springs BMW dealer, where the service manager noticed the handguard was just touching the front brake lever—which had prevented the ABS from resetting and caused me to ride 900 miles without ABS or servo-assist.

Following Kevin's recommendation, I did a circuit through a Colorado Springs park called Garden of the Gods, a stunning area of erosion-sculpted red sandstone. I described it in my journal as "a bit of southern Utah."

Back in 2002, before our Denver show on the *Vapor Trails* tour, Michael and I had ridden our motorcycles up and down Mount Evans, which, at 14,130 feet, was "the world's highest paved highway." This time I was determined to ride the Pikes Peak Toll Road to its summit, at 14,110 feet. (In the late nineteenth century, Denver and Colorado Springs were competing for tourist dollars, and after the Pikes Peak cog railway and carriage road started drawing visitors to Colorado Springs, the mayor of Denver sponsored the building of the Mount Evans road, finished in 1927.)

Pikes Peak itself was named after General Zebulon Montgomery Pike, who "discovered" the mountain in 1806. The carriage road was built to the summit between 1886 and 1888, the cog railway following in 1891. In 1893, a visiting teacher, Katharine Lee Bates, was so inspired by the view from the top, that on the evening of her return to Colorado Springs, she wrote the lyrics for "America the Beautiful."

"O beautiful for spacious skies," is the familiar opening line, then "amber waves of grain." (That used to be the slogan on Indiana's licence plates. Now they use the state's Web site address, which is not so poetic. Same with Pennsylvania, who used to have a slogan I really liked, "You've got a friend in Pennsylvania." Now the bottom of their plates said "pastate.gov," or something dull like that.)

After "For purple mountain majesties, above the fruited plain!" the first verse (of *eight!*) ends nicely with, "From sea to shining sea!" But then things get a little turgid, with patriotic breast-beating and more superfluous exclamation points. "Thine alabaster cities gleam, undimmed by human tears!," and "God shed his grace on thee, Till souls wax fair as earth and air, and music-hearted sea!"

And even 112 years later, what about the concluding lines? "America, America, God shed his grace on thee, Till nobler men keep once again, Thy whiter jubilee!"

Thy whiter jubilee?

Perhaps the best-known modern version of the song is by Ray Charles, who chose to leave that verse out—in fact, he chose to leave out *six* verses. No alabaster cities, no music-hearted sea, no whiter jubilee.

I pulled up to the ranger station at the bottom of the Pikes Peak Toll Road (opened in 1916) and paid my $10 fee. The ranger warned me there was rain at the summit, possibly turning to snow (on June 29!) and it would be muddy. I saw a few signs for the famous Pikes Peak Hillclimb, the second-oldest automobile race in America (after the Indy 500), which had been held the previous weekend. The hillclimb course ascended twelve miles, and included 156 turns.

The nineteen-mile toll road started out paved, climbing through the various climatic zones—Eastern Plains, with wildflowers and grasslands; the Foothills Zone, with scrub oak, sage, and juniper; the Montane Zone, with forests of Douglas fir, pines, and aspens; the Subalpine Zone, above 10,000 feet, with dense forests of Engelmann spruce, and ancient bristle-cone pine (up to 2000 years old); and finally, above the treeline to the tundra of mosses and tiny plants in the Alpine Zone.

The last nine miles of the climb turned to muddy gravel, zigzagging across the mountainside in tight hairpins that kept my progress slow and careful. Slipping and sliding through all that, with a drizzle coming down, I was glad my ABS was working again. The summit was obscured by clouds and rain (no "purple mountain majesties" for me), though I did pause to buy a couple of souvenir bumper stickers of "Pikes Peak, Colorado, Elevation 14,110," with different slogans: "REAL MEN DON'T NEED GUARDRAILS," and "GETTING THIS HIGH WOULD BE ILLEGAL IN MOST STATES!"

Having made it to the top, I felt an irresistible sense of urgency to keep moving. As always on a show day, I was nervous about getting to work, so I was content to turn around and head back down again, back to pavement. A ranger station at the bottom was checking cars to make sure their brakes hadn't overheated, and in an amazing coincidence, I recognized the same bearded ranger who had told me about my lost luggage case the previous day.

He recognized me, too, and asked if I had found the case. I said I hadn't, and asked him if it had landed on the road, or tumbled to the side. He said it had fallen pretty much on the line between the two lanes, and cars had been veering around it, so maybe someone had picked it up for safety reasons.

If so, I had to wish they'd just left it at the side for me to find, unless the intention had been to steal it.

"Well," I said to the ranger, "I'll just have to hope it was picked up by a Good Samaritan."

The ranger nodded and wished me luck, and I rode on, continuing to follow Kevin's recommended route.

Turning north, I followed little Highway 67 to Buffalo Creek, then 126 up through Pine, and the whole way was perfect, sublime mountain riding, with hardly any other traffic. It was also enjoyable to be riding solo for once, setting my own riding rhythm without having to keep an eye out for Michael in my mirrors. I surrendered to a perfect "groove," an aggressive eight-tenths pace from one curve to the next, through dense trees and rock formations and past occasional fast-moving rivers, for the entire 180 miles of that day's commute to work.

In response to a message Dave had left on my cell phone, I gave him a call when I got close to the venue, and he rode out on his Harley to meet me and guide me in. Watching Dave riding ahead of me, negotiating the tight road winding into the park, I admired the way he handled that big bike.

Red Rocks Amphitheater was a legendary outdoor venue, though somehow Rush had never played there before—we had always played at the arena downtown, or another, larger suburban amphitheater, Fiddlers Green. Red Rocks had been built in the late 1930s by the Civilian Conservation Corps, one of Franklin Delano Roosevelt's New Deal agencies for unemployed young men, and it utilized the natural setting of red sandstone monoliths, Creation, Stage, and Ship Rocks framing steep rows of redwood benches. Featured artists at Red Rocks ranged from Igor Stravinsky in 1948 to the Beatles in 1964 (the only show on their first American tour that wasn't sold out), and the venue's fame grew with a filmed concert by U2 early in their career, in 1983. An ongoing spectrum of performers, from Bruce Springsteen to the Grateful Dead (who still held the record for the most appearances at the venue), had performed there.

Even the backstage area had been built into and around the natural rock formations, tunnels connecting the offices and dressing rooms. The Bubba-Gump room was like a cave, with sandstone boulders forming one wall. Around soundcheck time, dark clouds and a menacing wind had the

crew scrambling to cover the equipment with plastic sheets, but fortunately the storm passed away to the south.

From the moment we took the stage that evening, the entire event
felt special, and later I noted in my journal:

> Carefully chosen word, *special*, as that's how I felt about the place,
> the audience, us, and even *me*—even the ride there. Remember sit-
> ting onstage thinking, "Colorado, all is forgiven," after my frustration
> with the drivers there, and what I considered at the time to be my
> stolen luggage case.

An unusual feature of the natural amphitheater's layout was that the
first row of the audience stood right in front of the stage on the same
level, then rose up steeply between the high walls of eroded sandstone.
Thus I had the feeling of playing out and up to the audience, rather than
the usual feeling of looking down and out, as it were. As I sat leaned over
the drums, I had to bend my neck *way* back to see the farthest rows of
people, a line of figures silhouetted against the sky at the top. The lack of
a roof was unfortunate for the audience when it rained, but there were
only a few brief showers through the evening.

Because of that steep rise, the whole audience seemed relatively
close, and during the early part of the show, while it was still daylight, I
had the feeling of being able to see each of the 8,561 people individually. I spotted Kevin and Rebecca and their friends up on the stage-left side
of the mixing area (still clad in plastic against that threatened rainstorm).
The last time we had played Denver, at the Fiddlers Green amphitheater
on *Vapor Trails*, I had looked out during "Vital Signs" and seen Kevin
with his arms flung wide, singing along. When I wrote to him about that
later, he was a little embarrassed, but I told him I had felt proud to see
that someone like Kevin derived such obvious pleasure from our music.
"The praise of the praiseworthy."

One unforgettable sight that night at Red Rocks was a row of handicapped fans in wheelchairs up on the stage-right side. They sang along
with "Roll the Bones," "Why are we *here*?," laughing wildly with their
hands out to their sides, then pointing down at their wheelchairs,
"Because we're here!"

That was a strange and beautiful response to the song—and to us—

and an apt interpretation of those words. My smile of appreciation for their spirit was bittersweet.

Once again, it was simply a *magical* show, and would remain in my memory as one of the best nights of the tour. I was glad photographer Andrew was there, too, because he captured some memorable images— including the one that graces the cover of this book.

Later that night, Michael, Dave, and I slept on the bus in Green River, Wyoming, then began yet another memorable commute, heading for the next night's show in Salt Lake City.

On a bright, sunny Great Basin morning, Michael and I rode south on Highway 530 through the Flaming Gorge National Recreation Area, a monumentally scenic region surrounding a reservoir and dam on the Green River. A hero of mine, Major John Wesley Powell, was a one-armed Civil War veteran who led the first descent of the Colorado River in 1869. In May of that year, he saw the sun reflecting off the red rocks and named it the Flaming Gorge.

Brutus and I had explored the area from the other direction on the *Test for Echo* tour, in early 1997, starting in Vernal, Utah, which I always remember for its cleverly named dinosaur museum, "Remains To Be Seen."

This time, Michael and I rode south through the Flaming Gorge country, then west through the southwestern corner of Wyoming. The rolling grasslands and isolated ranches were only occasionally studded with tiny towns with names like Burntfork, Lonetree, and Mountain View. Later that day, Doofus impressed me by navigating us over some unpaved wagon roads, nameless and unnumbered, as we made our way toward Highway 150.

From there, we joined up with a bicycle route I have written about before as one of my all-time favorites—and one of the longest and most difficult. From Evanston, Wyoming, to Salt Lake City, it was 150 miles of mountainous riding, crossing the Uintas Mountains, and two 10,000-foot passes, including one unpaved one, Guardsman Pass, and a lot of high-elevation climbing.

The elaborate fold-out booklet in our *Counterparts* CD showed a small black-and-white photograph of me standing in front of the band's tour bus with my bicycle. (Beside it is one of me with the Mohawk, at the end of that tour, as described back in Chicago.) Andrew took that shot early on a frigid morning in the early summer of 1992, at a truck stop in

Evanston, Wyoming. I was just about to set off on my second ride over that arduous route, during the *Roll the Bones* tour.

Highway 150 was marked on the map "Closed in Winter," and in 1997, Brutus and I had been turned back from there by a "Closed" sign as late as June. But in July of 2004, it was open, winding high through the mountains, passing lakes and rivers, dense conifer forests, and bare glaciated rock below some of Utah's highest peaks. The sky was a deep translucent blue, the light clear and radiant.

Emerging at Kamas, Michael and I crossed a valley to Park City, the overdeveloped ski resort and site of the Sundance Film Festival. Then we climbed again, to the gravel road of the Guardsman Pass, above the tree-line, with a massive view of surrounding peaks and wooded valleys. We followed that road down the other side to pavement again, through the Cottonwood Canyon to the south side of Salt Lake City. Even with that combination of dirt roads and meandering routes, we covered 473 kilometers that day, almost 300 miles, and still got into town by early afternoon. We decided to stop by the BMW dealer.

In 1997, when Brutus and I had been stopped on that little Highway 150 by the "Closed" sign, we turned back to the interstate and rode straight into Salt Lake City. It had been too early to go to work, so we visited the local BMW motorcycle dealer for a look around. Back then, BMW of Salt Lake had been a small, BMW-only dealership, and we talked a while with the nice people there, who were especially knowledgeable about our GS model bikes. Before we knew it, we were buying new mufflers (lighter and freer-breathing than the stock ones) and sharing some burgers with the employees in their lunchroom.

Twice on my *Ghost Rider* travels I had stopped there for oil changes, new tires, and minor repairs. Later, in southern Mexico, I experienced some transmission trouble, and called the BMW of Salt Lake service manager, Chip, the most knowledgeable expert I knew on the GS model. Along with a few dealers in Tucson, Vancouver, and Toronto, BMW of Salt Lake earned a "thank-you" in the book, from my motorcycle and me.

A couple of years later, when the band played in Salt Lake City on the *Vapor Trails* tour, I didn't have time to stop by the dealership, but I asked Michael to give them a call and invite them to the show. They had been excited to attend, and had brought along some BMW "swag" for us.

This time, my 1200GS was due for its 10,000-kilometer (6000 mile) service, and I had called the BMW of Salt Lake service department from Denver to see if they might squeeze me in the next day. Knowing it was short notice and a fairly lengthy job, I told them who I was, and offered them tickets to the show if they could help me out. I sent the 1200 ahead with Dave on the trailer, asking him to drop it off at the dealer that morning. I was riding my old 1150 that day, as Michael and I made our way through the busy interstate loop to the north side of the city and up to the large, new facility—which apparently now had different owners and different staff, and certainly offered me a completely different experience.

If my previous visits to BMW of Salt Lake had been pleasant, low-key encounters with fellow BMW people, this one was more like a celebrity appearance, a "meet-and-greet," as Dave described it. As I stood at the counter shopping for new luggage cases (to replace the lost one) and maybe some new gloves, a series of employees appeared at the counter in front of me, laying out items to be signed—Rush CDs, old Rush LPs, a homemade painting of our starman logo from *2112*, and copies of *Ghost Rider*.

Of course, I signed them all willingly, but began to feel a little uncomfortable with all that attention. As I noted in my journal, "All nice people, but . . . embarrassing. Just wanted to deal with *bike* stuff, not *me* stuff."

And it didn't end there. Someone who worked in the dealership must have called a friend who might be called (accurately if uncharitably) a "rabid" fan. He got too close to me, right in my face, as they say, and stayed there too long, saying things like, "I've been waiting my whole life for this."

What can you say to that?

Then, someone in the back shop couldn't resist telling a delivery-truck driver I was "in the house," and he had to come and have a look for himself. Just that—a *look*. Dave, witnessing all this fuss and knowing how I would feel, said, "Next time you'd better just send me or Michael."

"But I just wanted to *shop!*"

In any case, the staff were indeed very nice people, and they took care of the 1200's service, as well as ordering me some new luggage cases (big aluminum boxes from an aftermarket company called Jesse), some new gloves, and (finally) a handlebar mount for my very own GPS unit. I immediately christened it "Dingus."

Sitting onstage that night at the Health Maintenance Organization

Amphitheater, looking out at the crowd, for a few seconds I flashed back to the wagon roads we had been on that day, far away in such a remote part of Wyoming, and to negotiating the unpaved Guardsman Pass. Or the previous day's ride, when I had been speeding along those curvy mountain roads into Red Rocks. I had a brief smiling thought: "These people have no idea what I go through every day on my way to work—and I still get to the show!"

Later, I reviewed that show in my journal. "Strangely 'lackluster,' but maybe just subjective, after what seemed like such a special show at Red Rocks."

I also reviewed my recent riding performances. "Riding so *well* these past few days, and in areas where it's so important and rewarding to ride well."

The next show, at an amphitheater near Seattle, was over 800 miles away by interstate. Even with a day off, I figured Michael and I would have to get as far as Boise on the bus to get a decent start and be able to take the back roads. That meant Dave had to drive a *long* way that night, and it was five a.m. before I heard the main engine shudder to a stop and the little generator hum to life. Then I would have three hours of peaceful, stationary sleep until the alarm clock beeped.

When I got up at eight, I noticed the lights in the front lounge were dim, and had to wake Dave up to reset a breaker switch. Then the usual juice, cereal, and coffee, before rattling the curtain over Michael's bunk.

"Yoo hoo, Michelle, rise and shine!"

At the end of that long day, the first of July, I tried to capture it in my journal:

Then . . . a great ride. Almost want to stop there—simplest description of indescribable day (as usual).

Just too damn much to remember, never mind record. Need "mental download," even of contents of memory *now*, after the ride. I could summon a lot of it up now, but not six months from now.

Solidly in the Vortex now, in the blinkered focus of the days—breakfast, ride, ride, ride, then motel and dinner on days off, or afternoon arrival on show day.

Anyway . . . *love* Idaho (*smells* so good), and eastern Washington in its way, too. Some *stellar* riding today, despite thick traffic around

Eagle and McCall (beautiful lake town) and Lewiston.

Twinge of regret today, thinking of how few great rides we have left, before it all goes bad—meaning, before it all goes *east*.

Still, some wonderful rides in the past five or six days. And covered some *big* miles.

Almost 2000 "big miles" in the previous five days—3200 kilometers—and 374 miles that day (599 kilometers) to the tiny farming town of Connell, Washington. I led us to the same little M&M Motel I had stayed at in early '99 on my *Ghost Rider* travels, and we had passed some other resting places from previous travels in Idaho—like Riggins, Lewiston, and Boise.

"LOOK BACK FROM THE FUTURE" was the day's church sign, and I tried to grapple with that concept. I hadn't seen too many church signs lately, perhaps because we had been in Mormon country. The Latter-Day Saints didn't seem to go in for inspirational messages in front of their churches and temples. They preferred to use television commercials to promote their faith. Not to mention the thousands of missionaries they sent around the world.

It was my first time riding with Dingus on the handlebars in front of me, and at first I just glanced down from time to time to see the little arrow that showed where we were (theoretically). Later in the day, I asked Michael to set it to show our route, displaying not only where we were, but how far to the next turning, and even how far to the next job-site.

Our radar detectors were also on full alert that day, as we saw police cars on patrol everywhere, even on the loneliest back roads. The Fourth of July weekend may have been the most dangerous time of the year on American roads, but because the police were concentrating on open stretches of empty highway rather than towns or intersections, it seemed much more like a revenue-gathering operation than a mission of public safety.

At one point we even noticed that one of the Washington state patrol cars was deliberately stalking us, like a predator (apt analogy), passing us in one direction when we had slowed down in response to the radar detector, then sneaking up behind, passing us as we cruised blithely just above the posted limit, and lying in wait around blind corners, hoping to catch us unawares.

When the bikes were parked outside our adjoining rooms at the M&M Motel in Connell, Michael and I performed the Macallan ritual, then split up to have our showers and quiet time. Turning on my cell phone to check for messages, I paused to listen to one from my brother, Danny, wanting to make arrangements for he and his family to meet us the next afternoon. I made a mental note to call him, erased the message, and listened to the next one.

It was a man's voice I didn't recognize, and after he gave his name, he went on to say he had picked up my luggage case, that it was "all intact," and he had drilled it open and found my phone book, with my cell phone number inside the front cover. When I realized what I was hearing, my mind went *electric*, and I thought, "Omigod—I've got to play this for *Michael!*"

He had been skeptical about my earlier optimism, and indeed, by that point I had resigned myself to the loss. Now I couldn't wait to show Michael there *were* good people in the world. My finger went down to save that precious message, but out of habit, shock, and fatigue ("fatigue makes you stupid"), I realized—even as my mind screamed, "No-o-o!"— I was pressing the "Delete" button.

My head dropped, and I stared at the phone and my traitorous finger in disbelief.

Even then, I didn't think it would be a big problem. Surely we could trace the number of that incoming call. Or the Good Samaritan might call back; he had sounded like a good guy.

I went next door to Michael's room and told him what had happened. He looked at me, shaking his head, and I said, "Shut up, man—he'll call back!"

Michael tried calling the cell phone company, but it was late in the day and he couldn't reach anyone who knew anything. He said he would try again tomorrow, and we went next door to Michael Jay's Family Restaurant. Michael pointed out that his middle name was "Jay" too, so the restaurant was named after him. I told him I would alert the local media.

He called me a cruel name.

Dinner for both of us, with appetizers, steaks, wine, dessert, and coffee, was less than $40, and it was pretty good, too.

We had crossed into the Pacific time zone at the Washington state line, and I was asleep by ten. Up before six, I felt an ache of fatigue from my neck, to my legs and feet, to the tips of my fingers. I walked back across the parking lot to Michael Jay's for breakfast. My neighbor, the other Michael Jay, slept on.

Both of us wanted to get to work early that day, as both of our brothers were going to be visiting. Also, the 1150 was due for an oil change, which I planned to do that afternoon, as well as hoping to wash the 1200. Its red and silver finish was beginning to disappear under a patina of mud and insects. I also hadn't checked my e-mails for several days, and hoped to get all that taken care of before Danny and his family arrived in the late afternoon.

However, it was Friday, July 2, and things were warming up for the big weekend—or at least, the *police* were. I had plotted a route over the most remote little back roads—first through the irrigated farmlands around the Columbia River in eastern Washington, then into the Cascades Range southeast of Seattle—but it seemed as though every highway patrol car, and every sheriff in every town in Washington, was on the prowl. Once again, it just seemed predatory.

Our radar detectors were going off constantly, and we didn't always catch the warnings in time. We were pulled over once in a little town that wasn't even on the map, but fortunately the officer was an amiable older man, a motorcyclist himself (Honda Goldwing), and a local cop rather than a hard-nosed highway patrolman. He said, "I'm not going to cite you—just take it easy from now on."

I asked him about the unusual crops I had noticed in the area, vines growing up wires and trellises, and he told me they were hops—apparently a much-coveted crop, as the growers were individually licenced to grow them.

A church sign offered a variation on a message I had noted previously, "Exposure to the Son Prevents Burning" (the other one had been, "To Prevent Eternal Burning, Use SON Block"). I began to wonder if there was some kind of book or catalogue that offered these churches a selection of such "inspirational" messages. There had to be, I thought, and if not, maybe I ought to write one. (Note to self . . .)

Despite the ubiquitous police, we had a glorious ride that day, across the sun-washed Great Basin on long, straight roads, then into the winding two-lanes through the densely forested Cascades. The snow-covered peak of Mount Rainier towered 14,410 feet above the surrounding mountains. (It is strange, many months later, to look over the map, following our route highlighted in yellow, and think, "I remember that turning," or "I remember that pass." I also notice great place names that we missed, like Sightly, Humptulips, Novelty, and the mountain named Storm King.)

Just a few miles before our destination, we were pulled over once again (the third time that week!), this time by a younger highway patrol officer. He said he had clocked Michael at 55 mph, right on the speed limit, and me right behind him at 82.

Unknown to him, the reason for that discrepancy was that Michael was wearing an earpiece plugged into the radar detector, so he could *hear* the signals, while I was still trying to get by with visual checks. (That day was the last time, though, as I finally understood the flaws inherent in that system.)

Michael tried to suggest there must be something wrong with the officer's equipment, that the disparity of our speeds didn't make sense, since I was following him. The officer was doubtful, saying he usually found it was pretty accurate. Michael casually let slip that we were on our way to the nearby amphitheater, and that I was a member of the band.

The cop was obviously excited by that, but kept his cool. He talked about how the local residents had protested against the building of the amphitheater, but he had supported it, and he liked going to shows there. "The parking is easy," he said, pointing to his badge.

Michael asked if he wanted to come to the show, but he shook his head, saying he had "family plans."

He turned to me, "But maybe I could get your autograph—on the ticket!"

He didn't seem to be joking, but he didn't give me a ticket or collect an autograph. He just casually brought the conversation to an end, and walked back to his patrol car. Michael and I looked at each other, then put our helmets back on and rode away.

We finally arrived at the White River Amphitheater (what—they couldn't get a corporate sponsor in Seattle to buy the name?) after 343 kilometers (214 miles). In the loading area, C.B. called me aside, looking serious, and said that Liam had been taken to the hospital in Seattle that morning with chest pains. They were keeping it quiet for now, but apparently he had severe blockage in his heart arteries, and the doctors had given him an angioplasty. He would be okay, but would miss the next couple of shows; he was flying straight to Los Angeles to recuperate.

Liam was only forty-nine, and the idea of him having a heart attack seemed unreal and unfair, unacceptable, really (as I'm sure it was to him). But typically, some people looked for a reason why it was his fault—because he was wound so tight, because he didn't get enough exercise, because he smoked. When the shadow of fear falls over us, we seek refuge in either faith or reason, trying to reassure ourselves a thing like that isn't going to happen to us, and that it's not *random.*

In reality, we should just feel lucky, but that is seldom enough. In an almost superstitious way, we have to feel that the victim has somehow brought it on himself, and we're too smart for such things to happen to us. As for me, I know I'm not that smart, but I know I have been lucky— most of the time.

The health-conscious C.B. assigned his diagnosis, "He's gotta stop that smoking," and I assigned mine, "I think it's *our* fault—we put him under so much stress all the time!"

Poor Liam. Losing his mother just a few weeks back, and now this. It did seem like he would be all right, but of course he'd never be the same again, either—always having to "live for his heart." He would hate that as much as I would.

Dave told me our truck driver Mac had borrowed my 1150, which I had told Mac he was welcome to do once in a while, and taken his teenage son Ryan out for a ride, so we started by washing the two dirty bikes. When Mac and Ryan returned, I changed the 1150's oil, then carried my computer inside to check my e-mails.

A half-dozen separate messages from Paul McCarthy aimed to settle final details of the reprint of that disastrous edition of *The Masked Rider,* and asked a few questions about the hardcover edition of *Traveling Music.* I sent off brief responses to those queries, as well as answering a few from friends making arrangements to attend upcoming shows in California. I wrote to Kevin Anderson to tell him about the latest developments in the lost luggage situation, and the previous day's delete error,

and he sent back a quick reply, under the title "The 7 Key" which cleverly referenced the delete key, and also contained some relevant references
to the news of the day:

> You may be able to check with your cell-phone service; even though
> you deleted the message, I think they archive messages for a certain
> amount of time. Good ol' U.S. terrorist paranoia, you know. Also,
> how else would the courts be able to grab the ancient cell-phone
> conversations of Kobe Bryant's accuser, and Scott Peterson and
> Amber Frey?

You would think so, but so far, Michael had been getting nowhere with
the phone company and we had decided to be proactive. After a local
investigator had failed to turn up any clues, or any witnesses, Michael
arranged to place an ad in the Colorado Springs newspaper, offering a
"substantial reward" for the return of the luggage case and giving Michael's
800 number. In Michael's case-hardened view of humanity, he figured the
guy would eventually find the valuable watch (in a zippered side compartment of my shaving kit), and change his mind, deciding, "Oh well, he did-
n't call back—it's mine." But I still had faith—or at least hope.

Business and bike stuff taken care of, I had a shower on the bus, then
was ready to greet Danny and Janette and their boys—Max, nearly eight
now, and Nick, just turned five. They had driven down from their home
in Vancouver, British Columbia, the day before, and were staying in a
nearby hotel. Danny was pleased that Dave remembered he liked beer. I
toured them all around the backstage area, then out on the stage to have
a close-up look at the equipment, especially the drums (no little boy of
any age could resist a set of drums!). The boys were also fascinated by the
rotating treasures in Geddy's Automat, a collection that continued to
grow as he found new bobble-heads, action figures, and pop-culture odd-
ments. We took a couple of family photos around the drum riser, then,
with soundcheck approaching, I led them all out into the house so they
could watch that daily exercise. Our sound engineer, Brad, kindly provided the boys with pairs of insulated headphones he kept on hand especially for visiting kids.

I saw them all again for a few minutes after soundcheck, then they
went off to find some dinner. Backstage, Danny ran into George, who he

had known since grade school, and George invited them to join him at crew meal in the catering room.

For me, the usual ritual—a fine Frenchie meal with the guys in the dressing room (discussing Liam's condition, of course, once again along the lines of "It's his fault," and "It's our fault"), with the usual baseball game on TV. Then a little quiet time on the bus, a phone call to Carrie, my warmup from 7:00 to 7:20, put on my stage clothes, and join the other guys in the dressing room. And again, we wait out the usual ten-minute "hold," giving all 11,854 people time to make it inside.

On the *Vapor Trails* tour in 2002, we played at the arena in Vancouver, and during the second set, I looked down to the stage-left side of the arena and saw Danny and Janette sitting there, each with a sleeping boy in their arms. Two years older this time, the boys apparently managed to stay awake for the entire show.

It felt like a *fairly* good show (I noted, "nothing special, but good"), but Danny's reaction indicates the difference between my night-by-night experience, and that of someone seeing the show once. Danny had seen us perform many times since I had first joined the band, and he told me later it was the best show he had ever seen. That was nice to hear. I was also pleased to learn that the boys had started to become real fans of the band, and were always wanting to hear our music in the car (much to their parents' distress). Max's favorite Rush song was "Ghost Rider," while Nick favored "Roll the Bones." Interesting choices.

A couple of in-jokes had been growing among the band and crew. Toward the end of the show, in the final chorus of one of our older songs, "The Temples of Syrinx," Geddy had started changing the line, "We are the priests," to "We are the pirates," and the theme had spread, especially to the sound crew members at stage left—monitor mixer Brent, and technician Beau. When we started that song, Geddy walked out with a stuffed parrot on his shoulder, everyone at stage left was wearing eyepatches, and that night Beau wore a spectacular pirate hat, floppy brim and big white plume. I broke up laughing at that sight, and again as I looked out to see a giant skull-and-crossbones flag waving from the front-of-house mixer.

Eventually, as that joke spread, the fans also started picking up on the theme. I would look out during that song and see people in the audience wearing eyepatches, skull-and-crossbones bandanas, and waving little pirate flags. That was great to see. In earlier years, Geddy had once changed that same song to, "We are the plumbers, who fix your sinks," and we had heard some grumbling feedback: "If you're not going to play it *right*, don't play it at all." Perhaps our fans had grown up enough not to take it all so seriously.

A little later in the set, another old song, "By-Tor and the Snow Dog," had a line describing the latter character as "ermine glowing," and Brent had once asked, "Who's Herman?" Now, every night just before that line, he donned a cap with "Herman" lettered across it.

These were the kind of nightly comic-relief episodes that arose more-or-less spontaneously along the way, easing the night-to-night tedium, and keeping us all entertained.

That night Dave drove Michael and me straight to the next venue, the Clark County Amphitheater (again, no corporate sponsor?) just outside Portland, and we parked there for the night. Dave had suggested this novel variation on our usual routine, because that way he could come riding with us the next day, maybe up toward Mount St. Helens.

Before crawling off to bed, I typed up a couple of e-mails I wanted to send off the next day, including one to my friend Doane Perry, confirming his invitation to the upcoming Hollywood Bowl show. Doane had been the drummer for Jethro Tull for many years, and our friendship began back in the '80s, when I read an article in *Modern Drummer* about Mark Craney, whose drumming with Gino Vanelli I had long admired. The article revealed that Mark was suffering from kidney disease, and needed donations toward a possible transplant. I sent a donation, enclosing a note to the effect that, "this business is hard enough without that."

Doane was a friend and neighbor of Mark's in the San Fernando Valley, and wrote to thank me for my donation. That began a correspondence that would continue off and on for many years, even though we never managed to actually meet—being busy touring musicians, and living 3000 miles apart.

However, when I moved to Los Angeles in 2000, Doane and I finally managed to get together, and since then, we had become good friends, meeting for lunch whenever we were both in town. One Sunday in 2004, I joined Doane in visiting Mark Craney at the UCLA hospital. Mark told me we had actually worked together once, on a multi-act show in Portland, around 1976. Mark had been playing with guitar player Tommy

Bolin. (Coincidentally, Mark was from Sioux Falls, South Dakota, while Bolin, who had made his name with early fusion music and a stint with Deep Purple, was from Sioux City, Iowa.) I remembered that show; we had been co-headlining with Styx at the Paramount Theater, and I saw Tommy Bolin backstage, not long before he died of a heroin overdose. I can still picture how yellow and waxen his skin looked.

Mark's problems, though, were not self-inflicted like that, but simply hereditary. And unfortunately, despite a kidney transplant, his health problems continued. After years of trying to keep playing and touring, seeking out daily dialysis on the road, he was forced into a life devoted to simple survival and occasional teaching. (He finally passed away in 2005, his life and music touchingly celebrated by a crowd of hundreds of musicians, friends, and family members.)

As Doane and I got to know each other better, we learned we had much more in common than just being drummers for veteran rock bands. We shared so many other interests "beyond the cymbals," in art, literature, fine cars, and a taste for Indian food. My message to Doane from the bus was datelined "Somewhere between Seattle and Portland," and started out, "Riding the bus after the show—you know the drill . . . "

A couple of passages from Doane's reply expressed a musician's shared understanding, and shared experiences. He was commenting on our *Rush in Rio* DVD.

I always enjoy the personal moments on these sort of things, often as much as the music, and I think we all like to get an insight into what is going on with the people behind the music. There were some pretty funny moments off and onstage and I appreciate seeing a band that has such a great sense of humor about itself. I would like to think that we too have a pretty good sense of humor about ourselves and that we manage to project that to the audience, although sometimes unintentionally!

I could not believe it when you went into "Girl from Ipanema!" The first time we played there many years ago, people would often ask us if we listened to, or were influenced by, Brazilian music at all. As a response, on the last night in Rio, during some very intense, raucous instrumental passage, we segued into eight bars of "Ipanema" very quietly, then back again to whatever we were playing like nothing had happened. This completely blew the audience's mind, and they went ballistic, so I had to laugh when you did the same thing and of course, the audience went completely nuts and got the joke too!!! Very, very entertaining.

By the time Dave parked at the Clark County Amphitheater, Michael and I were already asleep. In the morning, all the other trucks and buses were parked around us in the backstage area. Some of the crew guys were still sleeping in their bunks, others at work already, waving to us as we unloaded the bikes. The day was cool and bright, a Saturday, and we set off on a relaxed cruise, already feeling less urgent somehow—perhaps because we were leaving from our destination, as it were. The previous night I had highlighted a route of tiny back roads to the northeast of Portland, on the Washington side of the Columbia River, some of which Brutus and I had explored back in '97. Michael had programmed the route into his laptop, then downloaded it to Doofus and Dingus.

I took the lead that day, running ahead of Dave and Michael along narrow, winding roads rising and falling between walls of fir and spruce, up through Battle Ground (apparently named after "a battle that never took place," when some Klickitat Indians escaped from nearby Fort Vancouver in 1855, and were talked into returning voluntarily), Amboy, and Cougar. For the first time, I was trying an earpiece inside my helmet, hooked up to the radar detector, and once I found a comfortable place for the flat, foam-covered speaker, it gave me a wonderful sense of security—reinforced by picking up a few beeps that allowed me to slow down before passing a police car, whether lying in ambush or on the prowl.

We came up behind a phalanx of other motorcyclists—cruisers— some of them noticeably unskilled on their machines, and we were stuck behind them for several miles. Riding in sloppy formation, their heavy bikes wobbled around in the lane, sometimes running wide on turns, and their pace was slow and unsteady. Also, as I puttered along behind them, I noticed their bikes smelled bad, from the unburned hydrocarbons from badly tuned engines and unmuffled exhausts.

To anyone who has stood on a sidewalk and felt his or her nerves rattled by one of those open-piped beasts blatting by, or heard that concussive rumble actually activate car alarms (those "rebels" think that's a big laugh), or had their Sunday morning ease and tranquility interrupted by a passing doppler of unmuffled explosions, the noise just seems obnoxious, and tars all motorcyclists with a boorish brush. Their proud justification for such antisocial noise pollution is "Loud Pipes Save Lives," though there is no evidence that angering drivers and pedestrians can save your life. Skill and roadcraft were worth much more than making a lot of noise, and made no enemies.

As that day's church sign said, "YOU WON'T BE PERSUASIVE, BY BEING ABRASIVE."

That goes for those guys, and, equally, of course, for me too. As they say, it's a free country, and I realize that, like religion, I am not going to change the minds of those thousands of loud-pipe riders. You just have to say your bit, and hope someone listens.

In any case, Dave and I got a kick out of the figure cut by the three of us, the unlikely combination of two BMWs and a Harley-Davidson. Dave was an excellent rider, on his own and as part of a group, and if his pipes were a little loud, he didn't rev his engine just to annoy people ("look at me, look at me!"), and recently he had confessed to me that he was thinking of getting mufflers.

It was impossible for the three of us to pass that phalanx of noisy, smelly cruisers without being dangerous or impolite, so we just hung back and followed them along that tree-shaded road. I was relieved when we reached a T-junction at Yale, and they turned left while our route continued to the right. From there on, we were on a more remote road ("Closed in Winter," always a good sign) around the back side of Mount St. Helens. A couple of times I led us off the road and into wayside viewpoints, where we paused to look at and photograph some of the devastation caused by the volcano's eruption, plainly visible even after almost twenty-five years. Entire hillsides had been swept bare of trees, and much of the mountain's profile had been reshaped.

As we got deeper into the backwoods region, I was keeping a careful eye on our gas mileage, with special regard for Dave's Harley, which had less range than our BMWs. At a sideroad leading to the main overview of Mount St. Helens, I waved us over and got off my bike to talk it over.

We had planned to have a look at the view from the end of that sideroad, then turn back and take a different loop back to work. Juggling mileage, time, and fuel, I was thinking we had better change our plan. The one-way sideroad was about thirty miles return, and the nearest town, Randle, was about forty miles to the north, and by my "cipherin'," I was pretty sure Dave only had about fifty miles worth of gas left.

He nodded in agreement, and I suggested we go straight up to Randle, refuel, then come back and take that sideroad to look at Mount St. Helens. Then we should probably ride back toward Portland on the same route we had taken, to make sure we got back nice and early. All hands agreed (and not just because I was the boss!), and we headed north to Randle, enjoying a wonderfully scenic, fragrant, and entertaining ride on a mostly deserted road.

At the junction of Highway 12, we suddenly encountered a busy flow of cars, RVs, SUVs, and groups of motorcyclists, all out on this Saturday, the third of July. We were glad to fuel up and head back down our less-traveled little road. After 335 kilometers, just over 200 miles, we arrived back at the Clark County Amphitheater.

As I was replacing a burned-out taillight bulb on my bike, Mac came by with an older guy, saying, "You remember Gordon Scott the astronaut." Indeed I did, and smiled and shook his hand. A truck driver from several tours in the late '70s and early '80s, Gordon had been given that nickname simply because his name sounded like a typical astronaut's name. He used to travel with a dog, P.D. (for Puppy Dog), he had found abandoned in a truck stop, and somewhere I had an old photograph of P.D. sitting in the cab of Gordon's truck, reflected in the big mirror.

Another old friend came to mind in Portland, though he would not be coming to visit. In my Quebec house, I kept a "cabinet of memories" in which I displayed small reminders of lost friends and loved ones. Among them was a cheap chain necklace with a small pendant, a metal outline of Africa, given to me in Portland during the *Test for Echo* tour by the brother of my friend, Greg Gugel.

Greg and I met at the base of Mount Kilimanjaro in 1987, on my thirty-fifth birthday, as we began the five-day climb up and down the mountain. Among an international crowd of young travelers, Greg and I discovered we had the same rapid walking pace, and fell into step together, talking and laughing or just climbing silently in the dark on the final grim press to the summit.

Greg was a young American marine, in his early twenties, who had grown up in the Pacific Northwest, and was then studying at a university in Tanzania, hoping later to enter the diplomatic corps. He was a gentle soul, and a sensitive, likeable young man. It was hard to imagine how he had survived marine training, about which he told hilarious stories, but in fact that experience had been the making of him. He told me of his troubled youth and early teenage alcoholism, and how Alcoholics Anonymous and the marines had been part of his self-rescue.

Greg and I kept in touch after that, mostly by letter, though we met up once in Germany, while he was visiting his grandmother, and another time in Washington, D.C., where he was continuing his marine-sponsored education, and where he met his Namibian wife, Sarti, studying to be a dentist. Greg had been a student in several African countries, and had a deep affection for the continent and a wish to help make things better there. In the mid-'90s, Greg and Sarti moved to Namibia together, and Greg wrote to tell me he had bought a BMW motorcycle to get around on. In early 1997, I wrote to him, saying that Brutus and I were thinking about a motorcycle tour around South Africa and Namibia, and wondering if he might like to join us, and perhaps guide us through his adopted country.

Sarti answered that letter, saying that Greg had flown back to Seattle to be with his dying mother and something had happened—he had taken some of her medicine, and he was now in a coma. I got in touch with Greg's brother, Geoffrey, who told me they still weren't sure how it had happened. While watching over their declining mother one night, he and Greg had shared a few beers—which was unusual for Greg, as a recovering alcoholic, but he was very upset. Before they had said good night, Greg had gone in to see their mother once more, and apparently had taken some of her morphine, then passed out. Geoffrey didn't find him until the morning—too late.

Now he was on life-support, but could never recover, and the family was facing a horrible decision. Fortunately for them, if not for Greg, he succumbed on his own, and while I was making arrangements to meet Geoffrey in Portland a few months later, I wrote to him:

Whenever my conversations with Gregory touched on a sad subject, he had this way of saying "Ach" that filled that little Germanic word with so much feeling, so much compassion. I am haunted by that now, by the sound of it and the look on his face as he said it, for that must have been how he was feeling about your mother. And now it is how I feel about his passing. *Ach.*

Your letter also expresses feelings I share. Terribly sad that it had to be so, and yet a little relieved that no one else had to make that dread decision on his behalf.

Geoffrey had given me the little Africa pendant on the *Test For Echo* tour, in the spring of 1997, and later that year, when death's shadow fell closer to me, and again, I heard that little "Ach" many times, and said it myself. I still do.

Before going into the Clark County Amphitheater for soundcheck, I squeezed in a quick nap, then another after dinner, but the cheap replacement for my lost Swiss Army alarm clock was not as reliable, and didn't go off on time. Michael woke me up at five minutes after seven, five minutes late for my warmup. Dave was just climbing into his bunk to rest up for the night's drive, and I said to him, "That's all *I* want to do."

Dave shook his head and said, "No, uh-uh. You gotta go earn us some gas money!"

I felt groggy from then on, through my hasty warmup and the first set, feeling I was on autopilot for what seemed like minutes at a time. My after-show review read, "Pretty good show, after all, though I wasn't really *there* half the time."

As I ran onstage for the encore, tossing my towel back to Gump, I had a sudden attack of high spirits and did a "bounce" with one foot against the big sub-woofer cabinet behind the riser, before leaping up to the drums. My foot slipped on the polished wood, and down I went, falling sideways between the metal stands and hardware. I scraped the back of my armpit badly on a piece of protruding metal, and bruised my thigh landing on the corner of the riser, but got up behind the drums before anyone else even knew I had fallen.

The pain was surprisingly intense, setting all my nerves on edge, and for a moment I wondered if I was going to be able to play. A dull throbbing tightened my right leg, cramping the muscles, and a sharper, raw agony clawed at my right arm. I sat there in a tense paralysis, willing the pain away, as I half-watched Geddy and Alex do the T-shirt-throwing ritual. The agony continued as Alex started the feedback drone, but I counted in "Summertime Blues" as usual, forcing my body to do its job, just like every other night.

I had the front lounge of the bus to myself that night, as Michael was staying behind and flying with the other guys to Los Angeles. The next show was at the Hollywood Bowl, and Michael had been appointed party planner. Many of Carrie's friends and family members would be attending that show, and for once I had agreed to stay behind after and be sociable. Michael had suggested a bar in the Legion Hall near the Hollywood Bowl, where he and I had once gone for a drink, and we agreed it would be the perfect place for the after-party.

As the bus roared south down I-5 toward California, I kept the curtain open between Dave's driving area and the front lounge, and we talked a little as I cooled down with my Macallan. But mostly I was content to be quiet and alone, catching up on my journal notes and listening to Frank Sinatra's *Cycles.* I noted that I wished that CD, from 1968, had been included in the playlist in *Traveling Music.* Along with the classic *Watertown*, recorded a year later, *Cycles* was a true portrait of American life—not the familiar Sinatra with overcoat and lamppost outside an urban saloon, or the tuxedoed swinger of Hollywood and Las Vegas, but the Sinatra of real-life feelings and situations—the Midwest in "Little Green Apples," the West in "By the Time I Get to Phoenix," and the great American romantic restlessness in "Gentle on My Mind."

Stylistically, the music was New York and Los Angeles, and even high-end Nashville in the country-flavored songs, and in the arrangement of the title track. Like Joni Mitchell's masterly song, "Both Sides Now," the title song "Cycles" takes the philosophic overview, "There isn't much that I have learned, in all my foolish years/ Except that life keeps spinning in cycles, First there's laughter, then those tears."

I also wished I had remembered to write about what Frank could do with the simple consonant "d." On *Cycles,* there was a lovely example in "Pretty Colors," "But in my mind—there'll always be," where he lingers for a moment at the end of "mind," before sliding into the next word. He often used that technique, lingering on that soft consonant. In the title track on *September of My Years*, he sang, "And I find, that I'm sighing softly as I near, September," and the way he lingered on the "d" in "and," caressed it, used it to punctuate the phrasing, was sensual, strangely poignant, and uniquely his own.

Later that night, while I slept, Dave pulled over in Redding, California, and in the morning, helped me unload my bike. I was riding down to meet Carrie in Palo Alto, near where her mother, Marian, lived with her husband, Les, a retired computer science professor at Stanford University (and inventor of the first "Spell-check" utility—you can thank Les when you read about people "pouring" over books that "peak" their interest). Carrie's brother Ken would also be joining us, on leave from his training as a multilingual translator for the U.S. Navy.

I had programmed Dingus to navigate me to our hotel in Palo Alto, but there wasn't much navigating for the first 200 miles (follow I-5 south). When things did get tricky, near San Francisco, of course the stupid thing fell apart. After directing me to the toll booths for the Oakland Bay Bridge, the screen suddenly read, "Make a U-turn," forcing me to cut through to the other side and back to the I-680 loop running south through San Jose.

After a fairly tedious 387 kilometers (241 miles), Dingus brought me to the hotel. I parked the bike, unloaded my bags, and went to meet my long-neglected and much-missed wife.

That evening, Carrie and I joined Ken and Marian and Les at one of their neighbor's houses in Los Altos Hills, high on a hilltop with a view looking north toward San Francisco and south to San Jose. It was a backyard potluck barbecue to celebrate the Fourth of July, lots of families and children, and as the evening darkened we watched a series of different fireworks displays from far below.

Once again, Ray had been forced to give us two days off in a row, since the only available date at the Hollywood Bowl upset the rest of his careful routing. From Portland to Los Angeles was almost 1000 miles, a long haul for the trucks and buses. The day after the Hollywood Bowl show, we would play an amphitheater near San Diego, then turn around and travel 500 miles north again to the Bay Area.

On July 5, a holiday Monday, I set out to ride home to Los Angeles, while Carrie and her mom spent some time together, then drove Carrie to the San Jose airport for her more "civilized" journey home. Of the two more-or-less direct routes south, I preferred Highway 101—a little longer, but more scenic—but Dingus wanted so *badly* for me to take I-5, displaying constant messages urging me to take every exit I encountered, and either head inland to I-5 or make a U-turn.

As I traveled south, the traffic grew heavier, both lanes in each direction filled with cars, RVs, SUVs pulling tent-trailers, boats, ATVs, dirt bikes, personal watercraft, gliders, and dune buggies, or carrying surfboards, sailboards, kayaks, mountain bikes—all the paraphernalia of California life. Along the ocean, the beaches were lined with cars, surfers dotted the waves, and the colorful kites of parasailors and parasurfers floated above the infinite blue plane of the Pacific.

Pausing at a rest area just before Santa Barbara, I noticed a guy standing beside an old sedan with Oregon plates, holding up a sign saying, "Out of gas, please help." Seeing his family crowded into the car, and imagining their misfortune, I handed him a $20 bill as I passed.

Traffic was stopped dead around Santa Barbara, and I was glad lane-splitting was customary in California. I put on my four-way flashers and slipped carefully between the lanes of stationary traffic for several miles until I finally passed the accident (turning my eyes from that always-disturbing sight). Further south, around Ventura, traffic came to a long standstill once again, and as I kept moving by riding between the lanes, I thought about how awful it would be to be in a car that day, trapped in all that for hours.

Usually, if I was traveling south toward Los Angeles, I would cut over to the Pacific Coast Highway at Ventura and travel home by that picturesque route, but I decided that trying to ride past all those beaches on a holiday weekend would be a bad choice. Dingus, however, started clamoring for me to go that way, directing me toward Mulholland Drive and the PCH, which was a really dumb idea. I continued ignoring him.

After seven long hours and almost 400 miles (631 kilometers) I was home again. I had only been away two weeks this time, though it seemed like forever somehow. I realized this was the first time the 1200GS had ever been there (its odometer now showing 12223 kilometers, 7639 miles). Like me, though, the bike was home, and yet *not* home. We were still in the middle of the tour, still in the middle of the West Coast run, and still in the middle of the Vortex.

That was the uncomfortable conflict I always felt about being at home, physically, but feeling "at work" in every other way—caught between two worlds. On a day off, the conflict could be ignored, but not on a show day. On the morning of the Hollywood Bowl show, I felt disoriented and edgy, time trickling by as I waited for the car to pick me up in early afternoon. Of course, I would rather have ridden to work, and kept up as much of the usual routine as possible, but there was the party afterward, and that would certainly require the consumption of adult beverages. So I left my motorcycle at home, and took a town car to work.

As soon as I arrived backstage I went looking for Liam, and gave him a careful hug, so glad to see him back "with us," in every sense. He told me he was feeling okay now, a little sore from where they'd inserted the angioplasty balloon in his upper thigh. He admitted he was going to try to be more aware of his health and stress level from then on, and try not to smoke too much. "Maybe one or two a day."

Like Red Rocks, the Hollywood Bowl was a legendary venue that we had somehow missed in our thirty years of touring. Built in 1922 as a summer home for the Los Angeles Philharmonic, the roster of performers in the Art Deco bandshell (designed by Frank Lloyd Wright's son) over the years included Al Jolson, Billie Holiday, Nat King Cole, Judy Garland, Frank Sinatra, the Beatles, and the Who, not to forget a famous live recording by Monty Python's Flying Circus.

Standing backstage just before we went on, I was struck by another strange juxtaposition. The steep hillside behind the stage was covered in the typical chaparral of the Santa Monica Mountains—scrub oak, manzanita, and dry grasses all set against the unmistakable Southern California light, now fading into evening. It was the same kind of landscape and light I viewed from the windows of our house, and that I hiked through in Topanga State Park, yet it felt so very different.

It looked so much like home, and yet felt so much like work.

And unfortunately, it really *was* work that night, uphill all the way. The venue was great, the audience was great (the largest so far, with 14,100 people), and from the outside, I think we played pretty well. But on the inside, I had an awful time.

My mother has always complained that I don't smile enough onstage, and it is true that when I watch a Rush concert video, I wince to see such a grim-faced image of intensity and exertion. That is not *me*, not the way I feel in all the hours of my life not spent onstage—but that transformation is what it takes to do my job. For Mom's sake, I always try to smile in posed pictures, and somewhere I learned the trick of looking at the camera and pretending your *dog* was on the other side of that lens. That worked for me; the image of a goofy dog-face helped to bring a genuine smile.

However, behind those drums and in front of an audience, it was a different story. No imaginary dog-face could help me there. A big part of running onto that stage and sitting behind the drums was a kind of *surrender*; I allow myself to be possessed by the performing state of mind. If the word "enthusiasm" derives from "infected by the god," it is equally about being possessed by a demon, a demanding and unforgiving master that spurred and whipped me through every second of the performance.

Sometimes I could goof around with my bandmates during a burnout ending, where I wasn't playing a part or worrying about timekeeping and consistency. But generally, I could not afford to let down my concentration or my physical discipline for a second. That wasn't always easy, especially when Alex, the funniest man in the world, was wandering around the stage in front of me making faces and mouthing jokes. Laughter makes you weak, and I needed all my strength. Sometimes Geddy and I deliberately avoided looking at Alex, our faces angled in every direction but his, so as not to let him break our concentration—our *possession*.

Onstage, I had little room for other feelings or other thoughts, and it was simply impossible for me to perform properly without a total commitment—a commitment that demanded stripping away the barriers, the usual defences between oneself and the world.

Thus it was also a very *vulnerable* mental state, and everything was felt sharply—I always found that even my sense of smell was heightened, catching the whiff of someone lighting a cigarette backstage, or a joint in the audience. Anger and frustration were also very near the surface, and though I could suppress them offstage, up there, such feelings easily became rage, if something or someone interfered with my possession.

That emotional rawness could be personal, too. On a hike with Matt Scannell further west in those same Santa Monica mountains that framed the Hollywood Bowl, he and I once discussed how when we were onstage and someone we loved was in the audience, we tended to be playing for them, in a "dedication" sort of way. Carrie used to think I was oblivious to her when I was playing, but the opposite was true—I always looked for her in the audience, and liked to see her out there smiling and waving at me, my real-life "muse." Of course, primeval man to primeval woman, I was showing off for her.

Carrie was hosting about twenty friends that night, and inevitably, some of them showed up late. She felt obliged to act as hostess, to go over and greet each of the latecomers and see that they found their seats, so I kept looking out to where she was sitting and seeing her gone, or turning away to talk to someone. Yes, there were 14,099 other people out there, but I was playing for *her.*

So I was both nervy and distracted, and because of that, or in addition to that, I didn't think I was playing very well. By the intermission, I was feeling pretty steamed up, and vented to Carrie about it. She didn't really understand what else she could have done; under the circumstances, she felt she had to be the gracious hostess. But I didn't care—it was all about me.

After the show, Michael had arranged a car to take me straight from the stage to the Legion Hall, where I paused in a back room to dry off and change, still steaming and grumbling. I downed a quick Scotch and smoked an illicit cigarette (in a California public building!) in preparation for the next ordeal: the party. Carrie arrived in a separate car and went off to play hostess again, so eventually I took a deep breath and went out to face the dozens of friends and guests, feeling self-conscious and tense. Receiving congratulations from our friends, I was polite and appreciative, only confessing my personal dissatisfaction with the show to people who would understand—fellow musicians Matt and Doane. They assured me my negative feelings were entirely subjective, that it had been a great show, and I'm sure that was true. But their comments didn't make it *feel* any better.

Typical of an after-show party, there was something hallucinatory about the event, faces of friends and strangers swimming into view and saying complimentary things, with me trying to be gracious and sociable, and pay them proper attention, even while other faces swam up with smiles and congratulations. At the end of a party like that, I always ended up feeling dissatisfied with myself, as if I hadn't managed to *give* enough. But it was impossible to have a proper one-on-one connection with a couple of hundred people.

I noticed Nicolas Cage sitting at the bar wearing a nifty little fedora, and went over to say hello and meet his new girlfriend, Alice. On the *Vapor Trails* tour, Nicolas came to see us at the Office Supplies Chain Center Arena in Los Angeles, wearing an outlandish disguise of long wig, beard, and cowboy hat. (He looked bizarre—but at least he didn't look like a movie star, and was left alone. How terrible to be *that* famous.) He had been accompanied by his then-wife, Lisa Marie Presley, and asked me to sign his copy of *Ghost Rider,* which of course, I was honored to do (apart from his other great movies, *Raising Arizona* had been a band-bus favorite).

It was only later, with a twinge of embarrassment and regret, that I realized I had spelled his *name* wrong ("Nicholas"). This time, the first thing I did was apologize for that oversight. He dismissed my concern about it, and said he had been honored just to get my autograph. Imagine.

The surreality heightened as our conversation continued, Alice slipping away occasionally to go outside for a cigarette. Nicolas and I started talking about motorcycles and cars, and knowing he had a fabulous collection of exotics in a Santa Monica hangar, I said, "When can I come and drive your cars?"

"Anytime," he said.

Then, the conversation took a serious turn, as he began to confess that he was having trouble with his acting, "I've made three movies this year, and I've been forgetting lines and blowing them. I've been making movies for thirty years, and I *never* do that. I don't know what to do."

He referred to a documentary he had seen recently about the band Metallica, in which they apparently hired a psychologist for $40,000 a week or something to sort out their problems. "Maybe that's what I need to do," he said.

I suggested that maybe he just needed to break away in a different direction, do some stage acting, learn a play in a foreign language, or find a teacher to kick his ass a little bit. I told him how I had reached a similar crisis after thirty years of drumming, found a teacher—Freddie—and basically started all over. "Maybe you need to find someone like that."

He looked thoughtful. "Yeah, I think I know someone who might help me that way."

As I went off to circulate a little, I wrote down my phone number in my little Mont Blanc notepad and gave it to him, and he wrote down his (under "Nic"). I'm still waiting for that invitation to drive his Aston Martin Vanquish and Porsche Carrera GT.

Michael, the "gay party planner," had used his network of fellow security people to invite any hip celebrities who were in town. He introduced me to the actor and screenwriter Mike White, who had written and costarred in *School of Rock* with the great Jack Black (who couldn't make it that night, but would appear—big time—at a future show).

I told Mike how much I had appreciated *School of Rock,* and especially the part when Jack Black, as the substitute teacher molding his students into a rock band, hands the young drummer a CD of our *2112* album, saying, "One of the great drummers of all time—study up."

"My proudest ever testimonial," I told him. "Only comparable to the time I was mentioned by one of the robots on an episode of 'Mystery Science Theater 3000.'"

He laughed and nodded, appreciating the reference.

Carrie brought over the Canadian fashion photographer Norman-Jean Roy, who turned out to be not only a Rush fan, but a fellow motorcyclist, a Ducati rider. We talked two-wheel stuff for a few minutes, and Michael brought over the drummer from the Foo Fighters, a good band and a good drummer, with long blonde hair like a surfer. We hardly exchanged a word before I was drawn away by Rupert Hine, the English coproducer of our *Presto* and *Roll the Bones* albums. Rupert's bushy "fro" was white now, and he introduced his teenage son, Kingsley, who had been born while Rupert was working with us. I moved around the room and said hello to a few other friends I recognized, wanting to at least greet those I knew and liked, but before long, I had stretched my social skills to the limit. All at once, it seemed, I felt too drained, over it, and retreated to the back room again.

As Satchel Paige advised, "Avoid carrying on in society. The social ramble ain't restful."

Michael put Carrie and me in a car bound for home, and made sure we weren't followed.

The next day, Michael and I met up and rode together down to Chula Vista, south of San Diego, the Megabrewery Amphitheater a stone's throw from the Mexican border. We moved back onto the bus, and back into what had come to pass for normal life. The show went fine, with "no noteworthy flaws or virtues" for me, though the 7,870 people seemed to enjoy it, and that was still the important thing.

That night, Dave drove us north to Bakersfield, with a day off ahead before a show in Mountain View—at an amphitheater I had been able to see from that hilltop barbecue in Los Altos Hills four days earlier.

The morning ride took us over roads that had become familiar to me in the past few years, on my overnight motorcycle getaways into the Sierra Nevada. The day was already hot, approaching 90 degrees, but soon felt cooler as I led Michael up the Kern River on Highway 78. I turned off on the old Kern Canyon Road, now bypassed by a stretch of modern four-lane, and noticed it was becoming increasingly rough and crumbly with disuse and neglect. Up through Kernville, with the scenic Kern River to our left, forested mountains of the Sequoia National Forest humping up all around, and north and ever-higher through Johnsondale and Springerville, then onto little J37 through isolated ranches and live-oak woodlands.

Along there I felt a sudden pain on my neck, on the inch of bare skin between my helmet and leathers, and said "Ow!" out loud. It must have been an insect—a big one, judging by the impact—and my neck began to burn painfully. A little while later, Michael pulled ahead of me, then signaled a turn off the road. Following him over, I saw him rubbing at his neck, and he told me something had hit him in the neck, and "It *hurts*."

"I know," I said, "I got one of those too. But I just kept riding."

"You're just so much more *butch* than I am," he pouted.

"Oh, stop your whimpering or I'll give you something to cry about!"

He made his voice small and breaking, "You know I'm fragile."

I sighed. "I know, sweetie, I know."

At Exeter, we picked up Highway 198 toward Sequoia National Park, traffic growing heavy now with summer tourists heading into the mountains. We wound through the park, twisting up to 6000 feet, the air cool and fragrant among the giant sequoias and bare granite turrets, pale gray in the bright sun. Through the trees we caught glimpses of fabulous vistas to the west, over the flat farmlands of the San Joaquin Valley far below. Among groves of giant sequoias, we passed the General Sherman tree, 275 feet tall, said to be the largest living thing on Earth (the redwoods were taller, but the sequoias were thicker), perhaps 2000 years old.

At one point I noticed I hadn't seen Michael in my mirrors for a while, and pulled over to wait for him. I watched for his headlight, growing nervous as long minutes passed and he didn't appear. With rising anxiety, hoping he hadn't fallen, I turned around and headed back, only to see, with mingled relief and alarm, Michael astride his bike beside the road, behind a park ranger's SUV. I turned around and went back again to wait for him, just off the road, but the first vehicle I saw was the ranger's, who pulled up alongside me.

He said he had pulled over my friend because a park employee had radioed him that a motorcyclist "in a silver helmet" had passed him in a no-passing zone (obviously designed for slower cars and trucks, but which shouldn't *always* apply to quick, agile motorcycists—in Ontario, a double-yellow line was considered a recommendation, not an obligation).

"You don't fit the description," he said, "but just take it easy while you're in the park."

I nodded and said "okay," then when Michael pulled up, we set off again, more carefully now—especially while we were shadowed for miles by yet another ranger vehicle. We were forced to sit impatiently behind lines of slow-moving cars and RVs, not daring to pass them even when there was obviously plenty of clear road ahead.

We had planned to aim for Yosemite National Park that day and find a motel around there, but as the afternoon wore on, it was obvious we weren't going to get that far. Pausing in a little corner of Kings Canyon National Park, where I had stayed a couple of times on my solo journeys (once seeing a black bear bounding across the road ahead of me), we looked over the map, and decided to head down Highway 180 to Fresno and find somewhere to stay there.

It was another busy, winding two-lane road, and soon we joined a line of traffic behind a county police pickup pulling a boat with "SHERIFF" painted across it in big letters. As we descended toward the San Joaquin Valley again, the temperature rose back into the 90s, and it was a torment to dawdle along behind that line of smelly cars and trucks. But there was no point passing all of them only to end up behind the sheriff, and it would probably be foolish to pass him—he might not catch us, but he would certainly have a radio.

When we finally reached Fresno, hot and tired, Michael consulted Doofus's list of accommodations in the area. He led me around the neighborhood of the airport—low office buildings, light industrial complexes and warehouses, and a few motels. We settled on a Holiday Inn, because it was there, and checked in after 477 kilometers, almost 300 miles. Long miles.

I felt better after a drink, a swim in the pool, and a shower, and made some journal notes.

A new *low* for us—an airport Holiday Inn. In Fresno . . .

Both of us struck by stinging insects today—mine still hurts. Adding to my many scars now: left elbow scraped on a road-case or light as I ran offstage the other night, upper right arm and right thigh from my fall on the riser in Portland, those bedbug bites on my legs still lingering, and painful split calluses on my hands.

Probably officially the most tired I've been yet on this tour. On reflection, not the most tired *ever,* as I've definitely been "here" before.

I had definitely been in Fresno before, too, as we often used to play there in the "olden days." One memorable time, in the early '90s, I had rented a Range Rover in Los Angeles and driven with Liam up to Fresno for a show there, then, on a day off, got up early and drove to Yosemite National Park. At the Ahwanee Lodge, in the heart of that magnificent valley of granite walls and domes and spectacular waterfalls, I met up with my guide, Kevin Anderson. He still lived in California then, and also brought along his wife-to-be Rebecca, the first time we met.

It was March or so, with wisps of snow remaining under the trees, and very few people in the park. Kevin toured me around some of the main scenic attractions, and on some short hikes into the woods. It was and is one of the most beautiful places I've ever seen. In the late afternoon we said goodbye, and I drove the Range Rover on to Sacramento, where it would be picked up by the rental company and where I would play the next night.

This time, Michael and I left Fresno early on another hot morning, heading west across the irrigated farmlands of the San Joaquin Valley. Once, my eye was caught by the unusual sight of a peacock in a farmyard, presumably someone's decorative pet. A roadrunner zipped along the roadside, and a family of California quail dashed across the road ahead, their natty black plumes bobbing above their heads.

Picking up little Highway 33 (a favorite road of mine at its southern end, around Ojai), we ran north to Los Banos (which I once encountered in a crossword puzzle, with the clue "town near the geographical center of California." I had to look it up) and onto a short stretch of I-5. Doofus and Dingus were about to face their greatest challenge so far—with mixed results.

On my first overnight visit with Kevin Anderson, in Livermore in 1992, he had taken me for a morning driving tour up to the Lick Observatory, and I remembered a steep and winding road from the west side of Mount Hamilton. On the map, a gray line appeared to go all the way through from the east side of the mountain, and it looked extremely curvy and interesting. Michael had programmed that route into the GPS units, but on the day, they couldn't find the Del Puerto Canyon Road.

The road we had hoped was it ended abruptly at a construction site, a soon-to-be gated subdivision and golf course. We asked one of the workers about the Del Puerto Canyon Road, and he steered us right (the old fashioned Global Positioning System), sending us one more exit north.

The yellow grass foothills (the "lion-colored hills," I called them in *Traveling Music*) were dotted with the dark green of live-oak trees. We climbed higher into dense conifers, leaving behind the few isolated ranches, and seeing very few other vehicles. Steep canyons led off to the sides, Washington Canyon, Deer Park Canyon, Adobe Canyon, and the dry landscape seemed to shimmer and buzz with stillness and heat.

The Del Puerto Canyon Road ended at the San Antonio Valley Road, which ran south, then gradually turned to the west. Its curves became sharper and steeper as it led us up past the Burnt Hills to Mount Hamilton. Near the summit, we saw the huddle of domes and outbuildings of the Lick Observatory, then began to wind our way slowly down, switchback after switchback, on what was now called the Mount Hamilton Road. We encountered an occasional car climbing toward us, some of them widening the switchbacks by wandering carelessly, lazily, and alarmingly into our lane. As I noted later, "Color *inside* the lines, people!"

For about twenty miles it was one of the twistiest roads I had ever ridden, and again and again we negotiated slow, sharp turns with steep grades between them, always in first or second gear. By the time we descended into San Jose, the constant effort of braking and downshifting had my wrists and elbows aching. A short freeway jaunt carried us to work, and Doofus and Dingus handled that easily enough.

The Shoreline Amphitheater in Mountain View was one of the older purpose-built outdoor venues, under a tall white tent-like roof. When it was first opened under Bill Graham's name, in 1986, the Shoreline made a welcome alternative to the indoor venues in San Francisco, the aptly named Cow Palace, a horrible sounding barn of a place with no reserved seats, or the Oakland Coliseum across the bay, which was a nice enough arena, but it was in Oakland—a menacing inner city in the '70s and '80s.

As a band, we had a checkered relationship with San Francisco anyway, dating from the early days. Bill Graham had a chokehold on concert promotion in the Bay Area, and when we first appeared as an opening act for his company at the old Winterland Theater, Graham's people all seemed to treat us with a kind of superior, jaded, "cooler-than-thou" attitude. Typically, in a service industry, a hotel, a rock band, or a concert promotion company, the way management treats its staff is the way the staff treats colleagues and clients. Graham's people were peremptory, unfriendly, and seemed scornful of a lowly Canadian opening act.

When a stagehand carelessly toppled one of Alex's Marshall stacks after our set, all of their crew closed ranks against our crew and denied everything. When our road manager at the time, Howard, took it up with Graham's production office, wanting the damages added to our meager fee, the guilty stagehand had mysteriously disappeared, and they brushed us off.

We held a grudge against the "Bill Graham Presents" organization after that, and other gigs with them did nothing to change our first impression. I remember lining up for a crew meal one day, as we used to do before every show in those days (no Frenchie back then), and a stagehand in line behind me grumbled, "I thought this was supposed to be for the *crew*." Apparently the musicians who were selling the tickets weren't entitled to eat.

Another time in San Francisco, our van (the "Funcraft") was broken into and robbed of some personal stuff, which left a bad memory, and generally, in those days it seemed to us that we frequently encountered a passive-aggressive version of West Coast "mellowness" there.

A few years later, when we had risen to a headliner and were selling out two nights at the Cow Palace, Bill Graham asked our agent, Bill Elson (an unusually literate member of that oft-maligned profession, Bill introduced me to the novels of John Dos Passos), to bring him to our dressing room and introduce him. We were polite but cool toward the great Bill Graham, and he remarked to Bill Elson, "They're very quiet, aren't they?"

Over the years, I came to appreciate and even enjoy the city of San Francisco, for its scenic beauty, its culture, and (like Los Angeles) its *sur-*

roundings, but the city still remained a little tarnished by those early memories.

One time in the mid '80s, I asked the concierge at the downtown Hyatt (famous among us for a memorable scene in Mel Brooks's *High Anxiety*) if I could take my bicycle on the mass-transit system, MUNI, out to Golden Gate Park. He assured me I could, but as I lifted my bike over the turnstiles and into one of the subway cars, a stentorian voice came over the P.A., "Bicycles are *not* permitted on the MUNI system. Will the person with the bicycle please remove it *immediately*."

Yikes! Embarrassed, and feeling about two-feet tall, I carried my bicycle out of there, and rode out to the park instead.

That day I cycled around Haight-Ashbury and Golden Gate Park, then across the Golden Gate Bridge and back. While I was exploring under the bridge, around Fort Point, I discovered some abandoned concrete pillboxes from World War II. Crawling inside one of them and looking out at the ocean through a narrow slit, I imagined the soldiers in 1942 and 1943, watching through the fog for the expected fleet of Japanese destroyers. In that chilling setting, I could begin to understand the fear that gripped the West Coast back then, the feeling of defenselessness and paranoia that had led to the internment of people of Japanese descent in California (and in British Columbia, too, Canadians sometimes forget).

The first time we played the Shoreline Amphitheater, on the *Presto* tour in 1990, I arrived there by bicycle with my brother Danny, who had flown down from Vancouver (with his bicycle) to spend a few days traveling the West Coast with me by bus and bicycle. On a day off after that show, staying in Newport Beach, Danny and I rode our bikes down to the mission at San Juan Capistrano. I had heard about that place all my life, where the swallows returned every spring. (I had always wanted to write a song about that, until I learned there already *was* one—"When the Swallows Come Back to Capistrano," written by Leon Rene in 1939.) My maternal grandmother had a watercolor of the mission circled by swallows, painted by her Welsh father around the time of World War I (she also gave me his collection of poems by Tennyson, and I wish I knew more about him and his obviously artistic spirit).

Unfortunately, the mission of San Juan Capistrano itself betrayed my imaginary vision of it, for it was surrounded by commercial and suburban clutter. I realized that sometimes it was better not to visit the places of your dreams—better to leave them as exotic, soft-focus mirages of romance.

The next day on that 1990 tour, we began a two-night stand in Costa Mesa, the last two shows of the tour. Since the crew wouldn't have to break down and load out after the first night, we had a big party in a private section of a local nightclub. The theme of our party was the movie *Moon Over Parador* (another bus classic we could recite from memory), with the movie playing on television screens, and the DJ dressed like the puppet dictator.

On the fictional Caribbean island of Parador, the national cocktail was called a "puna," and when the military dictator of Parador died, the evil power-behind-the-throne, played by Raul Julia, scowled and said, "Too many damn punas." So naturally, the official drink of our end-of-tour party was the puna, whipped up with cases of strong drink and tropical fruits by our irrepressible lighting director (and former road manager), Howard.

Danny learned that night what too many damn punas meant, and the next day, when he was supposed to fly home, I had to go to his room and box up his bicycle for him while he lay in bed paralyzed and groaning. I cycled off to work, and Andrew, our assistant at the time, had loaded Danny and his bike into a car bound for the airport.

Michael and I arrived at the Shoreline in mid-afternoon, after a hard-won 341 kilometers (just over 200 miles). I changed my clothes, changed my oil, had a shower, checked my e-mails, and went into the usual show-day routine. The show that night went well, with 9,178 presumably happy people. (On the book tour side of things, I learned we had sold 132 copies of *Traveling Music* and thirty-five copies of *Ghost Rider* that night, and that was satisfying.) Frenchie made a dryers appearance wearing a skimpy orange-and-black ladybug costume, complete with black tutu. I caught an occasional glimpse of Carrie's mother, Marian, when the lights from the stage shone out on the audience. At the end, as I stood to wave, I gave her a personal smile and blew her a quick kiss before I ran for the bus.

As in Portland, Dave drove us straight to the next venue, an amphitheater in Concord only sixty-two miles away, and we parked there for the night. In a futile attempt to catch up on my pathetically skimpy journal notes of late, I wrote that usual lament, "What a ride to have absolutely *no* notes on! Falling so behind—missing so much."

For the next day, I designed us another "mystery tour," using the Northern California road atlas and highlighting tiny little back roads that didn't even show on the state map. We rode to the summit of Mount Diablo, joining dozens of bicycles on what seemed to be a common Saturday pilgrimage, climbing to a magnificent 3800-foot viewpoint overlooking the whole Bay Area. We twisted our way down to the south side of the mountain, and I led Michael on a return visit to the exquisite classic car museum at Blackhawk (richly described in a letter to Brutus in *Ghost Rider*).

From there, we circled back around to Concord on the narrowest of roads, often just one lane, winding through forests of eucalyptus and live-oak and isolated ranches. This time Doofus and Dingus rose to the occasion heroically, as they helped us navigate those remote little back roads— often unsigned and even unnamed—we could never have found otherwise. Even "the boys," as we were calling Doofus and Dingus by then, were sometimes a little strained by the effort, and might not figure out the right road until after we had taken the *wrong* one, but the map would have been no help at all. All things considered, those boys were okay.

By the time we got back to the bus, we had ridden only sixty miles, but I felt deeply tired, my right arm sore from two days of mountain riding, braking and shifting constantly. After a shower, I stretched out on my bed and passed out until my alarm went off five minutes before soundcheck. I got up and went straight to the stage, still rubbing sleep out of my eyes as I greeted the crew guys and my bandmates.

The Big City Newspaper Pavilion was another of the older amphitheaters, built in 1975 from a design by a then-unknown Frank Gehry (another Canadian living in Santa Monica), who also presided over its renovation in 1996. Best known for his adventurous, metallic structures like the Guggenheim Museum in Bilbao, Spain and the new Disney Hall in Los Angeles, Gehry had worked on some more ordinary buildings as well. To my eyes, this one didn't look any different from the other "sheds," as they were often called in the touring business. Sitting behind my drums at soundcheck, I looked out on the roofed-over part, then out across the lawn and way back to the yellow hills beyond ("Crayola gold," I called them)—such a familiar California sight.

During the show that night, the California theme continued. A couple of times, that heady fragrance of jasmine wafted across the stage from somewhere (flashing back to Sunset Boulevard and the opening of this story), and another time I was sure I could smell the perfume of the Sierra forests, a piney, sun-warmed spice.

The show was another good one—not magic, perhaps, but certainly competent—and the 9,877 people seemed to enjoy it too, cheering and smiling. Even though the show had gone well, it was still hard, and riding on the bus that night, I felt a deep fatigue and the physical ache of overexertion—after two hard shows in a row, and four in the past five days. My hands were especially sore, with a cracked callus on my left hand baring tender flesh to burning sweat (the Bag Balm was too gooey to put on unless I wasn't going to be *touching* anything, so that made it difficult—to read, for example).

Basically, I hurt everywhere, and all that pain was affecting my mood.

It didn't help that the bus seemed to be tired, too. The fridge had died that day, part of the ongoing electrical problems that had plagued us. When the air conditioner in my stateroom kicked on, it was like a particle accelerator suddenly sapping the electrical grid, dimming all the lights and spiking the television. We had also been afflicted by septic woes, a sulfurous reek rising from the holding tank that had to be subdued by equally acrid chemicals.

The stereo was continuing to be difficult, and when I tried to calm myself by playing a CD, it skipped and made a horrible digital scratching noise, butchering Jeff Buckley's music and increasing my irritation. I punched the CD player a couple of times, which didn't help, though I noticed the unit was inset a little further in its cabinet.

The clock in the main salon had never kept time. The coffeemaker was slow. We were out of Macallan!

What next? When I announced that I had given up, and was going to have a shower, Dave told me he was out of water, and needed to stop at a truck stop and fill up.

A journal note:

I am *weary,* body and soul. Walking the line, it feels like.

Look out world—or everybody in mine, anyway. I'm remaining cool, though, not freaking on anybody. Note that I seem to have a "check valve" lately that lets me get angry at a *situation* but stop short of blame.

Don't know why I always want people who work for me to be my friends—a good thing, but complicated and delicate. Friendship and loyalty are more important than just doing the job well—but all are preferable.

Dave parked that night in a truck stop near Salinas, and wanting an early start the next morning, I dragged myself out of bed at 7:30. After breakfast, Dave and Michael and I unloaded our bikes and rode together to the racetrack at Laguna Seca, where Brian Catterson had invited us to attend the Superbike races that Sunday as guests of his magazine, *Cycle World*.

Doofus and Dingus couldn't quite manage to navigate us to the racetrack on that foggy Sunday morning, telling us we had "arrived" as we rode past on a neighboring road. So we flailed around in the fog (literal and metaphorical) for a while until we found our way in. The fog burned away into hot sunshine, and Brian led us around the giant "rock festival" of the racetrack, the pit area, the midway of motorcycle manufacturer displays and aftermarket vendors, and various vantage points around the track itself, including the famous Corkscrew turn, which I had seen so often on televised races from Laguna Seca.

The racers themselves I could only describe as "heroic," for their awe-inspiring displays of bravery, talent, and technique. Through each split second of a twenty-eight-lap race, every shift, every braking point, every tactic, had to be performed at their highest mental and physical ability. They had to be *perfect*—a single missed shift, late braking point, or miscalculated lean angle could cost them a position, a race, a crash and painful injury—even their lives. Worse yet, they could be taken out just as easily by someone else's mistake.

So much of that close-quarter racing was psychological warfare, too, as the pursuing rider kept up a running attack, braking a bit later into a turn and passing for a few seconds, then surrendering as the other rider pulled ahead on a better line. It was all about sending a message: "I'm on you."

Inevitably, I compared it to drumming and performing, but the consequences were so much more severe—however bad I felt when I made a mistake, embarrassment wasn't liable to *kill* me. But I did think I knew how those guys would feel on a race day, or while waiting in their trailers for the starting time.

By the time Dave and Michael and I got back to the bus at the truck stop in Salinas and loaded the bikes back into the trailer, it was early evening and I was beat. As Dave drove north toward the next day's show near Sacramento, I sprawled on my bed, making a few notes ("So nice to be tired, and not have to *do* anything—then, it's a kind of luxury"). A delicious fragrance suddenly filled the bus, and I wondered, "Who's eating something good up there?"

Then I realized we must be passing through Gilroy, Garlic Capital of the World, and I went forward to see if the smell was making anyone else hungry. Michael was assigned to get on-line and find us an In 'n' Out Burger, and we completed our "all guy" day with a feast of burgers, fries, and milkshakes.

Dave parked the bus that night in Stockton, and I gave myself (and Michael) the luxury of sleeping in a little bit. In late morning, Michael and I headed up into the Sierras again, or at least the foothills, on another hot, sunny day. We rode through a lot of woodland and quaint little towns, including Nashville number four, another Auburn, the irresistibly named villages of Rough and Ready, and Cool, California.

We were also in Gold Rush country around there, Calaveras County (as in the Mark Twain tale about the "Celebrated Jumping Frog"), and we rode through Placerville (formerly known as Old Dry Diggings and Hangtown, for its brand of frontier justice), and Grass Valley, whose most famous mines, the Empire and North Star, had produced $150 million of gold in a century.

"SIGN BROKEN, MESSAGE INSIDE," was a repeat from Elkins, West Virginia, but the first church sign for a while.

That night's workplace was an amphitheater in Marysville, just north of Sacramento. We hadn't covered that much distance, 252 kilometers, 157 miles, but it had been a long, hot ride, much of it through fairly dense and demanding traffic.

On especially hot days like that, we sometimes called ahead and requested a special treat from Frenchie, giving him time to send the runner out for the necessary ingredients to make . . . strawberry milkshakes! (The first time I asked Frenchie if he could prepare that delicacy, on the equally hot summer days of the *Vapor Trails* tour, he told me that in all his years of cooking for touring artists, from Frank Sinatra to Pearl Jam, no one had ever asked him to make a milkshake.) As I savored the result, I made a journal note, "Hot day, lot of traffic, but well rested (for once) and good humored. Frenchie's strawberry milkshake—aah."

The corporate name of that venue was the Sleep Train Amphitheater, apparently after a chain of mattress stores. Michael and Dave and I were about to spend our fourth night in a row sleeping on the bus, and it occurred to me that *we* were the Sleep Train.

My friend Chris, from the Sabian cymbal company, visited that afternoon. He and I had met during my first visit to the factory in New Brunswick, and because Chris worked out of the West Coast office in Los Angeles, he became my main man at the company—and soon, a good friend. (No matter how hard I tried, I kept making new friends!) An Iowa native, a fellow motorcyclist (Ducati Multistrada), and a fine drummer in his own right (educated at Berklee School of Music), Chris's career path had led him into the musical-instrument "hardware" side of the business—one way in which a musician's risky livelihood could become more stabilized.

Q: What do you call a drummer without a girlfriend?
A: Homeless.

Another avenue for a determined musican was exemplified by Chris's companion that day, a mutual friend named Jamie Borden. Jamie was an excellent drummer who played with a Las Vegas lounge singer, part of a great band that specialized in classic rock covers, at one of the nightclubs in the Bellagio. Watching Jamie play was an inspiration to me, because he put such pride, energy, and art into his playing, and obviously derived such satisfaction from it. On the side, Jamie worked on original music and made instructional DVDs, and thus had made his own path to fulfillment and success. Before becoming a full-time musician, Jamie had been a policeman, of all things—"Before I crossed over to the dark side," as he put it. (I laughed and said, "The other way around, I would think!")

Jamie's band had a residency in Reno that summer, which Jamie was enjoying, as he was a keen outdoorsman. He told me a story about fly-fishing in a Sierra Nevada stream, and seeing a young bear sniffing around nearby. Before Jamie's astonished eyes, a larger bear came bounding down the hill, roaring loudly, and attacked and killed the younger one. Slowly and carefully, Jamie backed away and got out of there.

On the bus after the Sacramento show, I wrote down my review of the night's work, "Good show, happy audience, smiling girls, but kind of 'edgy' for me—never really settled."

I put on Sinatra's *Everything Happens to Me*, then James Brown's *Live at the Apollo*, skipping straight to my favorite, the extended version of "It's a Man's, Man's, Man's World."

Michael laughed at this juxtaposition, shaking his head. "I'd love to know what goes through your head when you're picking the music you're going to play."

I folded my arms and frowned. "You're criticizing me again, aren't you? Nothing I do is ever good enough for you. I just want to hear whatever suits my mood, that's all. Is that all right with you?"

He held up his hands, "Whoa, baby, yeah. Whatever you want. But . . . why don't you ever *dance* with me anymore?"

We both laughed, then soon crept off to our beds on the Sleep Train.

As soon as I looked out the bus window in the morning, I knew right where we were: a truck stop south of Bakersfield, near the junction of I-5 and state highway 99. I had often stopped there for gas on my solo travels. And once again, I would ride solo that day, as Michael and I went our separate ways toward home for the day off.

I didn't need any help from Dingus that day, but let him keep me company, showing distances and compass directions as I followed familiar, favorite routes toward Los Angeles. After a few miles on I-5 South, I turned off at Frazier Park and rode west on Lockwood Valley Road, a remote and sometimes rough route toward the aforementioned Highway 33, also described in *Traveling Music*, running south through the Los Padres National Forest to Ojai.

Tall clumps of brilliant yellow flowers lined that road, filling the air with a strong, heady fragrance that was almost intoxicating, like lilac and jasmine. For months I had tried to learn the name of those flowers, searching in field guides and on-line, until I finally found them in a book called *Roadside Plants of Southern California*. Spanish broom, they were called, and they had not shown up in the usual field guides because they were a Mediterranean species, planted along California roadsides in the

1920s. Like other such introduced plants—purple loosestrife in the East, or kudzu in the South—they were pretty, but soon dominated the native plants until they were considered a pest. I was sorry to learn that, but still loved their smell.

Then it was over to the coast at Ventura, and south on the Pacific Coast Highway, the ocean glittering beside me, to Sunset Boulevard once again, and back in my own garage. After 298 kilometers, 186 miles, the 1200's odometer now showed 14022 kilometers, 8763 miles. Added to the 2500 or so miles I had put on the 1150, I had now ridden well over 11,000 miles on this tour.

The next day, July 14, we played at the Cellular Telephone Network Amphitheater (one of the older such venues, formerly known as Irvine Meadows) down in Orange County. I was able to enjoy a leisurely morning at home before setting off in the afternoon to ride the sixty miles down to Irvine. I also collected a church sign in Venice, just to show all the dumb ones weren't in the so-called Bible Belt, "GOD DOESN'T CALL THE QUALIFIED, HE QUALIFIES THE CALLED."

After a long, boring freeway slog, I arrived at work and settled back into the bus. Dave was all disgruntled, and told me he had been stopped on his bike by the local constabulary just outside the venue, as he was setting off for a ride with a couple of local Harley riders. The cop had confiscated Dave's "beanie" helmet, illegal in California, with his collection of rude stickers, and Dave was upset about that and determined to get it back.

Michael told me Jack Black was coming to the show that night, and during the intermission, he called me out of the Bubba-Gump room to meet Jack. Shaking his hand, I told him how I had met Mike White the previous week, and told him how pleased I had been by the reference in *School of Rock*. Jack said, "That was *my* idea!"

I also mentioned how we had originally wanted him to play the part of the "awakening dreamer" in our opening film, the part Jerry Stiller had ended up doing ("What did they put in my tea?"). At the time, we had been told by Jack's people that he wasn't available, but typically, he had never even heard about it. He spread his arms and said, with obvious sincerity, "I am at your service."

Michael and I told him about the dryer ritual, how we sometimes had guests come out onstage to put quarters in the dryers, and asked if he would like to do it. He said, "Well, yeah!," and Michael said he would tell him when.

At the beginning of *2112*, I saw Jack come bounding out from stage left in an improvised pirate costume—skull-and-crossbones hat, eye-patch, and some kind of multicolored skirt thing—do a somersault, and strike some "rock poses" as the crowd roared its delight. He fell to his knees in front of Geddy at the front of the stage, acting out more rock poses, then came back to the dryers and started to take his clothes off. "Oh-oh," I thought, "Is this where somebody gets *arrested*?"

Fortunately he stopped at his boxers, then climbed on top of the dryers, just as the "starman" logo appeared on the screen. Standing on the dryers, his pudgy body framed in the lights and his boxers displaying the classic plumber's crack, he struck the same pose as the naked man on the screen, arms up and hands splayed in resistance to oppression.

While I played on, I looked over at him in profile, and saw his face intent against the lights, immersed in the role, then he jumped down again, gathered up his clothes, and did a somersault offstage. The audience loved it, of course, laughing and cheering, and Geddy and I exchanged head-shaking smiles of disbelief. Before the encore, when we stood backstage for a quick swallow of water and a towel-off, Geddy said to me, "That wasn't just an *appearance*—that was some kind of performance art!"

After the show, as Dave and Michael and I drove away, apparently Jack stayed behind for a long time with Alex and Geddy, totally "on" in a way that owed nothing to drinks or drugs, just his own inimitable personality. Michael told me that when he was escorting Jack around during the show, out to the front-of-house mixer to watch from there for a while, Jack had been *delighted* to be recognized, exchanging high-fives and rock whoops with audience members. The character you saw in his movies, from *Shallow Hal* to *Orange County* (coincidentally, as that's where our show was) to *School of Rock,* was, quite simply, him.

And that unforgettable performance from him was part of another memorable show from all of us. As I noted later, "If not *great*, then definitely really good."

That, of course, meant it had been another magic show.

And the next day's ride continued that streak, a day off that developed into an adventure I would later describe as "my favorite day."

We slept on the bus near Ehrenburg, Arizona, then ran north through the desert along the Colorado River, through dusty little Parker and the redneck Riviera of Lake Havasu City. A short ride on I-40 brought us to Kingman, where a brief shower cooled us off for a few miles, then onto a perfect stretch of old Route 66 (which appears in *Ghost Rider* and *Traveling Music*) through the bypassed ghost towns of Hackberry, Valentine, and Peach Springs.

Several times over the years, I had passed a sign along there pointing north to Supai, with a little road leading off, and I had always wanted to take that road. Edward Abbey, Wallace Stegner, and others had written about that place, where you parked at the rim of the Grand Canyon and were led on sure-footed horses down to Supai, on the floor of the canyon, part of the Havasupai Indian Reservation. Michael and I would not have time for the overnight experience, but at least we could ride up there and have a look at a part of the Grand Canyon I had never seen before.

I had thought there was a gas station near the turnoff, but when none appeared, and Doofus and Dingus said there were none nearby, we back-tracked a little to Peach Springs to fill up. Then we headed north on that empty little road, through an empty big country, for about sixty miles. The road ended at a parking lot, and we stopped to take in the "usual" breathtaking view of the canyon. Dozens of cars were parked there, but there was hardly anyone around—just a couple of cowboys, a few horses, and the occasional tourist helicopter circling overhead—so all those people must have already descended into the canyon.

Looking over the Arizona state map on the bus the night before, I had noticed a dotted gray line indicating an unpaved road across the Coconino Plateau, just south of the reservation. It seemed to continue for forty or fifty miles and emerge at the main highway that led from Williams up to Grand Canyon Village. But no matter how much Michael enlarged the CD-ROM map on his computer, it didn't show that road, and it wasn't shown on the official national park map either. But if a road existed, we were determined to find it.

On the previous tour, *Vapor Trails*, in 2002, when Michael and I had ridden with Brian Catterson between Gallup, New Mexico, and Salt Lake City, we had set out to find a similar little road across the Navajo reservation in northeastern Arizona. We soon realized that road wasn't nearly as evident on the ground as it had been on the map, and the ungraded track got rougher and rougher. Riding up out of a dry streambed, over eroded dirt and boulders, I did a gentle somersault off my bike, and Michael's rear wheel sank to the hub in soft sand.

An automotive journalist was writing about riding with a female rally driver. Their car slid off a snowy road and overturned, and while they were climbing out, she had said, "Adventures suck when you're having them." I knew that feeling.

At one point, our dwindling track simply *ended*, leaving us in the middle of the desert, apparently stranded. The highway we were trying to reach was visible through my binoculars, but there was no obvious way to get there. We didn't have enough gas to go all the way back, and Michael was half-joking about using the satellite phone to summon an airlift rescue. The resourceful Brian led us back to another little dirt track, which had looked unlikely, but eventually led us out to the highway.

This time, Michael and I found a small dirt road leading to the east off the Supai road, in the same general area as the one shown on the state map, so we started following it. The gravel track soon dwindled to a two-rut wagon road, then ended at a gate. The fence surrounded an apparently abandoned ranch, a yard around a small house and barn, and a couple of cottonwood trees.

The road *appeared* to continue beyond the gate, but we didn't like to go through what seemed to be someone's private property. No vehicles were parked near the house, so we finally decided to take the chance. We opened the gate, closed it behind us, then rode across the fenced-in area, and through another gate on the other side.

The Coconino Plateau, at 7000 feet, was completely treeless, carpeted in inches-high sage and grasses that rolled gently to the far horizon like a windswept prairie. We still couldn't trust that this was the right road, or if it was, that it actually went all the way through, so we rode forward knowing that we might have to turn back. On days like that I always carried my little red plastic gas can, filled with a precious gallon of spare gas and strapped on the back of the bike, and I constantly kept track of how much fuel we would need to backtrack to Peach Springs if need be.

Often Doofus and Dingus showed nothing but the arrow of our location on an unmarked screen, then they would suddenly announce, "Turn Left at Intersection, 1.25 miles." Sure enough, the wagon track would divide, we would follow the left tine of the fork, and for a while, our screens would show the route again.

We moved slowly eastward across that wide open country, the trail alternating from gravel to dirt, to rocks and stones, to occasional patches of mud. We rode through sunshine and patchy white clouds, but an ominous wall of darkness filled the eastern sky ahead of us. Occasional veins of lightning on the horizon made me even more nervous about this choice of route.

A herd of wild horses, a stallion and four mares, came trotting from the north, pausing to look at us for a moment, then galloping away with puffs of dust under their hooves. I smiled inside my helmet at that beautiful sight, and paused for a moment as Michael pulled up beside me. I asked him if he had his camera with him, and he shook his head, "No, I didn't bring it, but I sure wish I had. You?"

I shook my head, "Me too. Of all the days not to have a camera!"

A little later we passed another stallion and his harem, five wild horses silhouetted against the darkening sky. These ones ran along beside us for a minute or so, and made such a surreal vision in that dramatic light, before they veered away and off to the south.

We came to a stop at a "No Trespassing" sign blocking the way ahead, which appeared to end at a huddle of wooden ranch buildings. A dirt road branched off to the south, but we were pretty sure we wanted to go straight east—through that ranch. We paused to consider, and I said that maybe we had to go around that way, to the south. Michael did some computing with Doofus, and said it was 100 miles to go around, and that our route seemed to be clearly east.

Beside one of the ranch buildings, we saw a man loading hay bales into a pickup, and agreed that I would stay there while Michael went to talk to him. A few minutes later, he returned, saying, "He was just like the Marlboro man! I asked him about the highway, and he said, 'About twenty miles that way. Go ahead.' "

Much relieved, both for our "safe passage" and the knowledge that we actually *were* going in the right direction, we continued on. I was glad when we passed under a row of pylons and power lines (electricity for the park, probably), then over the tracks of the Grand Canyon Railway. Then, all of a sudden, we were back on pavement (yahoo!) and heading north for Grand Canyon Village.

Pines began to close in around the road, smelling so delicious in that high-elevation air, sharpened by the ozone of a recent storm. As further evidence, sometimes the roadside was lined with white patches of hail, melting away like old snow. Our luck held out, and we made it through that gauntlet of dark clouds and lightning. The parking area around the Visitor Center was packed, and Michael agreed to stay with the bikes while I walked the quarter-mile to get my "passport stamp."

Back in March of that year, when Ray had sent me the first version of the summer's itinerary, I noticed the day off between Irvine and Phoenix, and called Michael right away to try to book us cabins at the Grand Canyon for that night of July 15. Even four months earlier, accommodations had been scarce for that busy time of year, but he had managed to reserve a couple of cabins—though now, as we waited at the front desk of the Bright Angel Lodge, it appeared they had only booked one.

Eventually they came up with two cabins, and we hauled our gear over to them. I phoned to ask about a dinner reservation at the more upscale lodge, El Tovar, but the only sitting they had available was at six o'clock. That left us only half an hour for a quick Macallan, a shower, and a short journal note:

> 56 miles of dirt altogether—and we *made* it.
>> Exciting, especially, as usual, when it's over. At the time it's often just *scary*.
>> I thought of the phrase "my favorite day," and it may have been. One of them, anyway.
>> Pretty magical. And adventurous. And . . . successful.
>> And what a view—though I've hardly had time to look at it.

I gave Michael the crew knock, and we followed the asphalt walkway along the edge of the Canyon. I showed him the cabin right on the Rim where I had stayed for four days in December 2003, finishing the first draft of *Traveling Music*, and we passed the rooms in the Bright Angel Lodge where Michael and I had stayed during *Vapor Trails*. We laughed at a redundant sign beside a faucet on the lawn, "NON POTABLE WATER NOT FOR DRINKING."

The waitress wore a name tag saying she was Maria from Brazil, but when Michael asked her where in Brazil she was from, she said she was actually Eva from Greece. She laughed, "I guess they had this name tag left over!"

After dinner, we had a leisurely walk back along the Rim in the moonless night, the canyon still visible by the light of the brilliant stars. A bright dot of manmade light gleamed from the North Rim, ten miles away and 1000 feet higher (215 miles away by road), where all had been dark the previous December, the North Rim lodge closed for the winter. After such a long, hard day, 576 kilometers, 360 miles, we soon said good night and went back to our little cabins.

In bed by ten, I caught up on several hours of missed sleep and was still awake by seven, walking back up to El Tovar for breakfast. I was delighted by the cool morning air and the light-filled canyon under a translucent sky. On the way back, I bought a Coke from a vending machine and delivered it to Michael's cabin with a loud crew knock and a call, "room service!"

We were on the road again by nine, following the park road east along the South Rim, through the shadows of pines and junipers. We paused at the Desert View area to admire architect Mary Colter's final masterpiece, the Indian Lookout Tower. It was a tall, tapering cylinder of natural stone, a fantasy of the Native West like her Hopi House beside El Tovar, and the small stone lookouts along the Rim—Lookout Studio (which I had looked out on as a snow-frosted vision from my desk during that December writing retreat) and Hermit's Rest. We continued east to Cameron, then turned south toward Flagstaff. For some reason, Doofus and Dingus sent us around in circles there (operator error, I suspect), and as we finally headed south on the little road I had chosen, a thin gray line unnamed on the map, a line of rainclouds was clearly headed our way.

July 16 was another one of those significant days for me, Jackie's birthday (it would have been her forty-ninth). In recent years, I had been trying to keep those days to myself, not wanting to make others uncomfortable or, strangely, to upset myself with *their* sympathy. But one way or another, that effort didn't always work.

Earlier that year, on Selena's birthday of April 22 (would have been her twenty-sixth), we were rehearsing in Toronto, and I just tried to go through the day, not mentioning it to the guys at work. Alex's wife, Charlene, had dropped by the rehearsal hall that day with their little grandson in the car seat, and a cute little baby was not something I wanted to share on that particular day. When Charlene asked me how I was, as a polite greeting, I mumbled something noncommital, and I'm sure I just seemed rude—or at least, weird.

And in Flagstaff, when Michael and I stopped and finally got our route sorted out, I was grumbling as I pulled on my rainpants.

"Do you think they'll fit over your cranky-pants?" Michael said.

I had to laugh a little, then said, "I've got a reason to be cranky—it's Jackie's birthday today."

Michael nodded, "Hey, I never said you didn't have lots of *reasons* to be cranky!"

The rain came down heavily, though the riding remained enjoyable on a lonely road through forested hills and valleys, past the pretty Mormon Lake and the little towns of Happy Jack, Strawberry, Pine, and Payson. On that gloomy day, in my gloomy state of mind, I was thinking of something Michael and I had discussed a couple of nights before. He had mentioned a musician acquaintance of ours, and I told him that another friend of ours was working with him, and he was behaving like a "temperamental artist." I said to Michael, "I get the feeling he might be a *dick*."

Michael shook his head. "I don't know. When people don't know somebody, and he doesn't do what they want him to, they can think that. Hey—some people who don't know you think *you're* a dick."

What a terrible thought! No doubt it was true, if only because I didn't make myself available to all those who wanted a piece of me, but I hated the idea that people who didn't even know me could think badly of me. It rankled on my mind all that day, and remained a disturbing thought for many days after that, echoing in my thoughts sometimes as I rode through the day: "People who don't know you think you're a dick."

After a show, I made a journal note.

Thinking tonight how it bothers me that people should think ill of me. I give them *everything* onstage, every night, but some want—demand—more. Another unbridgeable divide.

Humphrey Bogart quote: "The only thing I owe the public is a good performance."

Our rainy route was descending gradually, from almost 7000 feet at Flagstaff to 5000 at Payson, then a more rapid fall to just over 1000 feet in the Phoenix megalopolis. As we went down, the temperature went up—*way* up. Closer to Phoenix, we were riding through the saguaro desert, and the rain didn't so much stop as *vaporize*, sucked away by the glaring sun and 105-degree heat.

As we rode into the heavy traffic orbiting Phoenix, crawling along the freeway, heat came up from the asphalt like a furnace. Usually I would have my faceshield open for ventilation, but in that kind of baking heat I had noticed it actually felt cooler to have it closed. We had to ride east to west across the full width of Phoenix's sprawl to get to the Cellular Telephone Network Pavilion (formerly more poetically known as Desert Sky Pavilion), and after 488 kilometers, 305 miles, we were glad to park the bikes in the shade of the bus's awning, and rest in the air-conditioned front lounge as we slowly peeled off our sticky riding gear.

The crew guys were full of stories about the previous day's golf tournament, titled "Pirate Golf," and it sounded like they'd had a great time—even in 105-degree heat. As usual, Michael and I had been invited, but when I had compared the options, it was, "Hmm, I could have a great motorcycle ride to the Grand Canyon, one of my favorite places in the world, stay there overnight, then ride through the mountains down to Phoenix. Or . . . I could play golf."

Unusually, it was an eight o'clock show that night, which I generally disliked. I preferred to get it over with and get on the road earlier, get to bed earlier, and feel better the next morning. However, having the show start a half-hour later had one advantage, as my journal noted, "Eight o'clock show only good for one thing: time for a nap before 7:30 warmup."

The heat abated a little in the evening, though it was still in the 90s when we took the stage. I never minded working in the heat, though— the muscles certainly worked better than when they were cold. I had once discussed that with baseball pitcher Randy Johnson, a good friend of Geddy's, and he agreed that he preferred pitching in hot weather.

As we were driving away from Phoenix, another good show ended, and only one more left on the West Coast run, I felt inspired to jot down some quick notes.

Minutes after show. Still sweating, first drink, first smoke, wrapped in towel.

Random thoughts:

Jackie's birthday—kept coming back to that all day, including several times during show.

Short, thickset guy doing "calisthenics" all night, dancing in a steady bouncing jog, fists in front of his chest. Girls singing along too—loved that one tonight who was singing along so passionately, but didn't know the *words*.

Had a moment during the show when I could actually visualize what it was like to be out there, looking up at us—how we appear, how we *seem*—to them. The unbridgeable fantasy, and perhaps it has to remain that way (as they sing along with "Limelight").

Colored lights, glamour, drama, all that—with my private, inner knowledge of physical strain, and what *day* it is.

Lots of "heart flutters" today (dear diary), even during the show. Hope it's just fatigue and stressful arrhythmia [it was], and not something like what Liam had to deal with.

But another thing not to be discussed with others.

Somewhere I picked up a *fabulous* line from a country song— "It's hard to kiss the lips at night, that chew my ass out all day long."

That night, we slept on the bus in Kingman, Arizona, and in the morning Michael and I set off on our last Wild West adventure—and it would be a good one. In the far northwest corner of Arizona, leading toward Nevada, a little gray line on the map led to the western corner of Grand Canyon National Park and ended at a point marked in red as Quartermaster View Point.

The red ink signified "Place of Interest," which would have been enough of a reason to ride there, but the location was also attractive because it was at the end of about forty miles of lonely-looking road, the last third of it unpaved, and then it simply *ended*. Our kind of road, to our kind of place.

We left Kingman on the busy divided four-lane of Highway 93, flanked by the low Cerbat Mountains and a sparse desert of sage and cactus. At Diamond Bar, we turned off on a winding paved road through a forest of Joshua trees, their spiky branches upraised like the prophet after whom the Mormons had named them. The area was marked in red on the map as the Hualapai Joshua Trees, the easternmost range of that characteristic high-desert species.

When the pavement ended, we slowed down to negotiate a graded track of dry gravel and dust, sometimes rocky, sometimes soft and sandy as it crossed a wash, then paved again for the last few miles to the Quartermaster View Point. As the landscape opened out wide all around, we saw two or three cars parked in a gravel lot and, off in the distance, a touring company's van beside a metal-roofed pavilion, with a few figures around a picnic table.

We parked the bikes, took off our helmets and gloves, and walked to the edge of the precipice. Transfixed by the sweeping majesty of the setting, we stood before a deep, striated gash cut into the earth, a spectacular creation of erosion and geological upheaval. Multicolored layers of rock were shaped into dendritic canyons, battlements, and deep gorges, all of it on a scale that staggered the senses. I thought of that Tennessee professor teaching that it had been made in three weeks—because "scripture trumps interpretations of physical data." Not my scripture.

Or the church sign, "Faith is a higher faculty than reason." Not my reason.

The sun was hot, but a cool breeze ruffled the low grasses and clumps of sage, the only disturbance in a vast silence. Puffy white clouds sailed across the wide blue sky. With his digital camera, Michael made a brief video of me walking out to another vantage point, then he swept across the panorama as I stood and took it all in. Or tried to, anyway.

We backtracked down to 93 again, and headed northwest. It was a long, lonely stretch of road, and we began to worry about our fuel. A side road led to a marina on the Colorado River called Willow Beach, its sign showing a fuel pump icon, so we gambled on finding gas there—but it only had a fuel dock for boats. As we neared the Hoover Dam, there was a roadblock for a Homeland Security inspection, a recent installation reflecting a fear of sabotage (for the same reason, no trucks or buses were allowed on that highway across the dam, and Dave had been obliged to go the long way around).

Traffic was backed up a long way there, and again in sight of the dam itself, where the police were regulating a slow flow, alternating in one direction at a time. The line of cars and SUVs stopped ahead of us stretched for a mile or so on the winding road down to the dam, trapping us in a sweltering, airless canyon as we straddled the bikes and shuffled forward.

The previous night, when we were plotting the route, Michael had said, with a certain defiant note, "I hope we're going to stop and have a decent look at the dam, not just ride by—the way you *usually* do."

Now he could savor those words, eat them at his roasting leisure, as we spent about half an hour looking down over the Art Deco towers of the dam, tormented by the cool-looking waters behind it.

Now Michael wanted to jump the line and go to the front, but I said, "I can't do that—I'm Canadian!"

Fortunately we picked up an hour crossing into the Pacific time zone at the Nevada border, so I didn't have to worry about time too much. We made it through that frustrating jam, stopped at the first gas station we came to, then rode onward into the glitter of sun and flashing neon known as . . . Las Vegas.

In most cities, an 18,000-seat arena would stand out among the other buildings, but not in Las Vegas. Like the map of Texas, the scale of those huge casinos was so vast you could be fooled—like if, say, you tried to walk from the Bellagio to the Mandalay Bay, as I once did. Thinking, "it's only a few hotels down," I marched through that neon wilderness, past the Monte Carlo, New York, New York, Excalibur, and Luxor, for about an hour.

As we had last tour, this time we were playing at the MGM Grand Garden Arena, the first indoor show of the tour. It was very different to pull up beside the buses and park outside an enclosed building, but after 200 hot miles, it was refreshing to change, shower, and walk into the cool darkness of the arena. We had played hundreds of arena shows on past tours, of course, but the past two tours had been mainly outdoors.

The Rich family, longtime friends of mine since the making of the Buddy Rich tribute albums in 1994, had made three separate requests for tickets this time, one group for Cathy, one for her son Nick, and one for her ex-husband, Steve. Cathy and Steve were still business partners, and amicable enough, and the three of them showed up together at 4:30 so I could spend a bit of time with them during that brief interlude after my day's "commute," and before the beginning of the workday.

Cathy had often traveled with her father, Buddy, and his band, and I had always thought she, of all people, would understand about the little routines of touring life. But the previous time in Las Vegas, when I said goodbye to them after soundcheck, she frowned and said, a little resentfully, "What is it you have to *do*?"

She must have thought I would join them for dinner or something before the show, but that was unthinkable—I had a routine to follow. It is true that some bands do their soundcheck and then go back to the hotel, or out for dinner, but we had never felt comfortable doing that. In the beginning, I think it was some professional fear, almost a superstition, that we wouldn't get *back* in time, but these days it was simply part of our daily routine. For myself, I was already edgy enough before a show without interrupting that one tenuous pattern of normality. Since I didn't hang around after the shows, when a lot of other musicians might do their socializing, that little afternoon interval was the only chance I had to visit with people. I could only hope my friends understood that, or that I could make it up to them another time.

I had been friends with Cathy and her family for ten years by then, sharing their lively sense of humor and enjoying their company whenever we got together. They had been very good to me during my aimless "Ghost Rider" travels, hosting me at their then-home in Palm Desert, near Palm Springs. But as with some other people who had been my friends through the period when I had no life—when they used to hear from me frequently, and even see me traveling their way once in a while—there were sometimes misunderstandings when things changed. When I got together with Carrie and had a life of my own again, I didn't need others so much. Sometimes, I knew, those friends felt a little jilted.

And at the time of the Vegas show, Cathy and I were in the middle of a supreme test of our friendship. Earlier that year, Cathy had talked to me about her wish to produce a film version of *Ghost Rider*. She had already been working on trying to produce a film about her father, and she told me she had a vision about making my book into a movie. But I wasn't so sure. I had no wish to see my life, especially *that* part of my life, made into a movie.

But I hated to say no to a friend. We had worked together well on the Buddy Rich tribute recordings, back in '94, but I knew this would be different. Finally, I gave Cathy a reluctant, qualified "okay," but told her up front that not only was I apprehensive about the idea, but I also hated to mix business with friendship. I would not want to be involved in any way myself, but would put her in touch with Paul, my agent for such matters, and only reserve the right to tender my approval of any project. Or not.

That afternoon, I spent a few minutes talking with Cathy about the movie project, and I saw how serious she was about it when she held her fist to her forehead and said, "I can just *see* how it ought to be." She continued trying to draw me into it, asking me again if I wanted to have any involvement in the movie.

"Just approval," I told her.

Unfortunately, in the subsequent months, the situation grew increasingly uncomfortable. I had told Cathy she had to deal with Paul, as my agent, and though he understood the friendship aspect, his loyalty was to me and he felt he had to play "serious." When they disagreed on terms and conditions, and Cathy and Steve wanted further concessions and exclusive rights to which Paul demurred, Cathy kept bringing *me* into it again, and I started to feel . . . disturbed. The final stroke came when some guy who was submitting a screenplay proposal to Cathy started seeking out my personal friends and even family members, wanting to interview them for his screenplay. These people, already wounded, became upset and contacted me, thinking I had something to do with it. That was disturbing enough, but when I learned that the guy had gone so far as to contact Selena's former boyfriend, a terrible line was crossed. Through Michael, I made my feelings known to the guy, and wrote directly to Cathy about how upset I was.

Soon after that, Cathy wrote to me that she had decided to shelve the project. She said she realized now that it was simply too painful for me to deal with. I breathed a silent "hurray," and wrote back to thank her.

As I accompanied the family into the MGM Grand Arena, I started roughhousing with Nick, who was nineteen now, and still the irrepressible teenager. Nick had always brought out the immature kid in me, just as Selena used to, and I teased him and punched him in the shoulders, and lifted him up and threw him around (though he wasn't so *light* anymore), then took them all up onstage to look at the new drumset.

After soundcheck, I went to say goodbye, and Cathy looked at me and said, "So that's it?"

I spread my arms, "Yes, I'm afraid that's it."

Carrie had flown in for the Vegas show with her childhood friend Joanne, and they had spent the day shopping and sightseeing. They came by and joined us for dinner in the dressing room, then amused themselves while I had some quiet time, and began my warmup ritual.

It was strange going onstage in utter darkness instead of in outdoor twilight, or the bright rays of descending sun. We stood in the dark behind a raised stage, then ran up a flight of stairs lit by flashlights from C.B. and a couple of other crew members. The show was undeniably more *dramatic* indoors, though, at least from a lighting point of view, with the smoke machines filling the beams in the still air, and the rear screen more vivid in a dark building.

The sound was very different, too, from the stage—bouncing back again, instead of just going out into the night. I especially noticed the added resonance in the drum sound, and it gave me extra inspiration for that last show before the break.

A couple of guys in horse costumes appeared onstage to do the dryers, and later, Pat McLoughlin told me they had been two friends of his from the area. One of them was a longtime Rush fan, and he was thrilled by the surreal moment of putting coins in the dryers in front of thousands of fans, glancing over at his musical heroes while wearing a horse costume.

All considered, it was another really good show, in front of a roaring crowd of 9,543 people, a fitting end to what had been a tough but successful West Coast leg. Magic shows and golden roads.

But this time at the end I didn't run offstage to the bus, but into a limousine, where I changed out of my sweaty clothes as we drove to the nearby airport. Dave would be driving the bus back east to his home in Nashville, and when I had talked to Liam about possible flight arrangements after the show, figuring I could maybe get a late commercial flight from Vegas to L.A., Liam suggested I take "our" chartered jet, as Geddy and Alex wouldn't be flying to Toronto until the following day.

"Well, okay," I said. "That sounds good."

He stressed that I would still have to leave right off the stage, as FAA regulations on the crew's flying hours required that they be "wheels up" by midnight if they were going to fly back and take the other guys to Toronto the same day. "No problem," I assured him.

Mere minutes after we had played the last ringing chord of "Limelight," the Gulfstream was taking off, rising swiftly up and over the glittering lights of the Las Vegas Strip. The zillion-watt beam from the top of the Luxor pyramid stood straight up, like a pillar of white light. I relaxed deeper into the soft leather seat, sipping my Macallan as the jet carried me home, the way my bandmates usually traveled. It was, to say the least, a very different experience.

Along with Michael and me, and Carrie and Joanne, we also carried two friends of the band's, John Kastner and his wife Nicky, back to their home in Los Angeles. Michael had arranged to have Carrie and Joanne's favorite cocktails—cosmopolitans—served on board, and everybody relaxed and chatted through the hour-long flight across the dark desert.

I was deeply tired, sore, and sweat-sticky, my muscles aching and my fingers burning around the calluses. I thought of all the sights that had passed before my eyes just in that one day, from the Quartermaster View Point to the Hoover Dam, to the colored lights on the crowd in the MGM Grand Garden Arena, to the view from that private jet as carpets of dotted lights appeared far below, from Barstow and Victorville.

The constellation of greater Los Angeles crept toward us, grids of white lights between the dark mountains, and edging along the blackness of the Pacific. As the plane began its descent into the Burbank airport, we took turns looking through the cockpit windows at bright orange wildfires burning in the San Gabriel Mountains.

The dark silhouette of the big-shouldered mountains was broken by three lakes of fire, like pools of molten lava, flames lighting the spectral waves of smoke that wafted high into the air. Those out-of-control wildfires devouring the Angeles National Forest, on the very parapet of the vast city, were eerily beautiful, and then the runway lights painted the golden road home.

east coast spirit quest

I believe I have a sunny disposition, and am not naturally a grouch.
It takes a lot of optimism, after all, to be a traveler.

Paul Theroux

On one side of the road, palm trees and dark green mangroves framed lagoons of turquoise water and white coral sand. On the other, I looked over the distant sweep of the dark blue Atlantic. Cormorants sat on pilings with their wings spread to dry in the sun, flocks of pelicans glided inches above the small waves, and a strong, sulfurous smell of low tide filled the humid air. Above, rain clouds bulged heavily on every side, though I didn't bother putting on my rainsuit. The occasional showers were a welcome relief from the oppressive heat.

Michael, Dave, and I were riding in formation down the Great Overseas Highway, 126 miles and forty-three bridges that would carry us to fabled Key West. First visited by Spanish explorers led by Ponce de Leon, in 1513, they named it *Cayo Hueso*, Isle of Bones, after the human remains they had found there. The name Cayo Hueso morphed into Key West, and by the 1850s, was home to a colony of "wreckers" who salvaged cargo from shipwrecks on nearby reefs. Later arrivals were cigar makers, sponge divers, fishermen, sea-turtle hunters, writers, presidents, and bootleggers. Always a place of extremes, it was the richest city per capita in the United States by 1889, and declared bankruptcy in 1930.

As one who has a deep affection for the United States, my adopted home, and one who has traveled so many of its roads, big and small, for thirty years, I have often said, proudly, that every state in the Union has some road worth riding, to something worth seeing.

Florida was no exception, but with so much of the state a flat, featureless landscape of mind-numbingly straight roads through swampy terrain or monotonous citrus groves, the interesting roads and places were few. The Gulf Coast had some nice areas, the Everglades region was fascinating to a nature lover, but none of what I had seen before could be as attractive as a road I had never ridden, to a place I had never been—the end of the road.

The southernmost point in the continental United States, home of Harry S Truman's "Little White House" in the late 1940s, and Ernest Hemingway in the 1930s, the setting for some of his stories and a novel, *To Have and Have Not*, and the one little corner of the United States I had never visited.

In all the years Dave and I had toured the mainland United States, together or on separate tours, each of us had traveled hundreds of thousands of miles around every corner of the country, but neither of us had ever managed to get to Key West. It was well off the typical concert-tour itinerary, so we had never worked there professionally, and even if we had a day off in Miami, the nearest major city, Key West was still pretty hard to get to—a long ride down the bridges and causeways of Highway 1, and all the way back again.

For a few years now, Dave and I had been waging a friendly competition to see which of us could get to Key West first. The previous year, during his time off, Dave had sent me an e-mail gloating that he was about to set off from Nashville on his Harley, heading south into Florida, and planning to end up in Key West. However, he confessed later that he had been turned back by bad weather, and never made it past Fort Lauderdale. So by 2004, neither of us had yet made it to Key West.

The next leg of the R30 tour would start in West Palm Beach on July 29, and it happened that a few days before that show, during our break at home, Carrie would be leaving to travel with her mother to attend a friend's wedding in Sweden. Seeing an opportunity there, I suggested to Dave that maybe he could drive the bus down to Florida a few days early and park it somewhere, then Michael and I could fly in, and we could all ride to Key West together.

That became the plan, marred only when Dave called to let me know he was having clutch trouble with his Harley, and it wouldn't be ready in time for him to leave. We agreed that he would ride my backup bike, the 1150, and on the night of July 26, we met at an airport hotel in Fort Lauderdale. The next morning, we headed south on I-95 and the Florida Turnpike through heavy traffic, humid heat, and occasional rain showers.

After all the miles Michael and I had ridden through the wide-open spaces of the West, the Florida interstate seemed claustrophobic. Dense traffic clogged both directions, through built-up areas of light industry, warehouses, and franchise retail outlets. Even the heavy-laden sky felt oppressive, pushing down on us as the surrounding landscape closed in.

In my experience, Florida was the worst state in the Union in which to drive a car, ride a motorcycle, or ride a bicycle. Turn signals seemed to be a deleted option on all vehicles; on multi-lane highways there was no such thing as a passing lane, and the general mood on Florida roads ranged from oblivious to discourteous to downright hostile. Those attitudes often prevailed elsewhere in North America, of course, from coast to coast, but nowhere as universally as in Florida. Even in other states, so often Michael and I would witness that kind of heedless driving, and point down at the Florida licence plate on the back of the offending car. When traveling overland in the Sunshine State, it was wise to assume in advance that no one *ever* looked before he or she changed lanes, made a turn, stopped, started, or pulled out of a driveway.

Most of Highway 1, the Great Overseas Highway, was narrow two-lane, and busy in both directions, so passing wasn't always an option anyway. But even where it widened into four lanes, people dawdled along in the left lane. It was hard to tell if they did it obliviously or defiantly, but there was no question they expected you either to go around and pass them on the right, or stay where you were.

The scenery was a compensation, though, riding through those Caribbean views of sea and sky, the water birds, the palms and mangroves, and the bridges connecting the tiny islands, many of them with pretty names. Key Largo, Plantation Key, Islamorada ("Purple Isle"), Upper and Lower Matecumbe Key, Fiesta Key, and Grassy Key, all made a linked poem, and for a while I entertained the thought of describing the

Keys as a string of pearls. However, the highway was often lined with brightly painted tourist traps selling tacky souvenirs, and later I modified my romantic metaphor in a journal note, "Keys not so much a string of pearls as a string of plastic beads."

Sometimes we passed broken pilings and bridge abutments, the remains of the railroad, built in 1912, that had once connected the Keys to the mainland. The railroad was destroyed in 1935 by a mighty hurricane that hurled 200 mph winds and an eighteen-foot tsunami at the Keys (where the highest ground was sixteen feet above sea level), killing 423 people. I remembered reading a powerful account of the devastation left by that storm written at the time, and on the scene, by Ernest Hemingway.

Traffic came to a complete standstill on Marathon Key, and the three of us straddled our bikes for long, hot minutes, going nowhere. Being on motorcycles, at least we could creep along the roadside and escape, and when we saw a policeman, we asked him what the trouble was. He said there was a tractor-trailer jack-knifed up ahead on the Seven Mile Bridge, blocking both lanes, and it would take at least an hour to clear it. We saw a restaurant called the Stuffed Pig and decided to park and have some lunch.

Good timing, too, as it was just after two, closing time, and people coming in after us were turned away. We enjoyed our lunch of sandwiches and chili and lemonade, relaxed in the knowledge that we couldn't go anywhere anyway. After lunch, as the little restaurant was closing and the staff were going home, we sat out behind at a shady picnic table, smoking and talking for a while, until we saw traffic finally start to move.

"THERE IS A GOD WITHIN US, AND IT GLOWS WHEN HE MOVES IN US," said the day's church sign.

No Name Key, Big Pine Key, Ramrod Key, Summerland Key, and finally, Key West. It was already bigger and busier than I had expected, as Highway 1 took us around the downtown area. The big box stores like Home Depot and Target seemed too mundane for a place I expected to be exotic. But that was just a romantic mirage, like San Juan Capistrano.

We were all hot and tired and glad to finally arrive, as it had taken us six hours to travel 195 miles. We passed the waterfront marinas and a few hotels, and Michael took the lead, with Doofus guiding us down Duval Street past dozens of bars and souvenir shops (T-shirt, "JESUS IS MY

HOMEBOY"). We turned onto a back street, between rows of houses in Victorian gingerbread and colonial architecture, every second one or so with a B & B sign in front. Luxuriant subtropical foliage shaded the street and spilled over walls and fences.

We pulled into the circular driveway of the Wyndham Resort and put our sidestands down. No sooner had we stepped off the bikes than a short, bearded, self-important man in a patterned shirt came over from a little booth. Apparently he was the valet parking attendant, and he said, "You'll have to move those bikes."

His tone was not welcoming or polite, and we were in no mood to be bossed around pointlessly.

"Okay, we're just checking in," I said. "We'll move them after we unload our luggage."

"No, you have to move them now, so other people can get in."

Dave pointed to the open driveway beside us and said, "I could drive a bus through there."

"I don't care. You have to move them."

Michael left his bike where it was and went inside to check in, while Dave and I ignored this unpleasant man. I was bristling a little, as this was obviously an anti-motorcycle attitude, and he was treating us like "scooter trash." That was always annoying. As Dave said later, "He was just pissed because he knew he wasn't going to get a tip from us."

The parking attendant started one more time, "You have to move those—"

Dave stood square in front of him and cut him off. "You'd better just get back in your booth."

"But I . . . "

Dave gave him a no-nonsense look and said, a little more sternly, "*Go back to your booth.*"

He turned around and went back to his booth.

Michael came out and said this was the wrong Wyndham, and ignoring the parking attendant, we mounted up again and followed Michael a few blocks to another one. And what a contrast. The young doorman greeted us with a smile and a welcome, and pointed to the hotel's private parking area, right beside the door, saying, "Y'all can park right there if you want."

That was more like it.

My room wasn't ready yet, so I changed in Michael's room, putting on the Hawaiian shirt he had bought for me, the first one I had ever worn. I walked out of the bathroom, and minced across the room, camping it up. "There, I'm *wearing* it, are you satisfied now?"

"Oh honey, that top looks so *cute* on you!"

"Are you sure it doesn't look too gay?"

"Well, yeah, but it's nothing to do with the shirt!"

"You'd better buy me a drink, or you'll be sleeping alone again tonight."

"How will I notice the difference?" he sniffed.

"I hate you, I hate you, I hate you."

We went to meet Dave at the beachside bar, and drank *strong* pina coladas. Soft reggae played from overhead speakers, enhancing the Caribbean view of sandy beach, palm trees, and turquoise water. We were starting to feel better. After we ordered our second pina coladas, Michael went off to the front desk to check on my room and Dave went to the men's room. I took out my journal and made a quick note—"Long, fairly nightmarish journey—not sure to *what* yet."

The turning point came when I was finally checked into my room, with a view of the beach, palm trees, and skittering shorebirds, then the Gulf of Mexico stretching away through shades of blue all the way to Cuba. I looked out a side window to a quiet little street, and saw two chickens bobbing their heads as they rambled slowly across the road. A minute later, a white-haired couple in a shiny red '65 Ford Galaxie convertible, top down, turned the corner and cruised gently by. Somehow, the wandering chickens and the old convertible, and their easygoing paces, suggested something unique about this place, something relaxed and West Indian, and made me feel that maybe I was going to like it there. After all, Key West was closer to Cuba (ninety miles) than to Miami (150 miles).

Before leaving home, I had done a little Internet research on Key West, wanting to make the most of the one day we would spend there. I saw something about Dry Tortugas National Park, which put me in mind of a Peter Matthiessen novel, *Far Tortuga*, and a reference in a Hemingway story, "After the Storm." Reading on, I learned that the national park was a chain of seven small islands seventy miles west of Key West, centered around a nineteenth-century fort, Fort Jefferson.

Apparently you could take boat and floatplane trips there from Key West.

Browsing the national park Web site, I noticed there were nine national parks along the East Coast, and I started to feel the spark of inspiration. I had been worried about that upcoming East-Coast run—not about the shows, but about the rides. Again, every state had at least one good road to someplace worth seeing, but in the East, I had ridden most of those roads, often many times, by bicycle and motorcycle. Familiar roads could still be enjoyable, but they didn't feel so *adventurous.*

But what if I tried to visit all nine of those national parks, collecting the "passport stamp" at each one, from Dry Tortugas in Florida to Acadia in Maine? That could give me a theme, a mission. Not much of one, perhaps, but it was something, and early the next morning, I would begin my East Coast Spirit Quest.

Michael decided to stay in and miss the boat trip, but Dave and I met in the lobby at seven a.m. and took a taxi to Conch Harbor. We boarded the *Yankee Freedom II*, a big diesel-powered catamaran, and settled on the upper deck as it burbled out of the harbor. A few dozen other passengers, couples and families, gathered in the sheltered cabin while Dave and I grabbed a bench among a few hardier souls on the upper deck, open to sun and wind. Dave wore his usual dark jeans and Harley T shirt, though a sleeveless one, his only concession to hot weather. Unlike most of the rest of the crew, who always wore shorts, and many of the drivers on that hot summer tour, I never saw Dave in shorts. He also said he had no plans to go snorkeling with me at Dry Tortugas.

Binoculars in hand (a new set of Zeiss glasses to replace the ones lost in Colorado Springs—still no word on that missing luggage case), I looked over the grid of yachts and sport-fishing boats, a forest of outriggers, flying bridges, and sailboat masts. A romantic "tall ship," the 130-foot schooner *Western Union*, had been built in Key West in 1939. Big gray navy ships lined the concrete wharf across the harbor, at what had been a submarine base in World War II, along with Coast Guard cutters ready to intercept drug smugglers or Caribbean refugees.

Once underway in open water, Dave and I picked up some rolls and coffee from the main cabin, then returned to the upper deck. A naturalist, Jack, stood in front of us and introduced himself over the boat's P.A.

system. He was a middle-aged salty dog with a thick beard and a way of talking, and even laughing, with a frown that was somehow jocular. I told Dave that Jack looked and talked like a longtime driver of ours, Pat Lynes, who had driven both buses and trucks for us in the '70s and '80s, long before Dave's time. Pat had been a good friend of Mac's, and he was always called "Number Nine," after the psychedelic song on the Beatles' "white album," though no one knew exactly why. One time, Nine came into our dressing room before a show wearing a T-shirt with a big "9" on it, accompanied by his father with a big "99," and his baby son wearing one with ".9."

Sadly, Nine was killed in a car accident in the mid-'80s, but his spirit lived on in many on-the-road expressions that endured among band and crew. After a long overnight drive, he would run his fingers through his thick beard and growl, "I gotta go wash off this diesel cheese." When the drivers had parked their trucks and buses at the venue in the morning, and were waiting for the production office to organize their rides to the hotel, Nine would be the first to let them know if he thought they were being kept waiting too long. In fact, Nine was the king of the backstage rabble-rousing he called "Whackin' the hive," first to protest any ill-treatment, real or perceived, and to stir up the other drivers and crew members with his disgruntled rebellion. From then on, whenever anyone on the tour started spreading trouble, in good humor or ill, it would be forever known as whackin' the hive.

The big catamaran picked up speed as it reached open water, a few storm-squalls on the horizon. Jack gave occasional talks about the birds, fish, and sea turtles in the area, and the histories of Key West and Dry Tortugas. The isolated scattering of tiny islands was first named Las Tortugas by Ponce de Leon, after the abundant sea turtles they found there during his search for the Fountain of Youth. None of those islets had any fresh water, and the "Dry" designation was added later to warn mariners of that fact.

After about two hours, the *Yankee Freedom II* began to slow as the Dry Tortugas came in sight. As we circled Garden Key, I scanned the massive brick walls of Fort Jefferson with my binoculars. A pelican was swimming near the boat, and I watched a gull land right on its back and pester the poor bird until it gave up the fish in its pouch. Jack told us more about the history of the fort and the bird refuge on Bush Key.

Attached to Garden Key by a spit of sand, Bush Key was closed from February to September to protect the nests of tens of thousands of sooty terns and a few thousand brown noddies. In 1832, famed naturalist and wildlife painter John James Audubon had visited Dry Tortugas to observe the bird and marine life.

A lighthouse was built on Garden Key in 1826 (its need attested to by the more than 200 shipwrecks in the area), then moved to nearby Loggerhead Key in 1858. The 150-foot brick tower was still visible, and still active, though automated now. I always lamented the passing of lighthouse keepers, because that was one of my early ambitions—which perhaps reveals something about my character, even as a child—after my wish to be a birdwatcher or forest ranger, and before history teacher and meteorologist.

The construction of Fort Jefferson began in 1846, and the intention was to make it the "Gibraltar of the Gulf," the largest coastal fort in America. The work continued for thirty years, with soldiers, slaves, and prisoners laboring at the massive six-sided fortress enclosing eleven acres, and using sixteen million bricks. But it was never finished, or even fully armed.

During the Civil War, Fort Jefferson was used by Union warships in their blockade of Confederate shipping, and as a Union military prison for captured deserters. After 1865, the fort held Dr. Samuel Mudd, who had been convicted as a conspirator for treating the broken leg suffered by President Lincoln's assassin, John Wilkes Booth, as he made his escape. Following Dr. Mudd's efforts in treating a yellow fever outbreak at Fort Jefferson, he was pardoned by President Andrew Johnson in 1869.

The Army abandoned Fort Jefferson in 1874, though it continued to be used as as a coaling station for warships, as evidenced by the pilings still visible on two sides of the fort. In 1898, the USS *Maine* departed Dry Tortugas on its fateful mission to Havana, where it mysteriously exploded, precipitating the Spanish-American War ("Remember the *Maine*"). The fort was used briefly during both world wars, but after 1908 it was mainly a wildlife refuge, designated as Fort Jefferson National Monument in 1935, and finally, Dry Tortugas National Park in 1992.

Looking over the massive brick walls as we approached the dock, and listening to Jack's account of the fort's colorful history, I was amazed to reflect that two weeks earlier, I had never even heard of Fort Jefferson, nor even of Dry Tortugas National Park.

The crew of *Yankee Freedom II* handed out snorkeling gear at the stern, and I collected a set before going ashore. A narrow bridge led across the moat—just one of the engineering challenges in the fort's construction—and my first stop, of course, was at the Visitor Center, to collect that all-important passport stamp in the front of my journal. Then I joined Dave and the other passengers on Jack's guided tour of the fort. As we walked through the inner yard, Jack gave an amusing and informative talk, pointing out the ruins of the barracks and other buildings, then leading us up through the cool, arched tunnels of bricks, bricks, and more bricks (all sixteen million of them delivered by sailing ships from Boston, Jack told us), to the bright sunshine at the top. From there, I had a great view through my binoculars of the nesting terns and noddies on neighboring Bush Key.

A simple picnic lunch was served in front of the fort, then I changed into my swim trunks and carried my snorkeling gear over to the beach. The snorkeling guide map handed out by the crew showed that I could swim along the "moatwall" of the fort, then out past some small coral heads and back through the pilings of the former coal dock. The water was warm and shallow, and I swam slowly through the undersea world, fascinated as always by the tiny, colorful fishes darting among the sea grass and coral. Angelfish, wrasses, and the larger, aptly named rainbow parrotfish nibbled at the coral and barnacled pilings with audible clicking sounds.

Changing in the bathhouse near the dock, I found Dave dozing in the air-conditioned cabin. I had to admit, it felt very refreshing after the onshore heat. We stayed there as the *Yankee Freedom II* set off again, pelted by a series of rainstorms as we sped back toward Key West.

Dave and I took a walk past the scores of bars and souvenir stores of Duval Street. Dave wanted a T-shirt from the famous Hog's Breath Saloon, so we stopped there for a drink, then caught a cab back to the hotel. With Michael, we went back to the waterfront for a good meal, then got our cab driver to take us along Duval on the way back, so we could at least look at the wild nightlife.

It had been a long day, and for me anyway, I was glad to get back to my room—though I had to make a grumbling note about the bedside "reading lights." More and more often I was encountering these low-wattage, fluorescent coils in hotels, even expensive ones. These lights might save energy, but it seemed a false economy when they were nearly useless for reading. I thought about having a leather shop make me a small foam-padded case in which I could carry around my very own 60-watt lightbulb!

The show in West Palm Beach was the next day, and based on our experience of getting *to* Key West, all of us were a little nervous about getting away the next morning. It had taken us six hours to ride from Fort Lauderdale to Key West, and West Palm Beach was another hour north of Fort Lauderdale. Dave would have to ride to the bus, load the motorcycle, then drive to the venue, so he was going to leave by seven a.m., while Michael and I decided to leave at eight, just to be safe. Also, I wanted to pick up one more national park on the way back, at Key Biscayne.

In the morning, Michael and I made a quick stop and photo-op at the marker designating "The Southernmost Point in the Continental United States" (Michael, who had spent much of his youth in Hawaii, sniffed at that). Cruising along the quiet backstreets, houses were tucked among lush trees and greenery, retaining the subtropical charm of what Key West must have been like seventy years ago. We paused at the former Hemingway home on Whitehead Street, peering through the dense foliage around the beautiful old house. It was too early for a tour, and in any case, we had no time—we had to get to work, and it was a long way away, with many potential obstacles in between.

Our return up the Overseas Highway became a long, dreary ride through intermittent rain, sometimes heavy. When the rain didn't slow us down, the Anti-Destination League of Florida drivers did. Time after time, I gave up and passed them on the right, swinging back into the left lane in front of them and spreading my left arm in the "hello" gesture. It never did any good.

When Michael and I were finally off the Overseas Highway, back on the mainland and away from the worry of possible delays, we stopped for breakfast at a chain restaurant in Homestead. While we ate, we managed to avoid one heavy rain shower, then we put on our rain gear again and set out to find Key Biscayne National Park.

During the break, I had told Michael I was thinking about trying to visit each of the East Coast national parks on my spurious Spirit Quest, and he had programmed their visitor centers into Doofus and Dingus. We followed a straight side road east past the massive Homestead Motorsports Complex, another shrine to the ever-growing popularity of NASCAR (and bringing yet more of the Deep South vernacular to southern Florida), then along swampy canals and tangled undergrowth.

Passing the sign for the park, with the national park service's arrowhead logo, we stopped in the visitor center lot at the water's edge. The sun blazed out between the clouds for a few minutes, and Michael waited with the bikes, smoking a Red Apple, while I ran inside to get passport stamp number two.

Unlike most national parks, Biscayne was mostly underwater, a marine sanctuary of reefs, small keys, and mangrove shoreline stretching between Key Largo and Key Biscayne, near Miami. Early in the twentieth century, parts of Biscayne Bay had been dying, stifled by pollution and the runoff from construction in the Miami area. Years of cleanup had been necessary to reverse the damage. Most of the park could only be experienced by boat, and the view from shore would be the extent of my visit, but still, I knew something I hadn't known before, and I had another stamp in my journal. Two down, seven to go.

We mounted up again, and headed west to the Florida Turnpike, back into the dense, hostile traffic, intermittent rain alternating with oppressive swelter. I noticed several Florida license plates with an anti-abortion message printed right on them (the presumptuous slogan, "CHOOSE LIFE"). They were obviously sanctioned and manufactured by the state, and I thought, "That ain't right." Reproductive rights are at least a political issue, if not a religious one, and that Florida state license plate was virtually a "church sign," preaching at people. However, when the president was the Florida governor's brother, I guess they didn't have to worry about quaint notions of separating church and state.

(Apparently ten or twelve other states offer similarly-messaged license plates, though I have never seen them on the road. A $25 to $35 surcharge is supposed to pay to counsel women with unwanted pregnancies to choose adoption, but some money apparently goes to anti-abortion activists. The plates have repeatedly been declared unconstitutional by federal judges; many of the states have been sued by the

American Civil Liberties Union; Virginia's governor Mark Warner vetoed the proposal in his state, and a Louisiana state senator tried to sponsor a bill to offer a pro-choice plate as well—but so far the church signs are winning.)

Riding north through Miami and Fort Lauderdale to West Palm Beach, we were slowed by lines of traffic at frequent toll booths, where it was Michael's job to fumble with gloves, tickets, bills, change, and receipts. Sometimes drivers behind us honked impatiently, as if we were holding them up on purpose.

At breakfast, Michael had said, "It's funny riding behind you and watching you try to 'school' every driver in Florida."

"Well, jeez, I figure you've gotta *try*."

He fixed me with a serious glare. "You know that getting a handgun in Florida is like buying a pack of cigarettes?"

"Oh . . . But it's not like I'm giving them the *finger* or anything. I'm just going, like, 'Hey, wake up!' "

"They don't know what you're saying in your helmet."

A sobering thought. Considering that as a warning, added to my realization that protests were futile anyway, I gave up trying to school the drivers of Florida. I would try to accept them as they were, and navigate among them as safely as I could without visible protest. (As in Colorado, that very year, Florida's police finally started to ticket drivers for that offence, calling it "failure to yield.")

That sense of menace, though, and the image of the drivers around me all carrying weapons, reflected the mood of returning from the almost idyllic outpost of Key West to the mainstream of Florida. The upcoming shows were in the two most urban areas, the Miami, Fort Lauderdale, West Palm Beach strip along the Atlantic, and the Tampa-St. Petersburg metroplex on the Gulf side.

Paul Theroux, quoted at the beginning of this chapter, echoed my own feelings when I was sometimes accused of being too critical of people I encountered on my travels. Theroux, one of the most adventurous and prolific of travel writers, once said that people always asked him about his favorite places, the ones he wanted to go back to, but never asked him about the places he disliked, the parts of the world he would be glad never to revisit.

It is one thing to describe why you love a place, another to explain why you *don't*. Generalizations are difficult and sometimes dangerous, and nearly everyone feels exempt from them anyway, so they are hard to put across.

I would start with the exculpatory generalization that most people everywhere are fairly nice. Being generous (just this once), I might allow that out of ten people you encounter in any given place, nine will be agreeable and polite, and only one will be miserable and rude. However, if you are accustomed to experiencing that sort of ratio among the people and places where you travel, and on the roads you ride, when you encounter an area where only eight of ten people seem to be nice, and two are nasty, you notice the difference right away. I know some nice people in Florida, but . . . there are the others.

I grew up in Eastern Canada, where a winter trip to Florida was considered by the snowbound working class to be a dream vacation, their closest alternative to a tropical experience (though no part of Florida, even Key West, falls between the tropics). I never made the trip myself, but groups of teenagers would get together in someone's car and drive straight through for a couple of days to get to Florida during Christmas vacation or spring break. I remember my parents making winter driving trips to Florida a few times with friends of theirs, and even now they have a winter home at a trailer park on the Gulf Coast.

My own first impressions of Florida were not very pleasant. On the band's first few visits down there, we stayed at cheap motels, the rooms slimy with mold and mildew, the bath water greenish, and the staff rude and unhelpful. That kind of nastiness seemed to affect the atmosphere everywhere we went in Florida, just that slightly higher ratio of eight to two instead of nine to one.

And unfortunately, despite those eight-out-of-ten *nice* Florida citizens, many visitors to the state go away unimpressed, to put it mildly. A whimsical Internet search turned up *pages* of other visitors' responses, and it even seemed that for those people, my ratio of nasty to nice was reversed. Many visitors seemed to leave the state feeling that eight out of ten Floridians they encountered were unpleasant and discourteous, especially on the roads.

Floridians claim that a similarly high ratio of residents in their state is made up of transplanted New Yorkers, mostly elderly, but that doesn't account for the driving habits. Driving in New York is nowhere near that bad. (Arizona can be close, it's true, at least around Phoenix, so perhaps one factor *is* age.)

It is also worth noting that Florida has the largest number of shark attacks in the world, whether it's because Florida's sharks are especially nasty, or just bad drivers.

In the same way outsiders can have a shallow impression of California as a statewide beach party on a Hollywood movie set, and that illusion could warp and oversimply a complex reality, if you said "Florida" to many out-of-state people, they would think spring break, Disney World, Cape Kennedy, oranges, alligators, and—if they were baseball fans—spring training.

In Florida's case, it had to be said that those stereotypes represented the brighter side, for there are many shadows in the Sunshine State.

Somehow Florida was not generally thought of as a "Southern" state, in the way that Mississippi and Alabama were, but certain regions of central Florida I had passed through, away from the beaches and Disneyfied resorts, were the most abject manifestations of Deep South you could find anywhere. Well away from the Mickey Mouse ears, the Art Deco theme park of South Beach, and the vulgar showplaces of the rich and tasteless, the locals could seem as inbred and xenophobic as those characters in *Deliverance*. The Confederate flag and gun racks decorated as many pickups and mobile homes as you might expect to see in Alabama or Mississippi, and place names like Yeehaw Junction, Dixie Ranch Acres, and even the Suwannee River are all found in Florida.

History had left its Southern scars, too. Florida had been a Confederate state, of course, though too far south to witness any major battles on its soil. After the Civil War, the Florida legislature passed its version of Jim Crow laws, called "Black Codes," that legalized political, social, and economic discrimination. The Ku Klux Klan had always been active in Florida, and in the early twentieth century, the state had the highest per capita incidence of lynching in the country. Even at the beginning of the twenty-first century, a slavery ring was uncovered in Florida, a combine of citrus farmers who recruited Latino workers in Arizona, then kept them prisoner in indentured servitude enforced with terror and violence.

In the little town of Lake Placid, in south-central Florida, a van company that operated a service to transport farmworkers to other states was attacked by armed gunmen for "taking their people." The drivers and passengers were threatened with death, windows were smashed, and the owner was pistol-whipped and left unconscious and permanently disfigured. That occurred in 2003.

The disparaging term for racist white trash, "Cracker," originated not in Mississippi or Alabama, but in central Florida. Cattle ranchers had moved there from Texas, and were called Crackers after the sound of the bullwhips they wielded—and it wasn't just *bulls* they were whipping. Those Florida Crackers also seem to have influenced an equally repressive state institution: the police.

Both objective and subjective experience gave South Florida law enforcement a bad reputation as far as I was concerned. Around 1982, Rush was scheduled to play a concert at the old Hollywood Sportatorium, a jai-alai arena outside Miami (surrounded by a moat rumored to be filled with vicious alligators). It was the first show after a ten-day break, which I had spent in the British Virgin Islands sailing on *Orianda*, and through a chain of bad weather and circumstance, I missed my flight from St. Thomas to Miami. A later flight would get me in before the show, so I found a Western Union office and sent a telegram to the venue (no cell phones, e-mails, or even production-office telephones in those days), booked a seat on the next flight, and waited it out.

However, if I was dealing calmly with the situation, the notorious Dade County police were not (the same guardians of the peace who had arrested Elvis Presley, Jim Morrison, Janis Joplin, David Lee Roth, and Tommy Lee at concerts for "public indecency"). My telegram didn't arrive, and in those pre-Homeland Security days, the airline I was flying on wouldn't release their passenger manifest. Fearing a riot inside the building, the promoter didn't want to open the doors until they were sure I was going to show up, but their failure to communicate that situation to the restless crowd waiting outside, and the overreaction of the Dade County police, very nearly caused a riot *outside* the arena. Helicopters circled and teargas grenades were lobbed into the crowd, who doubtless already had reason to distrust their local police.

When I walked off the plane, our assistant, Kevin, was waiting at the gate, standing at the pay phone with the receiver in his hand, ready to tell them if I was there or not. We raced to the venue, I went straight to the stage—teargas wafting through the arena—and feigned nonchalance to my bandmates as we kicked off the first song.

And again, that was not an isolated incident. Phil Lesh recounts in his autobiography, *Searching for the Sound*, that Florida police even managed to stir a Grateful Dead audience to a near riot, and sprayed them with teargas, too.

In 2004, my bandmate Alex was living through a more recent bad experience with Florida law enforcement. Earlier that year, a horrible, nightmarish encounter had left him severely battered, bloody, and facing serious felony charges. He and Charlene had bought a holiday home in a luxury property in Naples, Florida, and on the previous New Year's Eve, they attended a black-tie event at the neighboring Ritz-Carlton hotel, with their son, Justin, and his wife, Michelle. They were all having a wonderful time, enjoying a great meal and dancing wildly to the live band. Just after midnight, while the band was taking a break, Justin stepped up on the band platform to wish his wife a Happy New Year over the microphone. A grumpy keyboard player called hotel security to have him removed.

When they tried to escort him off the property, Alex stood up and told the security goons his son wasn't going anywhere. They decided to call the local sheriff's department. When the deputies arrived, they dragged Justin and Alex away into a stairwell, out of sight of witnesses (they thought) and security cameras. They started beating on Justin, shoving him down the stairs, and Alex, like any father, tried to intercede and defend his son—who was guilty, after all, of *talking into a microphone*.

In a nightmarish few seconds of unbelievable violence, Alex and Justin were both brutally beaten and shot by Taser guns, *ten times* altogether. Alex found himself face down on the landing in a pool of his own blood, his nose broken, then he was cuffed and hauled away to jail. In growing horror and disbelief, he was held for the two worst days of his life, and charged with several felony offences of assault against the deputies. He faced not only automatic prison time, but felony convictions that would ban him from the United States forever.

He was shown on CNN and other media being charged, wearing his orange felon's jumpsuit, and again when he was released, his white shirt covered with dried blood, and his nose visibly swollen. The criminal charges against Alex would not be resolved for almost a year and a half, when a plea bargain would result in a misdemeanor of resisting arrest, but the memories of that violence and injustice have haunted Alex ever since.

I spoke to him on the phone the day he was released from jail, January 2, 2004, and the emotional effect on him was apparent in his voice. He really could not believe what had happened, any of it, and he especially couldn't believe the behavior he was being accused of—like pushing a female deputy down the stairs. Anyone who knew Alex knew that however drunk he might have been, and however enraged, there was no way he did that.

Alex was shocked at the way he and the other prisoners were treated, even as suspects, not convicted felons. The jailers played psychological games, taunting the inmates with food, keeping the cells uncomfortably cold, flaunting their power, and making them feel small.

There is an American saying that "a liberal is a conservative who has been arrested." The comforting illusion that anyone in trouble with the law must be getting what they deserved could suddenly be opened to a darker reality. Not only was Alex appalled and permanently scarred by his own treatment in the Collier County jail, he was disgusted by the way the whole system was designed and operated, seemingly with the sole aim of degrading and humiliating the inmates. It had nothing to do with rehabilitation, justice, or the often-used euphemism, Department of Corrections. The accused were now the victims.

A year later, a witness finally came forward to corroborate Alex and Justin's story, as reported in the local Naples newspaper (which had, unbelievably, actually published Alex's home address in its first story about the incident). A former employee of the hotel said that he had seen the way Alex and Justin were treated, and that it had been "extreme police brutality." He also testified that it had been the female deputy who had thrown Alex down the stairs: "She grabbed him by the throat and he went falling backward."

It is sickening to picture the scene in that stairway, but the behavior of those Collier County deputies was all too believable. In the year 2004, three "suspects" would be *killed* by Florida police using Taser guns, one of them by that same Collier County sheriff's department. Miami's Dade County police would be criticized for using Taser guns on a six-year-old boy, and on a twelve-year-old girl (they said she was drunk). As I write this, Fort Lauderdale police have just been charged with "excessive force" in subduing a kindergartener with handcuffs.

Those are some of the reasons why Florida was widely considered a police state, and those are some of the reasons why I never felt comfortable there. It is safe to say that what happened to Alex could never have happened in Canada, or in most of the rest of the world, or in most parts of the United States for that matter. But it does happen in Florida. And all that baggage had to come to Florida with us, and onto the stage in West Palm Beach.

During the show, despite the intense heat and humidity, I felt fresh mentally and physically after the break, especially in my legs. Even back in the '70s, I used to notice that my legs lost their "snap" during a tour, and it would happen in the studio, too, after too much hard, fast playing. That night in West Palm Beach, sometimes that very freshness made me get *too* fresh, too adventurous, and later I noted that I "got lost" a couple of times but managed to recover. During the show, though, I did have the conscious thought, "Nothing *hurts* yet!"

It was also the *sweatiest* show yet, as I felt myself slipping around on the "throne" (I wonder if whoever coined that name did it to bolster drummers' self-image?), and the sticks were slippery in my hands. Between a few of the songs I had a long enough break to grab a swallow of water and towel off my hands, face, and sticks.

It was Geddy's fifty-first birthday that night, making both of us the same age for another six weeks. It was also the band's actual thirtieth anniversary, for I had officially joined the band on Geddy's twenty-first, July 29, 1974. While we were playing the instrumental "YYZ," I looked through the drums and cymbals to my left and saw a pair of girls in provocative pirate outfits walk out carrying a cake with candles. They set it on the dryers, and the crowd cheered when the overhead camera showed it on the screen, with "Happy Birthday Geddy" iced on it. The girls did the dryer routine, pretending to check the T-shirts and putting in more quarters, then from what I could see through the drums, they just hung around stage left, standing in front of the audience, maybe dancing a little. I was thinking, "Okay, that's enough—get off the stage!"

At the end of the first set, in "One Little Victory," we had a burst of pyrotechnics, columns of fire that punctuated the onscreen dragon.

Some stages, like the one in West Palm Beach, harbored a lot of insect life up in their rafters and rigging. After that firestorm, and when we started the second set, I noticed a lot of dead bugs landing on my drums, and a few live spiders, too. Near the beginning of my solo, the fast snare workout section, I felt a sudden pain on my shoulder, a burning stab like a spider bite. No way was I going to stop playing to brush it away, but later I noted, "What a test of will *that* was!"

During the intermission, while I relaxed in the Bubba-Gump room, Gump came in as usual to use the facilities and ask if I had any problems with the kit. We discussed the bass-drum pedal that had broken—an unusual and disturbing failure, and very difficult for Gump to change while I was playing. Brent also made his usual visit to change the nine-volt battery in my monitor radio-pack, and ask if I had any monitor problems. Both of them were facing me while I looked toward the door, and I saw someone else come in, someone I didn't recognize. He was short and hairy, wearing the expensive Rush baseball shirt, and he just stood there, staring.

I made a facial signal to Gump and Brent, and as Gump guided the intruder out of the room, he suddenly started yelling my name and whooping excitedly. Gump called Michael on the radio and told him what had happened, and Michael went to investigate. He returned a few minutes later to report that the guy had made his way through no fewer than three separate security stations, and a few people were being sent home.

"No harm done," I said. "It's just unnerving. What if I had been alone? What if he had been *armed*?"

"I know," Michael said. "Believe me, I know."

In describing the incompetency of some security people, Michael told me he had stopped putting "void" on the sample passes he handed out to backstage guards every night at the security meeting. At a show in Texas, one guard had been turning people away because their passes didn't say "void" on them.

On that sweltering night, Alex changed his shirt during intermission, then again during my solo, and when the two of them returned to the stage for "Resist," Geddy made a joke to the audience: "This guy's got more costume changes than Madonna. Or should I say, Esther."

I'm not sure how many people got the reference to Madonna's recent adoption of that name as part of her dalliance with Jewish mysticism, but I laughed out loud.

During Alex's story-telling session in "La Villa Strangiato," he went into a sorrowful tale about "Why couldn't it be *my* birthday," inspiring Geddy and me to start playing a slow blues pattern. Alex joined in with blues guitar licks and a blues-style vocal performance, the "Birthday Blues."

As always, it was up to me to choose the psychological moment to stop him. Sometimes Geddy and I would exchange a look, and I would start the long snare roll and count-in to bring us back to the song. Often, the moment I chose would make *Alex* laugh—realizing that although he hadn't been finished, he was finished. He would turn to face me and mouth, "Thank you!"

After the show, when Dave and Michael and I had been riding on the bus for an hour or so, and I had been through my post-show rituals, I was just about to get Michael working on the next day's route when I heard Dave call out, "Hey Mackel" (the best transliteration of the way he pronounced Michael's name).

Michael went forward to talk to Dave, then walked past me and down the corridor to his bunk. He came back a few minutes later wearing his "uniform": black paramilitary pants, black T-shirt, utility belt with flashlight, handcuffs, badge, and—yikes!—holster.

"What's up?"

"Oh, we're being followed. Dave's going to see if he can lose them, but if not, I'll go have a word with them."

That kind of thing happened from time to time, in every part of the country (and other countries), and it was nerve-racking for me. Like the kind of people who would show up at my house, I had to imagine that anyone who would do that was mentally unbalanced in some way, maybe in a *bad* way. Compared to that ratio of nice-to-nasty people in the general population, Rush fans scored *much* higher—more like 999 nice ones to a single individual who would be rude and invasive. It was always important to remember that I would never meet all those nice people, because they wouldn't think of forcing themselves on me in any way. I would just see them smiling in the audience.

And in the audience of 12,203 people at the Consumer Electronics Retailer Amphitheater (formerly Coral Sky) in West Palm Beach, say, that meant there were maybe only a dozen bad ones. One of them had wandered into Bubba-Gump at the intermission, and now some of them were stalking me in a car.

They might only want autographs, or they might want to discuss the secret messages in my lyrics. Either way, this was not the way to go about it. Every night Donovan spread an array of items in the dressing room to be signed, some arranged by Shelley for local radio station contests and such, but many of them CDs, LPs, and photographs mailed to the venue by fans. Every night we signed all of them, and Donovan mailed them back. As for the secret messages, surely they could be transmitted telepathically.

But some people would leave the show early, get in their car, and wait by the back gate for my bus to leave so they could fall in behind and follow us, sometimes for hours. One morning on the *Vapor Trails* tour, Michael and I climbed off the bus in the morning and walked back to the trailer to unload the bikes. Two young guys came running up and stood in front of me, excited and breathless, holding up their denim jackets to be signed. They had followed us all the way from the previous show, somehow escaping Dave's notice, and waited in the rest area all night in their car.

Keeping my feelings to myself, I signed their jackets. Though I could never be easy-going enough to be comfortable with that kind of behavior, once such people had succeeded at invading my life, I couldn't bear to be rude.

Still, it was a jarring way to begin the day, startled out of a sleepy routine and a day-off state of mind. (One time, on a family outing with Jackie and Selena, somebody asked me, "Are you the drummer from Rush?" and I smiled and said "Not today!" The girls had laughed.)

Dave tried pulling off at an exit to make sure the car really was following us, then tried to lose them at a toll plaza. But they simply waited up the road until we passed, then fell in behind again.

Finally Dave pulled over, and the car stopped behind us. Dave and Michael went back to try to reason with them. Especially in that part of the country, I was glad Michael was armed, but as long minutes passed, I began to worry—my overactive imagination feared sudden cracks of gunfire. (Unfortunately, as anyone who has survived tragedy knows, the psychological after-effect of bad experiences is that deep down, you're always half-expecting the *next* bad experience.)

After a nervous wait, Michael and Dave returned. Dave put the bus in gear as Michael told me the story. "They were armed, all right—with Sharpies. When we came up to the car, they held up their pens and CDs, thinking we had stopped so you could sign their autographs!"

Some people might simply have done that, I guess, and perhaps it would be easier, but I just couldn't stand to reward people for behaving like that.

Michael said there had been three of them, and while two had been shame-faced and apologetic, one was belligerent about getting what he wanted. The driver (in an Ozzy shirt, Michael told me) had challenged Michael, "Are you a *cop*?"

Telling me about it, Michael shook his head, repeating what he'd said with rolling eyes, "No, I'm not a cop, but I can have one here in about five minutes, if that's what you want."

Another time, a guy had forced that issue. Michael had called the police, and we pulled away while the officers ransacked the guy's car. Most young people who have just attended a rock concert wouldn't want that.

Michael and Dave had convinced the stalkers they weren't going to get any autographs that way, and tried to explain that what they were doing was *wrong*. But we doubted they understood. Dave kept an eye behind us after that, to make sure they really had turned back, and I made a final note in my journal, "Enough weirdness—let's plot the route."

We spent the night in a truck stop west of Fort Lauderdale, setting up Dave to head west on I-75, the Everglades Parkway, or Alligator Alley. Michael and I would ride south on some back roads to pick up the smaller east-west route, a two-lane called the Tamiami Trail. It would take us along the northern border of Everglades National Park, and through the Big Cypress National Preserve.

It was another hot, humid morning, and I started it with a couple of Bufferins along with my morning vitamins (remembering the previous night's note, "Nothing hurts yet"—now it did). Once we were rolling, though, I felt pretty good. The Tamiami Trail was another of my favorite routes in Florida, straight and flat, but carrying us along between swamps and canals and low greenery, with glimpses of exotic-looking ibises, anhingas, white egrets, and other waterbirds. Turkey vultures circled high in the blue-white sky, no doubt soon to discover the good-sized alligator that lay at the roadside, killed by a passing car.

One turnoff led to an observation tower, where the park brochure said, "bird and alligator viewing rank among the park's best." Other signs indicated the various hiking trails and boardwalks and airboat rides, all of which I would love to have done, but one of the frustrations of those on-the-fly visits to scenic areas and national parks was that we had to keep moving. Farther south, the map showed a road running through the most remote parts of the park, ending at Flamingo, on the southernmost tip. I knew there was a lodge there you could stay in, and I wanted to do that, too.

But we had a show that day, way up in Tampa, so we kept riding. We did take the scenic Loop Road, which gave us a somewhat wilder look at the Everglades, the "River of Grass" (the name is actually a corruption of "River Glades"), then farther west, we turned off to ride to Everglades City and the Gulf Coast Visitor Center. While I went inside to get passport stamp number three, a tour boat was just about to depart with a dozen or so tourists. I could only imagine the fascinating sights those people would see.

While Michael and I rested on a shady bench for a few minutes, taking a Red Apple break, I looked over the park brochure. It informed me that all of South Florida had surfaced during the last Ice Age, 6000 to 8000 years ago. At least that part of the world fit comfortably into fundamentalist Creation doctrine.

It was nearing midday, in midsummer, in the Florida Everglades—so of *course* it was hot and humid. Michael and I felt sticky and uncomfortable as we put on our heavy riding jackets, helmets and gloves, then headed north again, up little Highway 29. We passed through a lot more swampy wilderness, seeing a few signs reading "Panther Crossing." Later, Michael asked me if that was for real, and I assured him it was, though the Florida panther was now so rare the park brochure said naturalists believe only about ten survive in the Everglades, and only fifty to seventy in the ever-decreasing wild lands of south Florida.

The whole region was suffering steady attrition from developers, and the national park brochure described the Everglades as already "on life support," the historic flow of water that nourished the rich natural environment meddled with so much by canals and drainage. Later I read that developers around Miami were paying bargain prices for tracts of open land that were protected, then fighting to have the designation changed, so they could build 16,000 houses beyond the "urban development boundary."

An attorney acting for the developers asserted, "The line was never intended to be a line in stone. It's not intended to be permanent. The bottom line, which people aren't addressing in this debate, is what are we going to do with the people? We are blessed with beautiful weather and people like to come here. They are not going to stop coming."

A church sign seemed to comment on those local struggles. "CREATION WITHOUT DIVERSITY IS LIKE A SONG WITHOUT A MELODY."

Not really sure what that means, exactly, but it sounds nice.

Through Immokalee and Lehigh Acres, we circled over toward Fort Myers, then picked up little Highway 31 running straight north to Arcadia. That was another sentimental journey for me, as in 1985, I had bicycled that road on a day off in Fort Myers, during a spring training tour before the recording of our *Power Windows* album. Aiming for a Century, I had ridden fifty miles north to Arcadia, then on the way back, one of my tires had gone flat. When I pulled out my toolkit to repair it, I discovered the patching glue had gone dry during the long Canadian winter.

With no way to call for rescue, I ended up walking and pushing the bike the last ten miles back to the hotel—though I did learn the valuable technique of pushing and steering a bicycle with one hand on the saddle, which I have found useful from time to time since then.

From Arcadia, Michael and I cut northwest along a pleasant little road to the dreaded interstate I-75, then battled our way with fear and determination up to Tampa, after 461 hot kilometers (288 miles). When we arrived backstage at the Domestic Automobile Manufacturer Amphitheater, Dave told me he had dropped my 1150 at the local BMW dealer, because its alternator light had come on during his ride from Key West to Fort Lauderdale. He showed me a ripped-up alternator belt, the same mechanical failure that had stopped Michael's bike in Texas.

Dave said that one of the mechanics was a fan of the band, and of *Ghost Rider*, but couldn't afford to attend the show. Dave had fixed him up with tickets, and also invited the guy to deliver the bike himself, and thus be able to visit the backstage area as well as see the show. I signed a copy of *Ghost Rider* for Dave to give to him, and was glad to know we had been able to give a deserving fan that treat.

Pat McLoughlin came by with a boxful of hardcover copies of *Traveling Music*, the first ones, and they looked good. I started inscribing them and handing them out to friends, beginning with Dave, Michael, Alex, Geddy, and Liam, then working outward from there in subsequent days.

My journal notes gave a review of that night's show, in front of another large crowd, 12,486 people.

Another long, hard, hot, trying, painful, difficult, endless . . . *competent* show.

Best I could do, as always.

I hurt now—body and brain.

Finally able to play a CD properly, though, after following a *page* of directions from the shop.

Not even halfway through [tour] yet!

The next day was a day off, to be followed by a show in Atlanta, so Michael and I were going for national park number four: Congaree Swamp, in South Carolina. Mapping the next day's route on the bus that night, I was glad to put away the Florida map and take out its alphabetical follower, Georgia. I highlighted a complicated route cutting northeast through central Georgia and into South Carolina, while Dave faced a long 278-mile drive up I-75 to the dropoff point in Tifton, Georgia. Michael and I would have a bouncy sleep until five a.m. or so. During a lengthy fuel stop (it takes a while to pump 230 gallons of diesel), I seized the opportunity to have a shower in a stationary bus, so at least I would be clean as we bounced through the night.

"LUST BLINDS, BINDS, GRINDS," was the morning's first church sign, on a day which set an all-time record for them—so many in the towns of Georgia and South Carolina I couldn't begin to remember them all when we stopped. Though I was getting picky, only bothering with the intriguing or funny ones.

One that caused Michael and me some confusion and discussion was, "FREEDOM IS SIMPLY ANOTHER PERSPECTIVE AWAY." That just seemed too complicated for its own good.

I did laugh out loud at one I had first seen on a billboard near Ojai, California: "DON'T MAKE ME COME DOWN THERE," signed "GOD."

And there were the inevitable cute ones, like "A SMILE INCREASES YOUR FACE VALUE," and "AVOID THE CHRISTMAS RUSH, COME TO CHURCH SUNDAY," the hellfire-and-damnation ones, "THE PRICE OF OBEDIENCE IS NOTHING COMPARED WITH THE PRICE OF DISOBEDIENCE," and the inspirational ones, "ENCOURAGE EACH OTHER AND BUILD EACH OTHER UP."

That was nice, and a more worthwhile spirit to be broadcasting, I thought.

A meaner spirit was shown at a rural crossroads, where somebody had tacked up a bunch of handmade signs on a fence, too many for me to catch, but I did note "SIN WILL KILL YOU," and "SHACKING UP IS SIN."

The ride itself was an easy Saturday cruise, hot and humid once again, along quiet country roads. Gently rolling Georgia pine woods, the smell of needles baking in the sun, deciduous forests overhanging small brown rivers in a rhyming series: Willacoochee, Oconee, Ocmulgee, Ohoopee, Canoochee, and Ogeechee. Red-dirt farmlands, woods, and small towns—Lumber City, Cobbtown, Metter, and Rocky Ford—led us northeast to the Savannah River and into South Carolina.

Now we rode through that state's Piedmont region, where I had often bicycled in former years, between shows in Columbia and Greenville, to the North Carolina cities of Charlotte and Asheville, and from there up to Chapel Hill and Raleigh. The Carolinas provided some of the nicest bicycling country in the U.S., I always thought, with pleasant country roads and thick, dark deciduous woodlands, the terrain rolling up and down just enough to be interesting, but not too arduous.

Likewise, it was good motorcycling country, our route leading along those same country roads through dense woodlands arching over more brown rivers (Coosawhatchie, Salkahatchie, and Edisto), and long stretches of farms between small towns with names like Sycamore, Jamison, and Wateree.

Late in the afternoon we started looking for the park, which seemed to be a well-kept secret. When I finally saw the sign, I was a little worried to see it marked as Congaree Swamp National Monument. My quest was limited to full-blown national parks, and didn't include the relatively commonplace, second-tier national monuments—not to mention national battlefields, military parks, historical parks, sites, reserves, preserves, seashores, lakeshores, parkways, scenic rivers, trails, recreation areas, or wild and scenic rivers.

It turned out that Congaree Swamp's designation was so recent (only upgraded from monument to park the previous year, making it the nation's newest national park) that they hadn't yet changed the signs, nor even printed up the attractive little brochures other parks had. Even my national park directory still showed it as a monument, and only the Internet list had made me aware of its status.

Apparently the park protected the "largest contiguous tract" of old-growth bottomland (meaning it was periodically flooded) hardwood forest in the United States. Some of the tallest trees in the eastern U.S., they also formed one of the highest canopies in the world. The swamp had been named for the Congaree River, which itself was named, like many of those rivers, after a local Indian people, all but wiped out by smallpox in the nineteenth century. The park's Internet listing celebrated its old-growth pines and cherrybark oaks, and the flood-resistant tupelos and bald cypresses. The beautiful name "tupelo" came from two Creek Indian words for tree (*eto*) and water (*opelwu*), and for those who remember the classic Van Morrison album, *Tupelo Honey*, there really *is* such a thing, celebrated for its translucent purity.

The park also claimed to be home to many "champion trees," a species I didn't recognize. A Web search informed me that "champion" was not the name of a species, but an official designation for the biggest, tallest, and oldest of any particular kind of tree. Well-organized hobbyists around the world classified them by state and by species, and even by *nation*.

I was constantly surprised by the things people could get interested in—and by the things I was learning on my Spirit Quest.

Congaree was another park I would willingly have spent some time in, as it promised wonderful hiking and birdwatching, along with a raised boardwalk looping through the middle of the swamp. However, it was late afternoon now, and Michael and I still had to find a place to stay. We parked in the shade of some of the tall trees for which the park was celebrated, and went into the visitor center to fulfill the next part of the quest—the grail.

I immediately went to the counter and looked around for the passport stamp and pad, hoping they would have at least that all-important badge of national parkdom. I didn't see it, and had a sinking feeling. I gave Michael a mock-hysterical look. My *quest!*

I said hello to the female ranger behind the counter, and asked her where the passport stamp was.

"Why, it's right here," she said, reaching down to a shelf below and placing the stamp and inkpad on the counter, then giving me a teasing look, "where it belongs!"

I had my journal open already, and said, "Oh—they usually have them out in the open, for people to use."

"Not here," she said, cheerily.

After the usual practice run on a piece of scrap paper to make sure the stamp was right-side up, I pressed it carefully down beside the Everglades one inside the front cover of my journal. They made three pleasing pairs now, counting the Sequoia and Grand Canyon ones I had collected earlier that month, before the collection had become *serious*.

The ranger had been watching me, and I thanked her while putting the journal back into my beltpack, and turning to go.

"Aren't you even going to have a look around?" she said.

"No, I wish I could, but we've got to go."

"You're not even going to take a walk along the boardwalk?"

"No, I'm afraid not. I'd love to see it, but . . . maybe another time."

She kept pressing, seeming genuinely upset. "I can't believe you've come all this way, and now you're going to leave."

I spread my hands, "You don't understand—I'm on a *mission!*"

On our way back out to the bikes, Michael said, "I wonder if she's all right in the head."

I laughed, "Oh yeah, I'm sure she is—these people just tend to get into their jobs, and their parks, and can't stand the idea that you're not going to appreciate it."

For myself, I appreciated that we had made four national parks in four days, and that day I also turned 17,000 kilometers on the 1200—making about 13,000 miles altogether, on the two bikes. Oh, and twenty-nine shows. We were halfway through.

Late on a Saturday afternoon, the streets of Columbia, South Carolina, were quiet as we cruised the town, looking over the accommodations. Columbia seemed to be a nice little city (116,000 people), combining modern and historical buildings on tidy, tree-lined streets. (Apparently the 100-foot width of most of Columbia's streets was based on the eighteenth-century belief that mosquitos could not fly more than sixty feet without dying of starvation.)

Following Doofus's list and directions, we rode around the downtown past the imposing city hall and state house, then across the Congaree River, just downstream from where the Broad and Saluda flowed together to form it. A couple of motels along there were tempting, but there was no restaurant nearby, so we returned to the downtown area, to a Hampton Inn in the middle of a lively looking neighborhood of restaurants and bars. After 509 kilometers, 318 miles, we were (as usual) hot and tired.

In that kind of heat, I had noticed that whenever I was off the bike, like when I unloaded the bags and carried them inside, I moved with a certain economy of motion, as if to conserve energy metabolically, and avoid generating heat. I wouldn't move if it wasn't necessary, and if it was, I would move a little slower than usual. Like a hybrid car, I could feel each of my muscular motors shutting down when they weren't needed, and I wasn't sure if this physiological response to hot weather was learned or automatic. Adaptation to a hot climate, certainly, but on a deeper level, such a change represented that classic distinction between Nordic and tropical peoples. For myself, I always thought both were good, climatically and temperamentally.

After cleaning up, Michael and I walked along the side street beside our hotel, perusing the variety of places to eat and drink. A youthful, bohemian atmosphere suggested a fairly worldly clientele—the college influence, we guessed, as Columbia was home to the University of South Carolina.

The next morning brought another hot day, the 1st of August, and a Sunday. Downtown Columbia was deserted, but the road out of town led us past churches with full parking lots, and a myriad of inspirational signs. They were the usual variety of confusing ones, "GOD'S TIMING IS ALWAYS PERFECT," too-clever ones, "SATAN SUBTRACTS AND DIVIDES, GOD MULTIPLIES," fire-and-brimstone ones, "FLEE TEMPTATION, AND LEAVE NO FORWARDING ADDRESS," and amusing ones, "EXERCISE YOUR FAITH, WALK WITH GOD" and "THERE IS UNLIKELY TO BE A REDUCTION IN THE WAGES OF SIN."

That would still be death, then.

Once again, I had planned the day's route to join one of my old bicycle rides, this one particularly memorable and historic to me—the longest bicycle ride I had ever done in one day, 175 miles across Georgia from Augusta to Atlanta, back around 1986. At the end of that long day I had arrived at Atlanta's Ritz-Carlton hotel, a luxurious reward. But after Alex's brutal experience at the Naples Ritz-Carlton, on this tour we were boycotting that luxury chain and their owners, Marriott. Alex, Geddy, Liam, Donovan, and Shelley were often staying at Four Seasons hotels, while Michael and I were staying at Best Westerns, Hampton Inns, or on the bus. Given that difference in accommodation costs, not to mention the chartered jet, our expenses for a week were less than what they spent in a day. And I got to collect national park passport stamps.

Michael and I rode west from Columbia, through the Sumter National Forest, then across the Savannah River and into Georgia. We headed south (following the dotted line on the map indicating "scenic route") through forests and farmland, through Loco and Amity, to Thomson, where we joined that long-ago bicycle route. As I had so many years ago, we rode west through charming little towns like Eatonton and Monticello, often built around a central square, sometimes with an imposing county courthouse.

The temperature sign on a bank read 97 degrees, and I remembered it had been hot on that bicycle ride too, eighteen years before. I recognized the river, the Ocmulgee, where I had paused to dunk my head, and even the church I had rested beside, at a picnic table under a tree. Michael and I stopped there, too.

Sometimes I was struck by the difference of looking ahead at that road on the motorcycle, climbing and descending between dusty red cutbanks and stands of pines by a simple twist of the throttle. I pictured how it would have been on the bicycle, pedaling up those hills and coasting down them. I was reminded of a Hemingway quotation my brother Danny once sent me:

> It is by riding a bicycle that you learn the contours of a country best, since you have to sweat up the hills and coast down them. Thus you remember them as they actually are, while in a motor car only a high

hill impresses you, and you have no such accurate remembrance of a country you have driven through as you gain by riding a bicycle.

On bicycle rides, I had often found local people would tell you a particular road was flat or short, when from a bicycle saddle, it was definitely hilly or long.

Even on the motorcycle, that Georgia crossing seemed like a very long ride, and I could hardly believe I had bicycled it. That old "will" again. We arrived at the Atlanta fairgrounds and the aged-looking Consumer Electronics Retailer Amphitheater, after 400 kilometers, 240 miles.

The show that night was another hot and sweaty job, the temperature onstage a humid 90 degrees, even at night. We had another good-sized audience, over 10,000 people, and my after-show review said, "Pretty good show, good solo, happy audience," which was a rave review, of course, by my standards, though the overall reality was on my mind, too:

Tonight passes halfway point of tour—and I'm fed up already, big time.

Still some things I like: riding the bus after the show, riding the bike, arriving at a motel, the overall *activity* of the passing days.

But by now, it approaches *too much*.

The next couple of days were definitely going to be too much. My Spirit Quest, like the original Native American trial, became harrowing and hallucinatory as I stepped up the pursuit of the next few national parks. Dave had helped set the scene by asking if we might swing by Nashville after the Atlanta show, so he could pick up his Harley. I looked over the map of the Midsouth and realized that sleeping in Nashville would put Michael and me in reach of Mammoth Cave National Park in Kentucky, so I said, "Sure, let's do it."

After another long, bouncy five or six hours on the bus, Dave parked outside the headquarters of his employers, the Hemphill Brothers Coach Company. We woke up among a few other buses in the parking area around the big facility, though most of their fleet of about eighty buses was out on summer tours, several working the presidential campaign with candidates and media.

The Hemphills, Trent and Joey, had once been traveling entertainers themselves, in the family gospel music group, until starting up their charter company in 1980. Dave's father had also led a gospel group in Cincinnati ("I basically grew up on a bus"), and he had known the Hemphills since then. Dave switched from playing bass in gospel groups to driving buses in late 1992, then started driving for the Hemphills in '93.

I had toured the Hemphill shop on the previous tour in 2002, Dave guiding me through all the separate areas where the custom interiors and utilities were fitted—carpentry, plumbing, electrics, and mechanical. Bare-shell Prevost buses arrived (from Quebec, Canada) with only a driver's seat, then were converted to suit the wishes of clients ranging from Oprah to Cher to George W. Bush. The bus we were using this tour had previously been chartered by Beyoncé Knowles and Jay Z., last tour it had been Faith Hill's bus, and the time before that, Kurt Cobain and Courtney Love. If those buses could talk . . .

After breakfast, Michael and I immediately got on the road and headed for the interstate, then sped north on I-65. No scenic back roads, no old bicycle routes, no sentimental journeys, no messing around—we were going for three national parks in two days, and to do it we would have to ride more than 800 miles.

Doofus and Dingus were programmed with the visitor centers as Waypoints, and the routes between selected for "quickest way." We passed the National Corvette Museum near Bowling Green, Kentucky, which I would like to have seen (my boyhood dream car was a '63 split-window Sting Ray), and Michael would surely have enjoyed it, too, as he drove an '85 Corvette as part of his Hollywood private eye persona. But not this time—we had to keep rolling.

The parking lot at Mammoth Cave was packed with cars and RVs, the visitor center filled with people lining up for tours of "the most extensive cave system on Earth." Over 350 miles of underground passages had been surveyed in that porous limestone, many of the caves explored by slaves who had been brought there to mine saltpeter for gunpowder in the early nineteenth century. They and their descendants continued to act as guides for over 100 years.

Michael and I wouldn't see any of the cave's spectacular attractions, or walk any of the sixty miles of aboveground hiking trails, but I soon had my precious stamp, and we were off again. We rode back south a few miles to pick up the Kentucky Turnpike, then headed east for the next goal, Great Smoky Mountains National Park.

It was another hot day, 95 degrees, but we had the Parkway pretty much to ourselves, running fast through heavy deciduous forests on the wide, empty road, then onto a brief stretch of pretty two-lane through the Daniel Boone National Forest. Meeting I-75, we headed south for Tennessee again, and along there, I had a start when we passed a sign that read Cumberland Gap National Park. I pulled over to check on that, and confirmed that it was a National *Historic* Park. Those did not count!

Down to Knoxville, then a stretch of I-40, on which we had ridden 2000 miles at the beginning of this odyssey (I also noticed that our first show-to-show ride, from Nashville to Charlotte, had also taken us within a few miles of the park, that rainy morning leaving Sweetwater on the Cherohala Skyway). From there, it was south to the "Hillbilly Disneyland" around the towns of Sevierville ("Se*vere*-ville," Dave had corrected me), Pigeon Forge, home of Dolly Parton's "Dollywood" (the second most popular attraction in Tennessee—after the park), and Gatlinburg.

Given the area received nine million visitors every year (even Grand Canyon only got five million), including ten thousand couples annually joining in holy matrimony there, traffic was heavy on that hot second day of August. Michael and I sweated and shuffled through lines of traffic and red lights, past the hotels, resorts, amusement parks, sideshows, bungee jumps, water slides, gift shops, restaurants, and assorted tourist traps. Slowly we made our way to a brief but refreshing stretch of winding, tree-lined road, leading into the park and the Sugarlands Visitor Center.

Journal successfully inked with stamp number six, we had to turn around and fight our way back to I-40, then onto I-81, heading northeast toward Virginia. The next goal was Shenandoah National Park, on the way to the next day's show, at an amphitheater in Bristow, Virginia, just southwest of D.C.

That kind of riding was no way to enjoy such a beautiful area, of course, but fortunately I had traveled the back roads around there many times on past tours, from the famous ones—Deals Gap, the Blue Ridge

Parkway—to the nameless little mountain roads. So at least I knew what I was missing.

And there was a deeper level to what I, and everybody, was missing in that part of the world. Like all of the Eastern United States and Canada, that area had been logged and burned and plowed throughout the eighteenth and nineteenth centuries. All of the parks, from the Great Smokies to the Adirondacks to Ontario's Algonquin Provincial Park, had not been established to *preserve* anything, but to let it grow *back*. (During a visit to Canada in 1929, Winston Churchill had remarked, "Fancy cutting down all those beautiful trees to make pulp for those bloody newspapers, and calling it civilization.")

Even more lamentably, the most dominant tree in those primeval forests, the American chestnut, averaging five feet in diameter and 100 feet tall, and providing high-quality timber and railroad cars full of nuts every autumn, had been wiped out by an Asian fungus. The blight appeared in New York City in 1904, and within a few decades, virtually all of the American chestnut trees were dead. Barbara Kingsolver's beautiful novel, *Prodigal Summer*, was set in the area Michael and I were now approaching, the southwestern corner of Virginia, and described one character's attempts to produce a blight-resistant chestnut by crossbreeding it with the Chinese chestnut. Her fictional man's quest reflected the ongoing attempts of dedicated scientists and amateurs to bring the lost trees back to life.

Late in the afternoon, Michael and I were powerfully glad to pull off the highway at last. We stopped for the night in Bristol, Tennessee, right on the Virginia state line, after covering a frenetic 770 kilometers (481 miles). A sudden rainstorm had soaked us for the last five miles, which at least cooled us off, but the spray behind the big trucks was sometimes blinding.

Monday night was Karaoke Night at the Bristol Motor Lodge, and though the crowd was hardly more than a dozen locals, over dinner we watched a few of them get up and sing songs by Conway Twitty and the Judds. One girl in her twenties, introduced as Zeanna, short and pudgy with cropped hair, glasses, Harley T-shirt, and jeans, put out her cigarette and stuffed her hands in her pockets as she delivered an impressive if undemonstrative version of "Delta Dawn."

Michael had told me before he was an occasional karaoke performer, and this was his chance. He got up and sang a creditable version of Sinatra's "Summer Wind," then, with requisite Scotch and cigarette in hand, he crooned the classic saloon song, "One For My Baby." The audience clapped politely, and I promised Michael I would try it, too—someday. Altogether, Karaoke Night at the Bristol Motor Lodge was, as I noted in my journal, "quite a slice of life."

Virginia was the only state we would encounter where radar detectors were illegal, and the next day began with a long run up I-81, where we needed to make some time. We still had a long way to go to the day's venue, and I wanted to ride Skyline Drive, the 105-mile scenic road through Shenandoah National Park. Without our radar detectors, we felt vulnerable enough on the interstate, trying to keep our speed within acceptable limits, but in the park, the 35-mph speed limit was rigidly enforced, and we would have to ride painfully slowly. On such a beautifully engineered stretch of perfect pavement and tempting curves, I understood why it was necessary to discourage people with fast cars and motorcycles from turning it into a racetrack, but the slow pace was still frustrating—we could easily have ridden that road at twice the limit, and had a lot of fun doing it!

But we would try to be good.

The day was hot, the sky hazy with humidity, and once again we were crossing our own trail from the beginning of the tour. We passed the turnoff for the little road we had taken between Steeles Tavern and Rockbridge Baths on our ride from the overnight stop in Charlottesville to Elkins, West Virginia, that second day off. Those little "crossroads in time" were always strange to me, riding along and looking over at a little road and thinking, "Two months and twenty-seven shows ago, I was on this bike, on that road."

We entered Shenandoah National Park at Rockfish Gap, as we had on the previous tour on our way to the same venue. In 2002 we had spent the night in nearby Afton, following Michael's "offroad excursion" near Frost, West Virginia. He had run wide on a tight corner, falling down in what racers called a "low side" (definitely preferable to a "high side," where you go flying over the bike), and his GS had slid into a guard rail. Fortunately he had been wearing the armored leather suit, as always, and hadn't been hurt, but his front tire was split wide open, and he needed a flatbed tow truck.

In those narrow Appalachian gaps and hollows, we had no cell reception, and it was the one day Michael had forgotten our satellite phone. I had ridden off on a rescue mission to call the tow truck from a pay phone a few miles back in the two-building hamlet of Frost. I also asked Dave to meet us at the motel in Afton, bringing the spare motorcycle and picking up Michael's bike to have the tire replaced.

"Adventures suck when you're having them."

As we had that summer, this time we rode slowly, slowly through the park, past deep forests and trailheads and scenic overlooks above the Shenandoah Valley on the west and the Piedmont to the east. All of it was beautiful to my eyes, but with a constant edge—we had to get to work, and keeping to that speed limit was maddening. However, we also saw a lot of rangers on patrol. About halfway through the park, we stopped at the Byrd Visitor Center for the necessary stamp, then crept along for another twenty miles, until we turned east on Highway 211.

It was a splendidly winding little road, with no pesky rangers, and I zipped ahead of Michael for a while, until the highway flattened into the farmlands and small towns of the rolling Piedmont. After the longest show-day ride of the tour, 571 kilometers, 356 miles, so much of it slow-going, we didn't arrive at the Japanese Automobile Manufacturer Pavilion until four o'clock. Though there was still an hour until sound check, we were usually in between two and three, and Dave met us beside the bus, saying, "I was starting to get worried."

I told him what we had done, where we had been, how many miles we had covered in those two days (837), and showed him the three most recent stamps in my journal. Seven down now, two to go, but those last two, one in Ohio and one in Maine, would be the most difficult to get to, as they were *way* off our itinerary. I was reluctant to ask Dave to drive hundreds of miles out of his way just to humor my whimsical little quest, but I finally soothed my conscience the old-fashioned way—bribery.

Compared to downtown arenas, those rural amphitheaters were a lot nicer for Michael and me—and the truck and bus drivers—to get to, and I would have thought the same applied to the audiences. I saw the other side of the situation in an on-line comment about that particular venue, forty miles outside Washington:

It doesn't matter what time you leave. If you live in D.C. you WILL be late and you WILL miss at least some of the show. This has to be the worst-planned venue in the area, if not the country. Hopefully people will just stop going and promoters will stop booking acts there.

Nearly every night, minutes before we were supposed to go on, Donovan would get a call on the radio announcing a ten-minute delay. C.B. would make that decision based on how many people were still waiting in line to get in, but of course, we couldn't know how many people were still on the *roads* waiting to get in.

Onstage that night, I noticed an older woman, certainly in her sixties, watching us with a wistful intensity, looking both confused and earnest, somehow. I had seen people like that before in our audiences, sometimes older couples, sometimes stooped and gray-haired single men and women, and I had the feeling—perhaps informed by the shared understanding of a bereaved parent—that they had lost a child who had been a fan of ours, and were trying in this way to reconnect. My heart was touched by that.

During the intermission, I walked into the main dressing room after my Red Apple break in Bubba-Gump, and laughed to see both Alex and Geddy hunched silently over their Powerbooks. I guessed that Geddy would be on-line following box scores, both as a real-life fan and fantasy league player, but I asked Alex, "Are you checking *golf* box scores?"

He laughed and said, "No, just catching up on e-mails."

That's what a modern-day rock band does backstage between sets.

After the show, as we drove north, Michael told me about another client of his, a drummer, who had asked Michael to check on his wife's activities while he was away on tour. Michael had gathered enough information to know that she was having an affair with another man, and the evidence indicated that she seemed to be the one doing the pursuing.

Now Michael faced the unpleasant responsibility of having to tell the guy.

Later, in a bedtime attempt at catching up on some journal notes, I commented about that story—the nightmare of many a traveling musician—and continued with the same old lament.

Don't like that story . . .

So much to get down, but just can't do it. Yet another time when real life is overwhelming the time and energy needed to *document* it.

And typically, now that I've got time to write, I can't think of all the stuff I've been wanting to remember to get down.

Main engine just rattled down, somewhere near the Maryland-Delaware border.

Now we were in a part of the country where it was especially difficult to live up to my assertion that each state had nice roads to ride. With the next night's show in Camden, New Jersey, just over the river from Philadelphia, the map confronted me with the dense chain of metropolises along I-95. Eastern Pennsylvania had space and scenery and some good riding, but I needed to save it for later.

On the *Test for Echo* tour in early 1997, on our way to that same amphitheater in Camden, Brutus had found a ferry that ran across Delaware Bay, between Delaware and New Jersey, and we had enjoyed our ride through the Delmarva Peninsula (the name incorporating abbreviations of the state names). That region always evoked one of my favorite writers, John Barth, who lived on the Maryland side of that peninsula. Many of his great novels, like *The Floating Opera*, *Sabbatical*, and *The Tidewater Tales*, were set in the tidewater country of the Delmarva Peninsula, and on sailboats and showboats in Chesapeake Bay. Years ago, I had also been captivated by James Michener's *Chesapeake*, which typically brought the region's history to page-turning life. On other tours, I had enjoyed some nice riding on that peninsula, and a ferry ride was always an adventure, especially on the ocean.

On another hot August day, Michael and I rode south on a narrow two-lane, Highway 9, through saltwater marshes, cornfields, and shady forests, then on the busier four-lane to the ferry dock at Lewes. The crossing took a little over an hour, an enjoyable interlude of cool salt air, expansive views of blue above and below, passing seabirds and boats, and even time for a nap on a bench on deck. At the other side of Delaware Bay, we rode off at Cape May, New Jersey.

New Jersey did not have a scenic reputation, but most of that stigma had been established by New York City residents, joking about the raw and odoriferous parts of New Jersey bordering Manhattan—which did much of the city's dirty work in industry and waste-handling. But away from the often noxious strip from Hackensack to Hoboken, other parts of the Garden State were actually very attractive, from the northern woodlands and farming towns along the Delaware River across from Pennsylvania, and the Delaware Water Gap National Recreation Area, to the Pine Barrens in the south enclosed in the Pinelands National Reserve.

My only experience of the Jersey Shore was a 1974 show at a waterfront ballroom in Asbury Park, opening for the band Mountain—aptly named after their massive guitarist, Leslie West. During their set, Howard assembled the contents of our deli tray into one giant sandwich, and left it in Mountain's dressing room. Oh those juvenile hijinks!

These days, I would have been glad to explore the more remote coastline of beaches and slender islands, especially the littoral areas in the national reserve that looked so nice on the map, and had interesting names like Barnegat Bay, the Mystic Islands, and Loveladies. But not this time.

Michael and I rode around the back side of Cape May, a meandering little road which led us along the Maurice River, combining estuary, river, rural, and small-town scenery. Highway 47 emptied onto Highway 55, a busy four-lane leading up to Camden. Originally a Quaker settlement, like Philadelphia, its neighbor across the Delaware River, Camden had been the home of Walt Whitman in his last years. In the late nineteenth century, luminaries such as Charles Dickens, William Thackeray, and Oscar Wilde came to Camden to visit the esteemed poet, who was also friends with the great painter Thomas Eakins. A hundred years later, though, Camden had fallen on hard times.

Like the Jersey side of Manhattan, Camden was a dark shadow across the river from a more prosperous city. The City of Brotherly Love was connected by the Walt Whitman Bridge to its impoverished and menacing neighbor—recently listed as the most crime-ridden city in America. Michael and I made our way through the cratered streets and crumbling buildings to the waterfront, where Camden had attempted to revitalize its downtown area. The Consumer Electronics Retail Chain Amphitheater, built in 1995, was part of that effort, and we pulled into the backstage area after 318 kilometers, almost 200 miles (not counting the *nautical* miles).

The first time we had played there, on the *Test for Echo* tour in the early summer of 1997, Selena had flown in from Toronto to join Brutus and me for a few days, traveling with us from show to show on the bus and on the back of my motorcycle. She arrived at the Camden venue wearing a blue silk Chinese-style suit that day, looking poised and beautiful.

Camden held another sad memory for me. On the *Vapor Trails* tour in 2002, I had been visited in the afternoon by two old cycling companions, Henry, the "Prince Among Men," and Gay, who I had written about many times before. In *The Masked Rider*, when I commented on an unpleasant companion on that journey, I contrasted her with Gay, always good-natured even when she was struggling. Fair of skin and hair, round of feature and physique, Gay was not a natural athlete, but her gentle, maternal spirit coexisted with a drive to explore the world, and her chosen ways to travel were sailing and bicycling. While Gay slowly turned the pedals on a long, relentless climb to a mountain pass in the Alps or the Rockies, she would listen to a tape of inspiring music she called "Dumbo's Feather." If she couldn't make it all the way, she got off and walked, never complaining.

Early in *Ghost Rider*, Gay was one of the first people I wrote to from the healing road, rekindling a friendship that had begun ten years earlier (as recounted in *Traveling Music*), on my first bicycle tour in China. Gay and her friends Bob and Rosie were from New Jersey, and belonged to a cycling club called the Western Jersey Wheelmen. In later years, Bob and Rosie began designing their own tours over the Alps, the Pyrenees, and the Rockies, and I often joined their small, friendly groups, where I met Henry, who became my frequent roommate and another favorite traveling companion.

Gay's temperament could anchor the delicate balance of a disparate group, for off the bike, she had a quiet, dry humor and a way of giving her traveling companions what I always called a "gentle tease." She shared my habit of letter-writing, and over the years, Gay and I kept up a fairly regular correspondence from our homes and separate travels, writing about our lives and families. Early in 2004, Gay wrote to tell me that a misdiagnosis of pneumonia had been upgraded to cancer, and she would be starting treatment soon. She passed it off lightly, though she must have known how serious it was, for only a few months later she was gone. I only heard from Henry at the last minute that Gay's condition had become critical, and I sent her an e-mail on what turned out to be the very day she died.

On the afternoon of the show in Camden, this time Henry showed up alone, and his usual irrepressible humor (master of bad jokes that frequently required punches in the shoulder) was subdued by our mutual recognition of the missing Gay—no homemade cookies, no gentle teases.

My after-show notes reported, "Tonight's show dedicated to Gay, for me. Good one, overall. Couple of little things. Good solo."

Later that night, as the bus roared north, I finally finished highlighting the next day's complicated route, littering the floor with four different maps (New York, Vermont/New Hampshire, Massachusetts, and Connecticut) squiggled with yellow highlighted lines. They were ready for Michael to input the route into the computer (using his handy blue-filtered flashlight, which made the yellow marker stand out like Day-Glo) and download them to Doofus and Dingus. Patsy Cline played on the stereo, and I made another journal note, "The Gatorade Drama."

Those three words were intended to remind me of a certain on-tour syndrome, the tensions and conflicts that sometimes brewed between the production office and the crew. It resembled the common divisions between management and labor in business, between officers and enlisted men in the military, and a separation I had noticed in the farm equipment business and at car and motorcycle dealers, between the sales and service departments.

In our case, that division arose every tour, no matter who we had in the production office or on the crew. It was usually not a case of one side being right or wrong, but of each being on different wavelengths. The crew members thought their requests were important and urgent, and the production office felt overwhelmed with seemingly trivial requests and complaints, everybody thinking theirs was the most important.

Case in point: Gump liked to drink Gatorade in hot weather. Earlier in the tour, he had asked Karen to get him some bottles of Gatorade every night, but it never showed up. Similar things happened with our bus requests: if Dave or Michael asked for some groceries or other supplies late in the day, the request might not be treated with the same urgency as it would if I asked personally. If I wanted to be sure our stuff would be on the bus before we left, I had learned to write out our grocery lists and hand them to Karen myself.

In Deborah Tannen's book, *You Just Don't Understand*, she describes how a man will commonly miss the signal when, say, he is driving with a woman and she asks if he is hungry. He might simply say, "no," not recognizing that the question was in fact a statement (that *she* was hungry). Similarly, one afternoon before soundcheck Gump asked me if I liked Gatorade, and I said I didn't. Taking his question at face value, I missed the subtext entirely.

Sometime later, Gump and Dave must have had a talk, because I noticed that the supplies delivered to our bus every night—sandwiches, drinks, and salty snacks—began to include a few bottles of Gatorade, which Michael would pass to Gump the following day.

In my farm equipment days, a farmer once asked me about a part he had ordered, saying, "I don't want to be a pest, but you know how it is—the squeaky wheel gets the grease!" As a road veteran, Dave knew the squeaky wheel not only didn't always get the grease, it sometimes got replaced, and he had learned to keep the friction out of his wheels by using the dry, long-lasting lubricant of *strategy*.

The next day, we awoke in the parking lot of a shopping mall near Troy, New York. Riding northeast into Vermont on a warm, sunny morning, our route followed the map's thin red and gray lines, many of the roads not named or numbered, through my favorite part of the eastern U.S. The Adirondacks of New York, the Green Mountains of Vermont, and the White Mountains of New Hampshire were all part of the same Appalachian chain, the oldest mountains in the world. As I have said before, I imagine my soulscape like that, forested mountains with a few scattered lakes—and some winding gray roads.

My journal note described it later:

Not a far day, or a long day, but a *hard* day. Hilly, curvy, tree-lined roads, lots of driveways, trucks, tractors, dogs, deer, lawnmowers, linemen, road construction, tree-trimming, police, gravel, pedestrians, fishermen, camper-trailers.

So tired.

The "boys" were mightily confused by some of the route—though Michael must be responsible for the Agony Hill Road detour.

That would have been around Reading, Vermont, where we were supposed to turn left from one gray line to another gray line. Dingus told me to turn left onto a little road, and though it wasn't marked as the one we wanted, Highway 106, I thought perhaps it was one of Dingus's clever "shortcuts."

The road soon diminished to a one-lane gravel track running through thick woods, then a two-rut lane, then an overgrown, grassy path, like a cross-country ski trail in summer. No one had driven or ridden that way in a long time. Roots and rocks and muddy patches studded the trail, even a fallen birch trunk that I had to get off the bike and move, and eventually we found ourselves at the edge of a steep hill, which bumped its way down to what looked like a bog.

I stopped at the top of that hill, straddling the bike, and Michael pulled up alongside.

"Look at your screen," I said, pointing to Dingus.

"AGONY HILL ROAD," it read. That didn't sound promising.

Leaving the bike running, I put it in neutral, kicked the sidestand down, and got off. "Let's have a look before we go down this hill."

In our heavy boots, leathers, and helmets, we stumbled down the steep and bumpy hill, then looked ahead at a damp, overgrown, and forbidding trail. I said, "I don't think so. If this ends somewhere up ahead, and we have to come back, I'd hate to try to climb this hill on these big, heavy bikes."

Michael called me some hurtful names and insulted my manhood, until he ran out of breath on the uphill climb.

Back on paved roads and meandering our way north, we were trapped for a while in the tourist crush of Woodstock, Vermont, a quaint little "olde" town of antique shops and such (also the real-life setting for the Stratford Inn on the old "Newhart" TV show). North of there, Doofus and Dingus had a little trouble following an unpaved section of the route, and I had to use a combination of their occasional contributions, map-reading, and intuition, to navigate us over the mountain to Sharon,

Vermont, home of Joseph Smith, founder and prophet of the Church of Latter-Day Saints.

A church sign I saw that day seemed to comment on the mysterious gold tablets Smith said he found in the Adirondacks, translated with the help of the angel Moroni, then "lost" before anyone else could see them: "IF YOU'RE SEARCHING FOR TRUTH, THE BIBLE IS A GOLD MIND."

Crossing a small bridge to Hanover, New Hampshire, home of Dartmouth College, we settled for the night at the exceedingly average Fireside Inn and Suites in Lebanon, after 282 kilometers, 176 miles.

"Not a far day, or a long day, but a *hard* day."

The next day's show was in Hartford, Connecticut, at the former Meadows Amphitheater (now called the Ctnow.com Amphitheater, awkwardly, after a supposedly hip name for the local newspaper, the *Courant*) where we had played the first show on the *Vapor Trails* tour. We started out that morning on New Hampshire back roads, through forests, fields, and quaint little towns that reminded me of Quebec—and made me miss it—angling down through Massachusetts to I-91, and south to Connecticut through the usual hostile traffic of a Friday afternoon.

When we arrived at the venue, after another short ride (256 kilometers, 160 miles) that had somehow taken a long time (five hours), Michael took off to the local BMW dealer to get new tires while I climbed into bed for a nap. When I got up for soundcheck, Dave told me he had come out of the bus and found a group of fans standing in our trailer, taking each other's pictures with our motorcycles. Apparently they had snuck past another lax security staff. Journal note, "That's just *creepy*."

Before soundcheck, as I was collecting my dancing shoes from the Bubba-Gump room, Geddy came in and told me his friend since their teenage years, Oscar, had died that morning. Oscar had suffered a stroke earlier that year, and Geddy had helped look after him as he gradually faded away.

"Another good one gone," I said.

Geddy, his voice breaking, said, "Yeah, what's up with that?"

We shook our heads, shared a strong hug, and went to work. That was all we could do.

That night Michael, Dave, and I slept on the bus in the parking lot of a BMW dealer in Wilkes-Barre, Pennsylvania. My 1200 was due for another major service, having just passed 20,000 kilometers, and I had called the day before to see if they could take care of it for me. When the service department opened in the morning, I wheeled the 1200 inside, then set out on the old 1150, which I hadn't ridden in weeks. "Nice, but not *as* nice," I noted.

Wilkes-Barre (where we had opened for Blue Oyster Cult in late '74) was only about twenty miles from Scranton's Montage Mountain Amphitheater, which had followed Hartford on *Vapor Trails* too, the second show on that tour. Michael and I wouldn't be taking the direct route, of course—I had designed us a long loop to the west and north, through the Poconos. The weather was overcast and much cooler than we were used to, only rising to 66 degrees, and we had "a lovely loop of country roads, many narrow with no painted lines, rolling country, more sylvan than pastoral, arches of trees over road, 324 kms [202 miles]." That sums it up pretty well.

We passed a campground with a sign bearing the superfluous apostrophe that always made me wince, "CHRISTIAN CAMPING AT IT'S BEST" (whatever that might mean), and the day's church sign was another kind of groaner, "BE FISHERS OF MEN—YOU CATCH THEM, HE WILL CLEAN THEM."

It was a cold night onstage, and for the first time that tour, I never turned on the little squirrel-cage fans that usually blew on my hands and back. Among the sea of faces in the audience, I noticed the reflection of a pair of big round lenses, binoculars, pointed right at me from about twenty feet away. That seemed a little weird. As the show went on, many people in that audience seemed to spend half the time trying to sneak photographs, peering through their little viewfinders and flashing in our faces. One big reason why photography was prohibited at concerts was *not* to have flashes going off in our faces all night, and another reason was the "private property" aspect—of our music, our show, and our faces. Every night, Michael would spend time standing in the wings looking over the audience, catching people with tape recorders, video cameras, and still cameras, and removing their tapes, film, and digital media. One of Michael's frequent freelance jobs in Los Angeles was covering movie premieres, wearing night-vision lenses and watching for pirates.

At intermission, I scrawled down a half-time review, then picked it up again after the show.

Competent, but uninspired. Call it dull. Audience seems that way, too—maybe just projection.

Note that it always seems important to *run* onstage, at beginning, middle, and encore—to demonstrate energy, eagerness, urgency.

Though of course I always run *offstage* too!

That was intermission, now on bus. Once again, such a *long* show, counting down song by song—that old familiar feeling. Not particularly *strong* tonight, especially legs, but accurate at least.

Tambourine screwed up in "Waltz," wrecked the solo for me, but otherwise, it was . . . accurate.

I have thought several times this tour how easy the job would be if I played all night like in "Heart Full of Soul" [where I just tapped along with acoustic guitars].

I kept noticing this adorable little girl with thin blonde hair, fluffy pink earrings, dazed-looking smile, and strabismus [crossed eyes].

Guy in center with camera—brazen and annoying. I never mind the people I see snap off a "memory" shot, as that's understandable and tolerable, but this guy was *obnoxious*. Michael eventually took his chip away, and unfortunately it's also got a bunch of personal photos. Why would he do that, take that foolish risk? Then probably blame us.

That night we were setting up to return to the Spirit Quest on the following day off. Even though the next show was in Saratoga Springs, New York, 200 miles to the east, Dave drove us about 250 miles straight *west* on I-80, almost to the Ohio line. We slept in a rest area at the junction with I-79, north of Pittsburgh.

After barely five hours of sleep, I dragged myself out of bed at 7:30, and Michael and I were on the road before nine, heading west for Cuyahoga Valley National Park. I couldn't forget we had played right in the middle of that park almost two months before, riding in on that rainy June 10 with Tom Marinelli. But I didn't know then that two months later, I would need that passport stamp . . .

We still had over 100 miles to ride west on the interstate, and as usual on a Sunday, the highway was filled with amateur drivers and riders. We wove our way through them, and through Youngstown and Akron, then turned north through Cuyahoga Falls. The town's streets were empty, but the church parking lots were full.

"Only a Fool Fools With Sin."

Cuyahoga Valley was an anomaly among national parks, relatively small (33,000 acres) and suburban compared to most of the others. Designated in 2000, it was part of a program to establish more "urban" parks in the system, accessible to the eastern cities. It was named for the river that meanders through the valley, "*Ka-ih-ogh-ha*," or crooked river. In addition to being a natural sanctuary of woodlands, the park offered a fair summary of Midwestern American pioneer life, from the restored farms to the towpath from the Ohio and Erie Canal, and the railroad which eventually replaced the canals throughout the Northeast.

The affection of a native son for his own soulscape was described by Cleveland writer James Snowden Jackson. "I have admired the rugged fjords of Norway and the bald peaks of Yosemite. But I gain strength each day at home from the beauty of our own Cuyahoga Valley."

Back in 1786, Connecticut had "reserved" three-and-a-half million acres of northeastern Ohio for eventual settlement by its citizens. The area became known as the Western Reserve, a name that endures on area banks, businesses, and the Western Reserve Historical Society.

In search of the park's visitor center, Michael and I saw more of Cuyahoga Valley National Park than we wanted to, with so far to travel that day. We circled the whole park before Michael finally made some phone calls and got directions to the visitor center. In a small cabin beside a fruit stand, a friendly older ranger showed me the stamp and pad—national park passport stamp number eight. One more to go.

Michael and I retraced our route down to the interstate, and began the long charge eastward. The midsummer Sunday was warm and bright, green all around, and even the semis wore their Sunday best. "His Name Is Not The Man Upstairs, His Name is Jesus," was the stern message painted across the back of a big trailer. Another truck offered a sanctimonious presumption: "Hurting? God Cares."

When I was hurting, reeling under the unbearable weight of my double losses, how I had bristled at those kinds of smug and unhelpful (not to mention unsubstantiated) sentiments.

Though I did appreciate the humor on a bumper sticker, "WARN-ING: IN CASE OF RAPTURE, THIS VEHICLE MAY BE UNOCCUPIED." At least, I *hope* it was a joke, but it might have been serious. Apparently about one third of Americans believed that in these End Times, any minute now the Messiah will return and they will suddenly be trans-ported to heaven—the Rapture. Books and movies have told the story about the rest of us poor losers being "Left Behind." At least there was no doubt about the humorous intent of another bumper sticker, quoted in *Traveling Music*, "IF THE RAPTURE COMES, CAN I HAVE YOUR CAR?"

We paused for gas and a quick lunch at a franchise burger joint in Clarion, Pennsylvania, then rode onward, hour after hour. Late in the afternoon we finally left the interstate on little Highway 150, up through Lock Haven (where the band had also opened for Blue Oyster Cult in 1974) and across the Susquehanna River into Williamsport, where we stopped for the night after 604 kilometers, 377 miles.

I believe that night was the first time I ever dined at the restaurant chain called TGI Friday's (as in "Thank God It's," though they never use the full name as it might offend their religious customers). The meal was forgettable, but the name once helped me with a crossword clue, "Some thank God for it." The answer, of course, was "Friday."

The next day we cut northeast on small back roads, beginning on a glittery, dew-soaked morning in the valley of the Lycoming River. The road was stippled with sunlight through overhanging trees, and passing cornfields were framed by the forested, ridge-like mountains so charac-teristic of central Pennsylvania. Dingus was having some mental prob-lems that day, crashing every time I left the prescribed route, even for gas, but it didn't matter too much. Just into New York State, we began a long interstate blast, all the way northeast to Schenectady, then a slow run up to Saratoga Springs, 440 kilometers, 275 miles.

In the afternoon, I met with my friend Paul Siegel for a while, letting him gently try to talk me into making another instructional video. Paul and his partner Rob Wallis had been excellent collaborators on my previ-ous one, *A Work in Progress*, made in 1996 (*A Jerk in Progress*, to me and my friends), and I liked them both as people and as professionals. They were close to my age, and had sustained their own successful partnership for about thirty years, and in all those ways, I considered them very much as peers. We had been casually discussing making a video on the subject of drum-soloing, but being in the middle of one tough job, it was hard for me to contemplate taking on another one.

And this job, this life, was about to get even tougher. The next day was August 10, the anniversary of Selena's death, and I wrote in my journal, "Feeling down already." After seven years, that remained the worst day of the year for me, as it will be for the rest of my life, and there was no good way to handle it. During the planning of our *Vapor Trails* tour, Ray had asked me, through Liam (the chain of diplomacy), how I wanted to handle that date. I had said, "Just make it a day off and I'll hide out somewhere."

The Saratoga Performing Arts Center was nicely situated in a wooded park, and we played a good show, in front of 8,073 hopefully satisfied customers. After, Dave and Michael and I drove straight to a hotel in Albany, where I could "hide out." Drawing a veil over the misery of that day and night, my journal said the next day, "Let's just forget yesterday. And today."

As I had found on *Vapor Trails*, the following day could be even worse to get through, when I had to go back to work and face sympathetic or unknowing friends and coworkers, and find the strength to keep *doing* it. Michael and I rode on the bus with Dave from Albany down to Jones Beach, on Long Island, watching *Kill Bill*. (Michael already knew the movie by heart, but I hadn't seen it before. I liked how its chilling brutality was tempered by humor, style, and kitschy references to martial arts movies.) Predictably, Michael and and I started calling each other "Oren Ishii" and "Gogo."

Later, I crawled into bed and fell asleep, waking to hear Pink Floyd's "Comfortably Numb" blasting outside the bus. That was the song Brad played every afternoon to tune up the P.A. system, and it meant we were parked at the venue. I had been having an awful dream that I was backstage before the show, overwhelmed with grief, wailing helplessly in front of everybody. Drifting off again, I woke to hear the crew doing "line check," testing microphones and direct feeds, while rain pattered on the roof of the bus.

Jones Beach Amphitheater was among the oldest venues we would play on the North American part of the tour, as the site dated to a wooden structure in the 1920s. The original version of the current building dated, like me, back to 1952. Through the 1990s, as amphitheaters became more popular, additional seating was added, and Jones Beach also followed the current trend by allowing a pop-fashion brand to add its name to the marquee (for a price, of course).

No part of the main seating area was roofed-over, and I watched intermittent rain slant through the spotlight beams a few times during the show, feeling sorry for the people out there getting wet. (Though I later talked to a friend who was at that show, and he didn't even remember it raining—we *must* have been good!) While I played the encore, I could see the running lights on the bus and trailer behind the seating area to far stage right, and that meant it was a *long* run from the stage to the bus. I followed Michael and a couple of flashlight-wielding security guards down several flights of stairs, through a long, damp tunnel on raised boards, then up several more flights of stairs at the other end.

A *fair* show for me, but legs falling off badly (hard to write on I-95! [bouncy]), though I realize that's always been the case, even when I was *young!*

So *down* all day, everything so surreal.

Michael struggling with tomorrow's complicated route across Massachusetts, transfering it from map to Mother [our name for the computer program that was downloaded to Doofus and Dingus—I had once defined their natures as "Mother is wise and all-knowing, but the boys are clever and streetwise"] with blue flashlight on yellow highlighter, trying to match that to Mother's parameters.

Dave reports we've been followed for two hours now—again.

How can they think that's an okay thing to do?

One thing Michael and Dave had in common was their political leanings. When our front lounge television was on in the afternoon, and not tuned to the Weather Channel, it was always on Fox News, keeping me up to date on the conservative side of the summer's current events—the presidential campaign, the Hacking murder, the Florida Keys being evacuated for Hurricane Charley (I noted, "Imagine Highway One!"), Pamela Anderson's novel, and the smug opinions of Hannity and Colmes.

Lately I had been calling Dave and Michael my Elite Republican Guard, and once again it was time for them to take action, pull over at the roadside and go back to talk to the "followers."

Again I waited nervously, half-fearing the sound of gunfire, but they returned after another successful diplomatic mission. We continued on our way, Dave keeping an eye on the mirrors to make sure.

We parked that night at the same shopping mall near Troy, New York, where we had slept the previous week. Next morning, Michael and I set off on a more southerly route to the east, aiming for the day's show outside of Boston. The route was very promising, through scenic northwestern Massachusetts, classic little college towns like Williamstown and North Adams, the Berkshires, then a network of small roads through Emily Dickinson country, Amherst, and all the way across the state.

However, as always on a show day, my route choices were subservient to time, distance, and weather. After an hour of pleasant riding, Michael and I had to stop under a covered bridge to put on our rainsuits (a uniquely New England experience, at least). The little gray roads, a couple of them unpaved, were slow going under those conditions, and by the time we made it over to Deerfield (where my friend Matt went to school), we had to abort. We set Doofus and Dingus to "Quickest Way," and followed I-91 down to the Massachusetts Turnpike and all the way east to the Consumer Electronics Retail Chain Center for the Performing Arts (formerly more concisely and poetically known as Great Woods Amphitheater), 303 kilometers, 189 miles.

The show was another good one ("competent," in my demanding rating system, a rave review), in front of a fairly large audience of 12,844 people. Afterwards, instead of driving south toward the next show in New Jersey, Dave headed north toward Maine and the final station on my Spirit Quest, Acadia National Park.

The 200-mile drive north to Augusta would put Michael and me in reach of Acadia, with time to get headed back south again on that day off. Even following Doofus and Dingus's "Quickest Way," we were already more than 400 miles away from the next job.

A meteorologist might have described the day's forecast as "rain, heavy at times," and of course that complicated the journey. As did the traffic and road conditions, for we had to make our way on busy two-lane roads full of vacationers, out to Bar Harbor (how do you write that in a Maine accent, "Ba Haba?"), 100 miles each way, all the way back to Augusta, and south on I-95 just as far as we could get that day.

All of that in "rain, heavy at times," and road conditions I described as: "Traffic mostly awful—in fact, *always* awful. Holiday travelers."

A church sign editorialized on what was growing into the most important political issue in America, the shibboleth that some would say decided the next presidential election, "ONE MAN AND ONE WOMAN MAKES A MARRIAGE."

It was a Friday, too, making the mood of the roads especially tense. Under those conditions, coupled with my constant state of fatigue, finally getting to Acadia National Park was almost an anticlimax. *Almost.* As I stood dripping in the visitor center, I looked at those neat rows of stamps in the front of my journal, and I had a brief little smile of satisfaction. Then I put the journal away in my beltpack, tucked it under my rain jacket, and walked out into the teeming rain. I replaced my earplugs, pulled down my steamed-up helmet, and off we went again.

I had wondered about the name "Acadia," usually given to an area of Nova Scotia that had been settled by people from a part of France called La Cady, hence "La Cadiens." When the British gained control of eastern Canada in the eighteenth century, the French settlers who refused to swear allegiance to the British king were exiled to Louisiana (see Longfellow's "Evangeline"). Their name was eventually corrupted to "Cajuns," while those who stayed in Nova Scotia retained their heritage in isolated settlements even to the present day. Brutus and I had traveled around there, and heard people speaking their strange, antiquated Acadian French.

French explorer Samuel de Champlain had sailed by that part of Maine in 1604, and for the next 150 years, the French and British battled over the area, and everywhere else in the Old World and New. During that time another French explorer, Antoine de la Mothe Sieur de Cadillac, left the last of his names on a mountain in the park, and after the final French defeat in 1759, Cadillac went west to found the city of Detroit. Many years later, he would lend his name and coat of arms (both invented, apparently) to a luxury car once known as "the Standard of the World," and more recently notorious for a titanic SUV, "the Bling-Bling Whip."

Apparently in 1524, the Italian explorer Giovanni Verrazano had actually named that part of the Maine coast "Arcadia," after its resemblance to a part of Greece. The first settlement would not be established until 1761, by colonists from England, not from La Cady. (Those early Maine residents became known as "downeasters," because in order to travel east, they sailed down*wind.*)

The park was designated by Woodrow Wilson in 1919, the first national park east of the Mississippi, and was originally named Lafayette National Park as a tribute to its French heritage. In the 1920s, an English family donated 2000 acres to the park, but objected to its French name (*plus ça change*). It took an Act of Congress to change the name to Acadia, in 1929.

After 624 kilometers (390 miles) of rain, crammed two-lane, and tedious interstate, Michael and I took refuge at a Ramada Inn just off I-495 in Boxborough, Massachusetts. I described the day in my journal.

Bagged park number nine today, which is sort of cool—and sort of dumb.

So tired all day, and really tired and sore now.

Just had an imaginary conversation with myself in the shower, thinking, "Of all the missions you've come up with, that was about the dumbest."

I answered myself, "Hey, I know it's stupid, but it was either that or go insane!"

Once again I'm feeling a terrible gap between what I experience, observe, feel, and think, and what I've been able to get written down. Considering my ambitions for this book, it seems a feeble foundation.

Chapter theme: "Being Bubba."

The next day, under gray and black skies, we battled heavy Saturday traffic south on the interstate through Massachusetts and Connecticut, all the way through New York City via the Cross-Bronx Expressway, and across the George Washington Bridge to the New Jersey Turnpike. Fortunately we dodged the rain showers, visible all around us in dark curtains, but traffic was slowed and stopped so many times that it was nerve-racking, especially on a show day, and we were changing lanes constantly just to keep moving.

In a line of stopped traffic at a toll booth on the Jersey side, I pulled up beside Michael and started growling the opening theme from "The Sopranos"—"You woke up this morning, got yourself a gun."

Michael's helmet turned sharply toward me. "I can't believe you're singing that—I've been singing it for the past hour!" And no wonder, as we had been riding through the same bleak industrial wasteland Tony Soprano was pictured driving through as that song played over the opening credits of the TV series.

I was thinking that day that anyone who complained about Los Angeles traffic should drive around the Northeast for a few days. And, I thought uncharitably, at least in California traffic, chances were that at the end of your journey, you would end up somewhere *nice*—not in the less savory parts of New Jersey.

I did have to smile when I passed a car with the Christian "fish" emblem on the back, for in the middle of the chrome fish outline were the words, "and chips."

We arrived at the Financial Services Corporation Arts Center, formerly known as the Garden State Arts Center, after "another 'what a day' day," and 386 bleakly urban kilometers, 241 miles. Altogether, on that final Station of the Quest, we had ridden 631 mostly unpleasant miles. But I must admit, I showed all the guys at work my complete collection of East Coast national park passport stamps.

That afternoon I had a long mental list of things to do, from maintenance on the bike to a couple of urgent e-mails (it was sister-in-law Janette's birthday, for one, and I always tried to remember people's birthdays). I also needed to start sorting out all my stuff on the bus, especially the swag I had collected—T-shirts from venues and vendors; books, cards, and letters from fans. We had only a few more shows on the North American tour, and I would soon be moving off the bus that had been my home for the past three months.

At soundcheck, under the "mother-ship" ceiling of the Arts Center, like the underside of a giant flying saucer, Geddy came over to the drum riser and brought up a subject I thought we had settled a few days earlier. For the upcoming European tour, he wanted to add another old song, "Closer to the Heart," because it had been popular there. In my opinion, the show was already at least fifteen minutes too long (if not three *hours* too long), but not wanting to argue about it, I had tried to be agreeable, saying "Okay, what song do you want to drop?"

He said he didn't want to drop anything, because the set was great the way it was, but he thought we could just add it after the acoustic set. I tried to express my feelings in a way I hoped was decisive without being argumentative. I shook my head and said, "I don't wanna."

"You don't wanna?"

"I don't wanna," I said again.

Apparently, when I'm trying to avoid confrontation, I sometimes don't express myself *forcefully* enough. Now Geddy had come up behind the drum riser before soundcheck, and wondered if we could rehearse "Closer to the Heart" that day. I turned around, raised my drumsticks in a *faux* threat, made my face the mask of an attacking warrior, and said, "I'm so *over* all this, and I don't want to add any more!"

This time he got the message, and we went on with our regular soundcheck. Later, Alex told me he was glad I had vetoed the idea.

During my quiet time on the bus after dinner, Dave told me that during soundcheck he had been getting a massage (local therapists often set up a massage table backstage, for cramped-up drivers and crew members). The masseuse had told him her seventeen-year-old daughter had never heard of Rush, but the girl's boyfriend, a seventeen-year-old bass player, had said, "Aren't they the old guys with the world's greatest living drummer?"

I had to laugh at that—though I knew there were at least fifty drummers ahead of me on that list.

In return, I told Dave and Michael, my Elite Republican Guard, the joke I had read about George W. Bush, a fine example of the school of philosophy known as "Baseball as a Metaphor for Life."

"George W. Bush was born on third base, and thought he hit a triple."

They laughed politely at the boss's joke.

Michael was off to supervise the meet-and-greet, and warned me that they would all be passing right by the bus that night. He suggested I wait there until he came back for me. Just before going inside for my seven o'clock warmup, I made a journal note.

6:45 now, waiting on "meet-and-greet." Last smoke, and a few minutes of *peace* before . . . we do it all again.

That night, Dave drove us back up into New York State, a long way north to Albany, then another hour west to my chosen drop-off point, Canajoharie (I picked it for the name). Like many roads in the winter-battered Northeast, the New York State Thruway could be a rough ride, and many restless hours passed before I finally heard the death-rattle of the main engine, followed by the hum of the generator. Then I knew my bed would stay *still* for a while.

On a quiet Sunday morning, cool, hazy, and threatening rain, Doofus and Dingus led Michael and me away on perhaps the most complicated route yet, an ever-changing thread of thin red and gray lines across the map of Western New York. Our destination was Darien Lake, an amusement park and amphitheater near Buffalo.

The humid haze and attenuated light created a soft-focus effect on the rural landscape, burnishing the still waters of Otsego Lake, shadowing the woodland greenery around Glimmerglass State Park, and ghosting the quiet streets of Cooperstown, the mythical birthplace of America's Pastime. Midsummer smells of damp lawns, fields, and deciduous trees seemed to hover in the still air. All that morning, we rode through a suspended hush, through tiny, almost imperceptible towns, their names telling tales of history and nostalgia for places the pioneers had left behind—New Lisbon, South New Berlin, Glen Aubrey, Van Etten. That part of New York State had been unfamiliar to me, but it had a quiet, rural charm that reminded me of the part of Ontario where I grew up, and that Sunday in August felt like a day from a childhood summer.

We drifted through occasional showers, but the day was mostly just gray. The few cars and people we passed seemed to be moving in slow motion, going about their Sunday errands, visits, and religious rituals. Even the day's church sign was calm and good-natured.

"LOVE YOUR ENEMIES—IT WILL DRIVE THEM NUTS."

The route zigzagged south of the Finger Lakes, aptly named glacial scrapes in the rolling landscape, vineyards lining the sloping hillsides, through Watkins Glen, a picturesque little town at the southern fingertip of Seneca Lake. In my car-crazy youth, Watkins Glen was famous for sports car races, originally held right through the town's streets in the late '40s. A racetrack was built nearby in the mid-'50s, and starting in 1961,

Watkins Glen hosted the U.S. Grand Prix for twenty years. After some hard times in the 1980s, the track again hosted a variety of racing events, from NASCAR to vintage sports cars.

That racetrack was also once the setting for one of the biggest-ever rock festivals, in July of 1973, featuring the Grateful Dead, the Band, and the Allman Brothers. Apparently the Dead played for five hours, the Band for three hours, and the Allman Brothers for four hours, then all of them crowded onto the stage for a ninety-minute jam. Presumably the 600,000 people in the audience were high enough to enjoy all that.

By the time Michael and I met I-86, the north-south interstate, the morning was gone and we decided it was time to hit "Quickest Way." My original route would have continued west along the little roads, through Birdsall, Rushford, Freedom, and Java Center, but instead we turned north on the interstate, joining the more urgent traffic of holiday-makers and recreational boaters heading for the Finger Lakes.

Pausing at a rest area for a Red Apple break, I took a photo of a parked semi with the title of Geddy's solo album, *My Favorite Headache*, painted across its sleeper. Geddy once told me about the man who coined that title, the elderly Jewish father of a friend who was describing his long marriage, "Ve alvays got along pretty vell, except for once in a vile, when she vud haff a headache." Then a wry smile, "You know—her *favorite* headache."

Michael picked a small yellow flower and placed it on Dingus's handlebar mount, then brought out his camera.

"Hold it right there," he said, and snapped a photo of me reflected in the rear-view mirror, smiling with my helmet chin-piece raised, beside the little yellow daisy decorating Dingus.

I shook my head, "You are *so* gay."

He shrugged, "And your point is?"

In and out of one more rain shower, we cut west and a little north, the countryside flatter now in the alluvial plain that had once been a giant lakebed in post-Ice Age times. Suddenly the rural countryside ended in the busy, festive atmosphere of a huge amusement park, circling, zipping, screaming fairground rides and throngs of people crossing the road between parking lots, midways, and campgrounds. We threaded our way to the backstage area and parked under the bus's awning, where I hoped to do an oil change between rain showers.

Notably, so to speak, that was the one day on the tour I didn't make *one* note in my journal, except for the day's mileage (490 kilometers, 306 miles). Darien Lake was only about fifty miles from my hometown of St. Catharines, just across the border, so I would have some visitors that day. After a quick oil change, just finishing before another rain shower, I cleaned up in time to greet my sister Nancy and a damp group of giggly girls, nieces Hannah and Emma (thirteen and eleven) with four of their friends.

Then some of my in-laws from Jackie's family arrived—sister Deb, her partner Mark, and their seven-year-old son, Rudy, and brother James, his partner Tracey, and their teenage daughter, Timara. They had all camped overnight in their trailers, and spent the day on the rides. I showed them around a little bit, talked with Deb about how awful Selena's d-day had been for us both, took the traditional photograph of Rudy behind the drums, then sent them out to the house with the nieces and their friends for soundcheck.

In the middle of all that, a security guard handed me a note from a distant friend of a friend, someone I vaguely remembered meeting once in St. Catharines more than thirty years earlier. He wanted to come backstage with his friends and say hello. I made a face and crumpled up the note, with hardly any guilt.

Remember Satchel Paige, "Avoid carrying on in society. The social ramble ain't restful."

During the earlier part of the show, when it was still light, I picked out my other sister Judy smiling in the audience, with her husband John, my teenage niece Holly, and nephews Jason and Sean, both in their twenties. Sean had been born just a few months before Selena, and in past years he had been like a member of our family, joining us for summers at the lake. He and Selena had shared an evil humor in making fun of all the adults, with derisory nicknames for everybody, and all of us were "losers." When Sean, now twenty-six, saw me looking in his direction, he started grimacing and sticking his finger down his throat. I laughed out loud while I played, then mouthed back, "loser."

It was a wonderful feeling to be part of such a close, loving, supportive family.

The next shows would be a two-night stand at Radio City Music Hall in New York City, and that night we had an all-night bus ride, all the way across New York State and down to Jersey City, over 350 miles. Dave would be staying there on the Jersey side, saving him from having to drive the bus and trailer through Manhattan on a Monday morning. Michael and I took a town car to our posh, artsy hotel, the Mandarin, near Lincoln Center, feasting our eyes on the passing parade of the streets of Manhattan along the way. It was going to be nice to get off the bikes for a few days, and to stay in a *good* hotel for a change, and for three nights.

I was tired and scratchy-eyed after a restless, bouncy sleep on the bus (and just in general), but I had another busy day ahead of me. First a long lunch with my editor and agent, Paul McCarthy, at the Princeton Club, me telling war stories about my Stations of the Quest, and him showing me sample covers for the boxed set of my books we were planning to release.

Carrie flew in that evening and I met her at JFK, then took her out for an exciting night on the town—bowling. The North American part of the tour was nearly over, and we were taking advantage of these days off to have a party for the crew at a bowling alley on the Lower East Side. Bowling parties were a tradition going back many tours, and we always had a lot of fun, eating, drinking, and laughing at our ineptitude—and occasional lucky strikes. Balls thumping on the lanes and into the gutter, pins knocking in staccato bursts, loud talk and laughter, rock music playing, and drinks flowing freely. It was a good time.

If I had been in New York just for fun, I would have spent the next day marching around in Central Park, visiting museums, and taking Carrie out shopping and dining. But under the circumstances, I was glad to spend the next day indoors, enjoying the luxury of room service, looking out at our view over Central Park South and Columbus Circle, and being with Carrie. Sometimes it's good just to rest.

The last time we had played Radio City Music Hall was a five-night run in September of 1983, just before recording our *Grace Under Pressure* album. During those shows we had played two or three of the new songs, and I had just developed my "360-degree" drumset with the electronic setup at the back. However, I didn't have the rotating riser yet, so I had to play a couple of the new songs facing the *back* of the stage.

Back in '83, I brought my parents to New York City for the last show of that run, putting them up at the same hotel where we were staying, and bringing them with me to the venue in a limousine in the afternoon. Mom and Dad sat in the stage-left wings during the show, and the next night I arranged for them to attend another concert in the same theater—Linda Ronstadt singing standards with an orchestra. So they had seen both sides of Radio City Music Hall.

Earlier in 2004, I had been hoping to bring Mom and Dad to New York again, twenty years later, but when they were returning from Florida for my dad's third hip replacement, Mom tripped over his crutches and fell, breaking *her* hip. So they wouldn't be able to travel. Instead, I was working on arrangements to bring them to the Toronto show a few days later, setting up transportation from their home a couple of hours north, hotel, and special seating at the Megabrewery Amphitheater there.

On the day of the first Radio City show, I decided to arrive early in the afternoon so I would have time to look around the balconies and corridors of that beautiful Art Deco building. It was strange to arrive at the venue by car instead of whisking through a gate on my motorcycle, helmeted and anonymous. It was even stranger to hear a crowd of people yelling my name (in the corner of my eye I saw them behind a barricade on the sidewalk). Head down and tense, I strode from the car to the stage door and inside.

As always, along with my discomfort, I felt a little guilty. I like the motto, "Never Complain, Never Explain," but I guess that motto is only for generals or kings. For myself, I try never to complain, but I always find myself trying to explain.

Of course I know those people weren't there just to shout and wave—they *wanted* something from me. Probably most of them just wanted an autograph, but that wasn't what I was avoiding. Signing your name isn't hard. Over the years, I had signed tens of thousands of autographs, and every night in the dressing room before the show we scrawled our names on dozens of CDs, posters, and photographs for people.

"Fan" is short for "fanatic," and the kind of fans who would wait outside a building all afternoon were going to be the most fanatical of all. I know most of them would be very nice, polite, and appreciative, but there were the others. The looks on their faces, the things they would say to me, the jostling, the cameras flashing in my face, the sheer, surreal *embarrassment* of it. Ernest Hemingway said something that has always stayed with me, "Praise to the face is open disgrace." That's how I felt about it: disgraced. And embarrassed. Those people never seemed to understand that, but I've noticed in life that people who are not shy can never understand those who are.

Zen and the Art of Motorcycle Maintenance made its author, Robert Pirsig, a sudden celebrity, and in his next book, *Lila*, he wrote about the polarities and consequences of fame, especially in American society.

> Everybody wants their children to be valedictorians, but nobody is supposed to be better than anybody else. A kid who comes out some-where near the bottom of his class is guilt-ridden, self-destructive, and he thinks, "It's not fair! Everybody's equal!" And then the celebrity, John Lennon, steps out to sign an autograph for him. That's the end of the celebrity, John Lennon.
>
> Spooky. Until you're the celebrity you don't see how spooky it is. They love you for being what they want to be, but they hate you for being what they're not. There's always this two-faced relationship with celebrity, and you never know which face will appear next.

By contrast, one time in the mid-'80s we were playing at Madison Square Garden, and I arrived by bicycle, after a thrilling—not to say ter-rifying—ride around the mean streets of Manhattan. Pushing my bicycle up to the employees' entrance at the Garden, I went inside, anonymous and unnoticed. Later that day, on the dressing room TV, I saw an MTV report on our show (when Music Television still concerned itself with events in the music world). Standing in front of the Madison Square Garden marquee, with our name on it, an MTV reporter was talking to the camera. Behind him you could plainly see me walking by with my bicycle—just a guy going to work.

Several times I also rode my bicycle from Manhattan out to the Meadowlands arena, on the New Jersey side, riding up through Harlem and across the George Washington Bridge, then through the famous swamplands, where notorious bodies were said to be interred—like Jimmy Hoffa and countless gangsters and hit men. (One story we heard had Jimmy Hoffa buried in the foundations of the Brendan Byrne Arena at Meadowlands.) New Yorkers were shocked at the idea that I would ride my bicycle through Harlem, but I always told them that if you were on a bicycle, people automatically perceived you as a harmless eccentric—not a threat and not a victim—and I was always either ignored or greeted amiably.

One time, though, I inadvertently rode through some broken glass and got a flat tire. Several shards must have worked their way into the tire, so that every time I fixed a puncture, another would appear as I set off again. As I worked my way slowly across George Washington Bridge, my tires going flat again and again, I eventually used up all my patches and was stranded. I was always careful to leave for work early enough to deal with such unexpected disasters, still—this was a challenge.

On the Jersey side, in dismal Fort Lee, I found a motel (the kind with hourly rates and iron bars over the check-in window) and used their pay phone to call a taxi. Removing the wheels from my bicycle, I crammed it into the trunk of the yellow cab, and headed for the Meadowlands. When I finally arrived at the backstage ramp of the arena, the security guard said taxis weren't allowed in the building.

My laminated pass and increasingly frustrated arguments wouldn't budge him, and I eventually had to climb out in the middle of a bunch of clamoring fans, gather up the pieces of my bike from the trunk, and struggle down the ramp with my arms full of wheels and frame. I made some angry noises in the production office, and I believe that security guard was sent home early.

This time, however, I arrived at a New York show like a "proper star," in a black limousine, but I didn't like it so much. Once I was inside and had looked around the beautiful lobby, I still had more than an hour to wait before soundcheck, so I concentrated on trying to keep myself calm. (Like that works.) Inevitably, I was a little *extra* nervous before that show. All shows are important, but some just seem to weigh a little more— Toronto, New York, Los Angeles, London.

Reading had always been a good distraction, and lately I had been enjoying a book called *The Big Year*, by Mark Obmascik. It had been sent to me by a fan earlier in the tour, in an envelope passed backstage with a note thanking me for a postcard I had sent him in response to the gift of a book on the previous tour.

Later that year, I would name that book as my favorite of 2004, in an article for the Toronto *Globe and Mail*, and describe it as,

. . . a non-fiction tale of epic sweep and depth about a competition among, of all people, birdwatchers. In the birding Olympics, their quest is to list the highest number of bird species ever seen in North America in one calendar year, and their obstacles are many, both human and natural, woven into a surprisingly compelling drama of obsession, competition, strategy, resourcefulness, and human nobility and fallibility. The competitors strain themselves, their resources, and their jobs and families to catch even a momentary glimpse of a feathered rarity, as they race around the continent from the Aleutian Islands to Dry Tortugas, to the Colorado Rockies, to a garbage dump in a Texas border town.

No cooking was allowed in the Radio City Music Hall building, and Frenchie had to order in our meals. Something in the first night's dinner disagreed with me, and I had serious intestinal upset and cramps before the show. Then, during the first few songs, I had strange cramps in my hands as well. One of my ears had been blocking up sporadically lately, which made my in-ear monitors muffled and distracting.

With all that, my after-show review read, "Only 'fair,' overall, but good solo."

Alex gave a great little story that night in "La Villa Strangiato," adopting the persona of Paris Hilton facing a new day, "What shall I do today? Let's see . . . I guess I'll dress up and go shopping. Then I'll get my picture taken."

It was truly amazing how he could *do* that every night—dream up something completely different, tell a little story about it, and usually be very funny. Some nights, as Geddy and I played our little jazz riff behind him, we just smiled at each other and shook our heads.

Carrie was watching from out in the house that night, enjoying the opportunity to see us in a small theater (and only the second indoor show of the tour so far). She reported that somebody from the balcony above spilled a drink on the video control board, and down on her and the people around her, and the situation nearly turned violent. Ah, New York.

One New Yorker I had been trying to get together with was Mark Riebling, a longtime friend I had first met, like Kevin Anderson, through a fan letter he wrote to me. In the mid-'80s, Mark was working at

Random House as an editorial assistant, when he wrote to ask if I might be interested in publishing a book one day. Well, of course I was interested in that idea, though not just yet, but I sensed something in Mark's letter—intelligence and confidence in his own accomplishments—that made me take a chance on beginning a true correspondence, an *exchange*.

The little postcards I usually sent to fans were a gift, sometimes to those who wanted something from me, other times in thanks for a nice letter or a present. The presents were usually books, or sometimes single-malt whisky, which was more welcome than, say, religious tracts or copies of *The Book of Mormon* with a note saying, "This is what you're looking for." But, as with Tom Marinelli, in those very few cases where I had dared to include a return address, I had been rewarded by long and satisfying friendships.

Mark and I first met face to face when I was in New York City for a video shoot in 1986, and later he would visit me in Quebec many times. Every time Mark and I got together, we stayed up late smoking and drinking and talking about everything. "Saving the world," we called it. When Mark left Random House and struck out on his own, I was able to hire him as a freelance editor, and he taught me a lot as we worked through my early travel journals. One good example was Mark's forbidding me to use words like "beautiful" and "interesting," explaining that those words were meaningless to a reader who wouldn't know what I might consider beautiful or interesting. Another example was his editorial mark of an "H" with a slash through it, warning me away from writing like Ernest Hemingway. No sentences like "It was a good road." (Rod Serling once wrote that his early writing had been very much influenced by Hemingway's, and joked that all his stories began, "It was hot.")

I had also learned by vicariously sharing the experience of Mark writing and publishing his first book, *Wedge*, about the secret war between the FBI and CIA. Throughout the process of Mark's careful research, and the molding of that information into narrative, I observed and learned. It was also Mark who later introduced me to Paul McCarthy, saying, "You know how cheap I am, and I spend my *own money* to have Paul work on my stuff."

Recently Mark had become engaged to a smart and funny television personality, Stacey. She had a speaking engagement on our second night off in Manhattan, so I invited them to the first night's show, and to meet at our hotel after. Once Carrie and I were back in our room, and I was showered and enjoying room service drinks and snacks, we were also joined by John Virant from Rounder Records (distributor of our *Rush in Rio* DVD, and Carrie's *Rhythm and Light*) and his family. John's wife Katie, and their bright, confident, and entertaining nine-year-old daughter, Zoë, became our "floor show." As an opening number, Katie and Zoë performed a duet from *Annie*, "I Don't Need Anything But You."

Stacey worked on a TV show called "What Not to Wear," in which she and a male *fashionisto* supervised wardrobe and grooming improvements on style-challenged individuals, and Zoë now began auditioning for that show. She started by telling us all how she would dress Alex, Geddy, and me, and we had a good laugh when she pictured me in red leather pants, black leather vest, and a white leather cap. I could only protest that all that leather "might be kind of *warm* for me."

Before the next night's show, I met with Paul Siegel and Rob Wallis in the Bubba-Gump room for a few minutes to discuss our possible video project a little more, and I also asked for a doctor to have a look at my ear. He arrived just an hour before show time, and while checking my vital signs, he said something about one of the numbers in my blood-pressure reading being a bit high. I said that it might have something to do with the fact that I was about to go onstage at Radio City Music Hall. The doctor laughed and nodded, "It might."

He said my ear was a little blocked-up, did the suction-cleaning on it (ouch!), and prescribed a round of antibiotics, as the on-the-road doctors always seemed to do for every complaint. So often they would look at Geddy's sore throat, for example, and say something like, "It's *probably* . . ." then the next night, another doctor would look at it and say, "It's *probably* . . . " something else. Alex and Geddy and I started calling them the "Probably Doctors," and eventually we decided we were "probably doctors" too.

The second show went a little better for me, but I was long past the stage, so to speak, of feeling any elation or excitement, never mind a "magic show." It was enough for me to do a good job, and to see the audience enjoying themselves. I had reached the point in the tour where the best part of the show for me was the end, racing off the stage and into the waiting car, toweling off and struggling into dry clothes while we drove across to Jersey City to meet Dave at the bus.

It would have been a wonderful return to normality, only the bus was *dead*. An interior light had been left on, draining the batteries, and we knew from experience it wasn't easy to get a boost for the bus's twenty-four volt system. On the *Vapor Trails* tour, we had been leaving Toronto on a day off with Carrie aboard, planning to see if she would enjoy her first long bus ride (she didn't). The batteries were dead, and we were stuck there for hours trying to get a tow truck operator who actually had the right equipment, and didn't just *think* he did.

Every other night of the tour there would be three other buses around to get a boost from, but we had stayed behind on our own that time in Toronto, and now, once again, all the other buses were across the river in Manhattan waiting for the crew. Eventually Dave convinced one of the crew bus drivers (Lashawn, in fact) to come over and give him a boost, and we were finally on the road, heading north to Kingston, New York, and onward to the last two North American shows, Montreal and Toronto.

Just before that second Radio City show, I had made a note describing the future: "Will be glad to have this one behind me—though then come Montreal, Toronto, and . . . Europe." I was not looking forward to the pressure and fuss and demands, professional and personal, of those two hometown shows, but my feelings about the next part of the tour, Europe, were summed up in one word: "dread."

The reasons for that sense of foreboding will be explained more fully when we get there, but for now I can say that my most recent stay in Europe, after Selena's death, had been the worst six months of my life. In addition, many of my worst memories of touring involved Europe. But we'll get to all that.

Friday, August 20 would be our last day-off motorcycle ride in North America, and my last one with Michael, so it felt like an occasion. And at least it would be a good route, crossing south to north across the Adirondacks, along some of the few roads in the East where you could actually ride for twenty or thirty miles without stopping for towns, and through perfect scenery of forested mountains and lakes. I had ridden most of those roads before—some of them many times—when I had traveled between Toronto or Montreal and New York City, or when we did pre-tour rehearsals in Glens Falls for *Test for Echo* and *Vapor Trails*.

They were the kind of roads you would never get tired of, and the landscape I liked best in all the world.

When I passed Michael the map of New York State with the next day's route highlighted in yellow, he shined his blue-filtered flashlight on it, then was thrilled to show me that our four different routes across the state intersected to form the Chinese symbol for woman.

"You need to get *home*," I said

The day's weather report was "cool and cloudy, with occasional sunny breaks." Leaving the bus in Kingston and heading west, Michael and I rode into the Catskills, through quaint little Woodstock and Bearsville. At nearby Bearsville Studios, built in the late '60s by Albert Grossman, manager of Bob Dylan and the Band, we had recorded the drum tracks for *Test for Echo* during the "Blizzard of '96." In May of that year, I had also been there to shoot the instructional video, *A Work in Progress*.

Michael and I angled our way to the northwest past farms and forests, through West Kill, Prattsville, Pleasantbrook, and Cherry Valley, then crossing our route into Buffalo from a few days previously (though it seemed so long ago) in the euphonious Canajoharie.

The day's first church sign gave me pause, "DON'T GIVE UP, MOSES WAS A BASKET CASE TOO."

More farms and little towns, one after another—Salisbury, population 100, the home of Joshua Yale, inventor of the eponymous lock (apparently he became famous for his bank locks by demonstrating to bankers that he could pick any other maker's lock), and Sprout Brook, not even on the map, the birthplace of Henry J. Kaiser. Kaiser's construction companies had built the Grand Coulee and Hoover Dams, countless ships during World War II, and some interesting cars in the '50s, the last days of the automotive independents. There was the Kaiser-Frazer, the little Henry J (one of America's first compacts, also sold under the Sears brand in their catalog), and the Kaiser-Darrin, a sleek two-seater with innovative sliding doors, a three-position landau roof, and a pioneering fiberglass body—produced three years before the Corvette. The Kaiser-Darrin was not a commercial success, and its quirky, adventurous design and underpowered drive-train could stand as a fitting symbol for the decline of the other surviving independents, Nash, Hudson, Studebaker, and Packard. The individualists were caught in a futile and fading struggle against the overwhelming might of the Big Three.

Henry J. Kaiser had also been a visionary in providing complete health care programs for his construction workers and shipbuilders in the '30s and '40s. He claimed to consider his workers' health as an *investment*, and their sickness or injury as a business loss, but it was clearly more than that. His system was later adopted by other companies and governments, enduring even today as Kaiser Permanente.

He left some memorable quotes, too: "Trouble is just opportunity in work clothes," and "When your work speaks for itself, don't interrupt."

In early afternoon, Michael and I finally turned northeast into the real Adirondacks, long sweeps of open road through deep forest, and alongside Moose Lake, Raquette Lake, Blue Mountain Lake, Long Lake, and finally, Tupper Lake, where we decided to stop.

As I remarked in my journal, "It's a Friday, mid-August, in the Adirondacks—of *course* it's busy."

We had been seeing a lot of signs in front of motels reading "No Vacancy," and a few simply saying "Sorry," and I was getting a little worried. As far as we were concerned, the Park Motel and Cabins in Tupper Lake might well have been called the Thistle Dew, for "This'll Do." We stopped there because it had little cabins, which I always liked, but most of all, because it had little cabins *available*.

After 433 kilometers, 270 miles, and what I described as "feeling so *drained* inside," those little cabins would have been welcome no matter what, but they turned out to be quaint and charming once we got moved in. Overall, the Park Motel seemed the perfect summit of Americana to crown this part of the tour. Our little cabin, split into two rooms, had fake log siding and aluminum screen doors on the outside, and clean, simple interiors of pine wainscoting and linoleum floors, with a few Southwest-style rugs and decorations.

The air smelled of pines and cut grass, and out back, an old red American Flyer wagon was propped against a fishing boat. Under the lofty trees on the well-trimmed front lawn, a miniature Aermotor-style windpump was painted red, white, and blue, and hung with little flags. Beside it was a comically oversized wooden Adirondack chair, also painted in patriotic colors. The back window of a pickup truck had one of the ubiquitous bad-little-boy-urinating stickers, though instead of a rival truck manufacturer, this one was peeing on the name "Osama bin Laden."

Not as bad as the sanctimonious version I often saw in "church-sign country," depicting the bad little boy kneeling in the shadow of a cross.

Not as good as one I saw in Los Angeles, with the bad little boy wearing a sombrero, and urinating on "La Migra." In fact, during my last break at home, I had my own experience with La Migra—the U.S. Immigration and Naturalization Service—when I went to their office in Room 2050 of the Federal Building in downtown Los Angeles to pick up my final, official green card.

Even as the spouse of an American citizen, it had been quite an ordeal to secure that—the sequence of steps was set in motion in 2000, and it would be another six to eight months before I actually had the card, so five years was not much of an exaggeration.

Arriving in the early morning, per instructions, I sat for three hours on a hard plastic chair, reading the *Discover* magazine I had brought with me (with just that expectation). I heard a polyethnic symphony of names being called—Hispanic, Vietnamese, Chinese, Dutch, and who-knows-what, most of them spelled-out by the clerks.

Some of those clerks were pleasant, others were miserable, and I drew one of the latter for my first "summons." I applied fingerprint and signature to a form, submitted my passport, my expired temporary green card, and a booklet containing three three-quarter-view photos.

The unhappy, unloved woman told me I could sit and wait, or go for lunch, "It's your prerogative."

When I asked, "It will be an hour or so?" she frowned and said, "Oh yeah."

I went back to reading about the rings of Saturn, the brain chemistry of so-called recovered memories, the controversial science of sex and the spread of infectious diseases, and DNA and behavioral variations in twins.

In early afternoon, my name was finally mispronounced by a heavy-set, stubble-headed, dark-complexioned, mustachioed man, and I went up to the wicket. He showed me the fresh stamp in my passport that would attest to my status until I received the actual card, and explained that it would allow me to work and travel in the interim. Then he stuck out his hand and said, "I just want to say thank-you."

Surprised, I took his soft hand in mine, as he added, "For the music."

I just said "Thank you" back to him, smiled, and turned to go.

That was the whole encounter, and all he needed to say—it was an expression of simple appreciation, and it made me feel nothing but good. Especially under those circumstances, in that place.

(Interesting that at that point in our careers, those words had become an increasingly common expression of the way people felt: "Thank you." That felt good.)

At the Park Smokehouse Restaurant in Tupper Lake, New York, busy on that Friday night, Michael and I stood waiting for a table. I noticed that the Clash's "London Calling" was playing—"ominously and incongruously," I noted. Incongruous in a crowd of older people and families ("large families of large people"), while the state lottery played on television, and ominous because London *was* calling, just a few weeks away, and again, my keyword on that prospect was "dread."

Michael and I set off in the morning into pouring rain, and I groaned in my fogged-up helmet when I noticed that we were pulling out behind two huge logging trucks. They were crawling along, but just fast enough to throw up clouds of spray. We would have to go through those clouds to pass them, creeping out into the left lane and taking one at a time, racing ahead nervously on a wet road to get back over before another one appeared coming *toward* us. I watched in my mirror until I saw Michael's headlight safely behind me again.

"GOD CHOSE FOOLISH THINGS TO CONFOUND MIGHTY THINGS," said the church sign. That one so confounded *me* that I noted its source, First Corinthians, so I could look it up later. The quote turned out to be inaccurate, for one thing—in the King James Version, it was actually, "God hath chosen the foolish things to confound the wise; and God hath chosen the weak things of the world to confound the things which are mighty." The meaning, apparently, is something like the earlier one, "He is no respecter of persons"—it doesn't matter if you are wise and mighty; God will choose the foolish and weak.

(Dare one ask, "Why?")

The Adirondack roads were quiet on that Saturday morning, and the rain began to taper off. We stopped for breakfast at the crossroads hamlet of Bloomingdale, at a restaurant called Four "Corner's," with that unfortunate out-of-place apostrophe again. Then we continued east to

Plattsburgh and onto the interstate. With a border to cross, always an unpredictable undertaking, and the rain starting up again, we would head straight for Montreal.

After a wet and cold 235 kilometers, 148 miles, and a thankfully easy border-crossing, we arrived early at the fairly new arena in downtown Montreal. Opened in 1996, the Deregulated Telephone Company Centre, formerly the Megabrewery Centre, had replaced the venerable Montreal Forum, a building we had played many times over the years, and home ice for the Montreal Canadiens hockey team. Dave arrived just behind us, backing the bus and trailer down the ramp into the underground parking area, and he was being guided by a familiar-looking silhouette, stooped and limping—it was *Brutus!*

The stoop and limp were among the scars Brutus still bore from a long-ago motorcycle accident. At age nineteen, in St. John's, Newfoundland, he was riding as passenger on a guy's Honda when a taxi full of nuns pulled in front of them. Brutus came to lying in the road with his femur sticking through his jeans and his teeth through his upper lip, his back broken and blood everywhere, while the other guy, walking around at first, soon died of internal injuries. While Brutus spent a year and a half in hospital being put back together, the nuns refused to testify against the taxi driver, who denied responsibility. When Brutus finally got out of the hospital, he got drunk, and found himself standing in front of the convent, yelling up at the blank windows, "You bunch of fuckin' *penguins!*"

Brutus had arrived in Montreal the night before to visit with our Dave for a while. They had become close when Brutus was my riding partner on *Test for Echo*, and had stayed in contact since then. Now Brutus was going to start preparing to join me in Europe. He wouldn't be joining Dave, unfortunately, as we would have a European driver over there, and he wouldn't be joining Michael, as he wouldn't be traveling with us. But he would be joining *me.*

I gave him a big hug and hello, and started introducing him to what Nelson Algren called, in *The Man With the Golden Arm*, "the new way we have of doing things around here."

Brutus had the kind of personality that adapted to any situation he found himself in, from an American prison to a French restaurant, to a rock tour. He could always make himself and others comfortable, even to the point of being what he called a "chameleon drinker"—if you drank single-malt whisky, that was his drink; if you preferred beer, Brutus drank beer. In any circumstances, he was the opposite of the French expression, *il est mal dans sa peau*, "he fits badly in his skin"—Brutus was comfortable in his own skin, and people around him felt that, and somehow trusted his prominent blue eyes and easy smile.

Years ago, when Brutus and I first started traveling together, I had said we needed a name for our two-man gang, and it was Brutus who came up with it: "Scooter Trash."

Scooter Trash rides again.

That afternoon I was visited by Mark Love, from the Sabian cymbal factory in New Brunswick, his wife Dorothy, and their friends, a couple from Montreal. I described earlier how I had traveled to the factory the previous year, and worked with "alchemist" Mark to develop the Paragon line of cymbals. That night in Montreal was the first time Mark had heard me play our creations, and all through the show, knowing Mark was listening, I was keenly aware of each cymbal as I played it. But I knew they sounded great.

I had quite a few other guests that night, though I wouldn't see them—my Quebec property manager, Keith, and his friends, some neighbors from "the house on the lake," and a number of people who dated back to the days of Le Studio in Morin Heights, just north of Montreal. The studio was closed now, unfortunately, but the people remained friends—our longtime recording engineer, Paul Northfield, and his wife Judy, who had been the studio manager for a few years; Trevor, who had once owned the legendary Commons Hotel, watering hole to international stars and local lushes (until the roof collapsed from snow last winter); and André and Yaël, the former owners of Le Studio.

We had first gone to work at Le Studio in 1979, on our *Permanent Waves* album. Le Studio was set above a gravel road in the Laurentians, surrounded by those low mountains and thick boreal woods, and the studio itself was at one end of a kidney-shaped lake, the guest house at the other. You could commute to work by rowboat, canoe, pedal-boat, on foot, bicycle, or—in winter—by cross-country skis or snowshoes.

We liked it so much we did almost all our recording there for the next five years, and returned to record the basic tracks for *Counterparts*, in 1993. In the early '80s, we often stayed in the comfortable guest house for months at a time while we recorded, overdubbed, mixed, and even wrote and arranged new material.

During our second stay at Le Studio, while recording *Moving Pictures*, I fell in love with the Laurentian winter. The assistant engineer, Robbie Whelan, a curly-haired, bright-eyed, enthusiastic young Englishman, introduced me to cross-country skiing, and I used to follow him through the snow-covered woodland trails, learning how to "herring-bone" up hills, how to kick and glide along the flats, how to choose the wax to fit the day ("Looks like a blue wax day!"). When we approached a downhill section, I would hear Robbie's whoops of excitement up ahead as I went tumbling head-first into the snow, after narrowly missing a tree. (I still ski like that—clumsy, graceless, and frequently falling—and sometimes wonder why I don't wear a helmet, as I do so religiously on bicycle and motorcycle.)

Robbie's friends sometimes called him "Happy Hands," as he had a way of describing something he liked by waving his hands down at his sides, and the more excited he was, the higher he raised those waving hands. His enthusiasm was infectious, whether it was about skiing or music, and he always became totally engaged in whatever recording project he was working on. In those days, Le Studio attracted clients like the Police, David Bowie, Keith Richards, and Tina Turner.

On his way to work at Le Studio one morning in early 1983, Robbie was killed in a car accident. "Afterimage," from *Grace Under Pressure*, was written for him. In the cabinet of memories in my Quebec house, mentioned earlier, I have an elaborate sextant, with ivory inlays and brass-framed colored lenses, that was given to me by Robbie's widow, Carla. I still think of Robbie and his "Happy Hands" when I'm skiing through the Laurentian woods. I think of him every time we play Montreal, too.

It was Gump's turn for stomach trouble that night, and just before we went on, he told me he was suffering with diarrhea and cramps, and warned me he might have to "disappear" sometimes. I told him not to worry, and just to ask George to cover for him if he had to run. However, he made it through, and as always, did a perfect job.

I guess we all did. Montreal audiences were perhaps the most demonstrative anywhere, and like the city itself, our crowds there were always a passionate combination of English and French Canadians. Vocal and physical, those 14,120 people inside the Deregulated Telephone Company Centre gave us an irresistible wave of "feedback," and throughout the show, they were a happy, enthusiastic, appreciative audience.

The special guests on the dryers that night were the characters from "Trailer Park Boys," including a return appearance from "Bubbles," and the crowd was delighted.

When I ran onto the bus at the end, joining Dave, Michael, and Brutus, the police officer who was supposed to escort us through the post-show traffic came up to the bus door and wanted to get some autographs before we left.

While I was in the back of the bus starting to wriggle out of my sweaty clothes, I heard Dave and Michael up front, saying, "No, forget it," and to each other, "Let's just leave without him."

Later Dave told me he had seen that cop hanging around the back door all through the show, letting his friends in and out, and now he had a couple of them in the patrol car with him.

It was great to have Brutus riding with us, and we raised our glasses of The Macallan in a toast, but we had a lot of business to take care of—the ceremonial "Passing of the Doofus," we called it. Brutus had been provided with his own GPS unit for the European run, and I had christened it "Dork." Doofus, Dingus, and Dork—a fine trio.

While I highlighted a route for the next day, making it deliberately complicated as an object lesson (not to say ordeal by fire) for Brutus, he and Michael hunched over the computer, "Mother." Michael demonstrated how to enter a route onto the computer map, different ways to use the various digital tools, and how to download the completed route to the bike-mounted units. Brutus was a quick study with nearly anything, but seemed a little daunted by what he called "the steep learning curve."

On a warm, sunny morning, we unloaded the bikes at a truck stop in Napanee, and Michael, Brutus, and I set out to trace a zigzag route across Ontario's cottage country, the lake-studded woodlands of the Canadian Shield. After spending the past three months riding on roads and through landscapes that were more-or-less unfamiliar to me, these roads, small towns, and lakes had all been known to me since childhood.

All at once I felt a connection with real life, something outside the Vortex.

It was late August, almost the end of summer, and I had missed it all—the usual season of cottages, tents, picnics, barbecues, corn on the cob, campfires, mosquitoes, fireflies, convertibles, canoes, pines, thunderstorms, and swimming in the cool, silky water of northern lakes.

In earlier years, when Alex, Geddy, and I all had young children, we used to work what we called "schoolteacher years." We would plan our recording and touring schedules through the fall, winter, and spring, then have our summers off. Given the twenty-first-century popularity of outdoor amphitheaters, on the last two tours we had adjusted to the idea of working in the summer, and made the best of it (certainly much nicer for motorcycling!). But now, as I rode through those familiar summer playgrounds of Ontario, I was suddenly aware of what I was missing: a whole, precious, irreplaceable *summer.*

I hadn't consciously thought of that when I was in Ohio, West Virginia, Idaho, California, or Florida, but now it was poignantly in the front of my mind, watching all those people on their summer vacations, tanned and happy, driving around with canoes, kayaks, mountain bikes, and speedboats.

The words that came into my head were, "I want it back."

The summer, the past, all of it. But it was already gone.

Somewhere around Bobcaygeon (included on the route in tribute to the Tragically Hip's song of the same name), Doofus, Dingus, and Dork had some problems. They would send us along the shore of Sturgeon Lake, then decide that was the wrong direction and send us back the other way, then get confused again. During one consultation with the map, Brutus said, "I feel like I'm learning everything *not* to do!"

At that point, we set them all for "Quickest Way," and headed south. We all had a lot to do before that Toronto show: Michael and I had to get moved off the bus and trailer, pack up more cardboard boxes of swag to be shipped home, pack up our luggage, and say goodbye to people we wouldn't be seeing over there—like Dave. Brutus would have to prepare my two bikes to be shipped to Europe, sort out tie-downs for the pallets Dave had arranged for the three bikes, and gather tools and supplies from the trailer we might need in Europe. (Michael's bike would be trucked to California, via Nashville, with some of the equipment.)

We followed the main highways down to Toronto, then Brutus and I were separated from Michael when he followed Doofus on some strange route that we, as longtime residents of the city, knew was wrong without consulting Dingus or Dork. After 435 kilometers, 271 miles, my 1200 now showed 22,839 kilometers on the odometer as we parked in the backstage area of the Megabrewery Amphitheatre. The loading area was busy with more than the usual activity, as a series of trucks delivered containers for all the equipment that would be traveling to Europe, by ship, after this show.

During soundcheck, my friend Chris from Sabian came by, and even amid the day's tension, I was always glad to see the amiable Iowan. When I asked Chris what he was doing in Toronto, he told me, with a little embarrassment, that he was in town to speak at "Rushcon," a convention of Rush fans, about the evolution of the Paragon cymbals. He handed me a business card he had been given the previous night, and on the back of it was written, "Don George, Neil's first drum teacher," and an address in a small town near St. Catharines (sixty miles from Toronto).

I had often spoken of Don George in interviews in *Modern Drummer* magazine and such, and I had even written about him in *Traveling Music*, where I gave credit to my first teacher for giving me a solid foundation in drumming, and that all-important early encouragement. I hadn't heard anything about Don since he stopped teaching at the Niagara Peninsula Conservatory of Music more than thirty-five years ago, so I was excited to have this opportunity to get in touch with him again.

Only later did I learn the shadings of that story. After the show, I met at the hotel with my friends Brad and Rita, who lived in St. Catharines. I told them about the business card and Don George's address, and Brad didn't say anything at the time, but a few days later he sent me an e-mail under the title, "What Worries Me." Apparently the guy whose name was on the *front* of that business card was running tours of "Neil Peart's St. Catharines"—to houses my family had lived in, schools I had attended, that sort of thing. Each tour culminated at a local restaurant, with guests including one of the "movers" from the cover of our *Moving Pictures* album (wearing the red jumpsuit from the 1980 photograph), and . . . Neil's first drum teacher.

I felt a little uncomfortable with that scenario (who wouldn't?), and though I was still glad to be able to write to Don George after all those years, I would be wary.

There was also a shadow over that Megabrewery Amphitheatre for me. I would never forget that our show there on the *Test for Echo* tour, in July of 1997, had been the last show Jackie and Selena had ever attended. I remembered Selena waiting with me before the show, in the Scooter Trash room (now the Bubba-Gump room), then going out to sit with her friends and, she told me later, shooshing them during the drum solo. After that show, I had been driven straight home, joined a little later by Jackie and Selena and some of our friends. Jackie had come into our house saying it was no fair that after weeks of being annoyed and frustrated with me being away all the time, the first time she had to see me was "when you're onstage and being *great*."

In the final nervous hour before that hometown show, one you always want to be *especially* good, Michael, Dave, and Brutus helped look after Mom and Dad, meeting them when the car Michael had arranged delivered them backstage. I was glad to give them a (careful) hug and talk with them in the Bubba-Gump room for a few minutes, then they made their way out to their "special seating." They were both recovering well from their hip surgeries, and were fairly mobile now, but I hadn't thought they would be comfortable sitting in hard plastic seats for three-and-a half hours. So we (I mean Shelley) had arranged for them to have a pair of wheelchairs in the handicapped area, off to stage right. I told them I would be running straight back to the hotel after the show, and my guys would look after getting them home. I would see them the next day for lunch before my flight to Los Angeles.

As for all my other friends, relations, and courtesy passes (I always made it a principle to give free tickets to my doctor and my motorcycle mechanic!), I had told everybody to enjoy the show, and I would see them some other time. After this big hometown show, with *everybody's* relatives and friends attending, there would be some kind of social gathering, but I would not be attending—I knew I wouldn't have the energy for that. I was running on reserve now as it was.

"Avoid carrying on in society. The social ramble ain't restful."

The purpose of the Spirit Quest had been to preserve my sanity, and now, at the end, I was preserving the last sparks of my spirit to deliver the performance those 16,725 people, the largest audience on

298

the tour, expected of me, and the performance I expected of myself.

I had come to realize my physical and mental energy were a finite resource—renewable, but like an aquifer, they could only be replenished slowly, in unhurried time. Thus, every day, as my energy was depleted, I had to mete it out carefully and conserve what I didn't absolutely need to expend.

Enough to do the show, no more.

The show at the Megabrewery Amphitheater in Toronto might have been show number forty-three to us, with many more yet to come on that tour, but for most of those people out there, it was show number *one*.

That's the way we had to think of it and deliver it—as if it were the last show we would ever play.

Minutes before show time, Liam and C.B. reported the large crowd was unusually slow in getting into the venue (bottled up by the one little footbridge they all had to cross), and that show time would be pushed back a little later than the usual ten minutes.

I asked Michael to go let my mom know, so she wouldn't start crying yet. She could be so *emotional*.

When we finally took the stage, on a cool, clear evening on the shore of Lake Ontario, I noticed quite a few familiar faces in the crowd—not friends, but fans who had attended ten or twenty different performances throughout the tour, and were gathering for the last North American show.

When we started playing "Earthshine," a girl held up a sign saying, "THIS IS MY FAVORITE." Then, when we started "Roll the Bones," she held up another sign that said, "NO, THIS ONE IS." When we went into "Bravado," the sign read, "THIS IS MY REAL FAVORITE." I smiled with amusement and appreciation.

Some of the other audience members held up little signs at the end of each song, like Olympic scorecards, that read "10" or "15." When we played the *2112* "Overture," which had a rhythmic part with a final accent on the fourth beat, when the whole crowd always shouted "Hey," a few dozen people, scattered all around, held up little signs reading, "Hey!"

That was genuinely funny, and I loved to see imaginative crowd participation like that.

One guy who had been in the front row at dozens of concerts on this tour and others, always stood out, because he wore the turban and beard of his Sikh heritage. Michael had got to know that diehard fan a little, starting on the previous tour, and one time, Carrie asked Michael how that guy could afford to attend so many different shows, always with front-row tickets.

"What does he do?" she asked Michael.

"He's a doctor," Michael said.

"Yeah, he looks after Sikh people," I said, proud of my bad pun.

After the drum solo, when I sat behind the dryers with Gump, I saw Michael at stage left. I waved him over and gave him a pair of sticks to give to the Sikh doctor, and when I got back up on the riser, I saw the guy waving the sticks, smiling and mouthing, "thank you."

I gave him a nod, then kept on playing.

In the end, it was a very good show, maybe even another *magic* show, at least for the people in that happy audience. I was just too tired to feel it, too drained by the effort of *doing* it.

I ran behind Michael to the car to ride back to the hotel, the car windows steaming up from my sweaty clothes and overheated body. I was glad to have played well, but even gladder it was over.

A couple of weeks off now, then the long flight to London, and fifteen more shows in Europe.

For many reasons, I was apprehensive about that final part of the tour, but I was trying to remain optimistic, hoping the shows would go well, and that Brutus and I would have a good time motorcycling between them. As always, I would try to make the best of the situation and enjoy it as much as I could.

Like Paul Theroux said, "I believe I have a sunny disposition, and am not naturally a grouch."

It takes a lot of optimism, after all, to be a drummer.

Q: What do you call a drummer with half a brain?
A: Gifted.

eurotrash rides again

To be sure that your friend is a friend
You must go with him on a journey
Travel with him day and night
Go with him near and far

(Angolan Proverb)

In June of 1996, just after the band had finished recording *Test for Echo*, and before we had started that tour, Brutus and I shipped our motorcycles to Munich. We flew in to meet them, and rode down through Bavaria, Austria, and Italy, then crossed by ferry to Sicily and Tunisia. We wandered down into the Sahara a little, and had some scary adventures (Brutus's burned-out clutch near the middle of nowhere, and my anxious solo ride to the oasis town of Douz for a truck to rescue him). Then it was up through Sardinia, Italy, and France to Geneva. It was on that trip that Scooter Trash became "Eurotrash."

As a traveler, I have always appreciated Europe, and have enjoyed some wonderful journeys there by bicycle, by motorcycle, and by car. The Alps, the English countryside, the Greek Islands, Paris, London, Venice—so many beautiful places, and in the squares, piazzas, and cafés, such a gracious mode of living.

As a touring musician, however, I was not so enthusiastic about Europe. Work is, by definition, no holiday. We had first toured there in 1977, and my enduring memory of that and other early tours was of shivering in Britain's gloomy weather, riding in a drafty old Daimler limou-

301

sine ("Why do I have to sit in the middle?"), staying in drafty old hotels, and waiting in drafty old dressing rooms.

For the hour or so we were on stage in those days, though, the audiences were vocal and enthusiastic. European fans tend to be as rabid about their favorite bands as they are about their soccer teams (for both good and ill). However, there were all the other hours in the day, and the hotels and venues would often be surrounded by fans. In many cities, especially in Britain, you couldn't leave the hotel—sometimes you couldn't even look out the window without being yelled at. Every time we went in and out of a hotel or a venue, there were jostling crowds of people shouting and pushing and *wanting*. We had some frightening mob scenes after shows, people surging around us, shoving and pounding against the car as we tried to drive away, and it was not very pleasant.

Early on, wanting to do the right thing, we tried to handle that situation by lining up all the guys (they were, of course, almost all males, in long hair and denim jackets) after the show. We would sit at a table in a backstage corridor for an hour or more and sign an autograph for each of them.

A nice idea, young idealists that we were. But being overheated after the show, sitting in a drafty old theater with the doors wide open on an English winter night, signing endless autographs (a few greedy people kept sneaking back to the end of the line again and again to get *more*), we ended up with bad colds, and bad attitudes about being taken advantage of.

(Those British fans used to say some funny things, though—we still laugh about the young Geordie who asked us, in all seriousness, in his lilting accent, "Are you sorry to be leaving Newcastle?")

As a veteran traveler through many parts of the world, I am always willing to endure difficult conditions in return for what I perceive as a worthwhile experience, like exploring Africa or China. But I have never wanted to *work* in places like that. I figure the job is struggle enough, and I prefer the living and working conditions to be as easy, comfortable, and predictable as possible. That means North America.

We had toured in Japan once, Mexico once, and Brazil once, just for the experience, and we had toured Europe many times in the '70s and '80s. But the last time had been in 1992, and because we did have quite a few fans there, especially in Britain, Germany, and the Netherlands, we felt a little guilty about it. We had tried to fit in some European shows on the *Vapor Trails* tour, but after sixty-seven shows, and the final three in Brazil, we had had enough. Or I had, anyway.

However . . . I flew into London on September 6, 2004, full of misgivings.

Of all the cities I had come to know in the world, London had always been closest to my heart. Not that I loved it wholeheartedly (I didn't), or that I had always had a great time there (I hadn't), but London had simply been important to me. As a city, it was not as enchanting as Paris or Venice, not as exotic as Istanbul or Beijing, not as livable as Toronto or Vancouver, not as visually dynamic as New York City or San Francisco. But for all that, London had played the biggest part in my life.

It started when I was eighteen and moved to London with my drums in search of fame and fortune, then continued when I returned with Rush so many times, at first to perform, then later to record. Adding up all of those stays in London and at residential studios in rural England and Wales, we had spent *years* working and living there, in hotels, rented flats, and houses in Mayfair, Chelsea, or Kensington. I had ridden my bicycle to and from studios in Soho, Whitechapel, and Shepherds Bush, and over the years, we had played many times at the Hammersmith Odeon and Wembley Arena.

In September of 1997, a few weeks after Selena's death, Jackie and I traveled to London to escape, to hide, and to try to reassemble our lives. After a couple of weeks at the Dorchester Hotel, overlooking Hyde Park, in a country mourning the death of their own princess (Diana), we moved into a little furnished flat for the next six months, certainly the worst six months of my life. While Jackie withered and faded in unbearable, inconsolable grief, I grieved my own way, marching around London. I didn't like to leave her alone for long, so I walked fast. At first I explored every inch of the green kingdom of Hyde Park and Kensington Gardens, then farther, along the canals of Regents Park and Camden Town to the panoramic views from Primrose Hill, along the Thames to St. Paul's, or west through Chelsea and Kensington to see the albino peacocks in Holland Park.

I was learning to armor myself against the world, all those people and their ongoing lives, while my life stood still and dark. But Jackie never could face them. I could only manage to get her out about once a week, to see a therapist, or for a quick dinner in a neighborhood restaurant, early, before other people arrived. Trying to look after her, keep her alive, I learned to cook for her, courtesy of the Marks and Spencer department store on Oxford Street. Its Food Hall thoughtfully provided cooking instructions with every item, a printed label on every fresh vegetable and piece of fish, telling me how to grill, poach, steam, or bake it.

Even I could manage that. But it was not enough.

In February of 1998, we flew back to Canada, already knowing Jackie was riddled with cancer, a self-willed death sentence, and a few months later, she was gone, too.

So in September of 2004, I was returning to London with all that to face again, almost exactly seven years to the day since Jackie and I had arrived there in the wake of losing Selena. On the car ride in from the airport, I tried not to look around too much, not to take in too many reminders all at once. For that reason I had also chosen to stay at the Savoy Hotel, far away from the Park Lane and Mayfair area, where every street, shop, and restaurant was a touchstone for that nightmarish six months.

The Savoy was in the West End theater district, on the Strand, and combined the Victorian atmosphere of its establishment in 1889 with an "updated" Art Deco style from the '20s and '30s. Its original manager had been César Ritz, and the first chef was the celebrated Auguste Escoffier. The Savoy was associated with a clientele ranging from Sir Winston Churchill and Eleanor Roosevelt, to Charlie Chaplin, Elizabeth Taylor, and Marilyn Monroe. Apparently Laurence Olivier had met Vivien Leigh there in the 1930s.

Geddy and I had stayed at the Savoy once in 1987, traveling into London by morning train on a day off from recording at Ridge Farm Studios, down in Surrey. With separate plans for the afternoon and evening, we agreed to meet in the famous American Bar at the Savoy for an afternoon cocktail. Excited to have escaped from the country to the big city, for once we were not the guys at work, but just friends. We shared stories about where we had been that day, where we were going that evening, and just talked about our lives.

It seemed that maybe Geddy had been stirred by the same memory, as I was surprised to learn from Liam that Alex and Geddy would be staying at the Savoy as well. Despite my usual wish to stay apart from "the band," to avoid any attention we might collectively draw, for some reason, fans had never found us at London hotels—unlike New York ones—so I didn't worry.

Like Claude Monet, who stayed at the Savoy many times in the late nineteenth century, and made over seventy paintings of the Thames from its windows, I had requested a river-view room this time. In that room's old-world atmosphere of somewhat worn luxury, I stood at the window and looked out past leafy trees and manicured gardens to the Thames, running slow and greenish at high tide, dotted with barges and tour boats. Leaning out, I could see along its banks all the way from the dome of St. Paul's Cathedral downriver, to the Houses of Parliament and Big Ben upriver, all under a cloudless "California sky," as I could only describe it. The gigantic ferris wheel, the Millennium Wheel, towered above the newer buildings along the South Bank. It was spectacular in its way, especially at night, but somehow it seemed to upset the scale and atmosphere of the city—as perhaps it was intended to do.

Wanting to start adjusting to the eight-hour time difference, I fought off the waves of jet lag and stayed awake all day. Our longtime photographer, two-time personal assistant, and old friend Andrew was in London with his friend, Alex, and I met them for dinner in the Savoy Grill. Alex, an actor, had been performing at a drama festival in Edinburgh, and Andrew had flown in to meet him, and to photograph our Wembley shows.

The band and crew had planned a rehearsal for the next day, to give us a day to acclimatize and a chance to go through a few songs and check out the gear after its long boat ride. I rode in early with Liam in a Mercedes sedan with a driver, once again averting my eyes from Hyde Park Corner and Knightsbridge as we crossed London toward Wembley.

Out in the loading area behind Wembley Arena, enormous arches and cranes were rising over the new Wembley Stadium, next door. Brutus and Michael had the motorcycles unloaded and ready to go, and Brutus was getting the tie-downs and chocks installed in the new trailer, with help from carpenter George. Brutus had flown over a week early with his wife, Georgia, and teenage son, Sam, driven around western England and Wales, then spent a couple of days in London. His family would stay for the Wembley shows, then fly back to Canada.

Our new bus was there, big and shiny black, striped with silver graphics and the name of the company, based in Austria, Beat the Street. All of our European contractors went in for clever names: the trucking company (nine trucks instead of seven, as they were smaller) was called Stage Truck, with a slanted, angular "S" between the two words, to suggest "stage struck," and the catering company touring with us was called Eat to the Beat. With the addition of four caterers, two drivers, an additional audio technician, and Brutus, we now had fifty-eight people in our traveling circus.

The four buses were made by Setra, a Mercedes-Benz subsidiary, and ours had a matching little trailer, just big enough for the two bikes. Our driver, Mark, a burly, short-haired man who looked like a veteran rugby player, was from Sheffield, and he seemed accommodating and friendly. The bus seemed nice too, but different. In layout, it was almost a double-decker, with the driver's cabin and sleeper underneath, then luggage bays and engine compartment all the way back. The upper area was laid out more or less like our Hemphill coach—front lounge, small galley, a row of stacked bunks, head (no shower, alas!), and a stateroom in the rear. The whole interior was decorated in a kind of Scandinavian austerity, with glossy veneers, blue leather seating, and blue and orange carpet and bedspread. Apparently the previous occupant of that bus had been Cher, and Mark said she had demanded a special mattress that cost 3000 euros or "some silly money like that." I must say, it was very comfortable. I told Mark that Cher had just built an enormous estate on the Pacific Coast near Malibu, and when I got home I would stop by her house and thank her.

Originally known as the Empire Pool, Wembley Arena was built for the Empire Games of 1934, and it looked and sounded like a seventy-year-old arena. As I walked around inside, taped music blared over the P.A. system and echoed in the cavernous interior. The sound company crew chief, Jo, came up and said, "London is one of the two greatest cities in the world, wouldn't you say? There's New York, and there's London, right? Well, you'd think they would build themselves a new arena!"

In fact, that arena was finally going to be closed at the end of 2004, then torn down and rebuilt in 2005. About time, too.

After rehearsal, I rode back to the Savoy and met with my old friend Peter Brockbank. I had known Peter since my first stay in

London in the early '70s, and written about him many times. In *The Masked Rider*, I had called him "Simon," wanting to be discreet (as I told him later, "to protect the guilty"), and in *Ghost Rider* he was the "English friend" who suggested that I was luckier than some, who had lost their families and were poor, too (?). But by the time I wrote *Traveling Music* and told Peter's story a little more fully, there seemed no point in dissembling.

Peter had been a self-confessed villain all his life, a con man, bagman, and lovable rogue, always involved in one scam or another—the kind in which no one was ever hurt, but which earned him a few "holidays at Her Majesty's pleasure." In my poverty-stricken days in London, around 1971, Peter had been my benefactor, something like Abel Magwitch in *Great Expectations*. He had been "road manager" for the band I was in, a band that had no work, and I was getting desperate enough that I asked Peter if I could help him "on a job" some time. Unwilling to involve the innocent colonial in his illegal enterprises, Peter passed me a five-pound note a couple of times, keeping me afloat until I got a "real job."

I had never forgotten his generosity (though he had), and on two previous European tours, *Hold Your Fire* in 1988 and *Roll the Bones* in 1992, I had hired Peter as my personal driver. Having a rental car allowed me to travel separately from everybody else, and avoid as much of the hoopla as I could. For the first time, I would also be able to do the tour overland, which I preferred, while Alex and Geddy could fly, which they preferred. I would run straight off the stage and into the car, changing into dry clothes while Peter drove toward the next destination.

Early in the planning for the R30 tour, I had written to Peter to let him know I *might* be wanting his services again, but didn't want him getting his hopes up. That was apparently impossible, and when I let him know I had decided to do the tour by motorcycle, he was crushed. Eventually, he let me know it was okay that I wasn't going to hire him. I told him I was relieved to hear that.

Peter was waiting in the lobby of the Savoy, smartly dressed and complaining about the price of a drink and a "packet of fags." I invited him to my room for some refreshments and conversation. The last time I had actually seen Peter had been in 1992, at the end of the *Roll the Bones* tour, when he had dropped Jackie, Selena, and me at Southhampton, whence we would be sailing on the *QE2* to New York. In letters, he had warned me that he now weighed "eighteen stone," which is apparently a lot in those quaint Imperial measures (a stone is fourteen pounds), but he had been joking—twelve years later, he looked spry and fit, a little balder, a little grayer, but with the same good-natured personality and ready grin.

After Peter entertained me with tales of his latest ne'er-do-well enterprises for a couple of hours, we said good night. Still jet-lagged and wakeful, I stood looking out the window at the Thames, at the lights of the Royal Festival Hall and the theater complex on the South Bank. A large, lighted sign flashed ads for upcoming performances, and I was reminded of the summer of 1985, when I bicycled every day and night between the band's rented house in Mayfair and a recording studio in Whitechapel. I had pedaled along that Embankment each way, and passed that sign, then advertising Oliver Goldsmith's play, *She Stoops To Conquer.*

The theaters also reminded me of some memorable dramatic performances I had attended in London. In the '80s, while recording there, Geddy and I saw Dustin Hoffman as Shylock in *The Merchant of Venice*, and Sir Ian McKellen in *King Lear* (long before his fame as Gandalf in *Lord of the Rings*), with the Royal Shakespeare Company. (I don't remember why Alex didn't join us, but I wasn't the only one negatively affected by spending too much time in Europe. Our tours and long stays there made Alex turn xenophobic and reclusive. There are stories . . . but never mind.)

I would never forget those first exposures to the power of Shakespearean theater when presented at that level. In *The Merchant of Venice*, when Antonio spat on Shylock's robe, or in *King Lear*, when the Duke of Cornwall plucked out Gloucester's eyes—the audience around us gasped audibly, their disbelief completely suspended.

A copy of *Time Out*, London's entertainment guide, was in the room, and I looked through the concert listings, amazed at the number of '60s, '70s, and '80s bands and artists still slogging it out in London pubs and small theaters. Like them, we were dismissed by the hip young writers, and the listing for our two nights at Wembley Arena described us breezily as, "Geddy Lee's longhaired right-wing Canadian prog-metal heroes." Well, they got one thing right: we were Canadian.

The right wing nonsense had persisted for over twenty-five years, at least in the British music press. With four or five music papers to fill every week, the often bitter and resentful scriveners could be as lazy, irresponsible, and shameless as their counterparts in the celebrity tabloids. Around 1977, a pasty, scruffy, humorless, left-wing "intellectual" had written a sensationalized exposé, portraying us pretty much as standard-bearers for the Hitler Youth. To my shock and horror, he twisted the libertarian notions of an idealistic twenty-four-year-old drummer and lyricist into the darkly sardonic words above the gates of many Nazi concentration camps, *Arbeit Macht Frei*, "Work Makes You Free."

In future interviews in Britain, we dryly informed other journalists that sure, we were the only Nazi band with a Jewish bass player. (In fact, Geddy's parents *met* at Auschwitz, where that sign most notoriously greeted the doomed prisoners, making that claim even more outrageous.) But even after twenty-seven years, the sensational lie outlived the obvious truth, at least in England.

On the afternoon of our first show at Wembley, I rode from the Savoy with Liam again, and during the forty-minute drive through central London (still averting my eyes from familiar streets and parks), we talked about his move to Nashville and the ongoing misery of his divorce, but still not a word about his new romance. Famous for his reserve and discretion, he sure could keep a secret, even from his closest friends!

The previous week I had finally seen a copy of the new edition of *The Masked Rider*, carefully nurtured into print by Paul McCarthy, and starting that night, it would be on sale alongside the other two. Even in Europe, with several non-English-speaking countries, Pat would sell about seventy-five books a night.

The first London show went pretty well, I noted, "all things considered"—meaning after a couple of weeks off, the long journey for us and the equipment, and the adaptation to British electricity, which did cause me some technical difficulties. It seemed the transformers altered the voltage properly from 220 to 110, but not the cycles from fifty to sixty, and this caused my drum riser to rotate slower than usual, which wasn't a problem, but it also made my little squirrel-cage fans turn like *hamster*-cage fans, making them less effective, even stopping entirely sometimes. My hands would get sweaty and slippery, and I missed those little fans more than I would have imagined.

When we started playing the "R30 Overture," the first audience member I noticed was a young black woman standing front-row center and wearing a "Friends" T-shirt—perhaps the most unlikely type you could ever find in a Rush audience. Maybe she had won a contest, but when I glanced down at her from time to time, she looked like she was enjoying the show—"without seeming to *understand* it," was the way I described it in my journal.

Overall, the audience seemed a little subdued, older and even more male than our American audiences had been on that tour. I described the sound in that ancient arena as "brittle and reverby (though as usual in that kind of arena, powerful for drums)."

When I ran offstage at the end, a car and driver were waiting, and Brutus joined me for the ride back to the hotel. Just outside the backstage gates, I saw rows of bootleggers selling T-shirts and other pirated souvenirs. Such bootleggers worked our North American shows as well, but were much more prevalent in Europe, where their wares were cheaper and nastier. On an early tour I received a letter from an English mum, complaining that her son had bought a Rush scarf (like the ones the Brits favor to show support for their football teams), and the ink had run in the rain on his way home. I wrote back to tell her I was sorry, and explained about those nasty bootleggers.

On the day of the second show I woke up tired and sore, and supplemented the morning vitamins with Bufferins. It was September 9, Carrie's and my fourth anniversary, but I would have to try to call her later, as it was eight hours earlier in Los Angeles. That would be a constant obstacle to communications between us from Europe—often the only opportunity would be on the bus after the show, when I would have to hope we had good cell reception on the English "mobile" we carried.

My hotel room phone rang at one o'clock p.m., and a woman from the front desk, who could only be described as "snotty," asked if I was checking out that day. When I said I was leaving at two, she announced unpleasantly that the hotel was full tonight, they needed the room urgently, they were losing revenue (a lie, as check-in time was four, giving them plenty of time to prepare the room for another guest), and finally, a peremptory demand, "Could you check out at one o'clock—which is *now*?"

I put the phone down, and heard no more about it.

At two, on another clear, bright day (rare in England, but it happens), I rode in to work with Liam once again. I wanted to get there early, to get moved into my new traveling home, rearrange my luggage into the stateroom and the bike bags, and I was also scheduled to do an interview with an English drum magazine. (Though I rarely talk to the press in recent years, I sometimes made exceptions for motorcycle or drum magazines.)

That second show came easier than the previous night's had, though my shoulders and wrists were sore, and once again, the audience seemed dull and reserved. Maybe they were just jaded Londoners, because other European audiences, even in Britain, would be more demonstrative. (Though there had always been a tendency in Britain for the front rows to be filled with people who had connections, rather than those who really *cared*—who would stand in line for any amount of time, or pay any price to be there.)

And of the almost 10,000 people in that audience, front and center was a sulky teenage boy, slouching in front of a plump, balding man, probably his father. The kid seemed determined to have a miserable time, and all through the show, he just *stood* there, frowning and glowering—though not so much at us, as at everything. Apart from wanting to whack him on the head with a drumstick, I could only think, what a waste to have him there instead of someone who would appreciate it.

Once again, I envisioned the first twenty rows sent to the back, on my "conveyor belt" idea, while the next twenty rows moved forward. It really would be great for everybody.

After the show I ran for the bus as usual, and stood for a few seconds in the dark stateroom, looking for the light switch. Suddenly there was a man beside me, close, and in the light from outside I saw a bulky figure with long straggly blonde hair and coarse features. He was holding up a pile of LPs and a marker-pen, saying, "Just give us a signature, Neil."

At first I thought he must be one of the new drivers, or a crew member who didn't know any better—we had to race straight out of there to avoid the after-show traffic—so I was polite, "No, no, we're leaving right now. You have to go."

Then he said, with an accent that sounded suspiciously like the English Midlands, "Boot I've coom all the way from Rooshia," and I figured out what was going on. The adrenaline started flowing.

It was a fan, actually invading my one-and-only sanctuary, and my brain was suddenly buzzing with outrage, disbelief, and not a little fear—different versions of "what is *wrong* with this person?"

Apparently the guy had got hold of one of the orange hard hats the stage crew wore, and made his way into the loading area unchallenged. Unlike our American bus, the entrance door was behind Mark's driving compartment, and when I had run onto the bus and Brutus pressed the button to close the pneumatic door behind me, Michael had turned back toward the building, and Brutus to fix our drinks. At the last second, the guy must have jammed his arm in the door and dashed inside, following me all the way back to the dark stateroom.

Still confused, but feeling threatened and angry, I backed away, then faced him squarely: "Get *out* of here!"

Brutus heard the commotion and came back and put a hand on the guy's shoulder, trying to lead him away gently. But he still wouldn't leave. Again he held up the LPs and said, "I've coom all the way from Rooshia."

Between clenched teeth, I said, "I don't *care*, you're in my *house*. Get out!"

He still wouldn't budge, standing there holding his LPs out to me, determined to get what he came for. My temper was rising, and finally I yelled, "Get the fuck *out* of here!" and pushed him away. Bolstered by a show's worth of adrenaline, as well as my reaction to this nightmarish moment, I gave him a *mighty* shove, and he went over backwards, his LPs scattering across the floor. He lay there for a few seconds, complaining about his elbow, but I was furious now. "I don't care, just get *out* of here!"

In a strange gesture of automatic courtesy (and tidiness), I picked up the guy's LPs and put them in his hands as Brutus and Mark led him off the bus. They called for security, delivered the guy into Michael's custody, then Mark finally started up the bus and pulled out. I changed out of my sweaty clothes, still trembling with mixed emotions.

As I walked forward, I saw Brutus's pale face, eyes bugging and mouth agape.

"That will *never* happen again," he said.

"I know," I nodded, then looked straight at him. "But how *scary*."

He made a face and nodded back.

Of course, I didn't blame Brutus, or anybody really, except the guy himself; if a lunatic like that was determined to get *at* me, he would find a way.

Still in shock, I took a big swallow of The Macallan and lit a cigarette. It seemed such a violation. As I wrote in my journal later (once I had calmed down), "Those maniacs are why vigilance and overtight security are *always* necessary."

Then I added, "Lucky for him *Dave* wasn't there." ("You're gonna get a whole lotta somethin' you're not gonna like.") Dave would never have accepted someone invading his bus, and the guy would certainly have been treated a little more *firmly*. Like the panhandler who opened the bus door and met the business end of Dave's gun—"You just got on the wrong fuckin' bus."

A few minutes later, Michael called our cell phone wanting to hear exactly what had happened. He said he had the guy in handcuffs, and wanted to know if he had touched me. I laughed at that, as it was *him* who got touched. But to our shock and disgust, apparently Britain had no law against simple trespassing. Even if someone walked right into your home, if they didn't break or steal anything, or touch anybody, there was no crime. That just seemed wrong, if you imagined some stranger wandering through *your* home, and even threatening you. I told Michael to let the guy go—there was nothing to be done about it now.

Still, it was a bad beginning to our first bus ride in Europe, and episodes like that always left their scars. I would never feel as "at home" on that bus, would never have the same sense of sanctuary I had felt on Dave's bus.

Mark parked for the night in Liverpool, right next to the ferry dock, as Brutus and I planned to spend the day off on the Isle of Man. The European bus had no generator when it was shut down, so there was no comforting hum through the night. In the morning I could hear Brutus's coughs and groans as he climbed out of his bunk (Dave, who had slept on the bunk under Brutus's on the *Test for Echo* tour, did a great imitation of that painful unfolding of Brutus's battered body, groan by groan).

I had my own aches and pains that morning, rolling out of Cher's 3000-euro bed and swallowing a couple of Bufferins with my orange juice. We ate our cereal and drank our coffee at the front-lounge table, looking out on a cool, gray morning and the massive, ornate stone buildings along the Liverpool waterfront. By the time I was dressed and ready to ride, Brutus and Mark had unloaded the bikes. We mounted our tankbags and panniers and rode over to collect our ferry tickets, then joined the line of cars, trucks, and a few other motorcyclists.

In the weeks leading up to the European leg, when Brutus was planning how we might spend our days off in Europe, one of the few suggestions I had offered was a visit to the Isle of Man. In the middle of the Irish Sea, thirty miles long and thirteen miles wide, the Island (always capitalized by locals) was an independent country, a "crown protectorate," like the Channel Islands of Jersey and Guernsey. The Isle of Man also had the world's oldest parliament—a parliament that had allowed motor racing on its streets starting in 1904, when the British government would not.

Automobiles soon became too fast for the Island's narrow roads, but motorcycle races continued for the next 100 years, interrupted only by wartime. The world-famous Manx TT (for Tourist Trophy) motorcycle races were held there over a "fortnight" every June, attracting more than 40,000 spectators, most arriving by motorcycle on packed ferries. In perhaps the world's most dangerous road race, the riders ran separate time trials over a 37.3-mile course around the Island, between stone walls, trees, and buildings, at speeds up to 175 miles per hour. The current lap record, including twists and turns and hills, and famously bad weather, stood at 127.68 mph.

During the 2004 TT races alone, three of those racers were killed, along with eight amateurs—on the Sunday following the finals, the visiting bikers were allowed to ride the course on "Mad Sunday."

A Manxman once described the Island as "70,000 alcoholics clinging to a rock," and the Manx symbol, the Triskelion, depicting three spurred legs bent at the knee and joined at the thigh, was seen everywhere from light poles to pub coasters. It reflected the Island's motto, "Wherever you throw it, it will stand."

Brutus and I had always loved ferry rides, and had been known to go out of our way to cross a river, lake, or strait by ferry, even if a bridge was available. The day remained gloomy, dark and misty, as we sailed over the calm Irish Sea. Despite occasional showers, we spent much of that smooth, two-and-a-half-hour crossing on deck, smelling the brisk sea air and watching seabirds, cargo ships, fishing boats, navigational buoys, and other ferries pass to port and starboard.

Riding off the ferry at Douglas, the capital, we were also introduced to riding on the left. We had been a little nervous about that, but later I would note, "riding on 'wrong side,' with roundabouts, not too bad—fun, really, just have to think about it *all* the time."

The rain and fog grew heavier, and the air was damp and chilly, the town streets often smelling of coal fires. That acrid odor reminded me of my early days in London, thirty-five years earlier, when coal was still commonly burned there. When we stopped for gas, I noticed bags of coal for sale in front of the petrol station.

We set out to follow the TT course, which Brutus had programmed into Dingus and Dork. The narrow, wet roads curved between hedges and stone walls, many still clad with padding from the recent Grand Prix series (a less-prestigious race on the same course, held in late August). It was hard to imagine racing along those country roads at more than 100 miles per hour.

We ducked out of the rain at the famed Sulby Glen Hotel, and chose what seemed a highly suitable lunch, cod and chips with mushy peas. In the motorcycle consciousness that prevailed everywhere on the Isle of Man, the waiter asked if we would buy a pin to support the worthy cause of emergency helicopter rescue for downed riders. We bought two.

Up over the so-called Mountain Section, on Mount Snaefell, we were slowed by traffic as well as the continuing rain and fog. I remembered watching televised races where it was raining on the mountain and dry in Douglas. Altogether, it was daunting to imagine racing around that course at the limits of physics, skill, and nerve, and I thought of a DVD I had been given by my friend David Mills, called *One Man's Island*. It was a documentary about an amateur Canadian motorcycle racer, Mark Gardiner, who had a dream since boyhood to race the Isle of Man TT. In January 2002, at age forty-six, he moved to the Island and spent the rest of that winter and spring riding a mountain bike around the course, learning it as intimately as he could. On a borrowed race bike, he barely managed to qualify for the race, then came second-to-last in the time trials. Still, he had fulfilled the dream. And he didn't get killed.

When the TT course brought Brutus and me back around to Douglas, we headed south to do a little more exploring. We crossed the Fairy Bridge, where tradition recommends you say hello to the fairies if you want to have good luck on the Island (of course we did), then down through quaint little Castletown to Port St. Mary and "land's end," at Spanish Head. Dingus and Dork had some trouble navigating around there, once sending us through what appeared to be someone's driveway, though it did bring us out the other side and onto another narrow lane. Eventually we made it to a rainswept promontory, where we parked for a few minutes and looked out through fog and rain to a small island, the Calf of Man.

Something about that lonely, bleak prospect made me wonder about the Isle of Man's part in World War II. (Perhaps because it so resembled a scene from a British war movie.) Spies from both sides might have worked there, with hidden radios and coded messages, and maybe U-boats had cruised by in the Irish Sea. Later I learned that some German Jews had been interned there during the War.

Brutus and I circled back to our modest hotel in Douglas, which at least gave us views of the gray waterfront. That stretch of dark pavement, sand, and sea seemed too dismal and deserted to merit its "Promenade" name. Noting our mileage, I could hardly believe it—the day had seemed impossibly full for only covering 124 kilometers, 77 miles (again, not counting nautical miles).

My room also had a window I could open to the sea air, which was always a treat. A high-pitched foghorn sounded throughout the night, and a few times I looked out to see the tide receding far across the dark shoreline.

We were up before dawn, with an early ferry to catch back to Liverpool. Riding slowly up the deserted Promenade to its far end, then back to the ferry terminal, we waited in the cold darkness as more vehicles collected around us. The rain held off until we got the bikes aboard and tied down, and we climbed up to the enclosed passenger deck and claimed a couple of seats.

It was a Saturday, and the ferry was packed with families and groups of schoolchildren crowding every seat. Making a pillow of my rain jacket, I dozed against the window, feeling the boat start to heave on a rough sea. Brutus told me he had watched the stewards coming around to collect sick-bags, people sheepishly handing over their full paper sacks.

I took a walk on deck as we approached Liverpool, and a guy came up to me and asked if I was me. When I said I was, he said, with a note of disbelief, "I've got tickets to see you tomorrow night in Manchester!"

I smiled and said, "I hope you enjoy it!," and went below again.

From Liverpool, we rode south into Wales, Dingus and Dork leading us unerringly through ancient villages and along tiny lanes framed by stone walls, rain coming and going under looming skies. The navigation was more of an orienteering exercise, roads constantly changing names and numbers, and often diminishing to one-lane tracks beside green hillsides dotted with sheep—*thousands* of sheep.

Meandering our way eastward through geometric green valleys and dripping woods, pavement slippery and leaf-strewn, we were becoming more accustomed to riding on the left. Given the mirror-image nature of "overtaking" (English for "passing"), Brutus was the first to work up his nerve and start venturing into the right lane to get by slower traffic, and I soon followed, fearful and excited.

We turned onto the M-6 motorway to run a little south to Birmingham, once again adapting to the reversed pattern of lanes, and I began to notice something—*no one* dawdled in the passing lane!

I had truly forgotten that it wasn't necessary to endure the frustration Michael and I had suffered from Colorado to Florida; it wasn't necessary to be exposed to the danger of having to pass on the wrong side. That miraculous observation would hold true for the whole time Brutus and I rode in Europe. With one single exception (an old English lady in a Rover), every driver we encountered in 5000 miles of riding in Europe treated other drivers (and riders) with courtesy and respect. They were skillful, watchful, and predictable, moved over if you wanted to pass, and *always* used their turn signals. The word to describe European drivers, I noted, was "trustworthy."

Before long, I decided I wanted to send every driver in North America to Europe for a couple of weeks—to learn how to drive!

We also had our first (and last) experience with European police. As we rode through a construction area on the motorway, admittedly exceeding the suddenly diminished limit of 40 mph, a police Range Rover pulled alongside us. The driver leaned out his window, extended four fingers downward across the door, and mouthed, "It's *forty*."

We slowed down, he drove off, and that was the end of it. No ticket, no wasting everybody's time by pulling us over, no lecture, no attitude. A long way from the time Brutus and I were pulled over in a similar construction zone on I-40 in Arizona. The apoplectic state trooper had looked at our Canadian licences and sneered, "You come down here like that, *we'll bury you!*"

It was certainly true that most American police officers were less intense than *that* (except in Florida), but it was another revelation to me that during the rest of our travels in Europe, despite our tendency toward rapid transit, we hardly saw another police car. Like the absence of the Anti-Destination League, the discourteous and careless drivers, you had to wonder why it was so different there—why the European police didn't prowl the roads gathering revenue by citing victimless offences.

Thinking of the similarities and differences among different countries and cultures in Europe, I always remember a T-shirt I once saw in Greece. It presented a centuries-old portrait of European culture in all its variations: "HEAVEN IS: Where the chefs are French, the mechanics are German, the police are British, the lovers are Greek, and it's all organized by the Swiss. HELL IS: where the chefs are British, the mechanics are French, the police are German, the lovers are Swiss, and it's all organized by the Greeks."

Other countries have their own variations on that theme, but the generalizations are telling.

Brutus and I rode in circles around the massive complex of buildings outside Birmingham that made up the National Exhibition Centre, until we finally found the Arena. We would actually be doing two shows at that venue, but they were separated by a few days, due to hall availabilities. A crowd of fans was already gathering outside the backstage doors, but Michael was watching for us, and had an overhead door opened so Brutus and I could ride straight into the loading area. Once again, the mileage wasn't much, 238 kilometers, 148 miles, but the day had been full.

On the last two tours, when we had mainly played at the American amphitheaters, one thing I had come to appreciate was the enclosed parking areas backstage, private and secure. Any time I wanted to, I could walk from the bus to the stage, dressing room, or Bubba-Gump room, and I was free to work on the bike in the afternoons. In contrast, at most arenas in America or Europe, the bus would be parked in a public area, trapping me inside the building from arrival until after the show, so another aspect of the European tour I had been dreading was that claustrophobic restriction.

However, one advantage of having Michael on full-time security duty, and aware of my preferences, was that every day he smoothed our arrival at the building. He also tried to arrange it so Mark could park the bus near one of the backstage doors. Then I would be able to sneak out to the bus and back when I wanted to, and a small freedom like that made a huge difference in my quality of life.

Despite my dread going into it, I was beginning to think this European tour might not be so horrible after all.

The Midlands audience of 10,939 people was a little more demonstrative than the London audience had been, and the show went pretty well. Another difference with the "shift change" between Michael and Brutus was that Brutus could spend the whole show out in the bus, working on routes and accommodations for the upcoming days.

That night, Mark parked us in the English equivalent of a truck stop, "motorway services," and we woke up on a Sunday morning surrounded by coachloads of OAPs (old-age pensioners). While we ate our cereal, we watched white-haired people doddering in and out of the Road Chef restaurant. Brutus and I filled up with gas, oil, and air, and set off on a tour of a region called the Derbyshire Dales, between Sheffield and Manchester. The area also included Britain's first national park, Peak District, established in 1951 (though no passport stamps, apparently).

The day was cold, with intermittent rain, but the scenery was spectacular over high, bare green hills and down through neat valleys framing rocky rivers. A couple of times I noticed the roadside was lined with stands of pines, which seemed very un-English, but then we would ride through a huddled little village, between time-honored pubs and half-timbered shops. Typical rows of attached homes, called "terraced" houses, lined residential streets among tidy floral gardens overhung with leafy trees. (Another observation I soon noted, "Those Brits sure can *garden*.") The churches were dignified, venerable houses of worship for Anglicans and Catholics, but there were no "inspirational" church signs.

Once again, the day's route was more a matter of orienteering, complicated and tortuous, but the boys did wonderfully well, guiding us along narrow little roads between the inevitable stone walls (and sheep). Sometimes, instead of naming the road or lane we were to turn down, the screen would just say "Turn Left On Road, 100 Yards."

On that English country Sunday, I also had many opportunities to think about what I saw, and describe it to myself in "English" terms. People in hiking clothes were "ramblers," or perhaps "twitchers" (bird-watchers), carrying their binoculars and "rucksacks." We also encountered many groups of motorcyclists, all of them wearing brightly colored, race-style leathers and full-face helmets, crouched over the Japanese or Italian race-replica machines the Brits called "sports bikes" (a parallel to "sports cars," I guess, though they were just "sportbikes" to North Americans, who watched "sports" on television while the Brits watched "sport").

That was another example of how many things really *were* different in Europe. On a cool, inclement day like that in North America, chances are we would not have seen *any* other riders, but even on a sunny Sunday, they would likely have been "cruisers," rumbling along with their riders fashionably garbed in Marlon Brando *Wild One* jackets and open-face helmets (or *no* helmets, in states like Illinois and Wisconsin).

We made our way into Manchester from the east, the streets ever wider and busier, until we arrived in the middle of the "City Centre," at the Local Newspaper Arena. Once again, we had only ridden 155 kilometers, less than 100 miles, yet somehow it felt as though we had covered a lot of country.

Brutus was feeling bad by the time we arrived, afflicted by pain and swelling in the, shall we say, lower abdominal area. He had suffered from an infection there before, and a doctor confirmed that it was recurring. Brutus downed the prescribed painkillers and antibiotics, then took to his bunk for the rest of the afternoon and evening.

I was expecting a few visitors that night from different branches of the extended family. As usual, I had asked them to come to the venue at 4:30, so I would have some time to say hello before soundcheck. In the Bubba-Gump room, I greeted Jackie's cousin, Fiona, husband Andrew (a keen "sports bike" rider interested in the route Brutus and I had ridden that day), and their teenagers Charlotte and James, with a couple of their friends.

They were, as the English say, "lovely people," but it was a slightly painful meeting for me, and perhaps a little awkward for them. The last time I had seen Fiona and Andrew had been in London, seven years earlier, when they visited Jackie and me after Selena's death, and not long before Jackie's. The summer before that, their entire family, with Uncle Harry and Aunt Joyce, had visited the Quebec house, leaving the day before Selena left—forever.

Before that, the last time I had seen them had been on the 1992 tour, backstage at Wembley, when I had been tired and crabby and complaining about British labor troubles—a ferry strike affecting our logistics, I think it was. So I hadn't been very pleasant.

Carrie's brother Ken was also in town, on leave from his navy posting in Spain, but he and his friends didn't show up until almost five, so I could only say hello and take care of their tickets and passes. In cases like that, I could only hope people understood how limited my time and energy were.

That night in Manchester we had one of the largest audiences of the tour, 13,374 people, and they seemed a happy, enthusiastic bunch. At intermission I made a journal note, "Decent show—good first half."

I also noted, "Apparently it's my birthday."

As I had so many times in the past thirty years, I was "celebrating" a birthday, my fifty-second, onstage. A few of the guys at work wished me a happy birthday that day, and everybody had signed a card. During the second set, a cake appeared on Geddy's dryers, shown larger-than-life on the rear screen by the overhead camera. The audience cheered; I blushed.

That night we had Mark drive all the way north to Glasgow, parking outside the next venue, the Scottish Exhibition Centre, though we had a day off before that show. When considering destinations for that day's ride in Scotland, I had been thinking of John O'Groats, at the far northern tip of Scotland, but Brutus had shown me a book called *1000 Places to See Before You Die*. It listed a place in Scotland called Skibo Castle, and it looked spectacular. Originally built by Andrew Carnegie, the Scottish-born American industrialist, the Castle was now a private club, famous as the site of Madonna's wedding. The book said Skibo Castle offered guest accommodations, and I said to Brutus, "I think we've got to go there."

Geddy had given me a couple of wrapped presents that afternoon, and I opened them on the bus. He had always been one of the best gift-givers I knew, and these were no exception: a first edition of Tom Robbins's first book, *Another Roadside Attraction*, and a bottle of armagnac from 1952, the year of my birth. What a thoughtful friend.

The next day, Brutus and I had every kind of weather, sometimes all at once—sunny, rainy, cold, windy, and cloudy, with lots of rainbows in between. Starting north, we rode through dense forests, with glimpses of Ben Nevis, Britain's highest mountain, and the sparkling waters of Loch Lomond. Veering to the east, we rode winding, wet little roads, some of them one-lane tracks, their names unknown to Dingus and Dork. We passed shaggy dark-green forests and bleak, rounded hills, often dotted with sheep. (In those few days, I had already seen more sheep than I had imagined there were in all the world.) Ancient stone bridges led to tiny villages, coal smoke rising from the crooked chimneys of small, rustic cottages.

I had hoped we could manage to visit Craigellachie, the home of The Macallan (cue angelic choir), or at least pass by it, but as the day eased into afternoon, with continuing rain showers and slow roads, we decided to switch modes on Dingus and Dork to "Quickest Way." As so often happened, we were torn between a beautiful journey and a beckoning destination.

On the A-9 motorway, with its "dual carriageways" allowing safer overtaking, we sped north toward Inverness, then across the windswept waters of the Moray Firth and the smaller Cromarty Firth. Near there, we passed the Glenmorangie (rhymes with "orangey") distillery, home of my second-favorite single malt. Way up in the Scottish Highlands now, edging the North Sea, and with the sun at last emerging to glorify the landscape, we seemed to ride through a world of blue water, green fields, and white sheep.

Around three o'clock, we turned into an unpretentious gate marked "Carnegie Club" (a side entrance, it turned out), and followed a long, winding gravel drive between 200-year-old beech trees. We pulled up in front of an enormous castle of red sandstone, with turrets and battlements and crimson-ivied walls surrounded by lawns and gardens and trees. The flag on the main tower waved in the breeze, showing the Union Jack on one side, the Stars and Stripes on the other.

Perhaps comparable only to William Randolph Hearst's San Simeon, Andrew Carnegie's estate was created for the same reasons—a place for him to relax and play country gentleman, and to entertain guests royally.

Carnegie was born in Scotland's ancient capital of Dunfermline in 1835, and when his father, a weaver, was put out of work by growing industrialization, the family emigrated to the United States in 1848. Young Andrew began working in a Pittsburgh cotton mill, then for Western Union and the Pennsylvania Railroad. With daring and foresight, he began his own business, the Carnegie Steel Company, which launched the steel industry in Pittsburgh.

When he sold his company to J.P. Morgan in 1900 for $480 million, he became the richest man in the world. At age sixty-five, he retired to devote himself to philanthropy—a uniquely American invention, pioneered by Carnegie. He stated publicly that the rich had a moral obligation to give away their fortunes—"The man who dies rich dies disgraced." His intention, though, was not charity, which he abhorred, but to "help people help themselves." Before his death in 1919, Carnegie had established several foundations in the United States and Europe, built 2,509 libraries (at a time when few public libraries existed anywhere in the world), and given away over $350 million. (He probably still died rich.)

Andrew Carnegie was also a political idealist, an early champion of the "league of nations" idea, and he built a "Palace of Peace" in the Hague that evolved into the World Court. He considered the beginning of World War I the end to his dreams of a civilized, peaceful world. Although he lived another five years, the last entry in his autobiography was the day the War began.

Skibo Castle was built as a retirement home for Carnegie and his wife, Louise, between 1899 and 1903. The 7500-acre estate had originally been a Viking stronghold (the name derived from the Norse "Scytherbolle") in the tenth century, growing over the next 1000 years into an "average-sized estate house." When Carnegie's baronial castle was built, sparing no expense in labor or materials, in that splendid Highlands setting, Carnegie said, "If Heaven is more beautiful than this, someone has made a mistake."

Brutus and I would be inclined to agree. We were welcomed by the uniformed doormen, dignified, older men who seemed unruffled by our rough, road-weathered Scooter Trash appearance. They did tell us we were the only guests ever to have arrived at Skibo Castle by motorcycle. It already looked as though private jets, Bentleys, and Range Rovers would be more the style of the Carnegie Club's members (nonmembers were allowed to visit only once).

Once Brutus had checked us in, we were directed to the Stables to park the bikes (384 kilometers, 240 miles), near the elegantly rustic stone buildings of the Dairy, and picturesque residences for groundskeepers and other staff. A friendly young Scotsman, Andrew, in a flat cap and hunting clothes, picked us up in one of the club's fleet of dark green, monogrammed Range Rovers. As he drove us slowly through the grounds, pointing out the features, Brutus and I looked around, then at each other, thinking, and sometimes saying, "Wow."

The Castle was unusually full that week, with members taking part in a Pro-Am golf tournament (professionals and amateurs). We wouldn't be staying in the main building, but Andrew delivered us to our accommodations in the Lodge, a small stone cottage not far from the Castle, near the Swimming Pavilion, with its saltwater pool.

Though rustic on the outside, with climbing vines and lichen covering the weathered stone walls, the Lodge had been made *immaculate* inside, with lovely workmanship and comfortable furnishings. Every amenity was provided, from luxury toiletries to a bottle of Rioja, a variety of cheeses, bread and honey in the kitchen, and tartan laundry bags and bathrobes in the two bedrooms.

Already, my journal notes despaired, "My god—where to begin? Impossible, even to capture *this*, never mind the whole amazing day."

A small electric golf cart ("buggy," in Brit-talk) was provided for our use, and we immediately changed into our outdoor clothes, poured a couple of whiskies to go, and went for a cruise. The sun was still out, but we knew that could change any time. Brutus drove us along the tree-lined drive, passing the small Loch Ospisdale, the wide estuary called Poll na Caorach ("Pool of the Sheep"), the Monks' Walk, and out to the open greenswards of the Carnegie Links.

We paused at the Golf House for a look around, and I overheard a golfer's conversation with another golfer that I wanted to remember for Alex, "The front nine I played like a god; the back nine I played like a dog."

Back at the Lodge, we walked over toward the Castle, through the Walled Garden, beside the greenhouses, looking down over the fountain and lawns to the trimmed green fields. Around the grounds, individual trees had been planted by, or in honor of, visiting dignitaries, and I noticed a giant sequoia, from California, had been planted by Bill Clinton, "On his first visit to Skibo Castle."

Even then, we hadn't seen a fraction of the estate, and when we went back to the Lodge for a cleanup and nap before dinner, I was reading about some of the activities available. I noted, "Could easily spend *days* here—falconry, archery, skeet-shooting, off-road 4x4 tours, spa, saltwater pool, horse riding, birdwatching, library, and just *walking around.* Maybe I'd even take a golf lesson!"

Once again I was feeling something I had written in my journal earlier: "Make every minute *two*; once to experience it, and once to savor it."

Back in 1987, I had expressed the same yearning in our song "Time Stand Still"—"Freeze this moment a little bit longer/ Make each sensation a little bit stronger/ Experience slips away."

Cocktails would be served in the Great Hall at 7:30, and dinner at eight, so Brutus and I wanted to clean up for that. From the outset, we had planned on staying in the kind of places where you have to dress for dinner, and the Carnegie Club information sheet specified "jackets and ties required for gentlemen; smart attire for ladies." As soon as we arrived, I had taken my black Prada suit from the bike-bags and hung it up in the shower to steam the wrinkles out of it. Brutus discovered that he had left his dress-up jacket in London (he had a habit of losing track of things, usually temporarily, and when we traveled together one of his nicknames was "the Mean Misplacer"). The resourceful staff at Skibo Castle said they would find him a tie and jacket.

We strolled back up the gravel walk through the gardens to the Castle, and while Brutus was getting his wardrobe sorted out, I had a look around. My notes reflected my first, and most powerful, reaction: "The *library*—oh my!"

Its main room featured floor-to-ceiling shelves full of leather-bound volumes, a ladder on wheels to reach the higher ones, all centered on an impossibly wide window looking out over the formal gardens, lawns, and stately trees. A few card tables for club members did nothing to interrupt the sense of spacious peace, dominated by Mr. Carnegie's huge desk at one end. Behind the desk was a door to a small private dining room, seating four.

What a dream! A writing space surrounded by books, with views of

roadshow

gardens, lawns, and trees, privacy, silence, even elegant dining, all in one suite of rooms. I had never seen anything so wonderful, and was afflicted with a severe case of "office envy."

I followed the stairs down to what was called the "dungeon," and looked through the gentlemanly snooker room, and a gun room converted into a bar. A modern business center had meeting rooms and all the necessary technology to serve the modern tycoon.

Upstairs again, I joined the crowd in the Great Hall, sitting alone on a sofa by the coal fire with my journal. The Great Hall was massive, sumptuous, and ornate, the very image of baronial country splendor— intricate carved-oak staircase, paneling, and gallery, comfortable furnishings, mounted moose and deer heads, a huge carved wooden organ, its pipes rising up the full two stories (Carnegie so loved organ music that he donated more than 7000 pipe organs to churches and halls around the world). Butlers circulated with champagne and canapés (foie gras and "haggis balls," which I described as "sausagey and porridgey—glad they're small").

Making a note about the contrast between that night and the previous one, when I had been sweating through a concert in an arena and sleeping on the bus ("tonight I'm sleeping in a *castle*"), I saw Brutus across the room, looking smart in his "borrowed tie and jacket" (quote from our song "Test for Echo"). He was already engaged in conversation with somebody. "The man at ease," I noted.

The Great Hall was filled with the hubbub of cocktail chatter, and one of the managers we had met when we arrived, perhaps seeing me sitting alone, stopped by to talk a little about our travels, and about the Castle. At eight o'clock, a bagpiper marched in, dressed in full Highland regalia, pipes "skirling," as they say. He led us into the Dining Room, another baronial hall of intricate carvings and draperies, candles sparkling on crystal, china, and cutlery.

Brutus and I found our two places, marked with menu cards at a long table across the end, crosswise to the main table, and we sat down, introducing ourselves to our neighbors. The information sheet called this "dinner party style," and I had been wondering how it was going to be. Opposite me, Jim and Brenda sounded English rather than Scottish, and Jim was an older businessman, in his sixties, with groomed white hair and mustache. His wife, Brenda, was younger, perhaps in her mid-forties, fair-haired and athletic looking. She was playing in the following day's golf tournament, and the others made much of her having a handicap of 12, so that must have been good.

Beside them was Robert, a friendly Scot of about our age, and beside Brutus was Robert's dark, attractive wife, Paula. Both of them had the soft Scottish accent that is so unlike the oft-caricatured, coarse version (think Groundskeeper Willie in "The Simpsons"), just as there is a more genteel style of Southern American accent, more refined and euphonious than, say, Cletis the Slack-Jawed Yokel.

Once everyone was seated, a kind of jester/toastmaster with wild hair, wearing a combination of hideous tartans, rose at the head of the main table and welcomed everyone. In a comic monologue, he told the classic anecdote about George Bernard Shaw sending Winston Churchill an invitation to the first performance of his new play, writing, "Bring a friend, if you have one." Sir Winston replied that he would be unable to attend the first performance, but would like to attend the second, "If there is one."

When the multi-tartaned comedian sat down, and dinner service began, our table carried on discussing Churchill's famous dry wit, and I recounted my favorite story about him. At a dinner party, Churchill was seated opposite a woman, and he made some remark that caused her to burst out with, "Oh Mr. Churchill! If I were married to you, I should put poison in your tea!"

Sir Winston replied, "Madam, if I were married to you, I should drink it."

The menu of wild mushroom risotto, roast turbot, and chocolate fondant was accompanied by appropriate wines for each course, all served by attentive waiters. Brutus and I fell into conversation with our neighbors, and when questions were raised about us, I took a metaphorical deep breath and told them . . . the truth. I was a Canadian musician on a concert tour, traveling by motorcycle, with Brutus as my aide-de-camp and guide.

To strangers, a little story like that was not an answer, but an invitation to more questions. Kevin Anderson once told me how he dreaded being in the company of strangers and hearing the question, "So, what do you do?" If Kevin replied, "I'm a writer," raised eyebrows would inevitably follow, and "Oh! What do you write? Anything I might have heard of?" And so on.

Because Kevin, as a science-fiction writer, worked in a kind of niche of popular culture, as I did in my way, it would be unlikely if the stranger had heard of our work. But it all had to be explained; they would apologize for not having heard of you, you would be embarrassed, they would be embarrassed, and it was all just . . . not very interesting.

In Paul Theroux's *Blinding Light*, he described a writer facing that situation.

> He did not want to disclose that he was a writer on assignment. That kind of revelation always provoked questions and cast a shadow over a conversation, made some people inquisitive and bumptious, and others wary. At the very least it turned most people, including the writer on assignment, into bores.

And of course, authors from Stephen King to John Barth have reported on the cocktail-party experience of hearing, "Say, I've got this great story, maybe you could write it for me."

So, when Jim followed up my answer by asking who I played for, I self-consciously murmured the answer, too quietly. He leaned over the table and said, "*Rusk*? You mean like children eat?"

That clarified, they asked more about Brutus, and once again, he was master of any situation. He described his current profession at home, which might be defined as casual carpentry, in terms of providing custom-fitted cabinetry to the carriage trade, and made it sound very impressive indeed.

Brenda told us she and Jim had a home in Spain, and invited us—apparently sincerely—to come and visit them there. There was a wistful dissatisfaction about Brenda, it seemed to me, despite her 12 handicap. She seemed almost desperate, as if wanting more *life* in her life. A common complaint, alas, for many women. And men, too.

After dinner, Brutus and I adjourned to the drawing room (from "withdrawing" room, where ladies used to go after dinner and leave the gentlemen to their cigars, brandy, and "serious" talk). A white-tied pianist sat behind the Bechstein grand piano, a thick songbook available for high-class karaoke (if only Michael had been there!). A loud, self-amused American led a couple of half-hearted sing-alongs of '60s pop songs with two or three other guests. Delighted by the great time he thought he was having, he roared, "Those fuckers in the Gun Room don't know what they're missing!"

After a coffee and cognac, we decided to investigate those mysterious "fuckers" in the Gun Room, now that we knew what they were missing. There we encountered Jim and Brenda and Robert and Paula again, and we all nodded and smiled. Brutus and I helped ourselves to a selection of cheeses and ports. We learned later the Gun Room was supposed to be for members only, but no one protested.

My journal note capped the day with, *"What a night!"*

After a deep (not to say comatose) sleep, I was awake at 6:30. Brutus wanted to sleep a while longer, so I walked up to the Castle, through the dew-soaked gardens in the radiant early morning to "Mrs. Carnegie's Dining Room." However, first I paused for one more look around Mr. Carnegie's library, the morning sun slanting through the wide picture window, framing that magnificent view.

I really would have to think about joining the Carnegie Club (if they would have me—see Groucho Marx—and if it wasn't 6000 miles from my California home), just to be able to hang around that room.

At seven o'clock, I was the only guest in the small, exquisite dining room, though the golfers may have been on the links already. My oatmeal and poached eggs were served on Royal Albert china (Lady Carlyle pattern, I noticed on the bottom, like a good reporter) with Sheffield cutlery.

The morning was sunny, but cold. A mass of dark clouds to the east threatened the showers that would cover us most of the day on our ride back to Glasgow. We circled Inverness and picked up a small road to the south of famed Loch Ness, avoiding the main road on its north shore. The Skibo doorman had warned us that road was often crowded with tourist coaches—though of course we would always choose the smaller road anyway. The clouds began to close in, bringing mist and showers, as we rode past more of those shaggy green forests and tiny cottages. The lonely little road was sometimes two-lane, sometimes one, with hardly another vehicle on it. The thick woods obscured any view of the Loch, but it was still a lovely ride.

At the far end of Loch Ness, we arrived in the busy little tourist town of Fort Augustus, and finally had a view of the misty waters that harbored that famous monster. Fueling up, we continued southwest past Loch Lochy ("Lake Lakey?") and out to the western shore of Scotland, riding along a series of misty lochs and firths, then back inland, through forests and farmlands (and sheep). As I noted later, "So many quaint little villages and cottages. So many sheep. So much rain."

Looking around at rural Scotland and thinking of Andrew Carnegie's father having to emigrate because of poverty and hopeless unemployment, I realized that the people who moved from Europe to North America in the nineteenth and early twentieth centuries hadn't necessarily wanted to leave, they *had* to. In a growing population, if there was nothing to do but, say, herd sheep, then all the shepherding jobs were soon filled.

Many Scottish emigrants settled in Canada, and even in that country of displaced persons, the Scots always seemed the most loudly sentimental about their homeland, especially when in their cups. Still, many Europeans behaved or felt the same way. To other people in their adopted countries who might not have such an overdeveloped sense of "heritage," an attitude like that could seem demeaning to the place they called home now—like living with someone who is always talking about a former lover. I used to think, "If 'home' was so great, why did you *leave*? And why wouldn't you just go back?"

A song of ours called "Territories," from 1985, was about nationalism of all kinds, and one verse talked about the way that syndrome played out in North America, Africa, and Australia, with an additional joking reference to how it seemed that everywhere the band traveled, locals told us they made the best beer in the world.

We see so many tribes overrun and undermined
While their invaders dream of lands they've left behind
Better people, better food, and better beer—
Why move around the world, when Eden was so near?

But of course, their Eden was played out, and they had to look for other gardens, always comparing them unfavorably to the one they had left. Generously, you might say these people were just celebrating their background and ancestry, but for myself, as a rootless earthling of uncertain derivation, I would say, as with religion, "Who needs it?"

Like religion, that kind of patriotism definitely causes a lot of trouble.

That day in Scotland I was also noticing how much I was obliged to depend on Dingus lately. Since I didn't draw out the routes myself, as I had in North America, I sacrificed that dimensional sense of the day's journey. As I noted, *"Have* to trust the damn thing. Though they haven't let us down, now that we know how to think like they do, and compensate."

With the rain and the highly technical riding on those wet little roads, even 407 kilometers (250 miles) felt like a long day. As we approached Glasgow, reflecting on all the good riding and the unforgettable experience of our night at Skibo Castle, I was thinking that as a commute to work, it was hard to beat.

At dinner with Alex and Geddy, I brought out my computer and showed them some of the photos I had taken of the Castle, and told Alex about the golfer saying he had "played the front nine like a god, and the back nine like a dog." Alex also confirmed that Brenda's 12 handicap was indeed impressive.

And although Brutus and I hadn't made it to Craigellachie, the cradle of The Macallan, it happened that before the show that night in Glasgow, The Macallan came to *me*. A lady from the company, who had heard of my fondness for their product, as expressed in *Ghost Rider* and *Traveling Music*, had arranged through Shelley to present me with a bottle of their new blend, called Fine Oak 15-Year-Old.

On the bus after the show, Brutus and I had a sample, and I pronounced it, "Very nice. Delicate-like."

After show. Once again, so many thoughts go through my head during the show—and then they're gone.

Sense of bizarre extremes again onstage tonight, like where I was at eight o'clock *last* night: being piped into dinner, after champagne, foie gras, and haggis balls (!), in my Prada suit.

So-so show. Sore wrists and tired brain from above-described exertions. A few clumsy errors, in the mental/physical interface. Pretty good solo, though—and whole show, really. I'm just being picky.

And why not.

Before *2112,* Lerxst told me there are nine more shows—I thought eleven. So that's good.

During the "spacy" intro, while we had a minute to catch our breath, Alex usually came over to the drums and shared a comical "look" with me. At that point every night, nearing the end of another show, we had also started holding up our fingers to count down the remaining shows.

Later that night, Mark, Brutus, and I slept at another "motorway services." Our target for the day was the Lake District, another area I had requested that Brutus include in our travels. During my early-'70s time in England, a band I was in played a couple of small-time gigs in that area, in Kendal and Whitehaven, and I had always remembered it. The region was also designated a national park, and was the historic home of poets William Wordsworth and Samuel Taylor Coleridge, two of the Romantic poets. During one of our previous stays in Britain, I saw a television movie about Coleridge, with David Hemmings playing the opium-addicted poet, set in the breathtaking scenery of the Lake District.

In the summer of 1797, in a cottage in Southern England, Coleridge fell into an opium-fueled dream and conceived the poem "Kubla Khan." He said the poem had emerged full-blown in his drugged mind, in hundreds of lines, but while he was trying to write it down he was interrupted by "a man from Porlock" at the door (on *business*, note!), and the rest of it evaporated.

In the summer of 1976, in a cottage in Southern Ontario, I was working on the lyrics for a song called "Xanadu." (I didn't have any opium, but I might have smoked a little hash.) The song idea was originally inspired by the movie *Citizen Kane*, and its main character, Charles Foster Kane, and I had planned to build something on that theme. At the beginning of the movie, the opening lines from "Kubla Khan" were quoted, "In Xanadu did Kubla Khan, a stately pleasure dome decree." As research, I looked up the poem, and I was so powerfully impressed by it that the poem took over the song. In the end, there was entirely too much "honey dew" in it—too much Coleridge, that is to say—and though musically the song was one of our earliest big "epics," I never cared much for the lyrics.

However, it happened that the song "Xanadu" would be the one that gained us our earliest television exposure in Britain, when a video of us playing it was shown over the closing credits of a music program called "The Old Grey Whistle Test." We were playing part of that eleven-minute epic on the R30 tour, part of a medley with a couple of other old war horses, "By-Tor and the Snow Dog" and "Working Man."

Another line from "Kubla Khan," "woman wailing for her demon-lover," turned up almost twenty years later as "Daughter of a demon-lover," in our song "Animate," a Jungian tribute to a man's "anima," or female side. "Animate" was one of my favorites from our vast repertoire of hits and misses, and I was glad we had started playing it again on this tour, though the Coleridge connection hadn't occurred to me before.

Other connections with the Lake District came from my child-hood—the toy cars, Dinky Toys, I used to have of Sir Malcolm Campbell's series of land-speed racers, all called "Bluebird." Campbell and his son, Donald, had also raced speedboats on these lakes, and Donald Campbell was killed testing a jet-powered boat on Coniston Water in 1967, pursuing a goal of 300 mph on water.

I thought of that, too, looking over those peaceful lakes, their serene waters now marked only by the silver wakes of stately tour boats.

The day, once again, had a lot of "weather"—alternating sun, clouds, and rain. Under that ever-active sky, Brutus and I rode through a land-scape of open lands, moors, and hills (called "fells" in Northwest England, contrasting with the "dales," valleys), with forests, farms, and villages of ancient, slate-roofed cottages. The area's plentiful rain (oh yes) made everything green and lush, and the roads and lanes were often slick with moisture, winding through overhanging trees, ferns, and moss over dry-stone walls. There were also, of course, many sheep.

Tour buses jammed the villages, and tour boats crisscrossed the lakes, so the main roads and towns were filled with tourists. Brutus had done his homework on the route, though, and Dingus and Dork mostly guided us down the small, picturesque lanes, looping around and back to the M6 motorway. Then a long run south to Birmingham, for the second show at the National Exhibition Centre.

After 352 kilometers, 220 miles, we pulled inside the loading area at the NEC again. Both bikes were due for oil changes, but Brutus had some other assignments to work on for future routes and reservations, and since I was familiar with the oil-changing operation on both my bikes, I volunteered to do it. While I worked, I was visited by Brent and Beau from the sound crew, to talk about bikes (Brent would buy himself a BMW GS after the tour).

The show turned out to be the best of the British run, I thought, and certainly my favorite audience. There were more smiles out there, more people who seemed to be having *fun*. I wondered if that was because it was the second show in the same building, and all the people with "connections" had attended the first one, so all the real fans were able to get good tickets for this one.

In any case, it was a pleasure to play for those people (*work* for them, I always wanted to emphasize). I noticed an adolescent boy at the front, over toward stage left, and in contrast to the scowling brat in London, he was having a wonderful time. Chubby and bespectacled, he reminded me of "Piggy" from *Lord of the Flies*, and late in the show I sent Michael out with a pair of drumsticks for him.

At the beginning of *2112*, Alex held up eight fingers, for eight more shows, and in the "pirate" section, the audience joined in with pirate flags, balloons, bandanas, and eye patches. Great!

My after-show review of the European shows so far:

Playing very well this run, barring a few dumb mistakes. Legs remain very strong. Generally good feel and flows—for everybody, in fact.

After the show, I put on an Isaac Hayes CD, an old favorite of Brutus's and mine from the *Test for Echo* tour, with its extended versions of "Walk On By" and "By the Time I Get to Phoenix." As I tucked into another great Frenchie sandwich I mentioned to Brutus that if the narrator in that song had really been driving from Los Angeles to Tennessee, he would have taken I-40, like Michael and I did. Then the song would be "By the Time I Get to Flagstaff," which maybe wouldn't sound as good.

I had discovered a couple of new after-show treats in Britain, too: a kind of "biscuit" (cookie) made by McVities called Boasters, and little candy-covered chocolate pellets called Smarties that were great to nibble on while reading. We had those in Canada, too, but not in the U.S.

An English fan had sent me a book called *French Revolutions*, by Tim Moore, and I had been reading it for the past couple of nights, often laughing out loud. It recounted the adventures of an Englishman who set out to ride the course of the Tour de France bicycle race, without much of a clue about bicycles or bicycling, but armed with an outrageous self-deprecating sense of humor.

That night I slept straight through the bus ride to the ferry, the crossing itself, and didn't come to until Brutus woke me at nine o'clock, which was actually ten, following a time change. Apparently we were in *France* now!

I had been lost in a wilderness of bizarre dreams, and the only thing I remembered from the ferry was a loudspeaker barking announcements about duty-free shopping. In my sleep, I had thought we were still on the dock, but Mark informed me that those announcements had been broadcast all through the crossing. I couldn't believe I had slept through all that, but I guess I was tired.

Brutus had the bikes all ready to go, luggage cases and Dingus installed, oil and tires checked, so I just had to eat some breakfast, put on my riding clothes, and load my bags into the cases. We started out in sunshine, on a motorway, but were soon slowed by construction, and the inevitable rain had us scrambling back into our rainsuits.

We were also back on the right side of the road again, which required a little mental adjustment. We followed Brutus's complicated route along the Meuse River into Belgium and the forested mountains of the Ardennes, scene of heavy fighting during both World Wars. Looking at the deep river valleys, the dense woodlands, and the ancient villages, I couldn't help thinking of how many soldiers and civilians had died there. The Germans had battled in both directions, advancing and retreating, in 1914 and 1918, and in 1940 and 1944-45 (the Battle of the Bulge), leaving a terrible wake of destruction and death.

In the narrow, cobbled streets of the villages, sometimes the turns came too fast for Dingus and Dork to keep up with, but eventually they would set us straight and we'd be off along the river, or over the leafy hills. In the southern part of the Ardennes we entered Luxembourg, without ceremony, and traveled into that small, prosperous principality. Strange to think that the night before we had been in England, then started riding that morning in France, passed through Belgium, and now were in another country, Luxembourg. Only about 2500 square kilometers, Luxembourg had remained an independent Grand Duchy since 963, except for brief German invasions during the two World Wars.

We rode into the streets of the city of Luxembourg, a small, Old World capital of 76,000 people, and right up to our hotel, Le Royal, overlooking a large park. After a long day, 381 kilometers (238 miles), we sat on the terrace outside Brutus's room in the late afternoon sun, drinking a bottle of complimentary champagne. The hotel was modern and luxurious, if a bit Spartan, but our *real* reward came in the restaurant, the Pomme Cannelle (spiced apple).

I have said before that the two best things about touring are, one, lots of motorcycling, and two, with all the calories I burn onstage, I can eat anything I want. Traveling in Continental Europe would push both of those advantages to the maximum.

The Pomme Cannelle had a sleek, streamlined Asiatic-French décor, a tie-and-jacket dress code (Brutus now looking smart in my dark gray Hugo Boss jacket and spare dark red tie), and a menu with a similar fusion of Europe and Asia. I had the terrine de foie gras, tandoori lamb, and we shared an excellent bottle of Pommard, followed by a warm chocolate dessert with custard and sorbet, then coffee, cognac, and cigarettes (the three Cs) in the Piano Bar.

A journal note expressed my satisfaction: "I was so dreading this European tour—failed to give proper consideration to *days off*. Unparalleled."

Everything was so elegant, luxurious, and excellent, so different from the kind of day-off meals Michael and I were used to settling for in the U.S. in our usual backroad American accommodations, and likewise so different from the average Canadian restaurant. Though admittedly, the Pomme Cannelle restaurant in Le Royal hotel in Luxembourg was not average for Europe either.

Then I realized something else about those emigrants who fled Europe for the New World. A certain quality of European life never made it over with them, because, of course, only the *poor* people emigrated. There were a few people of culture and refinement, naturally, but most of us colonials were descended from struggling farmers. Even generations later when I was growing up, a special meal, a holiday feast, was still meat and potatoes and boiled vegetables.

Brutus and I made another early start on a sunny morning, bringing our bikes up from the garage behind the hotel. A burly uniformed policeman was blocking the forecourt, with others in position around the entrance, and the officer explained that the Grand Duke was arriving, and we couldn't go in. He spoke good English, as so many

Europeans did (the official languages of Luxembourg were German, French, and an ancient German dialect called "Lëtzebuergesch"). I explained that we were checking out of the hotel, and needed to pick up our luggage. He directed us to a far corner of the entrance, and told us to park there.

Near where we stopped, a man was just backing in a Mercedes sedan. He got out, wearing a stylish jacket and tie, and said, "You have to move." When I pointed to the policeman, and said he had told us to park there, the man said, "I don't care about him."

Annoyed by his brusqueness, I answered, "Well, I don't care about *you.*"

He said, "You *have* to care—I'm a policeman!"

I had to laugh at that, nodded to him, and told Brutus we had to move.

Just as we were riding away from the hotel, the Grand Duke's motorcade pulled up, and the tall, handsome aristocrat emerged from his Mercedes limousine and ducked into the hotel. The current Grand Duke, Henri (of the House of Nassau-Weilburg) was just a few years younger than I was, and had only assumed power in 2000 when his father, Grand Duke Jean, abdicated in his favor. Behind the hotel's front desk, I had noticed large photographs of him and his wife, Maria Teresa Mestra.

The day's ride took us northeast on a short stretch of autoroute to the German border (again, no formalities, just a sign), then onto a small road along the meandering Mosel River. The overcast was light, the sun peeking out from time to time, as we rode through neat villages clustered along the river, spreading trees shading their perfect streets—Germany was always so *immaculate.* Above the rooftops and steeples, a patchwork quilt of vineyards climbed the steep banks, crowned with a fringe of woodlands and occasional castles.

At Cochem, a busy, pretty little river town, we turned away from the Mosel, up and over a high promontory of woods and farms, then onto the autobahn. We still had a long way to get to work, and it was time to make some time. We liked to cruise between 150 and 160 kilometers-per-hour (between 90 and 100 mph), but that wasn't fast enough for the autobahn—we had to stay right most of the time, leaving the left lane open for the big Mercedes and BMW sedans, and occasional Porsches, that zoomed up behind us and went whooshing by.

The inevitable rain showers came in, cutting visibility and traction, so we maintained a fast but prudent pace up through the former capital of West Germany, Bonn, Köln (nicer in the French spelling, Cologne), then into Germany's biggest industrial area (as we had learned in high school), the Ruhr Valley. Our show was at an arena in Oberhausen, which was centered among Dusseldorf, Essen, Dortmund, and a host of other factory towns grown into one industrial metroplex—the largest in Europe, and the fourth-largest urban area too, after Moscow, London, and Paris.

So there was a lot of traffic around there, especially trucks, and the last couple of hours of our 370-kilometer (231-mile) day were slow going.

Despite being in the middle of all those cities, we attracted one of our smallest audiences of the tour, 5,644 people, and apparently many of those came from nearby Holland. However, I did note that the crowd "seemed livelier than the Brits—though mustn't say so, of course."

After we arrived, Brutus rode my bike to a nearby BMW dealer to get my tires replaced, and while he was gone, I laughed to hear a call come over the radio, "Did Brutus lose his glasses again? They're in production." Everyone was on to the Mean Misplacer. I had been kidding him lately because he would get himself all organized by writing out a list of things to do—then lose the list.

Just before soundcheck, I was talking to some of the crew members in the monitor pit at stage left, and heard about a big poker game they'd had the previous night (what to do on a night off in Oberhausen, Germany). Apparently Beau had been the big winner, raking in $1000.

Brutus had picked up a complimentary bottle of red wine back at Skibo Castle, and we agreed to give it to Frenchie. He had been delighted, saying, "Next day off, I'm going to get drunk and take advantage of myself!"

At dinner, I heard about Alex and Geddy's adventures, as they had spent the day off in Amsterdam. Alex had visited one of the city's notorious hash bars, and commented how the proprietors kept urging him to sample this variety, or that one. Geddy reported exactly the same experience in his visit to a wine merchant—"Oh, you must take a bottle of this, and a bottle of this."

Geddy had arranged for the video company to provide subtitles for the opening film, which would appear at upcoming shows in German,

Italian, Czech, and Dutch. Apparently the German for "What did they put in my tea?" was, "Was hat man in meinen Tee getan?"

Oberhausen was also the first show on the tour with "festival seating," a setup we usually avoided, but sometimes there was simply no choice—no seats. During the show, I noticed one audience member who was much taller than the others, and though the face looked feminine, under a *Roll the Bones* cap, something about the facial structure and stature seemed more masculine. After my solo, when I sat behind the dryers with Gump, we confabulated a story about "her" being a transsexual, testing the results of her hormone therapy by seeing if she still liked Rush.

"Could be," said Gump. "This *is* Germany!"

Even that late in the tour, I still found parts of the show to get excited about. I made a note about a bridge in the song "Red Barchetta," where we pounded out a repeating 7/4 riff leading from the guitar solo back into the verse—a classic "tension-and-release" moment: "Gave me goose bumps the other night, and always a great part, for us and the audience."

The next day was another day off, and we slept on the bus near Strasbourg, on the German side of the Rhine. Dingus and Dork had a bit of trouble getting us going that morning, as Brutus had programmed a couple of routes traversing that area for upcoming days, and the boys couldn't decide which one we wanted to take. Eventually we got that sorted out, and headed south through the Alsace region, historically sometimes French and sometimes German, along the levees of the Rhine, which divided Germany and France in modern times.

On that low-lying floodplain no villages had ever grown, or at least survived, and the fertile soil was lined with cornfields, woodlands, and occasional factories. With the levees and all, the landscape looked quite American, and reminded me of the banks of another great river, the Mississippi.

Except the drivers were better. And the signs had names on them like Marckolsheim and Breisach.

Another request I had made of Brutus was a stop at *le Musée National de l'Automobile*, in Mulhouse, France. I had visited it twice before, and it may have been the most spectacular car museum in the world, but its history was even more amazing.

In the 1960s and '70s, a private collection of more than 500 classic cars had been secretly amassed by Alsatian industrialist Fritz Schlumpf with help from his brother Hans, a banker. Hidden in one of Schlumpf's textile mills was an elegant salon, but on a *huge* scale, with rows of gleaming cars illuminated by 900 replicas of the lamps on Paris's Alexandre III bridge. Many of the cars were unique, and some of them were priceless.

Fritz Schlumpf favored European classics and sports cars, especially Bugattis, and spared no expense to collect the ones he desired. He established a network of agents, sworn to secrecy, as were the mechanics and bodyworkers who restored and maintained his treasures. Sometimes trainloads of cars would arrive at the textile factory by night, including an entire collection of forty classics, including ten Bugattis, or a shipment of thirty Bugattis from an American collection he had bought outright.

Rumors began to spread through the car-collecting world, but the growing hoard remained secret for many years, until 1977. Schlumpf's textile factories were failing, at least partly because of the millions he had siphoned into his obsession, and when a strike erupted among the dismissed workers, the Schlumpf brothers were forced to flee to Switzerland. The workers broke into the museum, and as a publicity gesture, burned one of the cars on the street outside (a worthless old Austin—they weren't fools!). The workers then occupied the museum for the next two years, the cars growing dusty and neglected, while admission to see them earned millions of francs for the union. Politicians and lawyers eventually arranged a settlement, whereby the French government agreed to classify 285 cars from the collection as historic monuments, thus paving the way for the formation of the *Musée National de l'Automobile* in 1982. The remaining cars were auctioned off in massive sales that rocked the car-collecting world.

Fritz Schlumpf died in 1992, bankrupt and still in exile, but the core of his collection remained intact, visited by millions of admirers from around the world. My own first visit, in 1986, capped a year in which I saw all six of the Bugatti Royales, each of them with unique coachwork and a separate, well-documented history—perhaps the world's most valuable cars. Of the two examples in the Schlumpf collection, the Coupé Napoléon, once Ettore Bugatti's personal car, had been valued at between $30 and $40 million.

The Royale was engineered and designed specifically for royalty, every potential buyer having to be approved by "Le Patron" himself, Monsieur Bugatti. Unfortunately, there were no potential buyers, royal or otherwise, especially in the early 1930s, and like the paintings of Vincent van Gogh, only one or two of them was sold during Ettore Bugatti's lifetime. The value of the Royales would not be appreciated until long after his death, in 1947.

The six Royales were brought together only once, in 1985, at the Pebble Beach Concours d'Elegance, despite the French government's reluctance to allow the two Schlumpf cars out of the country—fearing questions of legal ownership. That would have been the easiest way to see all six of them at once, but in 1986, the band was traveling on our *Power Windows* tour, so I had been more-or-less conveniently able to see two of them in Bill Harrah's vast museum in Reno, Nevada (a larger collection than Schlumpf's, but less exclusive), one in Briggs Cunningham's smaller museum in Costa Mesa, California, one in the Henry Ford Museum in Dearborn, Michigan, and two at *le Musée National de l'Automobile*, in Mulhouse. That year was probably the last opportunity for anyone to see them all, for within the next couple of years the collections of Harrah and Cunningham were broken up after their deaths, and their Royales were sold. One of those ended up at the Blackhawk Collection in Danville, California (which Michael and I had visited back in July), one remained at the Ford museum, one was said to be on display in a museum in Germany, but the other was hidden away in a private collection in Japan.

Ettore Bugatti insisted that every part of his cars had to be beautiful, even if it could not be seen, and consequently every gear and casting was exquisitely machined, lovingly crafted by hand. Bugatti's cars represented the ideal marriage of function and form in a machine of unsurpassed beauty (and performance—they were also the Grand Prix champions of the 1920s, paragons of speed, handling, and reliability). Ettore's son Jean was a gifted designer, and originated some of the most beautiful of all Bugattis, the Type 55 (the one from *le Musée's* collection I would have taken home), several versions of the Type 57, including the streamlined Atlantique and sleek Atalante, and the legendary Royale. Jean was only in his twenties when he designed all those timeless classics, and died at age thirty, while testing a Type 57 racing car on public roads near Mulhouse.

In 1992, on a day off during our *Roll the Bones* tour, I had visited *le Musée National* again with my driver, Peter Brockbank (though I took the wheel of the BMW 750 that day, racing through the Black Forest from Stuttgart to Mulhouse). Since then, a major redesign had transformed the museum, and the display was split into three sections. It started with a walk through a chronological history of the automobile, from 1878 to the present. Then came a selection of historic racing cars—Ferrari, Maserati, Lotus, Mercedes—displayed as if on a starting grid, and finally, the hall of "masterpieces," including all those legendary hyphenated names: Rolls-Royce (the largest collection in the world), Mercedes-Benz, Hispano-Suiza, and Isotta-Fraschini, framing the elevated platform showing the two Royales.

Jean Bugatti's designs were so well proportioned that until you stood beside the Royales, you didn't notice their sheer *massiveness*—the hood alone was seven feet long, the 38-inch wheels with their enormous tires were almost chest-high, and the engine was a twelve-liter straight-eight, so powerful that leftover units were adapted to drive Bugatti railcars.

Brutus and I emerged from the museum about one, eyes glazed by the sheer mass of automotive beauty we had seen. Once again we had a little trouble with Dingus and Dork, who kept wanting to circle back to the museum again. As I described it later, "another almighty flail from the boys over giving up the 'Waypoint' of the museum. Recurring problem for them—and thus *us*."

After going around in ever-widening circles for a while, we finally escaped from Mulhouse and headed east across the Rhine and into Germany, toward the Black Forest, the Schwartzwald.

For the first time on the whole European run it didn't rain that day, which was pleasant, but it was also a Saturday, which wasn't so pleasant. The sun was shining and the temperature was perfect—warm in the sun, cool in the shade—but as the road began to wind into the dark woods and fairy-tale villages of the Black Forest, it seemed we encountered every bicyclist, motorcyclist, hiker, sports car, and family sedan in southern Germany. (I did remark to Brutus, in my usual always-look-at-the-bright-side manner, that at least there were not too many RVs, trailers, trucks, or buses.)

For a couple of hours we wandered around the evergreen-shaded roads, passing occasional green meadows dazzled by sunlight, villages and towns so meticulously kept they seemed like models from a toy railway, all framed in lush greenery. As in Bavaria, to the east, the houses and even bridge railings were often lined with flower-boxes, giving the lie to the Germans' so-called severity.

Once in a while we escaped the traffic and enjoyed a burst of good riding, but as the afternoon wore on, we turned west to the autobahn. We blasted north the last fifty or sixty miles to our hotel, just south of Baden-Baden, making 375 kilometers, 234 miles for the day.

Reading guidebooks and choosing hotels is something of an art, and I knew from my many travels with Brutus that he was a master of that art. On this tour, one of the spare bunks on our bus was covered with European maps and guidebooks, and every day, once we had discussed the general direction of our next day's route and a possible destination, I would leave it to Brutus. While I worked for our gas money, he would spend those hours poring through the books and maps, plotting the best route to the most attractive destination.

At the end of that day, we left the autobahn and followed winding roads up into the hills that framed the northern limits of the Black Forest. At the crest of the ridge of dark conifers, we turned onto the main scenic road, the Schwartzwald Hochstrasse ("high road"), then into a meandering driveway through trees and gardens to a stone arch. We pulled up in a circular courtyard of paving stones set around a graceful fountain, in front of an ivy-covered grand entranceway. The Bühlerhöhe Schlosshotel.

With the whole Schwartzwald area to consider, Brutus had chosen well. According to *The Leading Hotels of the World* guide, the Bühlerhöhe Schlosshotel was "the premier spa resort in Germany." Schloss meant "castle," and this grand establishment, built in 1914, lived up to its name—a large, stately manor of natural stone and masonry in traditional Black Forest style. Its nineteenth-century grandeur was softened by pink and brown panels, delicate moldings, and mullioned windows in symmetrical blocks and curves, under a dark-colored mansard roof. It was magnificent.

As usual when we arrived at such a high-class establishment, we felt a little scruffy with our bug-encrusted leathers and dirty bikes, especially Brutus having to enter the dignified lobby to check in. The Bühlerhöhe

Schlosshotel staff immediately won our approval by allowing us to park right beside the front entrance, in the courtyard, among the Mercedes, BMWs, and Porsches.

Our rooms were gracious and well-appointed, and overlooked a stone-paved terrace, a massive, round-domed tower to one side, and before us, a cloudless sky over the deep green woodlands of the Schwartzwald foothills. Beyond was the Rhine valley and the plains of Alsace, and a line of dark hills in the west. I described those hills in a cocktail-time journal entry, "marching across the western horizon, to get all literary."

Once again, my first note that evening was, "Another impossible day to get down."

While Brutus was checking us in, I had made a dinner reservation, thinking it was for the Michelin-starred Imperial restaurant. However, after we were cleaned up and "suited" for dinner, and were enjoying a Kir Royale in the elegant bar, we were told there was a misunderstanding. We were actually booked in the *other* restaurant, the Schloss.

Depending on which staff member we talked to, the Imperial had been booked up for days, weeks, or since that morning, and I went to speak with the man at the front desk who had made our reservation. I told him it seemed to me that a guest of the hotel would expect to have a table for dinner at their *best* restaurant, as of course it was part of the reason we had traveled so far to get there.

He said he would see what he could do, and when Brutus and I returned to the bar, Brutus said, "You gave him just the right amount of attitude."

I laughed, "I hope so. But maybe it would have been better if I gave him just the right amount of money!"

Either way, the front-desk man returned to say he was sorry, but it was impossible to get us into the Imperial. He offered his sincere apologies, and said that at least they would take care of our drinks.

And no matter, for our meal in the Schloss restaurant was excellent. Brutus and I always liked to try local wines when we could, even in Tunisia or Sardinia (excellent reds there), and on the Schloss waiter's advice, we ordered a bottle of a local chardonnay, Bernard Huber Weingut, and enjoyed it very much.

The waiter also made us laugh when we asked about a confusing description in the English menu, and he said, "Oh no—that is a wrong mistake."

Brutus said, "I never heard of a *right* mistake!"

I chose an appetizer of scallops with tomatoes and green onions in a rich sauce, then an excellent salmon with baby vegetables, a dessert of elderberry parfait, followed by coffee, port, and a selection of fine cheeses.

As Mr. Look-on-the-Bright-Side again, I noted that our view during dinner, down over the lights of the Rhine Valley, was better than the view from the Imperial. My final journal note that day summarized my transformation, "Europe has . . . seduced me."

The next morning was cool and overcast, the air damp as Brutus and I loaded up the bikes in front of the grand entrance of the Bühlerhöhe Schlosshotel. Brutus said the day's ride to Stuttgart wouldn't be very long, so we took our time getting going, and kept our pace relaxed.

We rode south on the Schwartzwald Hochstrasse, with hardly any other traffic as yet on a Sunday morning, though I imagined it would be busy later. Once again, Brutus's route was almost too much for Dingus and Dork, and as we looped north on a tiny road through the redundantly named village of Bad Wildbad (sounds like a German heavy-metal band), suddenly our road diminished to a horse trail, a narrow gravel track through thick woods.

I was thinking, "It's Agony Hill Road all over again!" and eventually we came up against a barricade blocking the trail. Fortunately we could get around it, and back onto a *real* road on the other side. Then, in the town of Pforzheim, the boys got a little confused by some one-way streets, sending us in loops, but we made our way out by overruling them.

Riding north out of the Black Forest, the landscape opened into rolling farmland, and our one-and-a-half-lane roads were perfect ribbons of asphalt past farms and woodlands. We encountered very little traffic on such roads, and every field and building seemed impossibly neat. I noted later, "Perfect little villages, no shacks, no mobile homes, no junked cars or old appliances in the yards, no litter, no graffiti, no posters, no billboards, no 'yard sale' signs."

Nearer Stuttgart, things got a little rougher, with graffiti on bridges and the inevitable ugly parts of such a major industrial city (home to Mercedes-Benz and Porsche, whose museums I had visited on previous tours). Our route took us around much of the city, past factories and warehouses, to the modern arena called the Schleyerhalle, after only 175 kilometers, 109 miles.

We arrived early enough to give the shamefully dirty bikes a good wash, at least, though it was an indication of Germany's environmental laws that the building people wouldn't let us use their hose—apparently it was "verboten" to wash vehicles outdoors and let the dirty water drain away.

During the show, in front of a fairly small audience (4,051 people) I made some mental notes, things I had been trying to remember to record for a long time. I tried hard to hold onto them until after, so I could write them down.

Each second onstage so full of thoughts, concentration, observations, intimate evaluations of the performance, people's faces, moving lights, my own random "departures" into faraway places.

I've been wanting to get down about seeing people with T-shirts from *horrible* bands, and thinking, "They like them—*and* us?" Not a good feeling . . .

New 18-inch cymbal tonight, raw, dull, stiff in its motion [cymbals occasionally cracked and had to be replaced, but new ones needed breaking in], 20-inch last show the same, but getting better—opening up sonically, loosening up physically.

Blew that second-chorus fill in "Earthshine" again—it's supposed to be the *easy* one. [Wasn't me, actually, found out the next day.]

Lerxst held up six fingers tonight.

Good run of shows lately. Felt legs fading a little tonight, though only after seven shows already this run. Need them back for Frankfurt filming—that's going to be a high-pressure night, especially for *solo*, if I go ahead with video idea.

The upcoming Frankfurt show was going to be filmed for a possible concert DVD, and my instructional video collaborators, Rob and Paul, had arranged to have additional cameras on hand to focus on my drumming in particular. We were hoping that solo would be the basis for the video we were discussing, so there would be a lot of pressure on that night's performance.

After Stuttgart, Mark drove us to a rest area in Altdorf, well into Switzerland. When I looked out the bus window in the morning, I saw a steep green mountainside disappearing into low, dark clouds. The light was so dim I thought it was still night. While Mark and Brutus unloaded the bikes, I made our orange juice, took my vitamins, turned the coffee on, and poured a bowl of cereal ("Frosties") with sliced banana and rice milk (my favored bus breakfast). Brutus had the bikes ready, oil and air checked, and I thought of the slogan for an American motorcycle clothing manufacturer, "Ride, Eat, Sleep, Repeat."

Add in a little drumming, and that was us.

Our little road led us up that steep green mountainside, hairpins and switchbacks climbing slowly into dense fog that condensed on our faceshields. After a few miles, we emerged above the clouds into the sunshine, and into the wondrous Alpine landscape of the motorcyclist's Mecca: Switzerland.

Flower-strewn meadows, snow-covered peaks against an icy-blue sky, cows with huge cowbells, dark wooden farmhouses with attached barns, immaculate villages with flower boxes and narrow streets, perfect roads winding through deep green valleys and high barren passes. "Delightful Switzerland," I described it. I had fallen in love with Switzerland on my first visit, on a Rush tour in the late '70s, and had returned many times by bicycle, by car, and by motorcycle.

To my eyes, and to my soul, the most beautiful part of the world was the Alps, not just in Switzerland, but where they spilled into Germany's Bavaria, Austria, France, and Italy. Every time you crossed a mountain pass, or rounded a bend along a glacial river, another prospect of stunning natural beauty awaited—vertical walls of granite rising up to snowy peaks before you, or a serene valley of lush pastures and tidy homesteads falling away below. The air was a bracing cocktail of pines and snow, hayfields and wildflowers, with the keen edge of the high elevations.

And talk about riding through places and wanting to move there! In Switzerland, every town, village, and chalet in the Alps called to me that way. Someday, I may heed that call.

To a motorcyclist, the Alpine roads were the most challenging and rewarding in the world, and some riders, especially Europeans, would return year after year, "bagging passes." As entertaining as those tortuous roads could be, though, they were also plenty dangerous, and demanded a heightened level of seriousness, focus, and concentration. Balancing the throttle and brakes, choosing the gear and lean angle, placing the bike perfectly in your lane and arcing it around the apex of the corner, each one was a separate challenge, each a separate reward.

In one of those postcard-perfect Swiss villages, Brutus and I saw a goat loose and trotting down the street ahead of us, looking panicked, and we made our first ever GPS joke.

Stopped at a light, Brutus pointed at the goat and imitated its thoughts, in a rising, fearful voice, "Select Waypoint: 'Home!' "

I laughed and called back, "Go To—Quickest Way!"

Traffic was light on the small roads Brutus had plotted into *our* route, and from then on we rode in blessed sunshine. The high passes were cold, but the views! Truly breathtaking, looking over sharp-edged peaks of snow-streaked granite and impossibly twisty roads, wriggling down into the dark green valleys ahead of us and up to a distant pass—the road we were about to ride.

The verdant slopes of the Vorderrhein River valley carried us back west and up to the Oberalp Pass, at 2044 meters, 6704 feet (closed by snow from December to May), then down over the attractive-looking town of Andermatt. That was a town I would like to have seen more of— maybe for a year or two.

We stopped for fuel there, and Brutus was leading as we approached the Furka Pass, rising up to 2435 meters, 7990 feet. He graciously waved me by, knowing I liked to attack those corners with a little more aggression than he did.

Riding toward the next turn at the outside of the lane, using all the available road, maximizing my own visibility and the ability of other vehicles to see me, I would look through the corner as far as I could, appraise its sharpness, banking, and surface, then choose the turn-in point. Squeezing the tank with my knees and holding on, my hands were free to be as smooth as possible on the brakes, throttle, and clutch, as I settled my entry speed and gear, then leaned the bike into it, pushing on the bar and leaning on the inside footpeg, using my body to help the turn.

When the bike was heeled over and angling through the curve, I used the edges of my mirrors as guides, my peripheral vision keeping the tip of the inside mirror along the radius of the painted lines. I also used a trick I had learned from yoga, of throwing my senses *ahead* of me: when I was learning the "balanced poses," standing on one foot with the other limbs extended, a yoga instructor pointed out that it was helpful to focus on a distant point—to fix my concentration, my awareness, away from the space under my foot. The same concept worked for me on the motorcycle. Instead of thinking of the road under me, or just in front of my wheels, I tried to "send myself" farther ahead. By concentrating on a point well up the road, my movements on the bike and its controls became smoother, and I could go faster with less anxiety.

More excitement, less fear—an important part of my old formula, "Danger + Survival = Fun."

As we climbed through one set of steep switchbacks, I could look straight down at the road behind, seeing Brutus and a couple of sport bikes behind him, gaining on us. One was a Ducati, the other an MV Agusta, the two fastest, most exotic Italian road bikes, and when I saw their headlights coming up behind me, I waved them by—noting that it was the first time I could remember being passed by other motorcycles. But it was no shame to let those two by, and I silently cheered them on.

One more small road and high pass, the Nufenpass, at 2478 meters, 8127 feet, carried us to the main autoroute, and we took it south toward Italy. Switzerland was the one country in Western Europe that still watched its borders, and we were stopped for a while in a line of traffic, then showed our passports and headed southeast to Lake Como.

During my recent telephone conversations with Carrie, we had been discussing where to go together at the end of the tour. She was planning to fly in for the final show, near Amsterdam, and then spend a week with me somewhere while I recuperated, and before she had to oversee the production of her photography book, *Rhythm and Light*, at a printing company in Verona, Italy.

I wanted to find a luxurious Alpine retreat in Switzerland; Carrie wanted to go to Northern Italy. So we were going to Northern Italy. In discussions with travel agents, and some Europeans Carrie had met at her friend's wedding in Sweden, she was considering some recommended hotels in the Italian lakes. When Brutus and I were discussing our own overnight stop on the way to Milan, I thought it would be a good idea for us to scout one of those recommendations, the Villa d'Este, on Lake

Como. It was listed in Brutus's *1000 Places to See Before You Die* ("a grand hotel from which all others take their inspiration, the Villa d'Este is unrivaled for its regal décor as well as its majestic position on the verdant banks of Lake Como"), and in several other of his guidebooks, and Brutus thought it looked the most promising. I hadn't been able to reach Carrie the previous night to discuss the idea, but left her a message saying Brutus and I were going to check it out.

To echo the waiter at the Bühlerhöhe Schlosshotel, "That is a wrong mistake."

I wanted to make sure Carrie and I would be staying at the best place, while she thought that wherever we were staying, we ought to be discovering it together. When we talked on the phone later that night, I learned the error of my ways. Once again, that line I put in our song "Presto" back in 1989 gets truer every year—sometimes every day. "What a fool I used to be."

The Villa d'Este, on the western shore of Lake Como, was built as a cardinal's palace in the late sixteenth century, then passed through a series of colorful owners. In the late eighteenth century, an aging aristocrat from Milan bought it for his new wife, a ballerina at La Scala, and she spent a fortune on the villa and gardens. When the husband died, the young countess married one of Napoleon's generals. Hoping to distract him from the lure of the battlefield, she installed imitation fortresses and towers overlooking the gardens, where he could play war games with his cadets.

Then came Caroline of Brunswick-Wolfenbüttel, Princess of Wales and wife of the future British king, George IV, who apparently didn't like her. The princess left him and traveled around Europe, eventually deciding that Lake Como was an earthly paradise. She fixed her eye on the Villa d'Este, and prevailed over the countess's reluctance to sell the property. The deed recorded the sale as a "royal demand."

Opened as a hotel in 1873, the Villa d'Este became one of the most luxurious, elegant, beautifully appointed, and *expensive* hotels in Italy—maybe the world. Looking out on the steep, villa-studded shoreline of Lake Como, the Alps visible at the north end on a clear day, the public rooms were resplendent with marble columns, crystal chandeliers, vaulted ceilings, silk brocade draperies, frescoes, and statues, and the guest rooms were equally palatial. The 400-year-old Romanesque gardens were shaded by ancient trees, and decorated by ornate flower beds and grace-ful cypresses, fountains, and an imposing mosaic colonnade leading up to a Greek temple.

Brutus and I checked into our rooms in the annex, the Queen's Building (built in 1856). Below my balcony, lines of small sailboats and motorboats were tied up to a dock, swaying to the lake's gentle motion. Through the hazy distance, passenger ferries moved silently across the middle of the lake, in front of a steep green mountainside rising up from the villages and villas along the far shore.

We started taking pictures of the hotel, and of our rooms, thinking Carrie would want to see all that (poor benighted fools). The phone call to Carrie that evening gently disabused me of my illusions, but she did have to admit it sounded like a wonderful place.

Cleaned up and dressed for dinner, Brutus and I strolled along the gravel paths by the lake to the hotel's celebrated restaurant, the Veranda. It was walled on three sides by huge windows overlooking the lake and gardens. We were seated in the dining room amid a multilingual murmur of well-dressed diners, older couples and younger, more fashionable Italians, perhaps up from nearby Milan. While we enjoyed the attentive service and exquisite dinner, I caught up on some notes. Without think-ing about it too much, I invoked the refrain from Baudelaire's poem, "*l'Invitation au Voyage*," echoed in the title of a beautiful Matisse paint-ing, "*Là, tout n'est qu'ordre et beauté/ Luxe, calme, et volupté.*"

"There, all is only order and beauty/ Luxury, peace, and pleasure." That was the Villa d'Este.

Another amazing place to arrive—*luxe, calme, et volupté*—and another amazing journey getting here. 422 kilometers, 263 miles. Such a *severe* contrast to American touring: adventurous riding through spectacular scenery to a jacket-and-tie dinner. A long, *long* way from Best Western and Ruby Tuesday.

Now crepes Suzette, and choice of about six different interna-tional coffees—I chose the Papua New Guinea. And sambucca.

This whole European experience so different from how I imag-ined it. I forgot about places we could *stay*, and I underrated the places we could *ride*.

Especially with Munich out now, and two days off.

Yes, after the next day's show in Milan, we would have two days off in a row—which, for Brutus and me, would mean two days off in *Switzerland!*

Apparently some production problems were expected with the show in Milan, including a slow load-out, and the venue in Munich the next night promised difficulties with load-in and set-up. The drive for the trucks and buses from Milan to Munich would have been over 300 miles overnight, with the Alps to cross, so the trucks were sure to be late as well. All things considered, the promoter, Ray, Liam, and C.B. had decided it was best to cancel that show (and I certainly didn't object). The promoters were offering ticket-buyers in Munich a refund or tickets to the Stuttgart or Frankfurt shows instead.

I had first visited the Italian lakes in 1986, on my first bicycle tour with the friends I had met in China, Robert and Rose Marie Boysen, Gay, and a couple of their other cycling friends, riding from Munich to Venice. We crossed the Alps via the Simplon Pass, a tremendous climb, more than twenty miles up, on our fully-loaded touring bicycles (one of the times Gay had used her "Dumbo's Feather" cassette, and gotten off to walk when she couldn't pedal anymore). On the other side, we descended into Italy through a small town called Domodossola. After the meticulous, flowery perfection of Swiss towns and roads, the Italian town seemed as dejected as its name, which I guess recalled "dolorous" to me.

The previous day, just before crossing the Simplon Pass, I had stopped in a hardware store in Brig, Switzerland, looking for a new padlock for the cable I used to secure my bicycle. The older lady behind the counter had said, "You don't need a lock here."

"Well, I'm crossing to Italy tomorrow."

She shook her head, "No lock will help you there!"

On a later bicycle trip with the Boysens and Gay, and this time with Henry, the Prince Among Men, we rode from Munich to Istanbul, crossing the Austrian Alps via the Grossglockner and Plücken passes. Once again I had been struck by the contrast as soon as we entered Italy, leaving Austria's *ordre et beauté* on crumbling Italian roads lined with tumbledown buildings, and even passing a horse-drawn cart, as if entering another time *and* place. Sure, Northern Italy had its own charm, a casual rusticity, and the enduring treasure of Venice (not to mention the industrial arts of Ferrari, Lamborghini, Maserati, Ducati, MV Agusta, Moto Guzzi, a painting or two, and some great food and wine), but if I had to choose, I knew on which side of the Alps I would settle.

In the art of selecting accommodations from guidebooks, Rosie Boysen had the same instinct as Brutus did. While Bob designed detailed itineraries of every day's cycling, with distances, topographies, and side-elevation maps, Rosie sifted through guidebooks choosing the best places to stay each night. Even in expensive cities like Venice and Paris, she could find hotels that were reasonably priced yet perfectly located, and more than luxurious enough for tired cyclists.

On Lake Como, we had stayed in the picturesque little town of Bellagio, and after the kind of copious dinner only people who have crossed the Alps by bicycle can put away (it was not uncommon for us to eat a huge meal followed by *two* rich desserts), we had taken a motor-launch ride around the lake. Stuffed and sleepy, we admired the gracious villas and their fantastic gardens, stone walls, and boathouses along the ancient shore.

Bicycling in Italy could be breathtaking in a different way, with diesels belching black smoke, hordes of tiny cars and scooters zipping around us, and an extremely aggressive style of driving—it has been pointed out before that Italian men seem to drive with their flies open, as it were.

Brutus and I had experienced that same attitude on our motorcycles on our first "Eurotrash" tour, when we rode down from those same Austrian passes into Italy and all the way south to Naples, to catch the ferry to Sicily, and then Tunisia. On the autostradas, Brutus and I became impatient with the Italian drivers following right on our tails, and we would reach one arm behind us to wave them away. Because we were bigger than them, especially in our leather suits and helmets, they usually backed off. I had often noticed that if you stopped in an Italian workingman's bar for lunch, every man in the place seemed to turn and look you up and down appraisingly—as if deciding if he could beat you up or not.

Our female companions reported a similar feeling, though a different kind of "appraisal."

I did have one of the great motorcycle rides of my life in Italy on that tour, zooming through the winding hills of Tuscany one evening, when it seemed everybody else was off the roads. At first I was going fast because it was late in a thirteen-hour day and I wanted to get to our destination, but before long, I was going fast because it was *fun*. Leaving Brutus far behind, and barely glancing at the hazy patchwork hills of woods and farms, cypress trees, and villages of umber and ocher in the golden light, I surrendered to "the zone." Perfect shifting, braking, and turning, not one moment of panic (though lots of wide-eyed concentration), and so smooth through the tight corners. I kept talking to myself about hubris, not wanting to push it *too* far, but I had the feeling of being one with the machine, one with the road, in an adrenaline-fueled dance without awareness of time or distance. It doesn't get better than that.

Now Brutus and I were heading for Milan, and we made a fairly early start from the Villa d'Este. Almost immediately we found ourselves in slow morning traffic, jousting our way through the busy town of Como, which seemed to spread east all the way to the next town, L'Ecco. The narrow winding streets and roads were jammed with smelly diesel trucks and cars, buzzing scooters weaving among them.

Finally we turned away, following a tiny road into the foothills of the Italian Alps. The narrow, precipitous road circled around, clinging to steep hillsides, and opening to views of forested valleys and clusters of pale-colored houses with red-tiled roofs.

As we rode through one town, I pulled out to pass a slow car, and Brutus was stuck behind it for a mile or so. Where the town ended in a steep, forested valley, and there was room to pull over, I stopped to wait, but he didn't appear. I turned around and rode back to where we had been separated, but still didn't see him.

Meanwhile, Dingus was getting mightily confused, and it turned out that somehow "we" had missed the right turn Brutus had taken out of town. Now Dingus was sending me on a figure-eight loop through the town. I finally decided Brutus and I were probably separated for good, and stopped to change Dingus's settings. Selecting the waypoint for the Milan show, I pressed "Go To" and "Quickest Way," and set off, hoping Dingus would pull himself together.

However, on the next stretch of road through that narrow valley and overhanging trees, there was no satellite contact. The screen was blank for long miles before Dingus was able to finish "Recalculating" and let me know we were on the right route. Hopefully.

At the next village, a T-intersection, I stopped one more time, just in case Brutus and I might somehow reconnect. While I smoked a Red Apple and watched the roads in every direction, I noticed brake fluid was dripping from the front master cylinder. The cap was loose, apparently knocked by Dingus's mount, which had been jarred by the windscreen. I hoped not enough fluid had leaked out to affect the brakes, but the fluid itself was also corrosive, and could eat paint and other materials. After cleaning the helmet's faceshield with my bug-rag one last time, I used it to wipe up the drops of fluid on my fuel tank, side cover, and luggage case.

Hoping Brutus was going to be all right, I worked my way down to a busy artery road. Between rows of ugly industrial buildings, the road was poorly maintained, dusty, and crammed with trucks and aggressive cars. The heat increased in the lowlands of the Po Valley, enhancing the stink of diesel, industry, and sewage. After long, slow miles, I finally merged onto the autostrada and sped west toward Milan. Dealing with a toll booth myself for once, and relieved I had some euros with me, I followed Dingus's directions—with fearful optimism—south toward the airport, then off on a wide boulevard.

Dingus seemed to think a big white tent behind a high wall was the venue, and I doubled back to look for a way in—only to see Michael and Brutus waving and yelling, directing me to the backstage gate. I was very glad to know I was in the right place at last, and that Brutus was, too. We had only ridden 177 kilometers, 110 miles, but, as my opening journal note said, "Fair bit of drama today."

And what a scene backstage. It took a while to figure it all out, but apparently the venue was owned by gypsies, and they had an encampment of trailers all around us. The largest trailer had an awning across its front, sheltering a line of five cars, including a new red Ferrari 360 Modena and a Cadillac Seville. One of the crew guys pointed at some steel cargo containers, and said there were Russians living in them, painting posters for the circus that was usually featured at the gypsies' tented venue.

Michael's girlfriend, Jae, had flown in to meet him in Milan, and they had spent the day off together exploring some of his old haunts. Coincidentally, when Michael had lived and worked there as a model, our merchandiser Pat had been doing the same thing at the same time, even living in the same apartment building, but they had never met.

I always remembered when Jae first came to see us play, on the *Vapor Trails* tour in Milwaukee, and told me she liked my drum solo, memorably calling it "your cute little drum thing." I had laughed at that, and always tried to think of it that way. (Perhaps my instructional DVD, *Anatomy of a Drum Solo*, should have been called *My Cute Little Drum Thing*.)

The air in the backstage compound was sweltering, indoors and out, and the shore power to the buses was inadequate, not strong enough to run the air conditioning. Since the bus had no generator, I could only open the windows and rooftop vents, letting in the sound of dogs barking and children playing (both unusual sounds to hear backstage), so it was impossible to take a nap. The dressing room and Bubba-Gump were no better—small and unventilated.

It was September 21, the birthday of my young friend Nick Rich (Cathy's son, Buddy's grandson). I wanted to send him an e-mail, but of course there was no internet service. Liam had been desperate to keep up with his daily business (among other things, coordinating the logistics of the upcoming filming in Frankfurt, with film crews and recording trucks), and he ended up calling a server in the United States just to get on-line. I was able to send Nick a brief message on Liam's computer.

I remembered how twelve years before, on our last tour of Europe, we had been asked about playing Milan. Based on my bicycle travels around Italy, I had voted against it, saying, "Italy is a third-world country." An exaggeration, of course, but compared to the well-organized infrastructures of Northern Europe, not to mention North America, Italy could be . . . difficult.

Once, Brutus and I had arrived in Naples on a Friday afternoon, through the most insane traffic I had ever encountered—and that includes Paris, Beijing, and Mexico City. Caught in a steaming gridlock of honking, shouting drivers, we were starting to worry, as we were booked on a ferry to Sicily that afternoon. We began following the young Neapolitans on their scooters, taking to the sidewalks, the crosswalks, and the wrong way down one-way streets. It was exciting, and funny later, but nerve-racking at the time—adventures suck when you're having them.

When we finally arrived at the ferry dock and I went to buy our tickets, I was exasperated to learn they would only take cash, no travelers checks or credit cards. I could not believe it: a huge company sailing a fleet of large ferries to different countries all over the Mediterranean in the 1990s, and they only took cash. Our combined tickets for crossing to Sicily and Tunisia, then back through Sardinia to Genoa, added up to more than a million lira (only a few hundred dollars, but it *sounded* like a lot).

Of course, the banks were closed for the day, ATMs were still unknown in Italy, and I ended up leaving Brutus with the bikes and running through the streets of Naples trying to find some kind of bureau de change. The first one I encountered was closed, but I noticed the travelers-check company logo on a travel agent's window, and decided to take a chance. A calm young man in a brown suit looked up as I came bursting in, sweaty and red-faced, and said yes, he spoke English, and yes, he could cash my checks. "Just take it easy," he said with a smile.

Then ensued another lengthy drama at the ferry dock, waiting in lines and trying to get the cabins we had reserved. When I finally handed over the stack of lira notes, the ticket agent gave me second-class seats instead of the first-class cabin we had reserved for the overnight crossing. Now we learned that all the cabins were full. It all worked out in the end, and we really loved Sicily, but it had all been so chaotic and unnecessarily stressful. That was one of the times in my travels when I realized that the great challenge in traveling could be simply overcoming the obstacles that stood in the way of moving forward. And it was one time when I thought, "Italy bugs me."

At the Milan circus venue, Michael came by at soundcheck with similar feelings. Shaking his head angrily, he told me about the driver who had just dropped off Alex, Geddy, Donovan, and Shelley. Usually, before their arrival, Michael, Liam, and Donovan were connected by radio or cell phone to coordinate that event, but the driver had insisted he knew where to go—then drove up to the front entrance of the building in the middle of the waiting fans, who mobbed the car.

A few weeks before our Milan show, I heard through the Sabian cymbal company that Clive Bunker, the original drummer from Jethro Tull, was going to be working in Italy at that time. He wanted to attend our show with an Italian drummer, Sergio Ponti, who was a friend of his. I had been a fan of those early Jethro Tull albums Clive played on, even played some of the songs myself in early cover bands—and, of course, I was now good friends with Tull's current drummer, Doane. So I arranged to have Clive and Sergio come by in the afternoon.

A slender, bright-eyed, balding Englishman in his late fifties, Clive was what his countrymen would call "a lovely chap." He brought a gift for me, a copy of Bill Bryson's *A Short History of Nearly Everything.* I had read all of Bryson's other books and loved them, so that was a well-chosen gift, and endeared me to Clive immediately. I showed them around the stage and the drum kit, and they stayed for soundcheck. Before I went off to dinner with the guys, I gave Clive and Sergio signed copies of *Traveling Music,* in which I had mentioned Jethro Tull as an early influence. I told Clive how much I had appreciated his drumming back then, and how influential albums like *Stand Up* and *Aqualung* had been for me. He was very modest about his work, especially from more than thirty years ago, but seemed pleased to be remembered.

Clive and Sergio were planning to stay for the show, but I didn't see them again. The show had a late start, 8:30, which would have allowed time for a decent nap, but the bus was too hot and airless, the barking dogs too disturbing, and during my eight o'clock warmup, the Bubba-Gump room was a stifling sauna.

That night, when Jerry Stiller wondered, "What did they put in my tea?" the subtitles read, "Che hanno messo nel tè?"

The audience of 5,809 Italians was loud and enthusiastic, jammed up against the barricade, with a lot of pushing and shoving from side to side. Though they were certainly excited, that excitement wasn't always about us—sometimes they broke into what must have been their local football chant (I can hear it still), between our songs, and even while we were playing. Later I made a note, "Somehow when the Brazilian audience acted like they were at a soccer game, it was charming—here, it was annoying."

I guess I also expected a certain level of "sophistication," and I was looking out into the heaving, chanting audience thinking, "This is *Milan*? The capital of European fashion and style?"

Before *2112* that night, Alex held up five fingers.

After the show, when I ran onto the bus and into the stateroom to start peeling off my wet clothes, I noticed the bus wasn't moving. When

I was dried off and changed, I went forward to learn that we couldn't get out of the backstage area because the access road was blocked with parked cars. That had never happened anywhere in the world before, and I could only shake my head and sit down to have my Macallan and wait. Though once again I noted in my journal, "Italy bugs me."

At the beginning of the European tour in London, Brutus and I had been told there was a new law in Italy that motorcyclists had to wear those bright yellow plastic reflective vests. That seemed unlikely to me, given the semi-anarchic nature of the country as I knew it, but anything was possible. Brutus and I had picked up a couple of those vests just in case, but now, after a day's riding in Italy, I noticed we hadn't seen anybody on motorcycles or scooters wearing them. Brutus said, "Do you think that was supposed to be some lame European joke or something?"

I didn't know, but thought it probably was. That British sense of humor. Then I made a joke about the Mean Misplacer, "Hey, today you misplaced *me!*"

The next day we began our two days of freedom, and we didn't plan a strict route—just gave Dingus and Dork a couple of possible hotel waypoints, and the next show in Frankfurt.

The third and last of my travel requests to Brutus, after the Isle of Man and *le Musée National de l'Automobile*, had been contained in an e-mail with the subject title, "One Word." The word in that message was "Stelvio," the name of one of the most famous of the old-time Alpine passes.

Brutus's reply, once he had looked it up, was, "Whoa—will you wait for me at the other end?"

We began the day at a rest stop on the main autostrada near the Italian-Austrian border on a cool, sunny morning. We turned west, up and over the spectacular Jaufenpass, shown on the map as a series of winding loops, grades of 10 percent and 12 percent, climbing to 2094 meters (6868 feet), and closed by heavy snow from November to May. The next pass, the Passo del Rombo, or Timmelsjoch, showed 12 percent and 15 percent grades, and wound its way up to 2500 meters, 8200 feet. That one was shown as closed from October until June, and carried us over a high, barren summit of granite and glaciers. There we were waved through a small border post and into Austria.

The Ache River valley led us north through Alpine villages, pastures, and forests, and just west of Innsbruck, we turned west, along the valley of the Inn River. At Landeck, we stopped for gas, and I called over to Brutus, "Hey, what happened to the Stelvio?"

He looked thoughtful, and said only, "Oh."

I widened my eyes, mouth agape in feigned shock. "You misplaced the *Stelvio*?"

I turned away and finished filling my fuel tank. Brutus could tell I was going to sulk, so he pulled out the map, then started some computations on Dork. A few minutes later he said, "We can go get it—it's just about eighty kilometers south."

And off we went, continuing through glorious weather and spectacular scenery. At first, we rode southwest, following the valley of the Inn, then straight south and back into Italy over the Reschenpass, or Passo del Resia, at 1508 meters, 4946 feet. The arbitrariness of even those ancient borders was shown in the bilingual names of some of the next villages: St. Valentin auf der Haide/ San Valentino alla Muta and Schluderns/ Sluderno.

At Spondinig/ Spondigna, we turned southwest toward the Passo dello Stelvio, or Stilfserjoch, shown with 13 percent and 15 percent grades, and closed from November to May. It was either the highest or second-highest paved pass in the Alps, at 2757 meters, 9042 feet, and approaching from the east, as we were, there were forty-eight hairpin turns to climb, each of them posted with a number. As the road began to twist back on itself, Brutus pulled to the right to see if I wanted to go ahead, but I waved him on—somehow I didn't think I was going to be *aggressive* with this pass.

It started in a steep gorge, the narrow road cutting upward through walls of rock and trees, then quickly ascended above the treeline, looping sharply across and back. We could look up and see the next loop, or down to the previous one. At least we could also see any approaching traffic, and fortunately there were only a few cars, trucks, motorcycles, and bicycles (I didn't envy them, climbing up or going down) on that September afternoon.

Each turn was a quick switchback of almost 180 degrees, and the pavement was steeply banked. We would have to creep around in first gear, leaning sharply without much speed to give us gyroscopic stability, then accelerate into second gear, and brake and downshift again for the next one—forty-eight times.

Or, at least, thirty-eight. We were about to have another adventure.

As we approached the turn marked "10," a road-maintenance crew was working ahead of us. A yellow truck was backing down the next stretch of road toward us. Brutus tried to stop and see what the truck was going to do, but he was right on the steeply banked hairpin. When he put his right foot down, it was on the low side of the grade, so steep that his foot just kept on going. The top-heavy motorcycle passed the point of no return, and I watched with horror as Brutus tumbled away from the bike, and it went right upside down. I pulled to the edge of the road, kicked the sidestand down, and ran over to him. He was up already, saying, "Sorry."

Like I was worried about the bike!

We struggled to pull the motorcycle upright again, and surveyed the damage. The windshield was cracked, a piece broken off the right side, and the turn-signal was broken off (we could tape it back on for now), plus the hard plastic luggage case was split open. It looked like we could carry on, and we pulled ourselves together and set off again.

Brutus pulled over at the next corner, and I stopped behind him.

"There's something wrong with the brakes—when I pull in the lever, nothing happens, except fluid comes gushing out."

He pointed to where brake fluid was dripping down the side of the gas tank, and we soon determined the front brake-line connector had been broken in the fall. The bike had no front brakes at all.

Time to switch to crisis mode.

"The back brake is still okay," Brutus said, but I knew he couldn't ride those kinds of roads with only the rear brake. With the bike's weight shifting forward when you slowed, the front brake did at least seventy percent of the braking. There was no way he could ride down this pass with no front brakes.

I looked up above us, and saw a few buildings at what was apparently the top of the pass.

"I think we should try to make it up there. Maybe there's a hotel, and we can try to get help."

Fortunately, it was still only three o'clock, on a weekday, we had two days to get to Frankfurt, and there were several hotels at the top. Apart from the Stelvio's popularity with motorcyclists and bicyclists, at more than 9000 feet, it offered year-round skiing on the nearby glaciers.

At that elevation, nearing the end of September, it was also very cold up there. Clouds were drawing in like curtains across the nearby peaks, dimming the light. The summit of the pass was a barren, somewhat dismal cluster of hotels and souvenir stands. None of the hotels seemed particularly fancy, or even attractive, but we chose the one that looked like it would have the best view, the Hotel Stilfserjoch, and went inside. The young man behind the desk, in his thirties, was friendly and helpful, but unfortunately spoke no English (though he did have a *spectacular* hair-do, a thick dark helmet that was carefully arrayed atop his head like something from an '80s pop group, and was prominently displayed, always perfectly arranged, in the many photos of him—as a ski instructor—around the reception area).

Checked into our humble rooms, I dumped my bags on the bed with my helmet and jacket. I glanced out the window, all gray sky above darker gray mountains, and down to the loops of the pass we had just climbed. Then I unpacked the flask, got two plastic cups from the bathroom, and went to Brutus's room. I poured us each a drink, then sat back and watched the master at work.

He started by calling the Canadian BMW Roadside Assistance number, and they connected him to a British BMW help line, who directed him to a Swiss BMW club, who put him in touch with a dealer in the Swiss town of Chur (pronounced "Kur"). There, unbelievably, he found a lady who spoke English and Italian, and she helped connect him to a towing company in Bolzano, Italy, 100 kilometers away from us.

Although we were only a few hundred meters from Switzerland, we had to use an Italian towing company. Well, no problem—the main thing was, it seemed like it was going to work. A flatbed truck would meet us at the hotel in the morning, and take Brutus and the bike to the dealer in Chur, about 150 kilometers away. I raised my plastic cup to Brutus, "A masterly performance."

We clicked cups, and he said, "Thank you sir. Now I'm exhausted."

Naturally, my first journal note (of a *long* entry) was, "Adventures suck when you're having them."

Even with our day's ride cut short like that, we had still covered

281 kilometers, 175 miles, and much of that had been difficult, demanding riding. After what I described as a "comatose nap" (complete with dreams that were somehow relevant to our situation, but with the band and crew involved), I woke to see rain spitting against the window, the light dim through a heavy overcast. A single knock on Brutus's door roused him, and we went downstairs to see what dinner might bring.

During our travels in Switzerland, I had noticed other small hotels like that in out-of-the-way places, huddled at the top of a pass in the barren, glacial landscape, or isolated on a high Alpine meadow or rural village. I had stayed in similar places on the Boysens' bicycle tours. The rooms were always scrupulously clean and comfortable, the food was often wonderful, and the settings were so fantastic. I had been wishing Brutus and I might be able to stay in one of those on this tour.

Unfortunately, the Hotel Stilfserjoch was no more than adequate in the clean and comfortable department, and, most disappointingly, our dinner was one of the worst meals I have ever been served in continental Europe.

The large dining room was occupied only by the proprietor's wife and children at one table, and another table framed by a dozen fit young men in matching tracksuits. They were the Italian cross-country ski team, and their coach, apparently training on the glaciers and on the nearby roads, on roller skis.

The only language Brutus and I had in common with the elderly, stooping waiter was French, which we all spoke equally badly. We managed to get mushy potato salad, bland soup, something the waiter called "voo," which we eventually figured out was *veau*, or veal, dry and tasteless, with soppy green beans, buttery potatoes, and a syrupy wine. Dessert was a decent apple strudel with ice cream, and instant espresso from a machine.

We stepped outside for a look around, but the chill rain was turning to sleet, and except for lights in the few hotels, all was utterly dark. We stopped by the bar for a warming cognac, and saw the Italian cross-country ski team gathered around a television, watching videos of their roadwork while the coach scolded them.

One great part of the experience, though, was sleeping at that elevation, curled under a pile of blankets with my window open a crack to let in the cold, clean air (I have always wondered why people who lived in Alpine villages, or South Pacific islands, didn't live longer than other people).

However, in the morning my windowsill was lined with gray ice, and reefs of sleet lay on the ground. The temperature was near freezing, and the rain was, too, slicing down into dark puddles. One car moved slowly toward the descending pass, its headlights flaring in the dim light, the beams slashed with needles of rain.

I helped Brutus carry his bags and riding gear down to the lobby, and the young Italian tow-truck driver showed up a little before eight. He spoke no English, but we put on our rain jackets and went outside, hunched against the icy rain, and together we got the bike winched onto the flatbed and tied down. Above the hotel parking lot, skiers walked to the skilift with their skis over their shoulders, heading up to the glaciers of eternal winter. Posters around the hotel advertised "summer ski school," and I couldn't help thinking that in another decade or two, as the world's glaciers continued to recede, the summer skiing would come to an end.

Brutus posed for my camera at the truck's door, with the bike tied down behind him, then we waved goodbye, each of us nervous about what the day would bring. The truck pulled out and headed down the mountain, and I was on my own. I was in no hurry to set off, because we gathered that the tow truck was first going to take Brutus back down the Stelvio to the company's office, so Brutus could pay for the tow (ah, Italy!), then back around another way to Switzerland and up to Chur, where hopefully the BMW dealer's mechanic would start working on it. All of that would certainly take a few hours (six, in fact), so there was no sense in me racing up to Chur now to meet Brutus.

After a grim breakfast of stale bread, dry meat and cheese, and machine-made coffee, I hung around the room as long as I could, catching up on my notes.

"Sound of wind outside, a low moan. I'm a little nervous, leaving from here into who-knows-what, alone. Also hoping 'everything else' works out okay today. Where will we end up tonight?"

Looking over the map, I decided to loop south a little to St. Moritz, one of the possible destinations Brutus and I had been aiming for the previous day. My brother Danny had been there, and I hadn't, so that was reason enough to ride through it. My motorcycle was still in the hotel's garage, and I took my time carrying my bags down and loading everything, then programming Dingus to take me to St. Moritz.

Wearing full foul-weather gear, including my electric vest and winter gloves, I finally set off into the cold rain, only to pause again after less than a kilometer. A sign pointed right to the Umbrail Pass, a potential shortcut, but also a potentially treacherous one—a tiny squiggle on the map, with at least part of it unpaved. One of our guidebooks noted that the Umbrail Pass was "the highest border post in Europe," and, as one British traveler described the Swiss officers, "keen as mustard, they were quite hostile when we called in." I could see the small building that must be the Swiss border post, barely 100 meters away.

I straddled the bike in the rain, looking at the map under its plastic cover and considering the choices. The mystery of the Umbrail to my right, the adventurous route with possible bad roads and border hassles, or the sweeping turns of the Stelvio descending in front of me, the longer, "safer" way? After a couple of minutes of indecision, I finally gave the kind of sigh that says, 'you may regret this later,' and turned right.

The border post was unmanned that day, I was glad to see, and I began to pick my way down the pass, carefully and nervously, especially over the unpaved part, several kilometers that were "shiny and mucky." Down through the steep valley lined with soggy tamaracks, I waved at a pair of motorcyclists on their way up, then a pair of intrepid bicyclists, and finally descended into a tidy, damp Swiss village.

Back on a good paved road, under a steady rain, I settled into a smooth pace. Though still a little anxious about being separated, and worried about Brutus being able to get the bike fixed—parts availability, for example—at least I had the calm feeling of not being in a hurry. I enjoyed riding in the rain under those circumstances: I was already dressed for it, I wasn't on a busy highway, and I wasn't in a hurry.

That region of Switzerland was known as the Lower Engadine, in the country's largest canton of Graubünden. That German name seemed to mean "gray people," and the canton was called Grigioni in Italian, Grisons in French, and Grischun in Romansch, a relict dialect of Latin surviving in isolated Alpine valleys, and the *fourth* of Switzerland's official languages. (To think Canada has trouble reconciling two languages.)

Occasionally wiping the rain from my faceshield, I followed a green, misty valley called the Val Müstair through the middle of the Swiss National Park (its foundation inspired by America's Yellowstone) then up toward the Ofenpass, or Pass dal Fuorn, at 2149 meters, 7048 feet.

A line of traffic was stopped for a construction zone, and up ahead I noticed a familiar-looking truck, with an even more familiar motorcycle on top of it. I rode up and parked in front of the truck, then walked up to the passenger side. Brutus was sleeping against the window. I shared a nodding smile with the driver, then knocked hard on the glass. Brutus came to with a start, but just then, I saw traffic finally starting to move up ahead, and said goodbye again.

Now I knew where they were, anyway, and could tell they had at least eighty kilometers of fairly slow traveling ahead of them. But it was still not yet noon, so they should arrive in Chur in plenty of time to get the bike fixed—as long as the parts were available.

A little later, I turned southwest, back in the valley of the Inn River, following it up into the Upper Engadine, and about forty kilometers to St. Moritz. Feeling the same lazy sense of unhurriedness, I circled the town in the rain, admiring its setting above Lake St. Moritz, the great mountains all around, and wishing Brutus and I had been able to stay there.

St. Moritz was dedicated to winter, calling itself "the oldest winter resort in the world," and had hosted the Winter Olympics in 1928 and 1948. Despite that day's rain, the area also boasted 322 days of sunshine per year. The huge grand hotels were impressive-looking, though still closed for the season, but the town remained busy on that Thursday midday, going about its everyday, out-of-season business among the high-rise buildings and fashionable boutiques.

I paused and reset Dingus to take me to Chur, and headed north over the Julier Pass, 2284 meters, 7491 feet. Rounding a sharp turn, I saw a truck and trailer blocking the road ahead, where it had apparently slid into the side of the road on the next sharp curve. The long truck was angled across both lanes, stopping traffic in both directions, and I joined the growing line of cars and trucks at first, watching as a tow truck tried to move the big truck. I could see the operation was going to take a while, and, seizing an opportunity, I slipped by it and out the other side.

For an hour or so I rode through a momentary break in the rain, though the sky remained dark and oppressive. The wind was cold as I sped down a stretch of autoroute. On the outskirts of Chur, I stopped at a BMW car dealership to get the motorcycle shop's address and typed it into Dingus. I was still worried I was going to beat Brutus there, and was glad to see him when I pulled up. He told me they were already working on the bike, fixing the brake-line connector, replacing the luggage case and turn-indicator lens, and that it shouldn't take too much longer.

Discussing our options for the remainder of that afternoon, and the necessity to report for duty in Frankfurt the following day, we agreed to head north to one of the hotels Brutus had logged, in another part of the Schwartzwald. Dork was out of commission in the service bay, but I did some computations on Dingus, putting in "Go To" that hotel, and "Quickest Way." The calculations took a while, but eventually Dingus figured it was something over 200 kilometers. We decided to go for it.

In Switzerland, even the autoroutes couldn't avoid being beautiful. We rode north toward Germany past storm-tossed lakes (the Walensee particularly dramatic), ranks of mountains with clouds streaming down their sides (seen through "rain streaming on faceshield," I noted later), forests, villages, towns, pastures, and tunnels—"so many tunnels."

At one point I led us in the wrong direction at a junction of two autoroutes, and though Dingus and I soon realized the error, at least that brief detour took us into and out of Liechtenstein, another tiny principality, like Luxembourg, that had somehow survived among its bigger neighbors for hundreds of years. One of the smallest countries in the world, only sixty-two square miles, with 33,000 people, Liechtenstein's ties to Switzerland had helped it remain neutral through the World Wars, and develop one of the world's highest standards of living.

The list of countries we had ridden through on this tour was growing daily, to twelve now: England, Isle of Man, Wales, Scotland, France, Belgium, Luxembourg, Germany, Switzerland, Italy, Austria, and Liechtenstein.

With Brutus riding the rainy autoroute just behind me, I pointed up at a sign for an exit to Tuggen and Wangen, which somehow *sounded* obscene, like the town I had passed through earlier, Cunter.

I was even singing a bit during that blast through the wet Swiss landscape, for the first time in a long time, warbling my way through "Hallelujah," "By the Time I Get to Phoenix," and "Everything Happens to Me." We just hadn't been riding the kind of roads that allowed long periods of "freeway drone" to encourage my vocalizing state of mind.

Dingus and Dork earned their keep that day, navigating us unerringly through a busy knot of ever-changing roads around Zurich, Winterthur, and Schaffhausen, two-lanes, autoroutes, and slow industrial zones, with rain pelting us most of the time. We reached a border post, showed our passports, then hit another stretch of heavily trafficked roads on the German side. We turned onto a quieter route into the Black Forest, winding our way through the dripping pines and firs to Triberg.

After such a very long day, I could hardly believe I had only ridden 414 kilometers, 258 miles. Finally arrived at the Romantik Parkhotel Wehrle, my rain gear was hung to dry around my room, draped on the ornate furniture painted in intricate designs of blue and yellow, with multicolored carved and painted panels in floral and geometric designs, all trimmed in gilt. (Once again, so much for German severity!)

Catching up on some notes, I made my valediction to Switzerland, "still the most civilized country in the world, and perhaps the most beautiful."

I looked out at the rain pouring down on the famously pretty little town of Triberg, in the heart of the Schwartzwald. The rising main street had three- and four-storey buildings, neatly painted, with flower boxes under their windows. Behind the town was a dark mountainside of conifers hung with scraps of gray cloud. Somewhere up there was Germany's highest waterfall.

Once again we did a quick-change from disreputable-looking, soggy Scooter Trash (Eurotrash) to sophisticated, well-dressed dinner guests. We were welcomed to the hotel's restaurant, a small, cozy dining room of carved wood and antique furnishings, by an apple-cheeked, cheery young fraülein of ample proportions. In answer to Brutus's question, she told us the hotel was 400 years old, part of a chain of "Romantik" hotels, all in historic buildings.

After that long, cold, wet day, I started off with a hearty soup, and we ordered an expensive bottle of red wine—to cheer us up. A set of antique prints illustrating the seasons decorated the wall beside our table, and I especially liked the word for spring, "frühling." It had a blossoming sound about it. Summer was "sommer," fall was "herbst," and winter was . . . "winter."

Earlier, Brutus had put in a call to Michael in Frankfurt, just to check in, and during dinner our fraülein announced, in her thick accent, "Michael called, and you should call Lye-am, it's very important."

Then she said, "But your food is ready. Should I hold the cooking?"

"No," I said. "Whatever it is, let's eat first." (Priorities.)

But of course that message stayed on the table before us, as it were, while we devoured our main courses of wild boar and venison. I was concerned about what could be so important that we had to call Liam right away, and I worried . . . I don't know, that something might have happened to somebody, I guess.

Brutus went off to phone Liam, while I noted, "and I'm sitting here fearing the worst."

A few minutes later, Brutus returned to the table shaking his head. He said Liam's message must have been exaggerated in the transmission from person to person, and it was just something about a flight reservation for after the last show.

I noted, "Ach, phooey. It was nothing."

Just before turning off the light that night, I was thinking about our recent adventures, and noted the qualities that had allowed us to deal with the previous day's situation—"Judgment, acceptance, imagination." Judgment to realize that we had to stop and get help, acceptance of that reality, and imagination in figuring out how to deal with it. We had done well. And been lucky.

The rain continued into the following day, and later that afternoon I would note:

Last two days some of the worst weather I've ever experienced on a bike. This morning cold, heavy rain, then heavy fog—all at once— through Schwarzwald Hochstrasse. Terrible visibility—not to mention view!

Traffic light, at least, though a couple of logging trucks to get by.

Remembering an image I had of the Black Forest, from my first visits, of tall dark conifers overhanging the roads for miles. I never actually *saw* that exact image this time.

Twenty-five years later, maybe it's gone?

Maybe. Apparently the Black Forest had suffered badly from acid rain, and although the Germans tried to practice sustainable forestry there, logging and pollution were bound to have reduced the forest I had first seen twenty-five years earlier.

Brutus and I rode out of the rainy, foggy Schwartzwald and onto a long stretch of cold, congested autobahn. We passed the larger cities of Karlsruhe, Mannheim, and Darmstadt, rain still coming and going, past several areas of highway construction. Still, we arrived at the Festhalle by early afternoon, after 282 kilometers, 176 miles, in plenty of time for the necessary oil changes.

Brutus had to get a runner to take him to a BMW dealer for some more oil, and another turn-indicator lens (an unfortunate encounter that morning against a brick wall outside the Parkhotel Wehrle, just as we were setting off in the rain—he said some bad words). Brutus also had some Internet and telephone work to do on upcoming routes and reservations, so once again I volunteered to do the oil changes on both bikes.

The day remained cold and gray, but fortunately the rain let up as I had to work outdoors. Equally fortunately, the concrete parking area outside the arena was fenced off, so I could hide behind the row of buses, out of sight of fans gathering at the fence. Several extra trucks and teams of technicians, the film and recording crews, were parked by the door.

The Festhalle, with a huge glass-paned dome in the middle of the ceiling, was about 100 years old, and that meant, of course, that it was around during the Nazi era. As one who grew up during the '50s and early '60s, with the ubiquitous war movies in the theaters and on television, when I first visited Germany I couldn't help looking at the villages and towns and imagining swastikas hanging everywhere, and in the cities, parades of goosestepping stormtroopers. Every time we played the Frankfurt Festhalle over the years, stagehands and locals pointed out the high balcony where Adolf Hitler had shouted and gesticulated during the infamous rallies of the late '30s. There again, it wasn't hard to imagine the giant red banners and swastikas—and *our* cheering crowds as *his* cheering crowds.

During soundcheck, we played a few extra songs for the cameras and recording truck, and after dinner, I made a quick note about the upcoming event: "Filming and recording tonight, just to make it 'extra special.' Big pressure on solo particularly, if I go ahead with that instructional video. Oh boy . . . "

Sometimes that kind of pressure inspired us to rise to an exalted level, as had happened the previous tour in Rio de Janeiro, and for other performances we had recorded and filmed over the years. However, other times that kind of pressure had the opposite effect, making us tense and . . . lousy.

Frankfurt, sadly, was the second kind.

I had a cold coming on, and felt fuzzy-headed, and all of us were edgy, overconcentrating and overanalyzing. It seemed like we had to fight our way through the show. I made a nasty mistake right in the first song, the "R30 Overture," and never really recovered. Something bad happened in "Earthshine," and again in "One Little Victory," and at the time I thought they had all been my fault. (The next night, after I had tormented myself all day about it, gone over those parts in my head all day, and even rehearsed that part of "Earthshine" in the Bubba-Gump room before the show, Alex told me it had been Geddy in "Earthshine," and Geddy told me it was Alex in "One Little Victory.")

The show was still good, objectively, as we would expect after doing more than fifty now (Alex held up four fingers that night), but that Frankfurt show was not the effortless triumph we had wanted it to be. If only we could select it, like a waypoint on Dingus, "Go To—Magic Show."

I also had some technical and mental difficulties in the drum solo, the part I had particularly wanted to be perfect if I was going to use it as the basis for an instructional video. So, I was feeling pretty low after that show, down on myself about it. (Again, the recorded solo would prove to be fine, objectively, for use in the concert DVD and the instructional one, *Anatomy of a Drum Solo*. The unexpected changes only amounted to "variations on a theme." But still—it hadn't been what I wanted it to be.)

The next day started badly, too. When I rolled out of bed in a rainy rest area near the Czech border, feeling bad with that cold filling my head with pain and congestion, Brutus told me a carload of fans was parked behind us. We talked with Mark about it, and he tried driving the bus a little further and turning off the highway, but no—they were still there.

Exasperated, once again I asked Brutus the rhetorical question, "How can they think this is an okay thing to do?"

He just shook his head.

I felt trapped, helpless, and angry. I couldn't leave the bus without those stalkers coming at me, and once again, I wouldn't be able to be rude to them, but I hated to be forced to reward them for *their* rudeness. We couldn't even call the police, given the language barrier.

"Well, I'm not holding a meet-and-greet for them at eight o'clock in the morning," I said.

Brutus nodded. "No. I guess we'll have to go have a talk with them."

I sat there, tense and angry, while Mark and Brutus walked back to the car. A few minutes later they were back, and Brutus said the German followers were leaving. He had suggested to them that they ought to respect our privacy, and one of them had protested, "We do respect your privacy—that's why we're back *here*."

Typically, there was one stubborn one, with an unpleasant sense of "entitlement," while the others were reasonable, even ashamed. The one with the attitude said, "I have vaited twenty years—I vant my album signed."

While the guy continued to protest and demand, Brutus just shook his head, one side to the other with each simple answer, "No. No. No. No. No."

Perhaps the worst thing was that everyone involved was left feeling bad. Those fans were going away unhappy, probably resentful of me, and Mark and Brutus had been put in an uncomfortable position. I felt regret and self-blame, as well as resentment, and hated feeling that way. But, I had learned long ago that when people expected me to behave in a certain way, if it went against every grain of my being, I could not do it. A few times in the early years I had tried *acting* blithe and gregarious in such situations, but that felt even worse. Like the old song, "I've gotta be me." Even when it didn't feel so good.

Riding off into the rain, Brutus and I were now traveling through the former East Germany. We were heading toward the Czech Republic, a country the band had never played in, and a storied city I had never visited: Prague.

The band had played in Eastern Europe only once before, in Berlin, on the *Roll the Bones* tour in 1992, less than three years after the Wall came down. Driving through Eastern Germany with Peter Brockbank toward the once-divided city, I looked around at a green landscape that resembled Western Germany, of course, in its fields and woodlands, but the villages and roads were very different. It seemed a bleak, gray world of utilitarian buildings, crumbling roads, and ugly, smoky little cars. The abandoned watchtowers were still there, grim reminders of soldiers who stood on guard with their guns pointed, not at invaders, but at their own people, who only wanted to *escape.*

One song on that *Roll the Bones* album was called "Heresy," and I wrote the lyrics in response to the fall of communism. The song's tone shifted from a lament for all the lives lost, stunted, and wasted ("Who can give them back their lives, and all those wasted years?"), to outrage at the ideologues and thugs who had perpetuated such brutality, such stupidity ("All those precious wasted years—who will pay?"). Finally the song expressed my angry disbelief over the effect on my own life: ten years old and hearing about atomic bombs that the Russians might drop on nearby Niagara Falls, ("All the crap we had to take/ Bombs and basement fallout shelters/ All our lives at stake"), and how for most of my life, the world had lived under the shadow of nuclear war. Now we were supposed to simply accept that the twentieth century's "noble experiment" had been reduced to a failed ideology.

"All the fear and suffering—all a big mistake."

In 1992, in those early years of German reunification, I drove through the former East Germany, eyes wide open. The only bits of color were a few older BMWs, brought in from West Germany, on used-car lots, and a few tentative-seeming advertisements on village walls. Those colors of advertising might have been loud and garish, but they still said *freedom,* as did the few touches of paint among weathered shutters and doors. In the Western European countries, I had smiled to see those little Trabants and Skodas toiling and smoking their way around France or Switzerland, jammed with Eastern Europeans enjoying their first taste of unrestricted travel.

By 2004, it had been fourteen years since the fall of communism, and I was curious to see how these countries, these people, were faring now.

The first thing that surprised me on that Sunday morning was the line of cars at the Czech border, uniformed officers checking the documents of each one. I wondered what they were worried about, and leaned over to Brutus and joked that I was going to throw myself at them and say, "Help, I'm a refugee from California, please grant me sanctuary in the Czech Republic!"

After democracy returned to the former Czechoslovakia, in the "Velvet Revolution" of 1989, the country had split into two separate states, the Czech Republic and Slovakia, in an amicable divide called the "Velvet Divorce."

The Czech border officers were friendly, but spoke no English, and gave our Canadian passports a quick scan, then waved us through. Just over the border, we encountered the most "bizarre bazaar," the roadside lined with a series of outdoor stalls offering hundreds of garden gnomes, reflective globes, knockoff T-shirts, and Harley-Davidson wall clocks. Beyond that, we rode into a village, its shops replaced with strip clubs, all of it a welter of desperate capitalism, presumably hoping to attract German visitors.

As we paused to put our passports away and put our earplugs back in, Brutus pointed up at three large villas above the town. "Someone's making some money here." On our way back that night, on the bus, we would see the darker side of those borderland enterprises.

Rain continued most of the day, making my cold feel even more miserable, as we meandered along two-lane roads, through farmland and ancient villages of brick and stone, the land once called Bohemia. (Our modern use of the word dates from an eighteenth-century Bohemian king who ejected the gypsies, many of whom moved to France and were known disparagingly as *les Bohèmiens*. French artists and writers, feeling equally outcast, adopted the name, as in Puccini's *La Bohème*.)

The atmosphere around us varied between nineteenth century and medieval, and the roads were as poor and dejected as the villages and farmhouses, though we had some nice riding through a national park. We noticed a lot of the Trabants and Skodas we passed were dented and bashed up, and we encountered three accident scenes, so we were encouraged to ride cautiously.

The roads got worse, and busier, as we approached Prague, then we merged onto a bit of motorway and saw the city on the far side of the Vltava River. The rain had lifted, and the sun radiated through the overcast, glowing on a long row of colorful, geometric buildings along the tree-lined river bank, Gothic towers and spires rising behind. Following

Dingus and Dork across a bridge and through the cobbled streets and monumental stone buildings, we tried to look around as much as we could without falling prey to taxis, cobbles, or streetcar tracks. My mental picture of Prague, perhaps from Kafka, had imagined masses of dark stone battlements crouching over shadowy cobbled streets, but in fact the city seemed open and bright, wide streets and squares surrounded by buildings decorated in elaborate Romanesque and Gothic decorations, their façades painted and carved.

Prague dated from the ninth century, and by the fourteenth century it was the second-largest city in Europe, after Paris. In 1618, the Thirty Years War was started when some Protestants threw two Catholic governors out of the Prague Castle windows—an act delightfully called "The Defenestration of Prague." Through its long history, the city experienced much violence and war, from the Holy Roman Empire to the Austrian Hapsburgs to the Nazis to the Soviets. In the late '60s, a time known as the "Prague Spring," local communist leaders tried to create "socialism with a human face," only to find themselves invaded by five Warsaw Pact countries. The Czechs would have to wait another twenty years for the reforms and democracy they desired, until 1989, when the domino effect of the Berlin Wall's dismantling brought on the "Velvet Revolution."

By about three o'clock, after 348 kilometers, 217 miles, Brutus and I arrived at a large amusement park, the home of the Cellular Telephone Network Arena (another example of eagerly embraced capitalism). Michael met us outside the arena, and directed us to the bus parked along one side. Beside the bus, a cacophony of loudspeakers blared distorted music and hawker's voices from the rides and games.

Michael told us the trucks hadn't made it in until two o'clock that afternoon, as they had been completely stopped on the autobahn outside Frankfurt for most of the night, trapped in traffic by a bad accident. Since they had arrived so late, everything was running that much behind, and though C.B. thought the crew could get the show up on time, he said we shouldn't expect a soundcheck.

Michael seemed down that day, and when I asked him if something was wrong, he just sighed and said, "Will you fire me, so I can go home?"

"No way, Betty-Sue—if I have to be here, you have to be here!"

But I felt pretty miserable myself, tired and sick from the cold, and

I crawled into bed and went to sleep. Occasionally, I woke to hear the loud distorted voices of carnival barkers, in unintelligible Czech, blasting from tinny megaphone speakers. After a couple of hours, I got up and went forward to find out what was going on. Brutus was on the cell phone making ferry reservations for Scandinavia, and, as seemed to be usual in Europe, he was using the radio-operator's method of spelling my name, "Papa, Echo, Alpha, Romeo, Tango."

Hearing the last three, I thought, "What a great car name—the Alfa-Romeo Tango. ART!"

At dinner, Geddy told me he had taken a tour of the city that day with his wife Nancy, who was visiting and traveling with him for a few days. They had thought Prague was one of the most beautiful cities in Europe, and Geddy said their guide had told them the communist leaders kept that one city so nice all those years as a kind of "holiday camp," a theme park to send loyal party functionaries to, as a reward.

With regard to the state of progress in Eastern Europe, it is worth noting that in Prague, unlike in Milan, I was able to get on-line and send my nephew Max a message on his eighth birthday.

Our stalwart crew was able to get the show up on time for the eight o'clock start, and despite my illness, I had a great warmup in the Bubba-Gump room. And despite the lack of a soundcheck, the show went great, too—the best in Europe so far. The audience was the largest since Britain, more than 7,000 smiling and appreciative young people seeming so grateful simply because we were there. Anyone in that audience over the age of fifteen had lived under the yoke of communism, and no doubt they *were* grateful, for everything.

Despite their enthusiasm, most people obviously didn't speak or understand English, and either sang along phonetically, or just pretended to sing along. One young couple in the front row center just smiled and moved their heads all night, the girl pumping her little fist in the air to the beat.

One of the crew guys must have done some shopping at those border bazaars, because a ceramic garden gnome appeared on the stage in front of Alex's pedal-board. I noticed it as soon as the lights came up, and broke into helpless laughter.

During intermission, I said to Gump that I wished we had filmed the Prague show instead of Frankfurt, as I had originally wanted. Gump said,

"Yeah, we seem to do better *without* a soundcheck," referring also to the Rio show on the last tour.

When Ray first suggested the idea of filming one of the European shows, I had thought *Live in Prague* sounded more exotic than *Live in Frankfurt*, but it hadn't worked out that way.

Ray was in Prague for that show, and during intermission, he told me he got a kick out of hearing us play "The Trees" in a former communist country. That song was a parable about collectivism, in which the maples rebelled against the oaks for being so lofty and taking all the light, concluding with, "So the maples formed a union, and they passed a noble law/ Now the trees are all kept equal, by hatchet, axe, and saw."

Well, yes, I thought, we *were* there representing something, and I was proud of that. At the beginning of *2112*, a tale of individual resistance against collectivist oppression, Alex held up three fingers.

And against every obstacle, and still feeling ill, I was having a really good show. Who could ever figure it?

During the second set, merchandiser Pat and pyrotechnician Kevin came out onstage dressed in Czech and Team Canada hockey jerseys to do the dryers. In a tribute to the number of Czech hockey players who played in the NHL, they staged a mock hockey fight, rumbling around and pulling each other's jerseys over their heads.

Apparently other disputes that night were more serious. Michael told me later there had been several fights in the back of the hall that security had to break up. Whatever those fights were about, it was an example of how I could get a misleading impression from the small part of the crowd I could see. (The same was probably true of the country—or any country.)

Riding on the bus that night, back toward the German border, Mark told us to have a look out the windows. We were driving through the narrow, curving main street of a border town, and the shop windows were lit with a lurid red and pink glow. And in the middle of those lighted windows were real live *women*.

Like the red-light district of Amsterdam, and with the same apparent legality, or at least tolerance, prostitutes were posed in show windows to tempt passersby, presumably the same cross-border Germans as the bazaars. But no one seemed to be around on that Saturday night.

At the border, a uniformed guard came aboard the bus, looked around, grinned at Brutus and me, and said, "Nice!"

Sunday morning, I awoke beside the autobahn north of Dresden, hearing the cars wailing past. I noted, "not raining, but *looks* like rain." It was also cold once we got rolling, giving the day a fitting mood of cold-war bleakness, as we headed through eastern Germany and into Poland, then north and back west to Berlin. We had a day off before the next show in Hamburg, and Brutus and I were going to do what we called "some 'splorin'."

It was all too much for Dingus and Dork. Eastern Europe didn't seem to be well-plotted on GPS maps, and though Brutus had programmed our route for the day, often that route just appeared as a purple line on the blank screen, with no roads or names displayed. The gray arrow showed where we were, at least in terms of longitude and latitude, and we had to navigate by trying to keep that cursor somewhere near the purple line. It truly felt like an adventure that day, a "journey without maps," and I rode along with the constant awareness of our vulnerability, a sense of being "really *out there*, if anything should happen, mechanical or . . . medical."

We showed our passports at the Polish border, then followed a variety of roads from autobahn to tree-bordered two-lanes to cobblestoned streets through humble, drab villages. The landscape was mainly flat, and varied from small farms to a forested national park to many conifer plantations. The ranks of identical trees were obviously fifteen to twenty years old, and perhaps had been make-work projects from the last years of the dying communist regime.

The few people we saw on that Sunday morning seemed friendly, sometimes smiling and waving, but there was little traffic on the roads— a few farm trucks and tractors, and occasional cars, mainly older Volkswagens and Opels made in Germany by General Motors. Poland had joined the European Union just a few months before, and was apparently already being flooded by used cars from Germany.

The Polish villages looked like eastern Germany had twelve years earlier, still clothed in what I described as "widows' weeds," unpainted plaster and bare bricks, with little color or decoration anywhere. Under communism, people probably hadn't wanted to call attention to any luxuries in their dwellings, so hints of old-world style, half-timbered walls, carved doors, and graceful rooflines, had been deliberately underplayed by leaving them unpainted. Soon, no doubt, the color would return to those villages.

Ancient cobblestone streets, bumpy and slippery in the occasional rain showers, had often been retained in the villages as natural speed bumps. They worked. Some of the smaller country roads were also alarmingly bumpy, heaved, and potholed, jarring, bouncing, and shaking us and the bikes, and eventually rattling my headlight bulb to death.

The towns and cities seemed more prosperous, more colorful, especially one, Krosno Odrzánskie, near a large hydroelectric project. Rows of nineteenth-century mansions lined the river banks, perhaps surviving all those years as multifamily dwellings. They were a stately contrast to the many complexes of gray, cheerless apartment buildings—compounds we started calling "Communist Blocs."

There were areas of severe industrial blight, too, vast decrepit-looking factories and belching smokestacks. We paused for a Red Apple break beneath a line of power pylons of crumbling concrete and rusting iron. A sign displayed the international warning of the skull-and-crossbones, and the message, NIE DOTYKAC! URZADZENIE ELECTRYCZNE!

Whatever that was, we weren't going to do it.

The road signs were another challenge, of course, and after the last few days, in which we had traveled through a different language every day, from Italian to German to Czech to Polish, the European "Tower of Babel" had started to become dizzying. Bad enough were the signs pointing to places with names like Nowogród Bobrzanski and Zielona Góra, but there were a host of warnings and advisories coming at us on the roads, where we could only *hope* our ignorance wouldn't be fatal.

The day remained cold, and mostly cloudy, with a few spells of rain, and a few spells of almost-sunny glare. We crossed back into Germany at Frankfurt (the *other* one, on the Oder River rather than the Main), waiting in a line of traffic to show our passports. With its bustling shopping area, filled with cars and people, Frankfurt was noticeably more prosperous than the Polish towns on the other side of the Oder. As I had written in "Heresy" all those years ago, "The counter-revolution, at the counter of a store."

Still, Brutus and I had only traveled through a tiny part of Poland's vastness, and it made me want to see more—especially Krakow, which Geddy had told me was exceptionally beautiful. A few years earlier, he had taken his mother on a visit to her native country, along with his siblings, and it had been a powerful experience for them all. Brutus had tried to route us through Krakow, maybe for an overnight stay, but the distance was too great to get us back to Hamburg in time for the next show.

Instead, we were going to stop in Berlin, and we rode toward that city from the east, through tidy little villages with ancient, half-timbered houses, then returned to big-city traffic. Even though it was Sunday, there was a marathon being run in Berlin, so several streets were closed for the race, and there was also a lot of road construction. Dingus and Dork were back on the ball now that we were back in a well-mapped area, but they were no help against those kinds of obstacles. After 425 kilometers, 265 miles, we saw rather more of East Berlin than we wanted to, looping around the narrow canyons between drab buildings and finally stumbling on the back entrance to the hotel.

Ah—but what a hotel.

Once again, Brutus had done his homework. Despite arriving on dirty motorcycles, with our usual disreputable appearance and weary faces, the staff of the Hotel Adlon Kempinski welcomed us warmly. We handed over our luggage, and while Brutus went to check us in, I parked the bikes in the underground garage. My luxurious room overlooked Unter den Linden, the main street of the former East Berlin, and the Brandenburger Gate that had marked the division.

My first journal note described my usual frustration of trying to remember all I had seen and thought: "Almost *dreading* this—trying to get down all the notes I formulated in my head all day."

I also noted, "two days without a shower or shave," and was grateful for those small luxuries.

From my window, I saw a few souvenir shops across the Unter den Linden, and once I was cleaned up, I made a brief sortie to look for Berlin stickers, and maybe some from other countries. Along with some good stickers, I picked up a copy of *The Wall: The People's Story*, by Christopher Hilton, a well-written, almost novelistic oral history of the decades when Berlin had been a divided city in a divided country. With all my recent immersion in the former Eastern Bloc, I was more curious than ever about one of the most dramatic symbols of my lifetime, the Berlin Wall—its rise in the early '60s, and its sudden dismantling in the late '80s.

For the next few days I would spend every spare minute reading that book, fascinated by Hilton's interviews with the citizens of Berlin who had been caught on one side or the other, and the East German guards who had been responsible for carrying out the "shoot-to-kill" order (at least 200 Berliners were shot trying to cross that line). More than anything, I had been wondering, "How did it happen?"—how did that wall go up, and how did it come down? Both events seemed so mysterious, so surreal, and Hilton's book gave eyewitness accounts, hour by hour, as the Wall went up, overnight, on August 13, 1961, and came down overnight, on November 9, 1989. His witnesses also described the time in between—almost thirty years of life in a city divided by concrete, barbed wire, guns, and a discredited ideology. It was so sad.

Even with the small part of Eastern Europe Brutus and I had seen, clearly it was going to take a long time for those countries to catch up to their Western neighbors, both economically and in their quality of life. When I looked at the people on the streets of East Germany, the Czech Republic, or Poland, especially those around my age, I realized those men and women had been robbed of any opportunity to have a life of ambition, adventure, or achievement. That was the saddest thing of all.

But, they moved on.

In the lyrics to "Heresy," I had asked the rhetorical question, "Who will pay?" The bitter old men, misguided idealists, and brutal thugs who were responsible for that tragic repression were beyond the reach of earthly justice now. That almost made me want to believe in a karmic afterlife, where such evil and wrongheaded "leaders" could receive a suitable eternal punishment.

But . . . we move on.

Brutus and I got ourselves all gussied up for dinner once again, and had a wonderful meal in the hotel's excellent restaurant.

Living it up after a long, hard day, and—oh my—pure luxury. Ordering expensive wine, '97 Chassagne-Montrachet, curry-coconut-scallop soup, so "exquisite," and scampi as beautifully presented as any lobster.

Note "Heresy" much on my mind these past few days. Surprised to see "Karl-Marx-Strasse" just as we crossed from Poland back into

former East Germany. Those people certainly have no cause to celebrate *him*.

Have to wonder about those long-ago political theorists, like religious ones: were they evil, just stupid, or the inevitable combination—fanatics?

Some certainly used the "party line" in their pursuit of pure
power, not ideology. But not all—some had been true believers.

On another cold, intermittently rainy day, we made our way out of
Berlin to the north, through some nice forests and fields in watercolor
greens, and past some lakes with grim-looking resorts on their shores—
no doubt retreats for former East German cadres. During a roadside Red
Apple break, Brutus said he was curious about the sign we had seen for
the town intriguingly called Ludwigslust.

"Must be quite the place!"

"Say," I said, "What's the name of that town in northern Germany
where the Nazis were doing their rocket experiments at the end of World
War II?"

"Peenemünde," said the all-knowing Brutus, "It's not far north of
here, on the Baltic Sea."

At a fuel stop on the autobahn, I caught a glimpse of my face in the
bike's mirror, and noted "Scary. Saggy, baggy, jowly, droopy-eyed. Still, no
one looks their best when they're cold and wet. And worn out."

After 374 kilometers, 233 miles, we arrived at the Sporthalle in
Hamburg, a school gymnasium in the northern part of the city. Michael
was all excited that day, as during the afternoon he had discovered the
local police training in the neighboring building. He had somehow talked
his way into joining them, and spent a few hours rappelling from the
arena ceiling and having his photo taken with the rest of the class.

That night we played before the smallest audience of the entire tour,
2,824 people. At least it wasn't hard to see them all, and during the intermission I made a note:

People's faces, as individuals picked out of a crowd. Sometimes like
someone I know, or used to know.

Good physical playing tonight, but trouble concentrating.

I . . . drift away sometimes.

However, we did play really well that night, and for me, the solo was particularly strong, confident and inventive, one of the best of the tour. After I ended it with the big gong sample (the only possible conclusion to all that bombast), I climbed down and sat behind the dryers during the acoustic interlude. Gump gave me his rare praise, "Nice one, man," and I said, "Why wasn't *that one* caught on film?"

Gump must have talked to the video crew about that, because at the next show, Bob from the video crew gave me a DVD of the Hamburg show. It was only an arbitrary view from a couple of their cameras, and a rough mix off the board, but still—at least it was captured. (And would appear on *Anatomy of a Drum Solo*, as a "sidebar.")

During that acoustic interlude, while Alex and Geddy were playing "Resist," I noticed the audience clapping along with that song's 3/4 lilt, on the "one" of every second bar. That spontaneous audience participation didn't happen every night, interestingly, but the small Hamburg audience nailed it nicely.

At the beginning of *2112*, Alex held up two fingers with a big smile.

On the bus after, I mentioned to Brutus that those general admission audiences seemed faceless, somehow. They were a deceptive mix of people, too, not representative of the whole audience. Those who pushed to the front were simply the most aggressive, or most fanatical, while the quieter, smaller, but equally dedicated fans were pushed back. (Though as I had learned from Michael's story about the violence at the Prague show, even that could be deceptive.)

We had a second driver riding with us that night, in preparation for the long drive down from Stockholm to the final show in Rotterdam. Given the strict laws about the number of hours Mark could drive in a day, he wouldn't be able to make it on his own. The new driver was a short, wiry-looking Englishman with a shaved head, topknot, Fu-Manchu mustache, and tattoos, and he introduced himself as "Nasty." Apparently he had formerly been a professional kickboxer, and had changed his name legally to Nasty B'stard. He showed Brutus his passport to prove it. Despite all that apparent "badness," though, Nasty was actually a friendly and cheerful man.

Next morning we woke up in Denmark, in the rain again. While Mark and Nasty would drive north to catch the ferry to Sweden, Brutus and I headed west across the Jutland Peninsula. Denmark's North Sea coast was a low-lying resort area, largely deserted on this late-September Tuesday. Clusters of low cottages hunched under the gray sky, sheltered behind long stretches of sand dunes and grass, with no view of the dark, rough sea. The inlets we passed or crossed over were signed as fjords, though their shallow banks lacked the drama of the Norwegian variety. The day remained cold, and the highest temperature we saw displayed was 16 degrees C (64 degrees F), though it felt much chillier with the wind sweeping in off the North Sea.

Many large wind generators dotted the horizon, as we had seen in northern Germany, and apparently Denmark made 20 percent of its electricity from wind power, Germany 10 percent, and all of Europe 2.4 percent. Despite the many "wind farms" in California, the U.S. produced less than one percent of its power that way.

Danish drivers also conserved energy—by being the *slowest* drivers we had ever encountered. I decided that was because the country was so small they would never have far to go.

The villages, I noted, were "tidy and austere," which was a capsule description for the country. A neat little country of neat little towns, with neat little shops and neatly dressed people. After several days in Eastern Europe, Denmark looked prosperous and well kept. Although once we left the seaside and crossed the central peninsula, passing many dairy farms, we seemed to ride through the constant smell of manure (as noted in *Traveling Music*, the emblematic smell of my childhood on a dairy farm). At a stoplight, Brutus leaned over and made the inevitable joke from *Hamlet*, about "something rotten in Denmark."

We made it to the little harbor town of Frederikshavn in plenty of time for the ferry, and parked our bikes in the empty staging area, amid the seaport atmosphere of cargo ships, loading cranes, and hydraulic loading ramps. We laughed at one big cargo ship with "Green Reefers" on its side, and I said it must be on its way to Amsterdam, to make a delivery.

Once again, we seemed out of season for that ferry crossing, and the dockside restaurant and snack bar were closed, so we bought some sandwiches and chocolate bars from a little grocery store. The sky was clearing, though it was still windy and cold, and we sat on a sheltered bench in the sun, waiting for the call to board the ferry.

Not many travelers were crossing to Sweden that day, just some tractor-trailers and a few cars, so we had plenty of room on the big ferry. The sun was bright on a calm sea, and both of us dozed for much of the two-hour crossing.

Amid an archipelago of tiny islands, Göteburg came into view, an attractive city arrayed around its sheltered port, the largest in Scandinavia. We disembarked into heavy afternoon traffic, then followed Dingus and Dork in a complicated route around and up to our hotel, at the top of the city. Even without counting the nautical miles, it had been a long day, 443 kilometers, 276 miles, and while Brutus checked us in, I waited wearily outside the convention center, watching all the suited men and women emerging from the revolving doors. Brutus and I both noticed we felt "vibrated" that day, not only from all the riding, but from the low-frequency oscillation of the ferry.

The hotel was accommodating, convenient, clean, well-appointed (with a special nod to good bedside reading lights), but it was a business hotel attached to the convention center, and thus was as charmless as its American counterparts.

Likewise, the restaurant, though tasteful, nicely lit, and decorated in a style I called "haute Scandinavian," also seemed austere. The meal, though, was wonderful, and elegantly presented. We had a carnivorous feast of terrine de foie gras and rib-eye steak, with a fine '96 Caymus, followed by a delicate crème brulée and coffee.

The next morning we had a long, cold ride across Sweden to Stockholm, 466 kilometers, 291 miles, through a familiar-looking landscape of mixed boreal forest, lakes, glaciated rock, and a touch of autumn color—just how Ontario and Quebec would have looked at that time of year. The sky had been clear and translucent in the morning, but through the day clouds slowly rolled over, in a way that also seemed Canadian, somehow. A few drops of rain kept our European weather record going—something like eight days of rain in a row. In fact, other than the two days in London, before we started riding, there had only been about one day it *didn't* rain.

Way back in June, riding to Cuyahoga Falls with Tom Marinelli in that torrential rain, I had made the joking comparison, "Just like riding in Europe." Ha ha.

As in Denmark, we didn't see one police car all day, yet the people

seemed to drive so *slowly*, even on the four-lane highways. No complaints, though—they always moved over to let us pass. Nearing the end
of our European travels, after almost 5000 miles of motorcycling, I
thought about how few police cars we had seen—basically one, that
Range Rover in Britain with the cop waving four fingers and mouthing,
"It's forty!" Just as the concept of road manners was completely different
in Europe, so was the philosophy of law enforcement.

In North America, that overzealous speed-limit enforcement seemed to
have started with the bogus "energy crisis" in the '70s, bringing on the fed-
erally mandated 55-mph limit, and radar-crazed police departments to
enforce it beyond all reason. The Canadian equivalent was our switch to the
metric system in the early '70s, when rural four-lane highways with 70-mph
limits were suddenly posted at 100 kph, 62 mph. The only explanation given
was a spurious nod to "safety," and the enforcement was at least as strict as
in the U.S. (plus radar detectors were banned in several Canadian prov-
inces). Over the next thirty years, it seemed that Canadian and American
drivers simply got *used to* that kind of predatory revenue-gathering.

In the U.S., police activity of all kinds was naturally ratcheted up
after the terrorist attacks of September, 2001, and—consciously or not—
every local sheriff and state trooper realized that no one was going to
complain about it. In '98 and '99, I had traveled extensively around the
Western U.S., tens of thousands of miles, and between then and the
Vapor Trails tour in 2002, when Michael and I rode over 20,000 miles in
America, I noticed a big difference in police presence—revenue gathering, not terrorist chasing—on the roads.

That had never happened in Europe, and neither had its effect on
traffic flow, or manners.

On our way into Stockholm, we passed through the suburban town
of Sodertälje, where the band and crew had stayed on our first visit to
Sweden in 1977. I remember trying to order breakfast in the Esso Hotel
there, where no one spoke English, and I still remembered those few
words of Swedish, "ägg und skinka," ham and eggs. The other important
one was "för efterätt," dessert.

Stockholm itself had been beautiful, though, in early summer, and I
remember a photo of the three of us taken after the show, the sky still
light along the graceful waterfront, all of us smiling with our long hair
and late '70s clothes blowing in the wind. Geddy with his big glasses, me

with my big mustache, and Alex with his big—well, actually, he *wasn't* big
then (though he always thought he was).

This time, coming into the Globe Arena, a huge white ping-pong ball
on the south side of the city, Brutus and I didn't see any of the beautiful
parts of Stockholm. We rode into the underground garage, parked
between the trucks and buses, and I went straight to bed. I was still feeling lousy from that cold, and was glad for an afternoon nap.

Still, once again the show went really well, in front of the largest
crowd since Manchester, 11,265 people.

After the show, I noted,

> Felt awful, but played really well. *Perfect* first set, really, but for slip
> in "Bravado," caused by Lerxst's mistrigger. Somehow being a little
> "disengaged" isn't bad.
>
> Crowd 99 percent male, as far as I could tell, a lot of hockey-
> player types, shaved heads or longhaired.
>
> As Dirk said during break, "like a Canadian audience"—they had
> a good time, smiling and happy, just . . . reserved.
>
> Lerxst held up one finger before *2112*, with a *big* smile!
>
> Barrage of pirate balloons from stage left in "The Temples."
>
> Fusillade of water bottles—what song?

During the short movie that played at the beginning of "One Little
Victory," Alex drank down a bottle of water, and I often saw him throwing the empty plastic bottle at someone in the crew down on the stage-
right side. That night a bunch of crew members were hidden beside the
stage armed with empty bottles, and in the light from the screen, I saw
about twenty of them come flying back up at him. The late-in-the-tour
diversions and amusements were continuing.

For the equipment trucks, the drive from Hamburg to Stockholm
had been about 600 miles, and from there to Rotterdam (forty miles from
Amsterdam) was something like 900 miles, so the other buses had been
sent back to Austria. The crew had flown from Hamburg to Stockholm,
and then on to Amsterdam. Like Mark and Nasty, the trucks would be
teamed with double drivers, all of them driving through the night and
most of the next day.

When I woke on the bus at nine, we were parked at a ferry dock,

waiting for the short forty-minute crossing from the island part of
Denmark to the Jutland Peninsula. Brutus and I had our breakfast and
got organized during the crossing, then the bus pulled into a gas station
on the other side, so we could unload the bikes. The morning was sunny
and bright, but the inevitable clouds were looming in the west, and it was
cold on that last day of September, so we put on our rainsuits.

We said goodbye to Nasty B'stard, as we wouldn't see him again, took
some ceremonial photos with Mark, the bikes, and the bus, then set off
on the long ride to Amsterdam.

With almost 400 miles to cover, we would be sticking to the motor-
ways that day, plus I was especially eager to get to Amsterdam because
Carrie had flown in the night before and was waiting at the hotel.

Faster, Brutus, faster!

Unfortunately, the piece of the 1150's windscreen that had been broken off in Brutus's crash on the Stelvio caused him some buffeting from
the uneven windflow at autobahn speeds, so he had to keep his speed
down to about 80. South into Germany, we crossed the low, featureless
landscape of green and gray past Hamburg, then west through Bremen
and into the Netherlands, country number seventeen for us.

More low, flat landscapes of green and gray, broken only by the long
dike, Afsluitdijk, a thirty-kilometer, eighteen-mile, causeway between the
North Sea and the Ijsselmeer, leading down to the canals of Amsterdam.
Intermittent showers became a steady downpour as Dingus and Dork
guided us to the city, and then things went awry. Amsterdam was always
notoriously difficult to navigate, with all those canals, bridges, and narrow
one-way streets, and it's also possible Brutus programmed in the wrong
hotel (he hinted, but didn't exactly confess). We found ourselves fighting
through heavy traffic, cars, bicycles, and pedestrians, in the rain, trying to
follow the confusing directions that kept changing on our screens.

We even tried the old-fashioned way of navigating, stopping at other
hotels and asking for directions, but it still took more than an hour before
we finally pulled up in front of the Amstel Hotel, wet, tired, and exasperated, after 624 kilometers, 390 miles.

Brutus told me later that once we had checked in, parked the bikes in
the hotel's parking lot across the street, and I had gone to wake up the jet-
lagged Carrie, he got a call from the hotel wanting him to move the bikes
to a different part of the lot. He said some bad words, but obliged them.

Brutus rode to the venue early the next day, wanting to start getting organized to ship the bikes home and move off the bus. In the early afternoon I set off alone, "following dutiful Dingus." The day was warm and cloudy, then rainy, and I felt miserable, my cold now full-blown. I noted that it was the third time on the tour I had been sick at the end of a run. "Some unconscious trigger. And so much to *do* today."

It was Friday, October 1, 2004, at the Ahoy arena in Rotterdam, the Netherlands—the last show on the R30 Tour. Once again, time to move off the bus, pack up the riding gear into the luggage cases, the duffle bag, and a cardboard box, adding in another leg's worth of swag, T-shirts from our vendors, books, and CDs, then pack my clothes into the big suitcase for the next journey—an Italian holiday with Carrie.

Into the arena for soundcheck, say goodbye to the crew guys one by one as I encountered them, have dinner with the guys, then retreat to the bus for a little quiet time. A car was bringing Carrie and her luggage in from Amsterdam, as we would be leaving right after the show (as usual—I hate long goodbyes!).

At 7:20, I sat in the front lounge of the bus, realizing it was the last time I would do that this tour, and maybe forever. Who knew? Before going inside for the last warmup, I made a note, "Is this the last time I'll ever sit on a tour bus? Warm up before a show?"

Who knew?

In most ways, the last show of the tour didn't feel any different from any of the others. The same rituals, the same tension, the same walk from the dressing room to the stage. I waited with Geddy and Donovan at stage left (Alex went on from stage right) for the intro film to play through. When Jerry Stiller said, "Come on, it's show time!," we would run onstage, and Alex would start the "R30 Overture."

Then "The Spirit of Radio," "Force Ten," and onward, one by one. There was no time to think "that's the last time I have to play *that* song," as the concentration and energy required were still the same, and the importance of my own performance was still the same, last show, first show, or any in between.

And last show or not, it went very well, as we worked our way through the set, in front of an enthusiastic and smiling audience of 10,076 people. After the intermission, the final showing of the introductory movie, "That Darn Dragon," then into a tough series of songs, full of fast, high-impact playing: "Tom Sawyer," "Dreamline," "Secret Touch," and "Between the Wheels."

Then Gump spins the riser around, and I turn to play the back kit, enjoying a bit of a respite with "Mystic Rhythms" and "Red Sector A," both always a pleasure to play. Into the ultimate ordeal and challenge, the drum solo, then duck down behind the dryers with Gump for a break and a refreshing iced towel. Alex and Geddy play "Resist," then begin "Heart Full of Soul," as I hop back up on the drums.

From then on, it's all hard and fast. At the beginning of 2112, Alex holds up thumb and forefinger circled in a *zero*, and we share big goofy smiles. The last appearance of the "pirates," then "La Villa Strangiato," with Alex's last story-time, then through to the big ending. A quick drink and iced towel behind the stage, then run back on. In celebration of the last night, a dozen or so of the crew guys join Alex and Geddy at the dryers, helping to throw the T-shirts into the audience. Then we launch into the fast-paced trio of "Summertime Blues," "Crossroads," and "Limelight."

I put my drumsticks down on the floor tom to my right, stand up, bow and wave to the audience three times, then run for the car. Brutus accompanies Carrie and me to the airport, and hands me a Macallan while I wriggle out of my sweaty clothes. Our chartered jet is whistling on the runway, Brutus and I hug goodbye, and by two a.m., Carrie and I are in our room at the Villa d'Este on Lake Como.

Luxe, calme, et volupté—luxury, peace, and pleasure. I will sleep, I will order room service, I will read, I will do the crossword in the *International Herald Tribune*, I will dress up and take Carrie to dinner, or swimming, or on a boat trip up the lake to Bellagio.

For three months I won't feel like doing anything: no exercising, no writing, no motorcycling, and definitely no drumming. After forty years of banging on those pots and pans, it never hurts to put the drumsticks down for a while.

Though not without appreciation.

As Buddy Rich once growled to his friend (and my teacher) Freddie Gruber, pointing at a pair of drumsticks, "Just remember, you schmuck, those two pieces of wood have kept you out of the corner gas station and the electric chair."

And finally, one more drummer joke:

A drummer was dancing around, celebrating, when the guitarist came in.

"What's up?"

"I just finished this jigsaw puzzle," the drummer replied. "It only took me six months!"

"That's not very good," the guitarist said. "Why are you so excited?"

"The box says two to six *years!*"

on with the story . . .

On a tour of fifty-seven shows, in nine countries, I played in front of 544,525 people, and went through 257 pairs of drumsticks, one 20-inch cymbal, three 18-inch cymbals, six 16-inch cymbals, two China cymbals, fifteen drum heads, 21,000 motorcycle miles, nineteen countries, twelve oil changes, five sets of tires, one lost luggage case (including Patek Philippe watch and Cartier engagement ring—as Michael suspected, my fickle Good Samaritan must have found them and changed his mind; he never did call back), thirty-four bottles of The Macallan (my riding partners helped), four cartons of Red Apples (ditto), 18,617 words of journal notes, an immeasurable outpouring of physical and mental energy, and an undetermined amount of hearing loss.

I celebrated my fifty-second birthday, almost forty years of drumming, thirty years of making music with Rush, twenty years of bicycling, ten years and almost 200,000 miles of motorcycling, and four years of marriage.

I laughed, I cried, I ached, I sweated, I despaired, I was joyful, I was miserable, I hated it, I loved it, I made friends, I made enemies, I made music, I made gas money, I made time to live and love.

After all that, what can I do for an encore?

Well, write a 395-page, 154,605-word book about it, I guess.

Again I ask myself, am I ever going to do anything that crazy again? (The tour, not the book.)

Hmmm . . . I don't know. Many times over the years, at the end of a grueling tour, I would resolve never to put myself through that again. Back in 1989, after only fifteen years of touring, I had said "no" for the first time. But after much thought, I had finally acquiesced—out of a wish for our new album, *Presto*, to get heard, for one thing. No one else was going to publicize it if we didn't. I also felt a sense of loyalty to the concept of the band as a living, breathing entity (a *real* band plays live).

At least I knew better than to say "never," but with the passing years I had become ever more reluctant to spend six or eight months on the road, putting myself through that struggle night after night. In the early years all that performing in front of audiences had been great training, and had made all of us better players, as individuals and as a band. Nothing makes a band tighter than playing together in front of an audience—a few thousand times.

It used to be that as a tour went on (and on), I would at least feel the improvement in my playing, and the band meshing at ever deeper and higher levels, but those days were long past. I had reached a plateau in which most of the skills had been mastered—or at least my mental and physical limitations had been met—and any new frontiers would be explored when the three of us got together to record, and new music demanded new approaches. After thirty years of playing together, we *had* our tightness, and could activate that synchronistic drive when we needed it.

So no, I have no wish to ever again take on a challenge like a major tour. But I've said that before.

All of us have returned to what passes for normal life with us. Alex and Geddy are home in Toronto with their families; crew members and drivers are off on other tours; Michael is back to his Hollywood private eye business; Brutus has found himself a perfect niche as an assistant director for a Canadian TV show, "Creepy Canada," arranging travel plans, logistics, and locations. After the tour, Liam sent me a long e-mail about his new life with Lashawn in Nashville, and about how happy he is now. So that's all good.

For me, it is wonderful to return to the pleasures and chores of everyday life with Carrie and Winston (our golden retriever, the brilliant canine love-sponge), to get caught up with long-neglected friends and family, to have the comfort of a daily routine, to run errands, buy groceries, cook dinner, write letters, have an Indian lunch with Doane, or take a hike with Matt. It is also nice to work on something that won't disappear into memory as soon as I finish it, the way a concert, even a "magic show," necessarily fades into the ether, and is gone.

However, as the months pass since that last show, I *do* miss the guys at work . . .